COLLATERAL
DAMAGE

COLLATERAL DAMAGE
The New World Order at Home and Abroad

edited by
Cynthia Peters

South End Press   Boston MA

Typeset by Cynthia Peters and the South End Press collective
Cover photos from Impact Visuals:(top) Brooklyn unemployment office by Robert Fox; (bottom) Kurdish refugees by Tiet Hornbak
Cover design by Ty de Pass

Library of Congress Cataloging-in-Publication Data
Collateral damage : the new world order at home and abroad / edited by Cynthia Peters
p. cm.
Includes bibliographical references and index.
ISBN 0-89608-423-x : $30.00. -- ISBN 0-89608-422-1 (pbk.) : $16.00
1. United States--Foreign relations--1989- 2. United States--Politics and government--1989- I. Cynthia Peters, 1961- .
E881.C65 1992
#27.73--dc20 91-38397 CIP

South End Press, 116 Saint Botolph Street, Boston, MA 02115

99 98 97 96 95 94 93 92   1 2 3 4 5 6 7 8 9

Table of Contents

INTRODUCTION

Cynthia Peters

collateral *adj.* 1. Situated or running side by side; parallel. 2. Coinciding in tendency or effect; concomitant; accompanying. 3. Serving to support or corroborate: *collateral evidence.* 4. Of a secondary nature; subordinate.

damage *n.* 1. Impairment of the usefulness or value of person or property; loss; harm.

The Gulf War brought these words into the popular vocabulary, not because we were meant to think about their meanings, but precisely because we weren't. Normally, "collateral" is a word reserved for finance or law; it doesn't usually pertain to human matters. Thus it worked to deflect our imaginations away from the human suffering usually associated with war, and instead lined us up behind the concept of war as something technocratic, lacking in human agency and leaving behind no victims. It helped to focus popular attention on the smart bombs' supposedly surgically accurate accomplishments and *away* from the "parallel, coinciding, concomitant" meanings and effects of the fact that they were launched in the first place and that, having been launched, would land…somewhere.

Collateral is, in fact, a very interesting word that begs many questions. What *does* "run side-by-side" a smart bomb? Or a patriot missile? What are the policies and choices that led up to their launchings and what are their parallel effects? We know something about the direct hits from the video-game-like images that came to us via the television screen. But what do we know of the indirect hits?

How did they—the hits—"impair the usefulness or value of person or property?" What was the exact nature of the damage they caused? Who was killed? Who was hurt? Who died later as a result of the diseases spread through untreated sewage, poor drinking water, and general lack of services? Who died of these conditions in Iraq? And who died of them here in the United States? Does a smart bomb in Baghdad, wending its way through neighborhoods looking for its target, *have* any relationship to conditions in the United States? "Collateral damage" includes a lot more than the innocents who happened to be in the way of a smart bomb gone dumb or a pilot off-course. Perhaps the Bush administration would like us to think—assuming they would like us to think at all—that some human "loss" or "harm" is the expected collateral in a high-tech war, but that it matters little because it is "secondary" or "subordinate" to the technological perfection of a bomb that humanely guts infrastructure without hurting a hair on anyone's head. But even a beginning exploration of the concept of collateral damage tells us otherwise.

That is what this book is about. It is a study of collateral damage. It is an incomplete study, of course. Each of the chapters that follows could easily afford several volumes worth of attention. But it takes us in three important directions. It analyzes the circumstances—the coinciding tendencies—that led to the Gulf War; it analyzes the damages, in all their ripple effect; and it asks what we can do as activists, as people concerned not just about stopping the wars but also about undermining the institutions that cause them. It takes the Bush administration term, "collateral damage," and follows it to find out what we can learn about the context for and ramifications of war in the "New World Order."

The Gulf War—the way it started, the way it was fought, the way the media covered it, the weapons that were used in it, the people who participated in it and those who died in it, the people who challenged it, the international community's response to it, and the way it is recorded for history—offers key lessons about power in U.S. society and abroad. Some of these lessons are new and some are merely reminders of how our institutions function. Key among the lessons of the Gulf War is the relationship between domestic and foreign policy.

Racism, for example, is a powerful tool in the realization of both domestic and foreign policy. Without social and economic policy at home that consistently devalues non-white communities, there would have been no groundwork for the sudden demonization of Saddam Hussein (after he had long been considered a friend to the United States) and the total disregard for the many thousands of Arab lives lost to almost unchallenged U.S. bombing of civilian sites. It is no accident, furthermore, that as the minority prison population grows and as infant mortality rates increase in communities of color, so swell the ranks of people of color in the military and the U.S. government continues its most bloodthirsty and abusive policies in Third World countries.

Consider, also, the economy. A "free-market" system that values making profit over meeting human needs will do exactly that. An economy that centers around outlandish military spending, that holds out the armed services as one of the few available career choices for vast numbers of people, and that spends billions and billions of dollars on military research and development, will obviously lead to warmaking.

It is certainly noteworthy that one of the richest countries in the world cannot adequately educate, house, or feed its population, care for its sick, or employ all those ready and willing to work, but apparently *can* amass the resources for $500-million-a-day war. It is also interesting that as highly extolled as U.S. democracy is, it still has no room for viable opposition or any divergence of opinion outside the extremely narrow range of status quo debate. The First Amendment protects freedom of speech but the mainstream media consistently brings us only the voices of the rich and powerful.

As Holly Sklar argues, it was U.S. policy—not the evil doings of Saddam Hussein—that got us into the Gulf War and that governs its aftermath. In Part I of this anthology, Sklar looks at the "Brave New World Order" both at home and abroad. By drawing the connections between domestic and foreign policy, her essay serves as an overview to the book as a whole.

Part II functions as a history and analysis of the so-called New World Order. It is meant to look at some of the major factors—material and ideological conditions—that go into the creation of U.S. policy, particularly the fighting of the Gulf War. Noam Chomsky leads off with a profile of the victor in the Gulf War. He analyzes U.S. policy in the Middle East, our history in the region, and the role of U.S. institutions (such as the media) in assuring that "what we say goes," regardless of principle. Cynthia Enloe follows with a look at the role of gender in the playing out of international affairs. Abouali Farmanfarmaian analyzes the role of race and sexuality in imperialism. And Arthur MacEwan looks at the interplay between the modern U.S. economy and the war. Taken together, these four essays offer a glimpse of some of the major institutional and social forces at work in the creation and projection of U.S. power.

Part III is a glance at the Gulf War's "collateral damage" abroad. Joe Stork and Ann M. Lesch offer a brief history of colonialism and imperialism in the region, and offer their estimates of the economic damage wreaked on the area by the Gulf War. Eric Hooglund gives us an eyewitness account of the Gulf War's human toll, profiling the suffering not just of those hit directly by the bombs and those affected by the crippled Iraqi infrastructrue, but of the vast new refugee population, including Kurds, Palestinians, and many others. Joni Seager investigates the profound damage done to the fragile eco-systems of the Gulf region—collateral damage that will affect all species of land and marine life for generations to come. And Michael Klare explains the new war technology used on Iraq, claiming that the non-nuclear conventional weapons have similar killing power to the bombs used on Hiroshima and Nagasaki. This section, "The War Abroad," tells us something of the war's destruction to the Gulf region, but it is brief in comparison to the ramifications of such a full-scale assault. As we gain perspective on the political fallout of the war and the depth of the tragedy, U.S. analysts should devote more energy to exploring the devastating effects of U.S. aggression.

Part IV reverses the gaze and asks, what is the "collateral damage" experienced at the home front, and what are the connections between U.S. society and institutions and our sponsoring of wars on foreign soil? Randolph N. Stone sees a connection between two growth industries in the United States: the prisons and the military, African Americans being disproportionately represented in both. The expendability of certain groups in the United States teaches us a lot about how policy will be carried out abroad. Rachel L. Jones looks at minorities in the military, the racism that puts them there in the first place and the racism they experience in the ranks. Nabeel Abraham traces the growth of anti-Arab racism in the United States, linking it to Reagan's and Bush's foreign policy and seeing it as a critical factor in getting public backing for their foreign adventurism. Tod Ensign investigates the changes in the military since Vietnam, the new forms of resistance within the ranks, and the military's strategy for quelling dissent. Having learned from Vietnam that enlisted men and women and veterans alike can be powerful resisters, the military has had to restructure itself and put renewed attention into controlling the media portrayal of war efforts. Robert Warrior looks back over the generations of his family's participation in U.S. wars and points to the fight to control Native lands as the start of the battle over oil. William Hoynes looks at a key U.S. institution—the media—and explains the role it played in rallying support for the Gulf War. Together, the contributors to this section reveal the contours of the New World Order at home: the Orwellian doublespeak that characterizes our media, the injustice of our social organization, the racism and sexism so prevalent in our institutions. Again, the exploration of these issues is not definitive or complete. However, juxtaposed to "The War Abroad," "The War at Home" offers critical insight into the links between foreign wars and those being fought here at home.

Part V is about the lessons we have learned and the direction these lessons might take our activism. Rebecca Gordon admits these are "hard, dry times" but argues that critical reflection, creative hard work, and honest dialogue amongst activists of all stripes will better prepare us for the future. Salim Muwakkil gives us a history of the African-American community's response to U.S. foreign policy and suggests that now more than ever, Blacks are receptive to an analysis of the role of race in shaping domestic and foreign policy. Sandy Carter, in his interview of Roots Against War, explores how youth of color are responding to and organizing around the war at home as well as the war abroad. Ward Churchill proffers a satirical rallying cry to progressive movements: Unite behind Bush's goal of standing tall in the face of foreign aggression against democracy! U.S. out of North America! Leslie Cagan, national organizer for the January 26, 1991 march on Washington to end the Gulf War, critically reflects on the anti-war work done by the peace-and-justice movement. Michael Albert ends with an eloquent argument for continued struggle. Offering the perspective of one who started doing political work in the Vietnam era, his essay gives us valuable insight into the lessons we can learn about the meaning of social change activism, the pitfalls of organizing, key problems within the Left, and the need for vision.

This book was originally conceived in January 1991 when the Gulf War seemed imminent. At South End Press we felt we were well-placed to produce a quick volume that would be useful to activists needing analyses of and responses to the situation in the Middle East. It soon became obvious to us, however, that a quick, crisis-oriented book was not the most important contribution we could make. A lot of good material was being produced by the likes of *Z Magazine,* for example, that met the movement's need for rapid-fire response and analysis. We decided it would be important for us to do a more in-depth analysis of the Gulf War, the institutions that helped bring it on, the policies that start wars abroad and allow them to fester at home as well, and the meaning of this most recent U.S. adventurism for the so-called New World Order. Perhaps even more than depth, we felt that our approach would give us the advantage of perspective. Accordingly, this book has a wide scope—one that attempts to capture the breadth of the issues involved in the Gulf War and the role of the United States in the New World Order. This project also reflects our commitment to hearing a diversity of voices on the subject. Too often, the peace movement is divorced from domestic social justice struggles, and wars abroad are not linked to those at home. Unless we listen to the plethora of voices responding to, analyzing, and resisting the complex of institutions that govern life, unless we understand the intersection of all the many struggles, we won't adequately confront them, nor will we change them.

We also chose to work fast; this book was less than a year in the making. The war in the Gulf may have officially ended, but conflict in the Middle East, in the United States, and around the world continues. We must be able to understand and respond to U.S. foreign and domestic policy; we must be able to see the links between the two; and we must look for ways to organize ourselves. We have to be ready not just for the crises, the sudden wars, but for the ongoing war—the one that is felt by the victims of U.S. policy everywhere: from gangs in Watts to guerrillas in

El Salvador, from a public hospital in Los Angeles to a burn ward in Baghdad. *Collateral Damage* attempts to uncover the U.S. role in all these spheres.

Thanks are due to the South End Press collective and to Michael Albert and Lydia Sargent of *Z Magazine*. This book's conception and realization are in many ways due to their help and advice. A couple of the essays, particularly those by Noam Chomsky and Michael Albert, were based on work originally done for *Z* in the spring of 1991. I am particularly grateful to South End Press. During my eight years as an editor there, it has been an honor to struggle over forging a role as an independent, activist publishing house; to maintain a non-hierarchical, democratic workplace; and to walk the line between business and activism in such a way as to maintain political integrity at the same time we get our books out into the world. My tenure at South End Press as well as the support of fellow collective members gave me the insight and access to resources that enabled me to edit this anthology. I am glad to have this opportunity to be a South End Press author. Thanks also to the contributors, each of whom worked under near-impossible deadlines in order to help meet the goal of bringing this book out quickly. Their dedication and commitment to exploring, analyzing, and ultimately changing the social and political structures that give rise to war is obvious in their hard work.

Many others worked hard to make this book happen. Loie Hayes, Amy Hoffman, Shelly Kelman, and Nathan McBrien proofed, commented, queried, typed, and corrected draft upon draft. Paul Kiefer, my partner in so many things, designed the book, gave unstinting support throughout its making, and helped me complete the index in the last couple of days before the printer deadline. Those final days of book production also happened to be the last days of my pregnancy with our first child. This book is dedicated to Zoë Mae and to all of our children. May we learn from each other and do better.

PART 1

AN OVERVIEW

CHAPTER 1

BRAVE NEW WORLD ORDER

Holly Sklar

Behold the 90s. In a special "Survival Guide" to this "age of anxiety," *Newsweek* declared, "The party was over almost as soon as it began...We ushered in the decade celebrating the end of the cold war and an impressive seven years of economic growth. Now those sunny forecasts have given way to the dark prospects of war in the desert, a free-falling economy, and disarray in the Soviet Union...The gulf crisis shows the world has been made safe again for the use of all-out military force."[1]

We are experiencing the wrong kind of global warming. The 80s ended with the crumbling of the Berlin Wall and the U.S. occupation of Panama—one superpower shedding its empire in an effort to salvage its Union of Soviet Socialist Republics; the other Bushwacking a renewed Pax Americana. The expected post-Cold War American peace dividend was quickly rolled over into banking bailouts and war dividends.

The world of the 90s is not just post-Cold War and post-Warsaw Pact, it is increasingly post-Soviet Union. But, without a fundamental change of course by the United States, the yellow ribbon military budget will continue wasting lives and resources. President Bush's September 1991 initiatives to eliminate some nuclear weapons have the politically and militarily expedient objectives of prompting the Soviets to dismantle their own mobile tactical nuclear weapons ("loose nukes"), which many fear could be wielded by breakaway republics, and containing congressional moves to cut big-ticket programs, such as Star Wars, Sea Wolf attack submarines, and "Stealth" B-2 bombers that cost $870 million *per plane*. Bush's triage of redundant nuclear weapons is designed to preserve the triad of nuclear bombers, submarines, and intercontinental ballistic missiles under a Star Wars sky.

A *New York Times* advance profile of Washington's Desert Storm victory parade said: "Parked along the Mall will be a Noah's ark of Pentagon procurement: a pair of every fighter plane that flew in the war, plus Tomahawk cruise missiles, Bradley fighting vehicles, and M1-A1 tanks...'The idea is that people can get within petting range of these things,'" said parade director Daniel Denning, a General Electric lobbyist.[2] Gulf War costs (funded separately from the Pentagon's nearly $300 billion annual military budget) will, according to the U.S. Comptroller General, "ultimately total as much as $100 billion," only about half of it covered by allied contributions.[3]

"The war reaffirmed America's faith in its armed forces," Defense Secretary Dick Cheney exulted in the Pentagon's report to Congress on the Gulf War. "And in some small measure, Desert Storm also helped to reaffirm America's faith in itself, in American products, in American performance, in American purpose and dedication."[4] As former Secretary of State Dean Acheson, one of the "Wise Men" of the military-industrial National Security State, said about the Korean War, it "came along and saved us."[5]

Meanwhile, at schools like the Greenwood Elementary School in Boston's Hyde Park, teachers are holding bake sales to raise money for needed supplies like pencils, pens, and crayons. That's pencils, not computers. We're seeing more schools without enough teachers or textbooks and stripped of art, music, sports, languages, and libraries. What kind of schools are those? Violence is so bad in some areas that teachers have turned the laughable "duck and cover" nuclear drills from the 50s into lifesaving bullet drills for the 90s. And every day, in cities and suburbs and farm country, one out of eight American children under 12 goes hungry.[6] In Bush's America, there's money to bail out arms pushers and his son's S&L, not the nation's children.

Doublespeak and Doubledealing

"Who controls the past," ran the Party slogan, "controls the future: who controls the present controls the past."..."Reality control," they called it; in Newspeak, "doublethink."...

To know and not to know, to be conscious of complete truthfulness while telling carefully constructed lies, to hold simultaneously two opinions which cancelled out, knowing them to be contradictory and believing in both of them, to use logic against logic, to repudiate morality while laying claim to it, to believe that democracy was impossible and that the Party was the guardian of democracy, to forget, whatever it was necessary to forget, then to draw it back into memory again at the moment when it was needed, and then promptly to forget it again, and above all, to apply the same process to the process itself—that was the ultimate subtlety: consciously to induce unconsciousness, and then, once again, to become unconscious of the act of hypnosis you had just performed.

George Orwell, 1984 (New American Library, 1949 edition).

George Bush's Brave New World Order rests on double standards and doublespeak, befitting a former CIA director. Children are supposed to learn that two wrongs don't make a right. If Joe steals Billy's bicycle, the right response would not be for young George to help Billy firebomb Joe's house with his whole family inside.

Iraq's occupation of Kuwait was wrong. So was the U.S. rush to reverse it through war rather than sanctions and diplomacy. Sanctions and negotiated settlements require time, tact, and proportionality regarding ends and means. Too often, time is prolonged because of obstruction by powerful nations, as in the case of U.S. and British circumvention of various sanctions since 1963 against South Africa, which not only imposed apartheid at home, but occupied and plundered Namibia and waged war against Angola and Mozambique. Johannesburg has no fear of international military action to right its continuing wrongs; instead sanctions have been dismantled.[7]

In Iraq's case, sanctions should have worked relatively quickly, setting a positive precedent, because most countries were united in enforcing them. As celebrity journalist Bob Woodward belatedly disclosed, the chairman of the U.S. Joint Chiefs of Staff Colin Powell felt sanctions were "working. An extraordinary political-diplomatic coalition had been assembled, leaving Iraq without substantial allies—condemned, scorned and isolated as perhaps no country in modern history. Intelligence showed that economic sanctions were cutting off up to 95 percent" of Iraq's imports and nearly all exports.[8] If anything, sanctions were hurting faster than expected—"When sanctions were first implemented nearly everyone acknowledged that a year or even more might be required for them to succeed."[9]

However, a negotiated withdrawal from Kuwait, leaving Saddam Hussein militarily unbowed in Iraq, was portrayed as the "nightmare scenario" by Bush policymakers. Sanctions were used to weaken Iraq in preparation for war, not as a nonviolent alternative to war. According to the Pentagon report to Congress, "The embargo enforced at sea and imposed upon all routes to and from Iraq and Kuwait, continued to deplete the *civilian and military* capabilities of the Iraqis."[10] (Emphasis added.) Before the bombing began, Iraq was reportedly forced to stop training flights and reconnaissance missions because of maintenance problems due to shortages of spare parts and refined jet fuel.

Ultimatums substituted for diplomacy. Real diplomacy was widely dismissed as an annoyance or appeasement. Here's how CBS News anchorman Dan Rather depicted (February 12, 1991) Soviet efforts to negotiate Iraq's withdrawal before the ground war: "If you consider this a kind of Iraqi-Soviet Scud—diplomatically...[presidential spokesman] Marlin Fitzwater at the White House has fired what amounts to a diplomatic Patriot at it."

With the negotiations "nightmare" avoided, the Bush administration tried to avoid another: the "nightmare" of a post-Hussein Iraq without a reliable authoritarian regime to keep it whole and pro-West. While cynically encouraging the Iraqi people to overthrow Hussein, U.S. (and Saudi) officials privately acknowledged they wanted a military coup, not successful popular rebellions by Shiites and Kurds. The Kurds earlier met disaster as U.S. pawns in 1972-75 when the CIA and the Shah of Iran armed them as a "card to be played" against Iraq, and then betrayed them. According to the 1976 report of the House Select Committee on Intelligence chaired by Representative Otis Pike, "Documents in the Committee's possession clearly show that the President, Dr. Kissinger [secretary of state] and the foreign head of state [the Shah] hoped that our clients [the Kurds] would not prevail. They preferred instead that the insurgents simply continue a level of hostilities sufficient to sap the resources of [Iraq]. This policy was not imparted to our clients." The day after the Shah and Iraq agreed to improve relations, Iraq "launched an all-out search-and-destroy campaign," killing many Kurds and prompting thousands to flee, whereupon the U.S. refused humanitarian assistance to the refugees and denied them political asylum. Kissinger told the Pike Committee, "covert action should not be confused with missionary work."[11]

Washington continues playing the endlessly changing lethal game, "the enemy of my enemy is my friend" or "the enemy of my old friend turned enemy is my friend at least until my enemy becomes my friend..." Yesterday, tilting toward Iraq. Today, toward Iran and Syria. As the U.S. tilts, the Middle East teeters atop powderkegs of militarism and subjugation (territorial, ethnic, religious, gender, economic).

Having used the Gulf War as a testing ground and trade show for new military equipment, Washington immediately sought big weapons deals for its Middle East strongholds. Purposeful proliferation of high-tech weaponry creates a self-fulfilling logic for new U.S. spending to keep ahead in the perpetual arms race. The U.S. is the world's Number One arms pusher; its share of the global arms market rose to 40 percent in 1990, while the Soviet Union's fell to 29 percent.[12]

Rhetoric and Real Estate

The Cold War era saw frequent hot wars. Of some 130 wars since World War II, all but four were fought in the Third World. About 22 million women, men, and children suffered war-related deaths. The civilian death toll jumped from about 50 percent in the 1950s to 74 percent in the 1980s to as much as 90 percent in 1990.[13] How many millions more will die if the world is "safe again for the use of all-out military force?"

We are not seeing a post-Cold War shift to North-South conflict, but an intensification of North-South conflict. Twentieth-century U.S. intervention in the Third World was not a sideshow to the anti-Soviet crusade. Washington used the Cold War to justify longtime economic, political, and military intervention in the Third World. The self-ordained right to intervene has been cloaked in many doctrines since the genocidal wars against Native Americans: Manifest Destiny, Monroe Doctrine, Truman Doctrine, Nixon Doctrine, Carter Doctrine, Reagan Doctrine. Now, it's the New World Order.

Beneath all the rhetoric about freedom and democracy, most intervention revolves around a simple proposition: What's mine is mine, what's yours is mine. That was clearer with colonialism. Then came neocolonialism, allowing nations their own flags but not their own economies. As then-U.S. Secretary of State George Shultz (longtime principal of the Bechtel superconstruction corporation) put it on a visit to occupied Grenada in 1984: "The terrain is more rugged than I imagined, but it is certainly a lovely piece of real estate."[14]

When the United States intervenes in other countries, government officials don't proclaim, "We're off to secure our lovely pieces of real estate, with their lovely beaches, cheap labor, and resources." Instead, the imperial right to intervene is promoted with propaganda taking two basic forms: We must protect civilization from the barbarians. We must civilize the barbarians (the "half devil, half child" inferiors of Kipling's "White Man's Burden"). During colonization the official barbarians were Africans, Arabs, Asians, and the indigenous peoples of the Americas. For most of the twentieth century, the official barbarians have been the Soviet Union and its alleged communist-international-terrorist offspring in the Third World.

For the post-Cold War Order, Third World people are being granted more independent official barbarian status under convenient categories like narcoterrorist (used as a cover for counterinsurgency abroad and civil liberties rollback at home), ecoterrorist, and Arab Hitler, which works better than oilmonger.

Dictator clients like Panama's Manuel Noriega and Saddam Hussein are transformed instantly into dictator barbarians with the help of racism. The *New York Times,* for example, ran an unusually large cartoon titled "The Descent of Man" across the top of its op-ed page on February 1, 1991. It showed, in descending order, Clark Gable, a guerrilla, a monkey, a snake, and a fly-infested Saddam Hussein.

The United States has a long history of portraying nonwhite enemies as less than human—from Indian "savages" to "yellow Jap rats" (the racist difference in war stereotypes of Japanese and Germans is apparent when you imagine redoing "Hogan's Heroes" in a Japanese prisoner of war camp) to Vietnamese "gooks" to Iraqi "camel jockeys" and "sand niggers," an even more disgusting term when you consider the high number of African-American Gulf veterans.[15] U.S. soldiers, following Vietnam War practice, commonly referred to the Gulf battlefield as "Indian country" or "Injun country."

Jingoism abroad fuels racism at home. Japanese-Americans were rounded up into detention camps during World War II. "A Jap's a Jap," said Lieutenant General John DeWitt, Military Commander of the Western Defense Command, in charge of internment on the Pacific Coast. "It makes no difference whether he's an American or not." Greed played a role. "Justice Frank Murphy noted in his dissent [against the majority upholding detention] in the *Korematsu* case that 'special interest groups were extremely active in applying pressure for mass evacuation.' For example, Austin Anson, the managing secretary of the Salinas Vegetable Grower-Shipper Association said, 'It's a question of whether the white man lives on the Pacific Coast or the brown men. They came into this valley to work, and stayed to take over...the white farmers can take over and produce everything the Jap grows. And we don't want them back when the war ends, either.'" Half a century later, Arab-Americans (and their businesses) were subjected to blanket FBI suspicion and harassment and increased racist slurs and violence. A popular Gulf War t-shirt showed aircraft attacking an Arab on a camel, and was captioned, "I'd Fly 10,000 miles to Smoke a Camel."[16]

War brings out the worst kind of "love it or leave it" politically-correct patriotism. Nearly one out of four Americans thought the government should have banned anti-war demonstrations and 57 percent favored more Pentagon control of U.S. war coverage.[17] Many Americans saw no contradiction in telling anti-war protesters to shut up because the soldiers in the Gulf were defending their right to free speech.

The Gulf War tested the ecoterrorism pretext. Saddam, killer of seabirds vs. the Pentagon, protector of greenpeace. We're supposed to ignore the Saudi estimate that 20 to 30 percent of the Gulf War oil spill resulted from U.S. and allied bombing. Never mind the unprecedented U.S. bombing of operational nuclear reactors. Never mind the U.S. defoliation and poisoning of Third World lands in the name of fighting narcoterrorism in counterinsurgency countries like Guatemala. Never mind U.S. obstruction of international action to stop global warming—while consuming 25 percent of world oil with only 5 percent of the world's population.

The reality is that both war and "peacetime" militarism destroy the environment. The U.S. military produces more toxics annually than the top five chemical companies combined. And the world's armed forces are together planet earth's largest polluter.[18]

Smart Bombs, Dumb Bombs, and TV Bombs

> There is, of course, no reason why the new totalitarianism should resemble the old...A really efficient totalitarian state would be one in which the all-powerful executive of political bosses and their army of managers control a population of slaves who do not have to be coerced, because they love their servitude. To make them love it is the task assigned, in present-day totalitarian states, to ministries of propaganda, newspaper editors and schoolteachers.

> Aldous Huxley, foreword to *Brave New World* (Bantam Classic edition).

In the oft-parroted euphemistic language of the Pentagon, weaponry is described more humanly than people. U.S. missiles are "smart" and have names like "Tomahawk Cruise" and "Patriot." An SDI program riding the Patriot missile is called G-PALS, for Global Protection Against Limited Strikes. G-PALS relies on missile-bombarding satellites called "Brilliant Pebbles."

Dead and wounded civilians are "collateral damage." Or, as *Time* magazine put it during the first week of the war, it's "a term meaning dead and wounded civilians who should have picked a safer neighborhood."

In Pentagonspeak there is no war zone, but a KTO or Kuwaiti Theater of Operations. For many Americans, especially those without friends or family in the Gulf, the war was a six-week Desert Storm miniseries or a Smart Bomb Super Bowl—highlighted by football's actual Super Bowl Sunday, reputed to be the worst day of the year for violence against women. The Pentagon picked NFL (National Football League) Films to produce a Gulf War highlights video. Television commercials promoting the 1991-92 NFL season feature headless soldiers in desert camouflage doing a marching drill about upcoming football games.

A May 27, 1991 *People* magazine story on Democratic presidential candidate Paul Tsongas asserted, "A lot of [people] will want to know that in the event of war, he can be counted on to provide more great Persian Gulf-style television."

News was manipulated to serve propaganda and profit. A Gannett Foundation Media Center report concluded, "Often reporters and news organizations, with a few exceptions, lapsed into cheerleading the war effort instead of striving for more balanced news and historical perspective."[19] Fairness and Accuracy in Reporting (FAIR) notes that "in an effort to increase ad sales, CBS executives 'offered advertisers assurances that the war specials could be tailored to provide better lead-ins to commercials. One way would be to insert the commercials after segments that were specially produced with upbeat images or messages about the war, like patriotic views from the front.'"[20] Four days into the bombing, ostensible reporter Dan Rather "turned to the camera and raised his right hand to his forehead in a slightly awkward but unmistakably earnest military salute" to the troops in Saudi Arabia.[21] CNN's mass market video, "Desert Storm: The Victory," narrated by new anchor Bernard Shaw, could have been produced by the Pentagon.

Pentagon propaganda experts know that television loves a good photo opportunity—however censored—and first images leave lasting impressions. Military briefers thrilled their audience with Top Gun videos of supposedly civilian-friendly "smart bombs" whizzing through doors and down air vents. Many reporters made it appear as if Tomahawk Cruise missiles were flying around Baghdad streets, pausing to ask civilians, "Pardon me, is that the Air Force headquarters?" Examples of Orwellian doublethink abound. On January 20, NBC's Tom Aspell marveled over Tomahawk cruise missiles, "accurate to within a few feet," right after reporting that a missile had "hit the hotel employees' compound."[22] Fewer civilian casualties appeared in the war "news" than on television "entertainment" shows.

The most publicized civilian carnage, the killing of hundreds of people, mostly women and children, when the United States bombed a public shelter, was blamed on Hussein and quickly forgotten lest Iraq reap a "propaganda" benefit. Though publicly the Pentagon insisted it was a military command and control center, privately U.S. officials admitted it was targeted as a shelter used by high-level Iraqi officials *and their families.* Defense Secretary Dick Cheney later told reporters, every Iraqi target was "perfectly legitimate," adding, "If I had to do it over again, I would do exactly the same thing."[23] Being American Means Never Having to Say You're Sorry. During the 1988 campaign, Bush had refused to answer a question about the U.S. Navy's shooting down of a civilian

Iranian airliner in the Gulf on the grounds that he would "never apologize for the United States of America. I don't care what the facts are."[24]

In the Pentagon's greatest hit videos, buildings and vehicles exploded and burned, not people. Other footage was censored by the military and/or news and photo agencies. For example, when award-winning journalist Jon Alpert, a longtime NBC stringer, "came back from Iraq with spectacular videotape of Basra [Iraq's second largest city with 800,000 residents] and other areas of Iraq devastated by U.S. bombing, NBC president Michael Gartner not only ordered that the footage not be aired, but forbade Alpert from working for the network in the future."[25]

The War is Peace PR image of "surgical" smart bombing endures, undisturbed by reality. In fact, most of the bombs dropped by the U.S. military on Iraq and Kuwait were "dumb" bombs, with an acknowledged *miss* rate of 75 percent. Only about 7 percent of U.S. bombs were "smart bombs," and many of them went off course. How many is still not known. According to *Boston Globe* military correspondent Fred Kaplan, writing in late January 1991, U.S. officials acknowledged that about 60 percent of the U.S. laser-guided bombs dropped in Operation Desert Storm had hit their targets "and the other 40 percent have missed." Laser-guided bombs are thrown off course, sometimes by miles, when the laser beam hits smoke, dust, clouds, or rain—hardly rare phenomena, especially in a war. U.S. Air Force Chief of Staff General Merrill "Tony" McPeak later told reporters that "on the order of 90 percent" of laser-guided bombs hit their targets.[26] Reviewing the F-117 stealth fighter, the Pentagon report to Congress says, "over 80% of the precision guided bombs released were hits." No target accuracy estimate is given for Tomahawk cruise missiles: "A total of 288 Tomahawks reportedly were fired, 276 by surface ships and 12 by submarines...282 are assessed to have successfully transitioned to a cruise profile for a 98% launch success rate...Based on a preliminary assessment, strategic targets struck by Tomahawk suffered at least moderate damage."

Over 100,000 combat missions were flown against Iraq by fixed-wing aircraft. U.S. planes dropped a reported 88,500 tons of bombs on Iraq and Kuwait. According to the Pentagon, the combined miss rate for smart and dumb bombs was 70 percent.[27]

Deliberate Damage

The Coalition military campaign will be remembered for its effort, within the bounds of war, to be humane...planners spared legitimate military targets to minimize civilian casualties. Tens of thousands of Iraqi prisoners of war were cared for and treated with dignity and compassion. The world will not soon forget pictures of Iraqi soldiers kissing their captors' hands.

> Secretary of Defense Dick Cheney, *Conduct of the Persian Gulf Conflict,*
> July 1991.

The officials said Bush assumes that the American public will be mainly concerned about the number of U.S. casualties, not the tens of thousands of Iraqis who stand to die or be maimed in a massive air assault, and that even the killing of thousands of civilians—including women and children—probably would not undermine American support for the war effort.

> Jack Nelson, *Los Angeles Times,* December 28, 1990.[28]

The modern U.S. military combines "smart" weaponry, with imperfect but improving accuracy, and conventional wide-area munitions such as cluster bomb units and fuel-air explosives, designed to have the destructive force of tactical nuclear weapons.[29] Superior air-land battle technology (including advanced radar, satellites, night vision, electronic countermeasures) provides an unprecedented ability to pursue the strategic warfare objective of striking directly at the economic, military, and/or psychological core of the opponent's society—witnessed in the bombing of London, Dresden, Tokyo, and Hanoi. Of Dresden, historian Walter LaFeber writes: "At Churchill's prodding, bombing attacks were increased—partly to break German morale, partly to impress the [Soviet] Red Army with western air power. The most infamous bomber attack occurred on February 13, 1945, when the magnificent—and militarily unimportant—city of Dresden was destroyed and 35,000 German lives lost. The next day, U.S. Mustang fighters machine-gunned refugees trying to flee the still-burning city…The systematic bombing of civilians…had become an accepted act of war."

Months later, when the United States dropped nuclear bombs on Hiroshima and Nagasaki, Truman propagandized, "The world will note that the first atomic bomb was dropped on Hiroshima, a military base. That was because we wished in this first attack to avoid, insofar as possible, the killing of civilians." In reality, the United States sacrificed tens of thousands of civilians (and future generations) to speed Japan's unconditional surrender and preempt the Soviet Union.[30]

After months of yellow ribbon victory celebrations, Pentagon officials acknowledged that civilian destruction in Iraq was deliberate policy. As reported in the *Washington Post* in July 1991,

> Some targets…were bombed primarily to create post-war leverage over Iraq, not to influence the course of the conflict itself.

Planners now say their intent was to destroy or damage valuable facilities that Baghdad could not repair without foreign assistance. Many of the targets in Iraq's Mesopotamian heartland…were chosen only secondarily to contribute to the military defeat of Baghdad's occupation army in Kuwait. Military planners hoped the bombing would amplify the economic and psychological impact of international sanctions on Iraqi society, and thereby compel President Saddam Hussein to withdraw Iraqi forces from Kuwait without a ground war. They also hoped to incite Iraqi civilians to rise against the Iraqi leader…

The worst civilian suffering, senior officers say, has resulted not from bombs that went astray but from precision-guided weapons that hit exactly where they were aimed—at electrical plants, oil refineries, and transportation networks. Each of these targets was acknowledged during the war, but all the purposes and consequences of their destruction were not divulged.[31]

The United States violated the laws of war in both letter and spirit. Proportionality and the protection of noncombatants are fundamental principles of the laws of war, as codified in the Hague and Geneva Conventions; "the right of belligerents to adopt means of injuring the enemy is not unlimited" (Hague Convention IV, 1907). Claiming to have adhered to the laws of war with "the most discriminate military campaign in history," the Pentagon acknowledged, "As a general principle, the law of war prohibits the destruction of civilian objects not imperatively required by military necessity and the intentional attack of civilians not taking part in hostilities."[32]

As *The Nation* editorialized (February 18, 1991), "Nothing in the traditional rules of war has survived the introduction of strategic air power, which by intention makes civilians the object of violence. The concept of 'collateral damage' is a monstrous sophistry—in Anglo-Saxon criminal law, a man who throws a hand grenade into a crowd is rightly presumed to have intended the death of everyone he kills, not merely the individual he may have been aiming at." In the Gulf War, the United States was often aiming at the crowd.

The thousands of direct bombing casualties among civilians merged with the victims of U.S.-provoked epidemics, hunger, civil war, and displacement. Drawing on U.S. and foreign government sources, relief workers, and press reports, Greenpeace estimates that as of July 1991, there were 62,400 to 99,400 war-related Iraqi civilian deaths, including 5,000 to 15,000 deaths during the air war. The estimated Kuwaiti total of civilian and military dead is 2,000 to 5,000.

The U.S. military anticipated a war with much higher civilian casualties, another indication of lack of proportionality. "According to a leaked copy of the 'civil affairs' annex to the Desert Storm war plan, the US military estimated in autumn that up to 40,000 Kuwaiti citizens would be killed in the war, and that another 100,000 would be injured [in a population of 2 million]. But two thirds of the population fled Kuwait before the air war began."[33]

The intentionality and lack of proportionality of U.S. actions must be clearly understood. Unfortunately, Greenpeace's valuable compendium, *On Impact,* is undermined by surprisingly misleading assumptions and conclusions. For example, the report states, "Through the repudiation of civilian attacks, albeit perhaps only in the context of an otherwise highly successful war, the US and its allies tacitly behaved in accordance with provisions of the Geneva Protocols...Iraq's gross behavior, particularly its devastation of the natural environment, serves as a sad contrast." Later the report asserts, "What this 'hyper war' demonstrates is that the idea of a war in which non-combatants are safeguarded is no longer credible...If this war is to be the model for the level of effort that 'hyper war' demands in the future...then it is the unintentional effects of war that now needs to move more to the center of our concern..."[34]

The *intentional* assault on Iraq's civilian infrastructure caused mass death and misery. A May 1991 Harvard Study Team reported that infant and child mortality had already doubled since the start of the Gulf crisis. (Nearly half the Iraqi population is under 15; about 20 percent is under five.) The study projected "that at least 170,000 children under five years of age will die in the coming year from the delayed effects of the Gulf Crisis...These projections are conservative. In all probability, the actual number of deaths of children under five will be much higher...[A] large increase in deaths among the rest of the population is also likely." The report states, "The immediate cause of death in most cases will be water-borne infectious disease in combination with severe malnutrition...Throughout Iraq gastroenteritis, cholera, and typhoid are now epidemic. The incidence of water-borne diseases increased suddenly and strikingly during the early months of 1991 as a result of the destruction of electrical generating plants in the Gulf War and the consequent failure of water purification and sewage treatment systems."

The report concludes that "Contrary to the statements of both the Iraqi government and Western journalists that the health situation is stable and will continue to improve, the study team finds that the state of medical care is desperate and—unless conditions change substantially—will continue to deteriorate in every region and at nearly every provider level."A followup 1991 study reported that the child mortality rate was 380 percent greater than before the Gulf Crisis.[35] A study by Tufts University focusing on southern Iraq, "confirmed the existence of chronic malnutrition. They report that nearly half the 680 children up to the age of five they examined in Basra and 12 neighboring villages were suffering from chronic malnutrition."[36]

As for Iraqi soldiers, often demoralized draftees, estimates of 100,000 to 200,000 dead in 43 days reveal one-sided, rapid lethality reminiscent of the Gatling gun vs. the bow and arrow, with even higher killing ratios. In September 1991, *Newsday* reported that the U.S. army used tanks with plows and other earth movers to bury thousands of Iraqis—many of them alive—in the front-line trenches.[37] Official U.S. casualty figures as of June 24, 1991 (which like those in previous wars, such as Grenada, may leave out some special forces and other casualties), are 148 killed in action, 458 wounded in action, 138 non-battle deaths, and 2,978 non-battle injuries, the vast majority of whom have returned to duty. Estimates for other coalition casualties are 192 killed in action and 318 wounded in action. At least 20 American and 11 British combat deaths resulted from what is euphemistically called American "friendly fire."[38]

The ability and willingness to carry out one-sided slaughter is a traditional feature of empire. As historian Paul Kennedy recounts, "In the year 1800, Europeans occupied or controlled 35 percent of the land surface of the world; by 1878 this figure had risen to 67 percent, and by 1914 to over 84 percent" aided by supremacy in firepower, especially in open country wherever machine guns and heavier weapons could be deployed. "Perhaps the greatest disparity of all was seen at the very end of the century, during the battle of Omdurman (1898), when in one half-morning the Maxims and Lee-Enfield rifles of Kitchener's army destroyed 11,000 Dervishes for the loss of only forty-eight of their own troops."[39]

The Pentagon intentionally exaggerated Iraq's comparative strength—portraying the Iraqi army as one of the world's strongest, rather than one of the Third World's strongest—both to mislead Iraq and set the stage for a more heroic looking victory. One reason there was little artillery fire from the Iraqis who survived the air war, besides shell-shock from the unprecedented 24-hour-a-day rain of steel and fire, was that the U.S. had the ability to locate artillery positions as soon as they fired and launch an immediate counterstrike. For Iraqis, shooting was not survival, it was suicide. U.S. pilots described the slaughter of an estimated 25,000 people on the Kuwait highways "to hell" jammed with Iraqis in full retreat as "shooting fish in a barrel." Widely published photos of this carnage showed only the corpses of the vehicles.

The Pentagon says, "The Coalition succeeded in what Sun Tzu calls the greatest achievement of a commander, defeating the enemy's strategy." It does not fully quote Sun Tzu, the Chinese general who elaborated

The Art of War over 2,000 years ago, when he says, "For to win one hundred victories in one hundred battles is not the acme of skill. To subdue the enemy without fighting is the acme of skill. Thus, what is of supreme importance in war is to attack the enemy's strategy." Sun Tzu also said, if armed force must be used, then victory should be gained "with infliction on the enemy of the fewest possible casualties."[40]

Mutilation is Not Surgery: Mistaken Mystiques From Low Intensity to High Tech

The only thing surgical about the U.S. bombing was the surgery used to save the wounded. "Surgical" should not be accepted as a euphemistic term for bombing strikes, whatever their accuracy or inaccuracy. The Greenpeace report asserts, "ironically it was the efficiency [sic] of the allied military destruction, even within what the war planners considered to be their exemplary and unprecedented care, that ultimately caused vexing devastation. Surgical war had finally arrived, and the patient was skillfully carved and disemboweled." The word for that is not surgery; it is mutilation.

While military analysts like Paul Walker and Eric Stambler of the Cambridge-based Institute for Peace and International Security rightly concluded "This was not a surgical war; it was a slaughter,"[41] others jumped on the "surgical," "technowar" bandwagon, adopting Pentagon euphemisms. "Surgical" terminology is mystifying and demobilizing instead of mobilizing and demystifying. (The same is true for "Low Intensity Conflict" lingo discussed below.) "Technowar" jargon focuses on smart bombs while forgetting dumb bombs, death from war-related disease and malnutrition, and air/ground war deaths, thereby distorting the overall picture. Pretending to see the war in greater complexity, Technowarspeak oversimplifies.

A *Mother Jones* article titled "Bomb Now, Die Later," grandly asserts: "At the threshold of the third millennium, the United States has succeeded in introducing an entirely new concept of warfare, one that does not involve frontline battle or produce direct civilian casualties as a result of bombing, but that, more insidiously, knocks out all of a country's infrastructure and nerve centers—electricity, communications, transportation. This has been, in the words of Dr. Jack Geiger of Physicians for Human Rights, a 'bomb now, die later' war."[42]

Historical knowledge does not seem to be a requirement for Gulf War observers declaring an "entirely new concept of warfare" anymore than it was for "Low Intensity Conflict" critics (who didn't seem to read Clausewitz or other war theorists). Recall William Tecumseh Sherman, the Union Civil War Commander who, lacking the invention of aerial bombardment, burned Georgia's infrastructure in a campaign to destroy Confederate supplies, disrupt communications and transport, and break civilian morale.

The Gulf War was a Bomb Now, Die Now *and* Die Later war. It was not, as Erika Munk called it in *The Nation,* a "high-tech, low-gore war."[43]

In the 1980s, anti-war activists developed a mystique around "Low Intensity Conflict."[44] Low Intensity Conflict (LIC) is a military term which, in the words of the Pentagon's Joint Low Intensity Conflict Project, "emerged as a euphemism for 'counterinsurgency' when that term lost favor."[45] The term expanded to include, in the Orwellian language of the Pentagon, insurgency/counterinsurgency (e.g., contras, El Salvador), counterterrorism (e.g., bombing Libya), peacekeeping (e.g., U.S. intervention in Lebanon in early 1980s), peacetime contingency operations (e.g., invasion of Grenada), and counternarcotics (e.g., intervention in Bolivia and Peru).

Many anti-interventionists misread LIC doctrine and practice and mystified it as a new politically-oriented war of attrition that would avoid the pitfalls of Vietnam by precluding the deployment of U.S. ground troops. For example, in a problematic analysis of the implications of the "mid intensity" Gulf War, Sara Miles writes, "'Low Intensity' wars are not simply less of a big war; they are qualitatively different *kinds* of wars, fought in different ways, with different logics...It is a kind of war where military escalation is usually counterproductive."[46]

The Vietnam War became the standard touchstone for contemporary war, but it was not typical of U.S. intervention in that the United States lost after paying a very high human, economic, and political price. The Pentagon's enduring lesson from the Vietnam War (not always followed) is that if U.S. ground troops are used in combat, they should not be deployed gradually, but with overwhelming force to rapidly crush the opponent.

Before Vietnam, with exceptions such as the Bay of Pigs invasion, Washington had a long record of victory in counterrevolution and counternationalism, employing a mix of covert and overt economic, political, and military intervention, with and without U.S. special forces and combat troops. It has had substantial, if sometimes partial, success since Vietnam, from Angola to Jamaica and Nicaragua.

In the Nicaragua case, Reagan planners first envisioned the contra war as a quick and dirty rout, not a prolonged war of attrition. As one official put it, "We were going to knock off these little brown people on the cheap." The initial U.S. strategy, whereby the contras would seize "liberated territory" and receive direct U.S. military support for their provisional government, was defeated by Sandinista resistance, public opposition in the United States, and regional peace efforts which put obstacles in the path of escalation. On December 20, 1983, following the failure of another contra offensive and feeling the flush of victory in Grenada, the Special Inter-Agency Working Group on Nicaragua decided "to bring the Nicaragua situation to a head in 1984." At a National Security Planning Group meeting on January 6, 1984, Reagan approved the recommendation to "proceed with stepped up intensity." CIA commandos and clandestine U.S. military forces such as the Army Intelligence Support Activity (ISA) and Task Force 160 helicopter "Night Stalkers" attacked military, economic, and civilian targets and mined Nicaragua's harbors. The mines caused a political explosion in the United States, which resulted in the temporary Boland amendment cutoff contravened by the Reagan-Bush administration. While U.S. troops in Honduras served as the contra rearguard, a possible direct U.S. invasion during Reagan's second term was derailed by the Iran-contra scandal.[47]

While the anti-intervention movement focused largely on supposed "low intensity proxy war" in Central America and, to a far lesser extent, the Philippines and southern Africa, the 1980s saw the repeated use of direct U.S. military force, including the routinized use of military force against "narcoterrorism," and the expansion of intervention forces from aircraft carriers to special forces and light army divisions. Many anti-war activists missed the point that, in the Pentagon's view, the invasion of Grenada was "low intensity," just like the larger invasion and occupation of Panama. A 1990 report by the U.S. General Accounting office, *U.S. Weapons: The Low-Intensity Threat is Not Necessarily a Low-Technology Threat,* noted that "the range of potential situations and locations where U.S. armed forces may be called on to take direct action is global."[48]

In a briefing following the 1986 National Defense University Low-Intensity Warfare Conference, then Deputy Assistant Secretary of Defense Noel Koch remarked, "One of our defense thinkers suggested rather than calling it low-intensity warfare, we should call it high-frequency warfare." My shorthand definition of LIC is "Let's Intervene in smaller Countries." Investigative journalist Chip Berlet calls it "Low Attention Warfare" because many Americans pay little heed when Third World people do most of the dying.

Our language should communicate, not obscure, the human toll of war. Nicaragua and El Salvador suffered death tolls of 30,000 and 70,000, respectively. A proportionate U.S. toll would be over 5 million people. Angola's U.S.-abetted death toll may be as high as 500,000, nearly 4 percent of its people—equivalent to nearly 10 million Americans. Mozambique's 1 million dead by war and related famine is a monstrous one-fifteenth of its population. These wars are not low intensity. The Gulf War was not surgical.

From Vietnam to the Gulf Syndrome

U.S. officials rewrote old history as they produced a censored version of new history. "By God," said Bush, "we have kicked the Vietnam Syndrome once and for all" in the desert sands because, unlike Vietnam, "we didn't fight this war with one arm tied behind our back." The United States lost in Vietnam, the official propaganda story goes, because the anti-war movement and the supposedly adversarial media prevented the military from winning, not because the war was wrong and many U.S. soldiers knew it. Some of these anti-war veterans have also "kicked the Vietnam Syndrome." Senator Bob Kerrey, a liberal Democrat presidential hopeful from Nebraska who won the Medal of Honor and lost a leg in Vietnam, said U.S. success in the Gulf would accelerate the process of Democrats shaking off the Vietnam Syndrome. He said, "When Nelson Mandela, Vaclav Havel and Lech Walesa addressed Congress to thank Americans for their willingness to fight for their freedom, I knew I had been wrong to doubt the moral cause of Vietnam."[49]

The official story has become the only story for many Americans born since the 1960s. Newspapers juxtaposed photos of a U.S. helicopter evacuating the American embassy in Saigon and a helicopter landing marines on the embassy in Kuwait City. The Vietnamese had the compelling cause of national liberation and terrain less favorable to one-sided air war than the desert. Still, this supposedly one-armed war took 58,000 American and 2 million Vietnamese lives (some in the Operation Phoenix mass assassination program). Napalm, B-52 carpet bombing, and "Only we can prevent forests" Agent Orange—with its continuing chain of death in increased cancer and birth defects among the Vietnamese and American veterans and their children—defoliated and cratered such a large portion of the country that environmentalists called it ecocide. One-third of the country was made wasteland.[50]

General William Westmoreland, Schwarzkopf's Vietnam counterpart, says the United States won the war because "Vietnam is a basketcase."[51] Two decades later, the United States is still fighting the Vietnam War with economic embargo and Cambodian proxies.

In reality, the only arm tied during Vietnam was nuclear, and even that was seriously considered by American war planners. The "nuke Vietnam back to the stone age" attitude was expressed this way by Ronald Reagan in October 1965: "We should declare war on North Vietnam...We could pave the whole country and put parking strips on it, and still be home by Christmas." According to a CNN-*Time* poll taken shortly after the Gulf War began, 45 percent favored and 45 percent opposed using nuclear weapons. *Tonight Show* host Jay Leno amused his audience on January 15, 1991 with the "joke":

Q: What do Hiroshima, Nagasaki and Baghdad have in common?

A: Nothing...yet.[52]

Presidents Reagan and Bush paved the way to Iraq through Grenada, Libya, and Panama. The public rationales for war have grown more Orwellian: hostage rescue operation, punishing terrorism, arresting a drug dealer. The little-known mission of the 1986 U.S. bombing of Libya's capital Tripoli was to kill Colonel Qaddafi and his family. At least 17 persons died, including Qaddafi's fifteen-month old adopted daughter, and over 100 were injured in the veiled assassination mission widely applauded in the United States as a blow against "international terrorism."[53]

Now, we're seeing a "Gulf syndrome" of jingoistic military triumphalism, whereby many Americans will assume the morality, legality, necessity, and low-risk winnability of future offshore wars. The common reaction to Hussein's crushing of the Kurdish and Shiite rebellions, tacitly approved by Washington, is not a reappraisal of the merit or morality of the Gulf War, but the insistence that the United States "should have finished the job" by annihilating Iraq's army, killing Saddam Hussein, and possibly occupying Iraq.

American dissidents will find it much harder to prevent, protest, and reverse the next war. It will be harder to warn that the next war might bring high American casualties, much less argue against U.S. self-righteousness and the immorality of slaughtering others. As the motto painted on a U.S. armored vehicle put it, "Killing is our business, and business is booming."[54]

Secretary of Defense Cheney knows that this war was tilted to the United States in many ways, not just in the size and strength of the armies. "We benefited greatly from...the long interval to deploy and prepare our forces—that we cannot count on in the future. We benefited from our enemy's near-total international isolation and from our own strong coalition. We received ample support from the nations that hosted our forces and relied on a well-developed coastal infrastructure that may not be available the next time. And we fought in a unique desert environment, challenging in many ways, but presenting advantages too. Enemy forces were fielded largely in terrain ideally suited to armor and air power and largely free of noncombatant civilians." The last point is a further indictment of U.S. strategy to take the war to civilians in the cities as well as the desert.

Cheney continues, "We should also remember that much of our military capability was not tested in Operation Desert Shield and Desert Storm. There was no submarine threat. Ships did not face significant anti-surface action. We had little fear that our forces sent from Europe or the U.S. would be attacked on their way to the region. Chemical warfare and biological warfare, though threatened, were never employed. American amphibious capabilities, though highly effective for deterrence and deception, were not tested on a large scale under fire. Our Army did not have to fight for long. Saddam Hussein's missiles were inaccurate...Future adversaries will seek to avoid Saddam Hussein's mistakes..."[55]

Cheney offers fit-for-public-consumption lessons about the need for a continued march toward presidential authority, high-tech weapons, highly motivated forces, and global power projection. The lesson the Pentagon leaves unstated is that with the help of a saluting media, the American public has a large tolerance for using overwhelmingly lethal force to achieve violent victory with disproportionately low U.S. casualties. No Third World countries can match the United States in "conventional" forces, much less nuclear. The United States might again get bogged down in jungle or mountain warfare once the decision is taken to intervene directly in a guerrilla war with large-scale U.S. forces, but I wouldn't assume it in the current world balance of power.

In an article titled "America's New Combat Culture," complete with Robocop graphic, Tony Cordesman (ABC News military analyst, congressional adviser and professor of national security studies at Georgetown University) described the Air-Land Battle doctrine this way:

> The new strategy stressed initiative, agility, depth of operation, and synchronization of all four services and their branches. New tactics stressed avoiding battles of attrition and accepting risk, using night and poor-weather operations, attacking enemies' specific vulnerabilities, and keeping the battlefield "fluid" through continuous operations so that foes would be kept off balance and forced to move in desired directions.
>
> The new culture implied a new civil-military relationship. This unwritten bargain said the military would never again willingly fight a major war if it did not have full political support, if it could not

use all its force to win quickly and decisively, if gradual escalation and political bargaining deprived it of the ability to maintain momentum and if politicians tried micro-management.[56]

In other words, the "new civil-military relationship" assumes no diplomacy or public debate over ends and means once war is launched. It echoes fascist war themes such as expressing the national will through a supreme commanding leader.

At the end of the Gulf War, Schwarzkopfmania had a wider run than Olliemania. Norman of Arabia would come home and make the trains run on time (his father, Norman of Persia, helped set up the Shah of Iran's police force in the 1940s and participated in the 1953 CIA coup to reinstall the Shah after Prime Minister Mohammed Mossadegh led the parliament's nationalization of the Anglo-Iranian Oil Company).[57] Bantam books won the "bidding war" for Schwarzkopf's memoirs for nearly $6 million.

Republicans and Democrats alike sought to make Schwarzkopf a political candidate. Americans have a long tradition of generals in the White House from Washington, Jackson, Taylor, and Grant to Roosevelt ("Speak softly and carry a big stick" Theodore) and Eisenhower—not to mention officials associated with Generals Motors, Electric, and Dynamic.

Madonna ended her 1991 Academy Awards rendition of "Sooner or Later (I Always Get My Man)" with the line, "Where are you General Schwarzkopf?" Liberal feminist columnist Ellen Goodman crowned Schwarzkopf a new model of male leadership: "Desperately seeking a man who is caring but, well, commanding?" Schwarzkopf, wrote Goodman, is not strong but silent John Wayne, sensitive but wimpy Alan Alda, "brawny no-brainer Rambo," or "just The Thinking Woman's Oliver North." Schwarzkopf is "a man who is on speaking terms with his emotions, willing to express his fears, but not paralyzed by them. Someone who isn't afraid of violence, but doesn't like it." The military, wrote Goodman, "was long one of the touchstones of maleness. Vietnam sullied the image of soldier with that of 'baby killer.' But Schwarzkopf, who had done much soul-searching about Vietnam put it behind him. And maybe behind men…A good man, as they say, is hard to find. Make some room for men who are still strong but no longer silent."[58]

Pax Americana, Pax Trilateral

Bush declared in his acceptance speech for the 1988 Republican nomination: "This has been called the American Century because in it we were the dominant force for good in the world. We saved Europe, cured polio, went to the moon, and lit the world with our culture. Now we are on the verge of a new century, and what country's name will it bear? I say it will be another American Century." *Fortune* magazine heralded "The New American Century" with a red, white, and blue special Spring/Summer 1991 issue.

The New World Order is a one-superpower order, with the United States as Top Gun. Just Say Uncle Sam. Even the *New York Times* noted in an editorial (January 20, 1991), "'New world order' is an unfortunate phrase, reminiscent of Nazi sloganeering."

Washington is using militarism, like aging empires of old, in an attempt to humble the oil-poor economic superstars, Germany and Japan, and preserve U.S. preeminence in the increasingly hegemonic trilateral alliance.[59]

Trilateralists in the Atlantic-Pacific Triangle of the United States (and North American junior partner, Canada), Western Europe, and Japan want to realize their dream of interdependent "collective management" over the world economy, not relive the nightmare of economic nationalism and possible war among the capitalist powers. Pax Trilateral would follow the Pax Americana that had succeeded Pax Britannica.

The New World Order of Pax Americana I was constructed on the World War II ruins of European and Japanese imperialism with the guiding blueprints of the U.S. Council on Foreign Relations' War and Peace Studies Project, originated in 1939. War and Peace Study Groups worked with the government to develop U.S. war and post-war objectives. In 1940, the Project's Economic and Financial Group did a study to determine how much of the world's resources and territory the United States required to maintain its power and prosperity. As summarized by Laurence Shoup and William Minter,

> The world was divided into blocs and the location, production, and trade of all important commodities and manufactured goods were compiled for each area...The self-sufficiency of each major region—the Western hemisphere, the British Empire, Continental Europe, and the Pacific area—was then measured...The self-sufficiency of the German-dominated Continental European bloc was found to be much higher than that of the Western hemisphere as a whole. To match this economic strength the Western hemisphere had to be united with another bloc...
>
> The degree of self-sufficiency of the new region, initially called the Western hemisphere, British Empire, and Far East bloc [including both China and Japan], was substantially greater than that of any other feasible union...The Council planners thus concluded that, as a minimum, the U.S. "national interest" involved free access to markets and raw materials [in those regions].

The so-called "Grand Area" was considered a core region. The ideal new world order would have a one-world economy led by the United States. In 1941, the Economic and Financial Group noted that "formulation of a statement of war aims for propaganda purposes is very different from formulation of one defining the true national interest." They advised, "If war aims are stated which seem to be concerned solely with Anglo-American imperialism, they will offer little to people in the rest of the world, and will be vulnerable to Nazi counterpromises. Such aims would also strengthen the most reactionary elements in the United States and the British Empire. The interests of other people should be stressed, not only those of Europe, but also of Asia, Africa, and Latin America. This would have a better propaganda effect."

The Council on Foreign Relations developed plans for new economic institutions to manage the post-war economy (leading to the International Monetary Fund and the World Bank) and advocated a United Nations body as a way to maintain effective international control while avoiding, in an age of rising nationalism, "conventional forms of imperialism."[60]

By the late 1960s/early 1970s, the Pax Americana was under challenge by growing rivalries with reconstructed Europe and Japan; the Soviet superpower; Third World national liberation struggles against both colonialism and neocolonialism; the OPEC exercise of "commodity power" which galvanized the Third World movement for a New International Economic Order; and what a 1975 Trilateral Commission report termed the internal "Crisis of Democracy."

The Trilateral Commission was formed in 1972-73 by then Chase Manhattan Bank Chairman David Rockefeller, future Carter National Security Adviser Zbigniew Brzezinski and other multinational corporate executives, bankers, academics, and past and future government officials as a transnational response to Nixon's attempt to reassert U.S. economic primacy with nationalist protectionism. At the government level, trilateralism was institutionalized with the so-called Western summits (including Japan) begun during the Ford administration.

Trilateralism was mistakenly dismissed as dead in the 1980s by those who treated it as omnipotent or unimportant, rather than an influential, tension-ridden transnational elite process of collective "management of contradictions."[61] In fits and starts, trilateralism has advanced far down the paths laid out in the 1970s:

- Integrating Japan into the "collective management" of the world economy, especially the Asia-Pacific region.

- Forging a United Europe (along with the overlapping and more secretive European Bilderberg group founded in 1954[62]) closer to a United States of Europe than a United Europe of Socialist and Social Democracies.

- Reintegrating the so-called "dropouts"—China, the Soviet Union, and Eastern Europe—into an increasingly one-world capitalist economy. Writing in 1980, I noted, "trilateralists are confident they can win the ideological and economic 'competition' with the Soviet Union. They believe that the Soviet economy is declining and will reach a crisis state in the 1980s."[63] In a 1989 Trilateral Commission report, former President of France Valery Giscard D'Estaing, former Prime Minister of Japan Yasuhiro Nakasone, and former Secretary of State Henry Kissinger provided advice that would be followed in 1991 at the so-called G-7-and-a-half summit (the capitalist powers plus the Soviet Union) when Gorbachev begged for more economic aid and faster full admittance to the International Monetary Fund, capitalism's economic enforcer: "We do not favor financing the Soviet Union as a political entity. We do propose to support, and perhaps to finance, those changes in the Soviet Union's economic structure that will make it more compatible with Western practices and values—provided the Soviet Union caries out a major reduction of its military expenditures and conducts a conciliatory foreign policy...Our countries should welcome Soviet and Eastern European participation in international economic institutions when these countries are ready to assume the obligations of such institutions and can meet the normal tests for entry. In the meantime, we support their admission to observer status."[64]

  U.S. policy risked the re-Stalinization of the Soviet Union by those seeing U.S. military and economic triumphalism as the modern equivalent of the World War I Versailles Treaty with Germany. But the failed August coup speeded the demise of the old Soviet political entity. It remains to be seen whether demagoguery or democracy will reap the whirlwind.

- "New Influentials" or "International Middle Class Countries" like Saudi Arabia and Mexico, backbone of potential Third World "commodity power," have been co-opted, split, and strangled in debt. Instead of fueling a New International Economic Order, OPEC's petrodollars have been largely recycled to Western banks, corporations, and military suppliers.

- Virtually all national liberation governments and movements from Angola to Zimbabwe, Jamaica to Nicaragua, have been co-opted or destabilized. Still strong movements like the South African ANC and

Salvadoran FMLN have been forced to significantly lower their economic and political expectations. With Russian approval, U.S. officials are contemplating when, not if, Cuba will be reunited with Miami.

- Carter's human rights policy was rooted in the trilateralist notion that "a minimum of social justice and reform will be necessary for stability in the long run."[65] After failing to preempt revolution by replacing dictators (like the Shah and Somoza) with so-called moderates, more success is apparent in post-dictatorship Chile and other countries in the southern Cone (Brazil's Workers' Party presents the strongest challenge there).

- The domestic items on the trilateral agenda included reducing the economic and political expectations of the poor and middle class; reestablishing presidential authority in the wake of Watergate; strengthening the bonds among media, academia, and government; weakening labor activism and strengthening corporatist-style business-government-labor partnership.

The 1975 report, *The Crisis of Democracy,* complained that the president could no longer "govern the country with the cooperation of a relatively small number of Wall Street lawyers and bankers." The U.S. section of the report was written by Samuel Huntington, coordinator of national security on the Carter/Brzezinski National Security Council, 1977-78, and architect of the Vietnam War program of "forced urbanization," i.e., bombing, burning and strafing rural villages to relocate peasants into "strategic hamlets" and thus deprive guerrilla forces of support. The report laments the erosion of traditional forms of public and private authority and the widespread questioning of "the legitimacy of hierarchy, coercion, discipline, secrecy, and deception—all of which are, in some measure, inescapable attributes of the process of government."

The "crisis of democracy" was that too many people participated too much, or attempted to do so: "Previously passive or unorganized groups in the population, blacks, Indians, Chicanos, white ethnic groups, students, and women now embarked on concerted efforts to establish their claims to opportunities, positions, rewards, and privileges, which they had not considered themselves entitled before [sic]."

The *Crisis of Democracy* was unusually blunt about the distinction between egalitarian, participatory democracy and the limited democracy beloved by the Establishment: "The effective operation of a democratic political system usually requires some measure of apathy and noninvolvement on the part of some [i.e., most] individuals and groups." The greatest threat to democracy is democracy itself: "The vulnerability of democratic government in the United States thus comes not primarily from external threats, though such threats are real, nor from internal subversion from the left or the right, although both possibilities could exist, but rather from the internal dynamics of democracy itself in a highly educated, mobilized, and participant society."[66]

Trilateralist Jimmy Carter made fiscal conservatism the bipartisan "politics of less." Trilateralist Federal Reserve Chairman Paul Volcker put it bluntly in 1979: "The standard [of living] of the average American has to decline."[67] In a special 1979 issue on the "problems of empire," *Business Week* advocated guns over butter. Earlier that year, *Business Week* noted, "By the standards of today, the U.S. offers both cheap energy and cheap labor—and the all-too-rare plus of political stability...In Germany, the Netherlands, Belgium, and Sweden, average wages for manufacturing workers now exceed comparable U.S. wages by as much as 20%."[68] Cloaked in the holy mantle of The National Interest, Corporate America used recession and blame-the-victim, divide-and-conquer campaigns against the "special interests" (women, workers, people of color). I'll return to this point below.

Progressives should not take solace in the idea that the United States will not be able to afford another Gulf War, that it has become a "rent-a-global cop," that it can't afford the costs of maintaining empire. The United States, while in relative decline vis-à-vis Germany and Japan (whose World War II devastation left the United States in an extraordinarily dominant position) is still the richest nation and the only military superpower. And, together, the trilateral alliance is far stronger, and getting more so, than the rest of the world.

Whatever the long-run outlook of U.S. empire, the United States is still resilient economically and militarily. If necessary, the United States can raise significant cash by taxing its rich at rates closer to Europe and Japan, whether to use for militarism or economic reinvestment or, if politically necessary, to buy the "minimum of social justice and reform necessary for stability in the long run" that the New Deal was all about. Or the United States can become more repressive in defense of empire and wealthy elites.

As always, trilateral nations are both partners and rivals, and the United States swings between the trilateral need for accepting collective management and reasserting U.S. predominance. When the Soviet Union unilaterally ended the Cold War the Bush administration found the chance to relive Pax Americana irresistible. But, however long Pax Americana II lasts it will be different in that its military leg will be much stronger than its economic leg. The best long-run hope for a thriving Corporate America is in trilateral partnership, not increasing rivalry.

If trilateralism breaks down it is much more likely that the United States and Europe will ally against Japan (or, less likely, the United States and Japan against Europe), than that Japan and Europe will unite against the United States. The hegemonic order for the foreseeable future will likely be a two-headed one: Pax Americana militarily, Pax Trilateral economically.

Recolonization

We are going back to the future: the recolonization of the Third World—legalized, if multinational corporate elites prevail, by lopsided GATT (General Agreement on Tariffs and Trade) and Free Trade Agreements, loansharked by the bankers' International Monetary Fund, disguised by pseudo-democracy, and policed by covert and open warfare.

Neocolonialism hid the interventionist principle—What's mine is mine, What's yours is mine. Now there's less pretense. An American t-shirt sold during the Gulf War shows a U.S. Marine pointing his rifle at an Arab on the ground, asking "How much is oil now?" Americans who easily claim Arab oil as "ours" would find it ludicrous if Arabs or anyone else asserted, "That's ours" about U.S. crops, coal, or other resources.

Western policy has largely been set by those who see the world as their farm, factory, market, and playground. Women are the cheapest labor on the multinational assembly line that stretches from the *maquiladoras* of Mexico and electronic firms of California to the "export processing zones" of Asia. Displaced from farming by agro-export business and discarded quickly by factories seeking a young workforce, some women turn to the "hospitality industry," the government-sanctioned sexual assembly line servicing multinational businessmen and U.S. military bases.[69] A *New York Times* article on Subic Naval Base in the Philippines observed, "For generations of American sailors...Subic had made possible a way of life that could never be duplicated on a Navy salary back home: Spacious houses with what are now $20-a-week maids, private white-sand beaches along the bay...privileges at a well-manicured, professional-quality 18-hole golf course, and a seemingly endless supply of available women and cheap beer."[70]

Now the workers of Eastern Europe are being auctioned off to the low-bid multinational corporations. The Soviet Union is readying itself to follow suit.

To "develop" their countries as cash-crop plantations and export-platforms for multinational corporations, western-backed Third World regimes went into heavy debt with multinational banks and agencies such as the International Monetary Fund. Like international loan sharks, the bankers encourage them to rob their people to service the debt.

According to UNICEF, "throughout most of Africa and much of Latin America, average incomes have fallen by 10% to 25% in the 1980s. In the 37 poorest nations, spending per head on health has been reduced by 50%, and on education by 25%." Taking into account aid, repayments of interest and capital, and the unequal terms of trade between the North's manufactured goods and the South's raw materials, "then the annual flow from the poor to the rich might be as much as $60 billion each year." The World Bank estimates that as many as 950 million people, nearly one out of five human beings, are "chronically malnourished"—double the numbers of a decade ago.[71] The 500th anniversary of Columbus' claim to the Americas' would be an appropriate time to recognize that the Third World "debt" has been paid many times over through colonialism, neocolonialism, and usurious interest.

Globally, new GATT proposals would devastate small farmers, speed up ecological crisis, and threaten the health and safety of workers and consumers. They would deepen Third World dependence, reward the production of cash crops for export over food needed for local consumption, and tighten multinational corporate control over technology and resources, including indigenous seeds and medicinal plants.[72] Free Trade Zones are zones where multinational corporations can operate free of taxes, unions, and health and safety regulations. With the expansion of GATT and Free Trade Agreements, corporations will be freer to exploit workers, consumers, and the environment, North and South, East, and West.

Making the World Safe for Hypocrisy

> I don't see why we need to stand by and watch a country go communist due to the irresponsibility of its own people.
>
> Henry Kissinger, June 27, 1970, voicing support for U.S.
> efforts to block Allende's election in Chile.

The new Pax Americana harks back to nineteenth century Manifest Destiny in the modern guise of Manifesto Democracy. To further its brand of political and economic correctness, Washington shores up repressive regimes with the flimsiest democratic façades and intervenes overtly and covertly in the most basic of internal affairs, the elections, of other countries. The underlying attitude is the same as that expressed by a U.S.

official in a 1927 "Confidential Memorandum on the Nicaraguan Situation": "We do control the destinies of Central America...Until now, Central America has always understood that governments which we recognize and support stay in power, while those which we do not recognize and support fall."[73]

Destabilization campaigns can culminate in invasions like Grenada 1983, or military coups like Guatemala 1954 and Chile 1973, or "electoral coups" like Jamaica 1980 and Nicaragua, where economic embargo, contra war, and increased internal opposition to the Sandinistas prevailed in 1990. Angola may be next.

Today's main electoral manipulators are the CIA, the National Endowment for Democracy (NED), and an interlocking set of quasi-private front organizations.[74] The National Endowment for Democracy—already involved in 77 countries from South Africa to New Zealand, Chile to Czechoslovakia—was established in 1983 as the public arm of "Project Democracy," a covert-overt intervention and propaganda operation coordinated by the National Security Council (NSC). The CIA-NED connection is personified by Walter Raymond, Jr., a CIA propaganda specialist who was detailed to the NSC in 1982 as senior director of Intelligence Programs; resigned from the CIA in 1983 to become NSC director of International Communications and Public Diplomacy, overseeing NED; and later became deputy director of the U.S. Information Agency. In Eastern Europe, NED has followed in the CIA's footsteps in working with fascist and anti-Semitic forces, for example, Hungarian emigre Laszlo Pasztor, a convicted Nazi collaborator.[75]

At the March 1990 NED board meeting, NED President Carl Gershman called the "victory of the democratic opposition in Nicaragua...a tremendous victory for the Endowment as well."[76] Imagine the leaders of the Soviet Endowment for Perestroika or even the Swedish Endowment for Social Democracy claiming victory in U.S. elections. It's unthinkable because U.S. law rightly prohibits foreign funding of U.S. candidates and such support would be politically suicidal. But Americans are so good at democracy doublethink, we get to participate in the "democratic elections" of other countries.

After democracy's "victory," exploitation worsens without fanfare. Nicaragua had only to look at Panama to see there would be no post-election bailout. Panama had only to look at Grenada. With a population of 110,000, Grenada was the perfect place for creating a low-cost theme park of corporate co-optation. Instead, Grenada (like Panama and Nicaragua) saw hollow promises and declining living standards. An August 1991 investment risk guide to 129 countries by International Business Communications ranked Panama a risky 75 and Nicaragua a riskier 109. Grenada was not ranked.[77] Washington insists that Iraq pay reparations to Kuwait, but refused to follow a World Court order to pay reparations to Nicaragua (with an estimated $17 billion in war-related economic damage). Instead, it pressured the Chamorro government to drop the case.

The National Endowment for Democracy is busy making the world safe for hypocrisy. The hollow democracy being exported by the United States is a Trojan Horse for controlling sovereignty and containing popular democracy. Freshly laundered, though, U.S. intervention in other nations' elections enjoys more political legitimacy now than before the CIA exposes of the sixties and seventies. Meanwhile, back in the U.S., you can buy a gun in many places more easily than you can register to vote.

A true crisis of American democracy is evident both in the Reagan-Bush campaign's alleged treasonable effort to swing the 1980 election by delaying release of U.S. hostages in Iran (October Surprise) and Democrats' fears they'll look like spoilsports if they seriously investigate while Bush is running for reelection. Willingly gullible Iran-contra watchdog Rep. Lee Hamilton has been put in charge of the House's reluctant investigation. The Iran-contra hearings should have led to the impeachment of President Reagan and then Vice President Bush. There were many more high crimes and misdemeanors than Watergate. But two presidential ousters in two decades were seen as too many. Instead, Congress beat around the Bush and preserved the coverup instead of the Constitution.[78]

American Disorder

We stand at a defining hour. Halfway around the world, we are engaged in a great struggle...We know why we're there. We are Americans...What is at stake is more than one small country, it is a big idea—a new world order...end of the cold war...hopes of humanity turn to us...We are Americans...If anyone tells you America's best days are behind her, they're looking the wrong way...a thousand points of light...We are Americans...the largest peacetime economic expansion in history has been temporarily interrupted. But our economy is still over twice as large as our closest competitor...reduced tax for long-term capital gains...if the playing field is level, America's workers and farmers can outwork and outproduce anyone, anytime, anywhere...control of the world's oil resources...Patriot missile...SDI...only the United States of America has had both the moral standing, and the means to back it up...The winds of change are with us now...

George Bush, 1991 State of the Union (Lite).

Post-Cold War America is being forged in cold cash, cold steel, and cold blood.

Each day, 40,000 children around the world die from poverty- and war-related killers such as malnutrition and disease. Their deaths, and many adult deaths, are preventable with a shift in government priorities. "The numbers stand in long rows like tombstones, monuments to the lives lost to society's neglect": 14 million children die yearly of preventable disease; 100 million people have no shelter; 900 million are illiterate.[79]

President Bush told the 1990 World Summit for Children, "I've learned that our children are a mirror, an honest reflection of their parents and their world." If the U.S. government were a parent it would be guilty of child abuse.

The New American Order is marked by growing inequality, polarization, and violence to the mind, body, and spirit. American children are dying because the United States is the only industrialized nation besides South Africa without national health-care protection. The United States has the world's Number One military and economy, but ranks only 24th in infant mortality.[80] Washington, Detroit, and Philadelphia have higher infant death rates than Jamaica or Costa Rica. Black America has a higher infant mortality rate than Nigeria. We have laws requiring newborns to leave the hospital in carseats, but none requiring full funding of WIC, the Supplemental Food Program for (pregnant and nursing) women and children.

The United States is the poorest richest country in the world. Even by the government's understated figures, nearly one out of four children is born into poverty—the highest rate of any industrialized nation. Poverty kills. The Maine Health Bureau found that poor children were more than three times as likely as other children to die during childhood.[81] Most poor families with children have one or more workers, employed full or part-time. But the ranks of the working poor are swelling as real wages are falling. Today's minimum wage ($8,840 a year) is a sub-poverty line wage.

The official poverty line for a family of four was $13,359 in 1990. According to Patricia Ruggles of the Urban Institute, the yardstick for assessing poverty is so outdated that it would have to jump to over $20,000 for a family of four and almost $17,000 for a family of three, just to match the standard of living provided by the original 1967 poverty line. (The 1989 median wage for full-time, year-round workers was $17,389 for Black women, $18,922 for white women, $20,426 for Black men, and $28,541 for white men.) The government sets the poverty line by using the Consumer Price Index to determine the cost of a minimally adequate diet and multiplying by three—wrongly assuming that a household spends one third of its budget on food and two-thirds can cover everything else. Today just two necessities, housing and food, take 85 percent of a typical poor family's budget.

By Ruggles' more honest measure the 1987 poverty rate would nearly double to about 24 percent overall—one out of four Americans. For children under 18, the rate would jump from 21 percent to 33 percent and for female-headed households, from 34 percent to 50 percent.[82] Since 1987, the poverty rate has risen.

Education, like health care, is rationed by income—in a country spending less public funds on education than the military, and more on military bands than the National Endowment for the Arts. The United States ranks only 18th in school-age population per teacher. Education disparities are widening as affluent cities and towns maintain decent schools while others slash public education along with other government services. The growing inequality of opportunity is illustrated by economist Robert Reich's comparison of three predominantly white Boston-area communities: In prosperous Belmont, the average public school teacher earned $36,100 in 1988. Only 4 percent of Belmont's 18-year-olds dropped out of high school and more than 80 percent of the graduating seniors went on to four-year colleges. In working-class Somerville, the average teacher earned $29,400; a third of the 18-year-olds did not finish high school; and fewer than a third planned to attend college. In Chelsea, the poorest of the three towns, the average teacher, "facing what is surely a more daunting educational challenge than in Belmont, earned $26,200 in 1988, almost a third less than the average teacher in Belmont." More than half of Chelsea's 18-year-olds did not graduate from high school, and only 10 percent planned to attend college.[83] President Bush, who was schooled at elite Andover and then Yale, calls himself the "education President." Jonathan Kozol, author of *Savage Inequalities,* says, "The worst thing is Bush saying that money won't make a difference...I'm embarrassed at the absurdity of arguing that money doesn't matter—that it's good for the rich but not for the poor."[84]

State university systems are being decimated. In Harvard's Massachusetts, state public higher education funding has been slashed by a third since 1988, leaving a $476 million budget—half the price of one B-2 bomber. Yale's Connecticut has the nation's highest per capita income, but public higher education spending has dropped to about $380 million, less per capita than Mississippi, the state with the lowest income. The proportion of the U.S. population attending college has actually begun to decline as reduced loans and grants means reduced access for lower-income students.[85]

Rising numbers of young people do not have equal opportunity, except, as the recruiting slogan goes, to "Be all that you can be in the

Army." On the front lines in the Gulf, Blacks and other people of color made up one-third of U.S. Army troops; nearly half of the over 35,000 military women in the Gulf were Black. On the home front, "In some areas of the country it is now more likely for a black male between his 15th and 25th birthday to die from homicide than it was for a United States soldier to be killed on a tour of duty in Vietnam."[86]

In the New American Order, more teenage boys, white and Black, die from gunshots than all natural causes combined.[87] More kids are killing and dying because society shows them violence is the way to settle disputes, in popular movies and popular wars, and makes guns more accessible than Head Start, health care, drug treatment, day care, job training, and college. The problem is not lack of prisons. The United States already has the world's highest imprisonment rate. It has more Black men in prison, per capita, than South Africa.

A 1991 Senate Judiciary Committee report calls the United States, "the most violent and self-destructive nation on earth"—leading the world in per capita murder, rape, and robbery rates. The 1990 murder rate was more than twice Northern Ireland's and nine times England's. Rates for violence against women were even worse. The rape rate was 15 times higher than England's and 26 times Japan's.[88]

The American Dream—always an impossible dream for many—is dying a slow death. Living standards are falling for younger generations for the first time since the Civil War. Average workers' wages are in a long-term depression. The dream of home ownership is fading with the twentieth century. Homelessness has become so visible it rouses little attention.

The earnings of nonsupervisory workers dropped 19 percent (after correcting for inflation) between 1973 and 1990. The inflation-adjusted median income for families with children headed by persons younger than 30 fell nearly one-fourth between 1973 and 1987.[89] With "givebacks" in health and other benefits, and an increase in involuntary part-time work (without benefits), the job scene is even worse. Not coincidentally, the share of unionized nonagricultural workers dropped from 35 percent in 1960 to 17 percent in 1990. Excluding government workers, union membership was 13 percent—less than in the early 1930s before the National Labor Relations Act established a legally protected right to unionize.[90] Unemployment is high, but the proportion of unemployed receiving benefits (37 percent in 1990) is smaller than any other recession since World War II and job programs are scarce. A drop in unemployment is declared when more despairing people stop actively seeking a job and are no longer counted.

Redistribution for the Rich

Wealth is not evaporating. Instead of "trickling down," it is flooding up to the Truly Greedy in a massive redistribution of wealth from poorer to richer. By 1973, the post-World War II trend toward a narrowing of income disparities was reversed. While wealthy households are taking a larger share of the national income, the tax burden has been shifted down the income pyramid, through cuts in the top personal income rates and capital gains and increases in regressive social security payroll taxes (up 30 percent since 1978), state and local sales taxes, and fees for public services.

While the average wages for most Americans are falling, for the richest 1 percent they more than doubled from 1977 to 1988, after accounting for inflation. According to *Business Week*, the average chief executive officer (CEO) earned as much as 41 factory workers or 38 teachers in 1960. By 1988, a CEO earned as much as 93 factory workers or 72 teachers. That year, the average CEO's total compensation climbed to over $2 million, far outpacing counterparts in Europe and Japan. According to *Fortune* magazine, "By 1990, the average CEO in manufacturing was making 119 times more than the average Joe," compared with 18 times more in Japan.[91] Meanwhile, the top personal income tax rate plummeted from 50 percent in the early 1980s to 28 percent, the lowest among industrialized nations.

According to an authoritative study by the Center on Budget and Policy Priorities, between 1977 and 1988, the average after-tax income of the top fifth of the population rose by an estimated 34 percent while the bottom fifth's share fell 10 percent. The wealthiest fifth now receive as much after-tax income as the other 80 percent. The average after-tax income of the richest 1 percent, adjusting for inflation, rose 122 percent from 1977 to 1988. The richest 1 percent of all Americans now receive nearly as much income after taxes as the bottom 40 percent—in 1980, the top 1 percent received *half* as much as the bottom 40 percent.[92] (Remember also that money begets money through interest, dividends, and inheritance.)

The Luxembourg Income Study, a comprehensive comparison of income levels, poverty rates, and government policies in the United States, Australia, Canada, Germany, Israel, the Netherlands, Norway, Sweden, Switzerland, and the United Kingdom, showed that American income is the most unevenly distributed and found "that the child poverty rate in the United States, after taxes and benefits are considered, was *more than twice that in Canada and four times the average child poverty rate in the other nations in the study.* It also showed that the poverty rate just among white children in the U.S. was higher than the poverty rate among *all* children in all other countries in the study except Australia.

"In short, the private economy in the United States generates more relative poverty among children than the private economies of many other western, industrialized nations—and the U.S. then does far less than the other nations to address this problem."[93] Forty percent of all poor people in the United States are children.

According to the Center on Budget and Policy Priorities, "Especially sharp reductions occurred in the Aid to Families with Dependent Children Program...From 1970 to 1991, the maximum AFDC benefit for a family of three with no other income declined 42 percent in the typical state, after adjusting for inflation. In fact...the average value of AFDC and food stamp benefits *combined* has now fallen to about the same level as the value of AFDC benefits *alone* in 1960, before the food stamp program was created" to combat hunger. According to the Children's Defense Fund, "In January 1990 the median state's maximum AFDC benefit for a family of three without other income was only $364 per month, 44 percent of the federal poverty level. Even with the maximum food stamp allowance, that family's income was still only 73 percent of the poverty level." What about the many poor families with earned income? The "disposable income of a mother who has two children—and who earns wages equal to 75 percent of the poverty line—was $3,100 lower in 1990 than in 1973."[94]

As the Children's Defense Fund's Marian Wright Edelman puts it, "We face a crisis of economic injustice...From 1982 to 1989, the number of U.S. billionaires quintupled while the number of children who fell into poverty increased by 2.1 million." In 1990, 2 million more Americans—including 800,000 more children—sank into poverty.[95]

According to economist Robert Reich, were the personal income tax as progressive as it was in 1977, "in 1989 the top tenth would have paid $93 billion more...At that rate, from 1991 to 2000 they would contribute close to a trillion dollars more, even if their incomes failed to rise."[96] In short, the Demon Deficit strangling social services, infrastructure repair, and other government responsibilities is a deficit of humanity, not money.

Populist Dreams or Nightmares?

In the early twentieth century, the vision of a future society unbelievably rich, leisured, orderly and efficient...was part of the consciousness of nearly every literate person...From the moment when the machine first made its appearance it was clear to all thinking people that the need for human drudgery, and therefore to a great extent for human inequality, had disappeared. If the machine were used deliberately for that end, hunger, overwork, dirt, illiteracy, and disease could be eliminated within a few generations...

But it was also clear that an all-round increase in wealth threatened the destruction...of a hierarchical society...

The essential act of war is destruction, not necessarily of human lives, but of the products of human labor...Even when weapons of war are not actually destroyed, their manufacture is still a convenient way of expending labor power without producing anything that can be consumed...The social atmosphere is that of a besieged city...

War...not only accomplishes the necessary destruction, but accomplishes it in a psychologically acceptable way...What is concerned here is not the morale of the masses...but the morale of the Party itself. Even the humblest Party member is expected to be competent, industrious, and even intelligent within narrow limits, but it is also necessary that he should be a credulous and ignorant fanatic whose prevailing moods are fear, hatred, adulation, and orgiastic triumph.

George Orwell, *1984.*

Writing two decades ago, conservative political strategist Kevin Phillips helped define *The Emerging Republican Majority.* Now, in *The Politics of Rich and Poor,* he describes "the triumph of upper America...No parallel upsurge of riches had been seen since the late nineteenth century, the era of the Vanderbilts, Morgans and Rockefellers."[97] Phillips predicts a populist swing in the political pendulum.

The failed American Dream can give way to a new American fairness or a neofascist nightmare. It depends on whose populism triumphs. Progressive populism. Or the reactionary populism of the David Dukes. That question is posed in the Soviet Union, where demagoguery is masquerading as democracy, and throughout Europe, East and West, where racist and fascist forces are resurgent.

Prosperous white American males are so intent on keeping their monopoly privileges of race and class they are resurrecting arguments, in the guise of countering "political correctness" and "quotas," that they and their "Western civilization" forefathers are superior to women and people of color and their ancestors. Instead of explicitly claiming genetic superiority, they imply that all women and people of color at top universities or corporate headquarters or Pulitzer prize winners owe their places to "standard-lowering" affirmative action "quotas." Except those whom, like Clarence Thomas, they anoint through affirmative tokenism.

While "glass ceilings" keep upper Corporate America an almost exclusively white male enclave, "quota" has become the current sexist and racist codeword.[98] As United Mineworkers President Richard Trumka put it at the June 1991 National Rainbow Coalition conference, "'Quota' is a substitute for Black, Hispanic, women…'Quotas are nice but I wouldn't want my daughter to date one…'"

We're not supposed to know that private universities have long had de facto affirmative action programs for the parentally correct offspring of rich white alumni. As Jim Hightower, former Texas Agriculture commissioner, said about Bush, he was "born on third base and decided that he'd hit a triple." A *Boston Globe* article on so-called "legacy admissions" noted that the acceptance rate for all Harvard applicants, class of 1992, was 15.6 percent while for children of alumni it was 35.2 percent. As the article put it, "far from being more qualified, or even equally qualified, the average admitted legacy at Harvard between 1981 and 1988 was significantly *less* qualified than the average nonlegacy."[99]

College is a ticket to higher wages, but not an equitable one. The average annual earnings of full-time workers 25 years and older with four or more years of college was $41,090 for white men, $31,380 for Black men, $27,440 for white women and $26,730 for Black women.[100]

The assault on multicultural diversity and "PC"—that's politically correct, not parentally correct—reflects the growing backlash as more women work outside the home and the United States evolves into a twenty-first century nation in which whites are a minority.

U.S. elites have carried out a mass redistribution of wealth and dismantling of social programs, laughing all the way to the bank and the FDIC as they divert, divide, and conquer with racism, sexism, homophobia, and xenophobia; young vs. old, poor vs. middle class, Black vs. Jewish, HIV positive vs. HIV negative, U.S. workers vs. Mexican and Japanese; Gulf wars, drug wars, and quota wars.

On an issue by issue basis, from national health and day care to affirmative action, a majority of Americans is often more progressive than their so-called representatives in Congress. A 1991 *Wall Street Journal*/NBC News poll showed strong support for deep cuts in the military budget; more than four out of ten Americans "believe American defenses could safely be cut in half by the year 2000."[101]

Too often voters are faced with a choice between timid Democratic tinkerers and hot-button pushing Republicans who thrive on divide-and-rule politics. Many Democratic politicians behave like defense lawyers who plea bargain every case, no matter the particulars of provable guilt or innocence. Who wants a lawyer—or politician—like that? Jesse Jackson forged populist Democratic presidential campaigns winning various 1988 primaries from Virginia to Vermont. The 1990 election saw significant progressive victories including the election of Democratic Senator Paul Wellstone, the 1988 Jackson campaign cochair for Minnesota, and of independent socialist Bernie Sanders as congressperson from Vermont. Iowa's Senator Tom Harkin built his 1992 presidential campaign on a populist platform.

At a time when more Americans see incumbency as incompetence, progressives have a good chance to make important electoral inroads. So do right-wing demagogues, who, unlike many leftists, don't default in disgust with electoral politics. Empowerment is a popular word among progressives. Too often though, it means protest against the powers that be without a real belief in the possibility of power. While advocating self-determination, many progressives succumb to self-defeatism: the self-defeatism of organizing as a permanent protest movement. The self-defeatism of trying to change policy through protest and lobbying without also trying to change who is making the policy. The self-defeatism of divorcing issue organizing from electoral organizing. The self-defeatism of piecemeal international solidarity without domestic solidarity. The self-defeatism of defense without offense.

In this time of fear and flux, progressive grassroots activists and candidates must reach out with commonsense talk about commonsense ideas.

Fair New World Order

The American political system is in a crisis of democracy—a crisis of too little democracy. We should abolish the globetrotting National Endowment for Democracy intervention and *endow participatory democracy* in the United States. We have to put a commitment to social and economic equality back into the definition of democracy. Workers, women, and others must reject their dismissal by elites as "minorities" and "special interests" and claim their rightful place at the heart of the national interest. We need to revitalize democracy with vigorous debate over who benefits and who loses from government policy, who gets bailed out and who gets locked in poverty.

Imagine a Congress truly representative of the American people, more than half female, with an ethnic and racial mix more like the Army's ground troops than the corporate board room. Essential elements of democracy include universal voter registration, free media for genuine debate among diverse candidates, and public financing for all campaigns at the local, state, and federal level.

We need *Fair Taxation with Representation*. Americans need to stop cutting off our noses to spite our faces with "No New Taxes" insurance for those who can afford to send their kids to private day care, private schools, private hospitals, and private colleges. If our schools are increasingly separate and unequal, children impoverished, and murder rates higher than nations with civil wars, it's not because we lack money, but the will to change priorities.

As Marian Wright Edelman puts it, "One of the most corrosive lies we face is the pervasive argument that 'nothing works,' the War on Poverty failed, social programs don't succeed. It is as though our entire nation has been put in one of those spirit-squelching, hope-destroying schools in which we bury so many students...These teachings inspired a 'can't do' spirit."[102] The Children's Defense Fund says it would have cost $26 billion to bail children and families out of poverty in 1988 and under $54 billion to eliminate all poverty.[103] That's far less than the price of bailing out S&L speculation and looting, "defending" Europe against a defunct Soviet bloc, or providing tax breaks and income redistribution for the rich. It's time to disband the educational and health care caste system, extend Social Security to children and the unemployed, and stop using our children's future as war collateral.

The United States must *shed its military-industrial complex and convert* to a socially- and ecologically-responsible economy. We should make rapid progress on comprehensive nuclear and conventional disarmament and demilitarize international affairs. We don't need Star Wars to shoot down nuclear missiles in space; we need nonproliferation and disarmament to dismantle them before they get off the ground. We should cut off spending for the NATO Cold War dinosaur, consuming half the military budget, rather than develop it into a global rapid deployment force for recolonization. Just one B-2 bomber costs more than the total gross national product (GNP) of Chad, Grenada, or Guyana; three B-2s cost more than the GNPs of Haiti, Nicaragua, or Zambia. For five B-2s you could double the GNP of Panama.

We should *outlaw covert action* as a threat to democracy at home and abroad. Recall that in 1947, President Truman approved both the National Security Act, creating the CIA and the Federal Employee Loyalty Program, which sowed the seeds for McCarthyism. The result of covert action has been illegal, immoral, and largely unaccountable terrorism and war abroad and the debasement of American democracy seen in the overlapping Iran-contra, BCCI, and October Surprise scandals.

A Fair New World Order would be safe not for "all-out military force" and covert action, but safe for all-out smart diplomacy, disarmament, and international law. In a real new world order the United Nations would serve the cause of nonviolent conflict resolution and international peacekeeping, not selective, veto-enforced, U.S.-directed police keeping. The World Court would be strengthened, so that international law could be applied without big power bias—to Iraq on Kuwait and the United States on Nicaragua, Panama, Grenada, and so on.

A Fair New World Order would be safe for human rights in their fullest sense, elaborated decades ago in the 1948 UN *Universal Declaration of Human Rights,* which embraced the right to an adequate standard of living, "including food, clothing, housing and medical care and necessary social services..." A decent job at fair pay should be a right, not a privilege.

A Fair New World Order depends upon a *Social and Environmental Compact for Sustainable Development.* Responding to the speeded up globalization of the world economy, broad coalitions of farmers, workers, environmentalists, women, consumers, and others (e.g., Fair Trade Campaign, Third World Network, Maquiladora Coalition) have formed nationally and internationally to promote equitable and sustainable development. The protection of earth's ecosystem is an essential element of security—personal, national, and international.

In the words of Mexican opposition leader Cuauhtemoc Cardenas, "The exploitation of cheap labor, energy, and raw materials, technological dependency, and lax environmental protection, should not be the premises upon which Mexico establishes links with the U.S., Canada and the world economy. We cannot be satisfied with the kind of future that would emerge from a simple economic liberalization. This would only extrapolate present trends and exacerbate present vices. Instead we should act with vision...Economic liberalization is not our objective, it is one of our tools. Development, social justice, and a clean environment are our objectives."[104]

Imagine a United States that is not a superpower for the superrich. Imagine a United States upbeat over educational progress, proud of rapid mobilization to sustain the environment, and euphoric over an end to unemployment and poverty.

If we can't imagine a fair new world order, we'll never get there. If progressives don't resist self-marginalization and Think Big (from grass-roots action to media to electoral politics), we'll always be marginalized.

Notes

1. "The Age of Anxiety," *Newsweek,* December 31, 1990, p. 16.
2. "No Comment," *The Progressive,* August 1991, p. 11.
3. Statement of Charles A. Bowsher, Comptroller General of the United States Before the Committee on Armed Services, U.S. Senate, "Defense Budget and Program Issues Facing the 102nd Congress," April 25, 1991, General Accounting Office, p. 26. Also see Center for Defense Information, "The Stealth Bomber: Just Say No," *The Defense Monitor* XIX:9, 1990 and "A New Military Budget for a New World," XX:2, 1991.
4. Department of Defense, *Conduct of the Persian Gulf Conflict: An Interim Report to Congress,* Pursuant to Title V Persian Gulf Conflict Supplemental Authorization and Personnel Benefits Act of 1991 (Public Law 102-25), July 1991, p. I-3.
5. Quoted in Bruce Cummings, "The End of the 70-Years' Crisis: Trilateralism and the New World Order," *World Policy Journal* 8:2, Spring 1991, p. 215.
6. Community Childhood Hunger Identification Project, *A Survey of Childhood Hunger in the United States,* Washington, DC: Food Research and Action Center, 1991. On school shortages and violence, see Diego Ribadeneira, *Boston Globe,* September 23, 1991, and Seth Mydans, *New York Times,* June 16, 1991.
7. See, for example, NARMIC, *Automating Apartheid: U.S. Computer Exports to South Africa and the Arms Embargo,* Philadelphia: American Friends Service Committee, 1982 and William Minter, *King Solomon's Mines Revisited: Western Interests and the Burdened History of Southern Africa,* New York: Basic Books, 1986.
8. Bob Woodward, *The Commanders,* New York: Simon and Schuster, 1991, p. 299.
9. Robert C. Johansen, "Lessons for Collective Security," *World Policy Journal,* Summer 1991, p. 563.
10. Department of Defense, *Conduct of the Persian Gulf Conflict,* p. 4-1.
11. See Bill Moyers Report, "After the War," Public Television, June 18, 1991; Stephen Hubbell, "The Iraqi Opposition: From Babel to Baghdad," *The Nation,* April 15, 1991; Jane Hunter, "Sowing Disorder, Reaping Disaster," *Covert Action Information Bulletin,* No. 37, Summer 1991, p. 25; William Blum, *The CIA: A Forgotten History,* London: Zed Press, 1986, p. 278; and Christopher Hitchens, "Minority Report," *The Nation,* May 6, 1991, p. 582.
12. See Center for Defense Information, "We Arm the World: U.S. is Number One Weapons Dealer," *The Defense Monitor* XX:4, 1991.
13. Ruth Leger Sivard, *World Military and Social Expenditures,* Washington, D.C.: World Priorities Inc., 1989 and 1991 editions.
14. Quoted in Philip Taubman, *New York Times,* February 8, 1984.
15. See Richard Drinnon, *Facing West: The Metaphysics of Indian-Hating & Empire-Building,* New York: Schocken Books, 1990.
16. Jamin B. Raskin, "Remember *Korematsu:* A Precedent for Arab-Americans?" *The Nation,* February 4, 1991, p. 117; Jennie Anderson, "Blame the Arabs: Tensions in the Gulf bring bigotry at home," *The Progressive,* February 1991. Also see reports of the Washington-based American-Arab Anti-Discrimination Committee and the New York-based Movement Support Network of the Center for Constitutional Rights.
17. "Harper's Index," *Harper's,* April 1991, p. 15.
18. Sivard, *World Military and Social Expenditures 1991,* p. 5; Political Ecology Group, *War in the Gulf: An Environmental Perspective,* San Francisco, 1991.

Saudi estimates on the oil spill in "America at War," *Newsweek* Commemorative Edition, Spring/Summer 1991, p. 79. On the environmental implications of narcoterrorism/counterinsurgency see, for example, Environmental Project on Central America, "Guatemala: A Political Ecology," *Green Paper* 5, San Francisco, 1990.

19. Everette E. Dennis, et al., *The Media at War: The Press and the Persian Gulf Conflict,* New York: Gannett Foundation Media Center, Columbia University, 1991, p. xi.

20. Fairness and Accuracy in Reporting *Extra,* Special Issue on the Gulf War, May 1991, p. 10.

21. Lewis H. Lapham, "Trained seals and sitting ducks," *Harper's,* May 1991, p. 10.

22. FAIR, Special Issue on the Gulf War, p. 5.

23. Barton Gellman, *Washington Post Weekly,* July 8-14, 1991.

24. Lewis H. Lapham, "Democracy in America? Not only the economy is in decline," *Harper's,* November 1990, p. 47.

25. FAIR, Special Issue on the Gulf War, p. 15. Also see Michael Hoyt, "Jon Alpert: NBC's Odd Man Out," *Columbia Journalism Review,* September/October 1991; Holly Sklar, "Buried Stories From Media Gulf," *Z Magazine,* March 1991; Moyers, "After the War"; FAIR, "'Slaughter' is Something Other Countries Do," *Extra,* May/June 1991; Ellen Ray and William H. Schaap, "Disinformation and Covert Operations"; and Paul Rogers, "The Myth of the Clean War," *Covert Action Information Bulletin* No. 37, Summer 1991.

26. Fred Kaplan, *Boston Globe,* January 29 and March 16, 1991.

27. Department of Defense, *Conduct of the Persian Gulf Conflict,* pp. 6-1, 2, 8; Tom Wicker, *New York Times,* March 20, 1991; Moyers, "After the War."

28. Quoted in Christopher Hitchens, "Minority Report," *The Nation,* March 11, 1991, p. 294.

29. See Michael Klare, "High-Death Weapons of the Gulf War," *The Nation,* June 3, 1991 and Paul F. Walker and Eric Stambler, "...And the Dirty Little Weapons," *The Bulletin of the Atomic Scientists,* May 1991.

30. Walter LaFeber, *The American Age: United States Foreign Policy at Home and Abroad Since 1750,* New York: W.W. Norton & Co., 1989, pp. 414, 425-28. Truman quote in Howard Zinn, *A Peoples' History of the United States,* New York: Harper & Row, 1980, pp. 413-15.

31. Barton Gellman, "Storm Damage in the Persian Gulf: U.S. strategy against Iraq went beyond strictly military targets," *Washington Post Weekly,* July 8-14, 1991.

32. William M. Arkin, Damian Durrant, and Marianne Cherni, *On Impact: Modern War and the Environment: A Case Study of the Gulf War,* a Greenpeace study, Washington, DC: Greenpeace, 1991, pp. 118-19; Department of Defense, *Conduct of the Persian Gulf Conflict,* p. 12-3.

33. "Deaths in the Gulf War at the One Year Mark," Greenpeace USA, July 1991. Quote on expected Kuwaiti casualties from Greenpeace, *On Impact,* p. 45.

34. Greenpeace, *On Impact,* pp. 145-49.

35. Harvard School of Public Health, *Harvard Study Team Report: Public Health in Iraq after the Gulf War,* May 1991, pp. 1-3, 18; Elizabeth Neuffer, *Boston Globe,* October 23, 1991. Also see "Report to the Secretary-General on humanitarian needs in Kuwait and Iraq in the immediate post-crisis environment," March 20, 1991, United Nations Security Council, S/22366.

36. Jean Mayer, "Iraq's Malnourished Children," *New York Times,* July 15, 1991.

37. Patrick J. Sloyan, *Newsday,* September 12, 1991.

38. Eric Schmitt, *New York Times,* August 10, 1991. For official casualty figures, see Department of Defense, *Conduct of the Persian Gulf Conflict,* pp. 27-31.

39. Paul Kennedy, *The Rise and Fall of the Great Powers: Economic Change and Military Conflict from 1500 to 2000,* New York: Random House, 1987, p. 150.
40. Department of Defense, *Conduct of the Persian Gulf Conflict,* p. 2-8. Sun Tzu, *The Art of War,* translated and with an introduction by Samuel B. Griffith, New York: Oxford University Press, 1963/1971.
41. Walker and Stambler, "And the Dirty Little Weapons."
42. Joost R. Hiltermann, "Bomb Now, Die Later," *Mother Jones,* July/August 1991, p. 46.
43. Erika Munk, "The New Face of Techno-war," *The Nation,* May 6, 1991. Also see the exchange of letters in the July 1 and October 7, 1991 issues.
44. See Holly Sklar, "Lick Low Intensity Conflict Doublespeak," *Z Magazine,* March 1989 and "Born Again War: The Low-Intensity Mystique," *NACLA Report on the Americas,* March/April 1987.
45. Joint Low-Intensity Conflict Project, *Analytical Review of Low-Intensity Conflict,* Fort Monroe, VA: U.S. Army Training and Doctrine Command, August 1, 1986, pp. 1-9.
46. Sara Miles, "The Gulf Syndrome," *War Watch,* Salinas, CA: Out Now, May 1991. Her LIC thesis was presented in "The Real War: Low Intensity Conflict in Central America," *NACLA Report on the Americas,* April/May 1986.
47. See Holly Sklar, *Washington's War on Nicaragua,* Boston: South End Press, 1988.
48. United States General Accounting Office, Report to the Chairman, Committee on Government Operations, House of Representatives, *U.S. Weapons: The Low-Intensity Threat is Not Necessarily a Low-Technology Threat,* Washington, DC: GAO, March 1990, p. 5.
49. *Boston Globe,* March, 31, 1991. I called Kerrey's office to confirm he had not been misquoted.
50. Sivard, *World Military and Social Expenditures 1990,* p. 30; Peter Korn, "Agent Orange in Vietnam: The Persisting Poison," *The Nation,* April 8, 1991.
51. *Boston Globe,* March 14, 1991.
52. Quoted in Margaret Spillane, "M*U*S*H," *The Nation,* February 25, 1991, p. 237.
53. See Seymour M. Hersh, "Target Qaddafi," *New York Times Magazine,* February 22, 1987.
54. Photo in *Boston Globe,* March 22, 1991.
55. Department of Defense, *Conduct of the Persian Gulf Conflict,* p. I-4.
56. Anthony H. Cordesman, "America's New Combat Culture," *New York Times,* February 28, 1991.
57. See Linda Rocawich, "The General in Charge," *The Progressive,* January 1991; *New York Times,* January 28, 1991; *Washington Post,* January 18, 1991; William Blum, *The CIA: A Forgotten History.*
58. Ellen Goodman, *Boston Globe,* March 14, 1991.
59. See Holly Sklar, ed., *Trilateralism: The Trilateral Commission and Elite Planning for World Management,* Boston: South End Press, 1980.
60. Laurence H. Shoup and William Minter, "Shaping a New World Order: The Council on Foreign Relations' Blueprint for World Hegemony," in Sklar, ed., *Trilateralism,* pp. 138-39, 145-46, 149. See the longer version of this chapter in their book, *Imperial Brain Trust: The Council on Foreign Relations and United States Foreign Policy,* New York: Monthly Review Press, 1977.
61. The term comes from Thomas Hughes, "Carter and the Management of Contradictions," *Foreign Policy,* Summer 1978.
62. See Peter Thompson, "Bilderberg and the West," in Sklar, ed., *Trilateralism.*
63. Sklar, "Trilateralism: Managing Dependence and Democracy—An Overview," *Trilateralism,* p. 34.

64. Valery Giscard D'Estaing, Yasuhiro Nakasone and Henry A. Kissinger, *East-West Relations,* Triangle Papers: 36, New York: Trilateral Commission, 1989.
65. Richard N. Cooper, Karl Kaiser, Masataka Kosaka, *Towards a Renovated International System,* Triangle Papers: 14, New York: Trilateral Commission, 1977, p. 10.
66. Michael J. Crozier, Samuel P. Huntington, and Joji Watanuki, *The Crisis of Democracy: Report on the Governability of Democracies to the Trilateral Commission,* New York: New York University Press, 1975, pp. 61-62, 93, 98, 113, 115.
67. *New York Times,* October 18, 1979.
68. "The Decline of U.S. Power: The New Debate Over Guns and Butter," *Business Week,* March 12, 1979, pp. 40-41. Previous quote from *Business Week,* July 9, 1979, pp. 50-52.
69. See Annette Fuentes and Barbara Ehrenreich, *Women in the Global Factory,* Boston: South End Press, 1983 and Rachel Kamel, *The Global Factory: Analysis and Action for a New Economic Era,* Philadelphia: American Friends Service Committee, 1990.
70. Philip Shenon, *New York Times,* September 29, 1991.
71. United Nations Children's Fund (UNICEF), *The State of the World's Children 1989,* New York: Oxford University Press, 1989, p. 15; World Bank cite in Robin Broad, John Cavanagh, and Walden Bello, "Development: The Market is Not Enough," *Foreign Policy* 81, Winter 1990-91.
72. See Chakravarthi Raghavan, *Recolonization: GATT, the Uruguay Round and the Third World* and Martin Khor Kok Peng, *The Uruguay Round and Third World Sovereignty,* both published by Third World Network, Penang, Malaysia, 1990 and available from Environmental News Network, Berkeley, CA, which has produced *GATT, The Environment and the Third World: A Resource Guide.* Also see, Robert Weissman, "Prelude to a New Colonialism: The Real Purpose of GATT," *The Nation,* March 18, 1991; Mark Ritchie, "GATT, Agriculture and the Environment," and other articles in *The Ecologist* 20:6, Special GATT Issue: Gunboat Diplomacy and the Uruguay Round, November/December 1990; *Multinational Monitor,* Issue on GATT, November 1990; Jeremy Brecher and Tim Costello, "Global Village vs. Global Pillage" and "A One World Strategy for Labor," *Z Magazine,* January and March 1991.
73. Undersecretary of State Robert Olds, "Confidential Memorandum on the Nicaraguan Situation," 1927, cited in Karl Bermann, *Under the Big Stick: Nicaragua and the United States Since 1848,* Boston: South End Press, 1986, pp. 292-94.
74. See Holly Sklar, "Washington Wants to Buy Nicaragua's Elections Again," *Z Magazine,* December 1989 and *Washington's War on Nicaragua*; Holly Sklar and Chip Berlet, article on NED, *Covert Action Information Bulletin,* Winter 1992; Beth Sims, *National Endowment for Democracy,* A Policy Report by the Council on Hemispheric Affairs and the Inter-Hemispheric Education Resource Center, Albuquerque, NM: The Resource Center, 1990.
75. Chip Berlet and Holly Sklar, "The N.E.D.'s Ex-Nazi Adviser," *The Nation,* April 2, 1990.
76. Draft Minutes of the March 29, 1990 Meeting of the Board of Directors, National Endowment for Democracy, p. 6.
77. *Wall Street Journal* special report, September 20, 1991.
78. Sklar, *Washington's War on Nicaragua,* especially chapters 12, 14, and 15.
79. Sivard, *World Military and Social Expenditures 1990,* p. 9.
80. "US lags in rates of infant deaths," *Boston Globe,* September 20, 1991, citing U.S. Centers for Disease Control.
81. Clifford M. Johnson, et al., *Child Poverty in America,* Washington, DC: Children's Defense Fund, 1991, p. 16.

46   COLLATERAL DAMAGE

82. Patricia Ruggles, *Drawing the Line: Alternative Poverty Measures and their Implications for Public Policy,* Washington, DC: Urban Institute Press, 1990.

Ruggles' data is summarized in Tim Wise, "Being Poor Isn't Enough," *Dollars and Sense,* September 1990.
83. Robert B. Reich, *The Work of Nations,* New York: Alfred A. Knopf, 1991, p. 275.
84. Quoted by Mary McGrory, *Washington Post,* September 30, 1991.
85. Reich, *The Work of Nations,* p. 258; Anthony Flint, *Boston Globe,* October 1, 1991.
86. Dr. Robert Froehlke, principal author of a Federal Centers For Disease Control report on homicide rates among Black men, quoted by Seth Mydans, *New York Times,* December 7, 1990.
87. Paul Taylor, *Washington Post,* "Guns are leading killer of teen-age boys," *Boston Globe,* March 14, 1991.
88. *Fighting Crime in America: An Agenda for the 1990's* and *Violence Against Women: The Increase of Rape in America 1990,* Majority Staff Reports Prepared for the Use of the Committee on the Judiciary, U.S. Senate, March 12 and March 21, 1991.
89. Johnson, et al., *Child Poverty in America,* pp. 18, 20.
90. Reich, *The Work of Nations,* p. 212.
91. Isaac Shapiro and Robert Greenstein, *Selective Prosperity: Increasing Income Disparities Since 1977,* Washington, DC: Center on Budget and Policy Priorities, 1991; Robert Greenstein and Scott Barancik, *Drifting Apart: New Findings on Growing Income Disparities,* Center on Budget and Policy Priorities, 1990; "The New American Century," *Fortune,* Special Issue, Spring/Summer 1991, p. 15; *Business Week,* annual survey of executive pay.
92. Shapiro and Greenstein, *Selective Prosperity,* pp. viii, x; and Greenstein and Barancik, *Drifting Apart.*
93. Shapiro and Greenstein, *Selective Prosperity,* pp. 22-23.
94. Ibid., pp. ix, 14; Children's Defense Fund, *Child Poverty in America,* p. 25.
95. Marian Wright Edelman, *Mother Jones,* May/June 1991; Center on Budget and Policy Priorities, "Two Million More Americans Become Poor As Recession Hits and Wages and Incomes Decline," press release, September 26, 1991.
96. Robert B. Reich, "The REAL Economy," *The Atlantic Monthly,* February 1991, p. 51.
97. Kevin Phillips, *The Politics of Rich and Poor,* New York: Random House, 1990.
98. See Sklar, "The Truly Greedy II," *Z Magazine,* February 1991.
99. Mark Muro, "Class Privilege," *Boston Globe,* September 18, 1991, citing work by Harvard graduate John Larew and others.
100. Barbara Vobejda, *Washington Post, Boston Globe,* September 20, 1991.
101. R. W. Apple Jr., *New York Times,* September 28, 1991.
102. *Mother Jones,* May/June 1991.
103. Children's Defense Fund, *S.O.S America! A Children's Defense Budget,* Washington, DC: 1990, p. 11.
104. Cuauhtemoc Cardenas, "The Continental Development and Trade Initiative," New York speech, February 8, 1991.

PART II

THE NEW WORLD ORDER

Same As It Ever Was...

CHAPTER 2

"WHAT WE SAY GOES"

The Middle East in the New World Order

Noam Chomsky

With the Gulf War officially over, broader questions come to the fore: What are the likely contours of the New World Order, specifically, for the Middle East? What do we learn about the victors, whose power is at least temporarily enhanced?

A standard response is that we live in "an era full of promise," "one of those rare transforming moments in history" (James Baker). The United States "has a new credibility," the president announced, and dictators and tyrants everywhere know "that what we say goes." George Bush is "at the height of his powers" and "has made very clear that he wants to breathe light into that hypothetical creature, the Middle East peace process" (Anthony Lewis). So things are looking up.[1]

Others see a different picture. A Catholic weekly in Rome, close to the Vatican, writes that Bush is the "surly master of the world," who deserves "the Nobel War Prize" for ignoring opportunities for peace in the Gulf. Bush "had the very concrete possibility of a just peace and he chose war." He "didn't give a damn" about the many peace appeals of Pope John Paul II and proposals of others, never veering from his objective of a murderous war *(Il Sabato)*. To the editor of Germany's leading daily, Theo Sommer of *Die Zeit,* the U.S.-U.K. reaction to the Gulf crisis was "an unabashed exercise in national self-interest, only thinly veiled by invocations of principle"—invocations that were proclaimed with due pomposity and self-righteousness as long as the interests of power were served thereby. The Jesuit journal *Proceso* (El Salvador) agreed, warning of the "ominous halo of hypocrisy, the seed of new crises and resentments." The hypocrisy "is extreme in the case of the United States, the leader of the allied forces and the most warmongering of them all."[2]

The *Times of India* took Bush's curt dismissal of Iraq's February 15 offer to withdraw from Kuwait as a demonstration that the West seeks a "regional Yalta where the powerful nations agree among themselves to a share of Arab spoils... [The West's] conduct throughout this one month has revealed the seamiest sides of Western civilisation: its unrestricted appetite for dominance, its morbid fascination for hi-tech military might, its insensitivity to 'alien' cultures, its appalling jingoism..." A leading Third World monthly condemned "The most cowardly war ever fought on this planet." The foreign editor of Brazil's major daily wrote that "What is being practiced in the Gulf is pure barbarism—ironically, committed in the name of civilization. Bush is as responsible as Saddam... Both, with their inflexibility, consider only the cold logic of geopolitical interests [and] show an absolute scorn for human life." The "Business Magazine of the Developing World" predicted that the Arab states will "in effect...become *vassal states,*" losing such control as they once had over their resources *(South,* London).[3]

These Third World reactions preceded the glorious "turkey shoot" in the desert and the "euphoria" and unconcealed bloodlust it evoked until the news managers thought better of the project and suddenly called it off.

Outside the West, such perceptions are common. One experienced British journalist observed that "Despite the claims by President Bush that Desert Storm is supported by 'the whole world', there can be little doubt about which side has won the contest for the hearts and minds of the masses of the Third World; it is not the U.S." (Geoffrey Jansen). Commenting on the world's "moral unease" as the air war began, John Lloyd noted in the London *Financial Times* that the United States and Britain are a "tiny minority in the world" in their war policy. *South* concludes that the French, Italians, and Turks joined the U.S.-British war only "to secure a slice of the pie in the form of lucrative reconstruction and defence contracts in a post-war Gulf, or in the form of aid and credits, or both." Reports from the Third World, including most of the neighboring countries, indicated substantial, often overwhelming, popular opposition to the U.S.-U.K. war, barely controlled by the U.S.-backed tyrannies. The Iraqi democratic opposition publicly opposed the war, and even the most pro-American Iraqi exiles condemned the "wanton quality of the violence" in Bush's "dirty and excessively destructive war" (Samir al-Khalil). The general division through the world was illustrated in South Africa, "as usual, split along racial lines," the *Mideast Mirror* reported: "Whites cheered on President George Bush while the black and Asian communities on the other side of the apartheid divide lined up behind President Saddam Hussein," against the U.S.-U.K. attack.[4]

Writing in a Chilean journal under a caricature of Bush in a bathtub filled with war toys, Mario Benedetti agreed that Bush has "succeeded in outdoing Saddam in hypocrisy." "When liberation fever hits the United States," he continued, "the alarms sound everywhere, particularly in the Third World," which lacks the Western talent to turn quickly away from "the liberated wreckage." He finds ominous resemblances between Bush's "New World Order" and the "Neue Ordnung" and "Ordine Nuovo" of Hitler and Mussolini. The "express intent" of Bush's Gulf War was nothing other than "to show both the Third World and its old and new European allies that from now on it is the United States that orders, invades, and dictates the law, period." For the Third World, "the combination of the weakening of the USSR and the [U.S.] victory in the Gulf could turn out to be frightening...because of the breakdown of international military equilibrium which somehow served to contain U.S. yearnings for domination," and the shot in the arm to western racist jingoism "could stimulate even wilder imperialist adventures." For the Third World, the only hope is to pray to every imaginable deity to "try to convince Bush and Powell not to come liberate us."[5]

The general mood in the Third World was captured by Cardinal Paulo Evaristo Arns of Sao Paulo, Brazil, who wrote that in the Arab countries "the rich sided with the U.S. government while the *millions* of poor condemned this military aggression." Throughout the Third World, he continued, "there is hatred and fear: When will they decide to invade us," and on what pretext?[6]

Before evaluating such conflicting perceptions, we have to settle a methodological question. There are two ways to proceed. One is to rely on the rhetoric of power: George Bush has "made it clear" that he is going to "breathe light" into the problems of suffering humanity; that settles the matter. Perhaps there are some blemishes on our record, but we have undergone another of those miraculous changes of course that occur at convenient moments, so we need not trouble ourselves with the documentary record, the events of past and present history, and their institutional roots. That is the easy way, and the path to respectability and privilege. An alternative is to consider the facts. Not surprisingly, these approaches commonly yield quite different conclusions.

"Surly Master of the World"

Adopting the second approach, we face some obvious questions. Consider the president's proud boast that *dictators and tyrants* know "that what we say goes." It is beyond dispute that the United States has no problem with dictators and tyrants if they serve U.S. interests, and will attack and destroy committed democrats if they depart from their service function. The correct reading of Bush's words, then, is: "What we say goes," whoever you may be.

Continuing on this course, we find no grounds to expect George Bush to "breathe light" into the Middle East peace process, or any other problem. In fact, why is the peace process a "hypothetical creature"? The answer is not obscure: The United States has kept it that way. Washington has barred the way to a diplomatic settlement of the Arab-Israeli conflict since February 1971 (coincidentally, just as George Bush appeared on the national scene as UN Ambassador), when Kissinger backed Israel's rejection of Egyptian President Sadat's proposal for a peace settlement in terms virtually identical to official U.S. policy, without even a gesture towards the Palestinians. The United States has regularly rejected other peace proposals, vetoed UN Security Council resolutions, and voted against General Assembly resolutions calling for a political settlement. In December 1990, the General Assembly voted 144-2 (United States and Israel) to call an international conference. A year before, the Assembly voted 151-3 (United States, Israel, Dominica) for a settlement incorporating the wording of UN Resolution 242, along with "the right to self-determination" for the Palestinians.[7] The NATO allies, the USSR, the Arab states, and the nonaligned countries have been united for years in seeking a political settlement along these lines, but the United States will not permit it, so the peace process remains "hypothetical."

In part for similar reasons, reduction of armaments has been a "hypothetical creature." In April 1990, Bush flatly rejected a proposal from his friend Saddam Hussein to eliminate weapons of mass destruction from the Middle East. One way to direct petrodollars to the U.S. economy has been to encourage arms sales. While deploring such sales, Bush announced a plan to sell $18 billion worth of arms to his Middle East allies, with the Export-Import Bank underwriting purchases, at below-market rates if necessary, a hidden tax to benefit major sectors of industry. Military victories by the United States and its Israeli client have long been used as an export-promotion device. Corporations may hire showrooms to display their goods; the government hires the Sinai and Iraqi deserts.[8]

Given the nature of the state-subsidized industrial economy in the United States, it is not surprising that U.S. arms sales to the Third World reached a record $18.5 billion in 1990, placing the United States far in the lead worldwide. The contradictions between fact and rhetoric cause some problems for the doctrinal system, however. Thus, *Times* correspondent Patrick Tyler observes that "gaps remain in the Administration's goal of stemming the Middle East arms race, even as Washington has become the dominant arms supplier in the region." The "goal" is doctrinal truth, established by official pronouncement; the sale of high-tech weapons is mere fact, too insignificant to challenge doctrine.[9]

There are no plausible grounds for optimism now that the great power that has kept the peace process "hypothetical" and has helped keep the region armed to the teeth is in an even stronger position than before to tell the world that "what we say goes."

The administration has in fact taken pains to present itself as "surly master of the world." As the ground campaign opened, *New York Times* correspondent Maureen Dowd quoted a leaked section of a National Security Policy Review from the first months of the Bush presidency, dealing with "third world threats." It reads: "In cases where the United States confronts much weaker enemies, our challenge will be not simply to defeat them, but to defeat them decisively and rapidly." Any other outcome would be "embarrassing" and might "undercut political support."[10]

"Much weaker enemies" pose only one threat to the United States: the threat of independence, always intolerable. For many years, it was possible to disguise the war against Third World nationalism with Cold War illusions, but that game is over and the real story is bright and clear: the primary target has always been Third World independence, called "radical nationalism" or "ultranationalism" in the internal planning record—a "virus" that must be eradicated.

The *Times* report makes no reference to peaceful means. That too is standard. As understood on all sides, in its confrontations with Third World threats, the United States is "politically weak"; its demands will not gain public support, so diplomacy is a dangerous exercise. That is why the United States has so commonly sought to keep diplomatic processes "hypothetical" in the Middle East, Central America, Indochina, and on other issues, and why it has regularly undermined the United Nations. Furthermore, political support at home is understood to be very thin. Naturally, one does not want to confront enemies that can fight back, but even much weaker enemies must be destroyed quickly, given the weakness of the domestic base and the lessons that are to be taught.

These lessons are directed to several audiences. For the Third World, the message is simple: Don't raise your heads. A "much weaker" opponent will not merely be defeated, but pulverized. The central lesson of World Order is: "What we say goes"; we are the masters, you shine our shoes, and don't ever forget it. Others too are to understand that the world is to be ruled by force, the arena in which the United States reigns supreme, though with its domestic decline, others will have to pay the bills.

Lessons at Home

There is also a lesson for the domestic audience. They must be terrorized by images of a menacing force about to overwhelm us—though in fact "much weaker" and defenseless. The monster can then be miraculously slain, "decisively and rapidly," while the frightened population celebrates its deliverance from imminent disaster, praising the heroism of the Great Leader who has come to the rescue just in the nick of time.

These techniques, which have familiar precedents, were employed through the 1980s, for sound reasons. The population was opposed to the major Reagan policies, largely an extension of Carter plans. It was therefore necessary to divert attention to ensure that democratic processes would remain as "hypothetical" as the peace process. Propaganda campaigns created awesome chimeras: international terrorists, Sandinistas marching on Texas, narcotraffickers, crazed Arabs. Even Grenada was portrayed as a mortal threat, with fevered tales of an air base that would be used to attack the continent, huge Soviet military stores, and the threat to Caribbean sea lanes. Only a year before Bush went to war in the Gulf, Manuel Noriega—a minor thug by international standards—was elevated to the status of Genghis Khan as the United States prepared to invade Panama to restore the rule of the 10-percent white minority and to guarantee continued U.S. control over the Canal and the military bases there. Government-media agitprop has had some success. The tourism industry in Europe has repeatedly collapsed while Americans cower in terror, afraid to travel to European cities where they would be 100 times as safe as they are at home, eliciting much derision in the right-wing European press.

In the Old World Order, the Soviet threat was skillfully deployed to mobilize public support for intervention abroad and for subsidies to high-tech industry at home. These basic institutional requirements remain a policy guide, and they have their consequences. During Bush's first two years in office, real wages continued to decline, falling to the level of the late 1950s for nonsupervisory workers (about two-thirds of the work force). Three million more children crossed the poverty line. Over a million people lost their homes. Infant mortality increased beyond its already scandalous levels. Federal spending dropped for education and for non-military R&D (research and development). Government, corporate, and household debt continued to rise, in part concealed with various budgetary scams. Financial institutions drowned in red ink, following the S&Ls, set on their course by the Deregulation Task Force headed by George Bush. The gap between rich and poor grew to post-war record levels. Civic services declined further while the United States took a healthy lead worldwide in prison population per capita, doubling the figure during the Reagan-Bush years, with Black males four times as likely to be in prison as in South Africa. And the "third deficit" of unmet social and economic needs (repairing infrastructure, etc.) is calculated at some $130 billion annually, omitting the S&Ls.[11]

The administration makes no pretense of addressing such problems; rightly, from its point of view. Any serious measures would infringe upon the prerogatives of its constituency. For the executives of a transnational corporation (TNC) or other privileged sectors, it is important for the world to be properly disciplined, for advanced industry to be subsidized, and for the wealthy to be guaranteed security. It does not matter much if public education and health deteriorate, the useless population rots in urban concentrations or prisons, and the basis for a livable society collapses for the public at large.

For such reasons, it is important to distract the domestic population. They must join their betters in admiring "the stark and vivid definition of principle...baked into [George Bush] during his years at Andover and Yale, that honor and duty compels you to punch the bully in the face"— the words of the awe-struck reporter who released the Policy Review explaining how to deal with "much weaker enemies."[12]

The principle that you punch the bully in the face—when you are sure that he is securely bound and beaten to a pulp—is a natural one for advocates of the rule of force. It teaches the right lessons to the world. And at home, cheap victories deflect the attention of a frightened population from domestic disasters while the state pursues its tasks as global enforcer, serving the interests of the wealthy. Meanwhile, the country continues its march towards a two-tiered society with striking Third World features.

The same *Times* reporter goes on to quote the gallant champion himself: "By God, we've kicked the Vietnam syndrome once and for all." The second national newspaper joined in, applauding the "spiritual and intellectual" triumph in the Gulf: "Martial values that had fallen into disrepute were revitalized," and "Presidential authority, under assault since Vietnam, was strengthened." With barely a gesture towards the dangers of overexuberance, the ultraliberal *Boston Globe* hailed the "victory for the psyche" and the new "sense of nationhood and projected power" under the leadership of a man who is "one tough son of a bitch," a man with "the guts to risk all for a cause" and a "burning sense of duty," who showed "the depth and steely core of his convictions" and his faith that "we are a select people, with a righteous mission in this earth," the latest in a line of "noble-minded missionaries" going back to his hero Teddy Roosevelt—who, we may recall, was going to "show those Dagos that they will have to behave decently" and to teach proper lessons to the "wild and ignorant people" standing in the way of "the dominant world races." Liberal columnists praised "the magnitude of Bush's triumph" over a much weaker enemy, dismissing the "uninformed garbage" of those who carp in dark corners (Thomas Oliphant). The open admiration for fascist values is a matter of some interest.[13]

For 20 years, there have been vigorous efforts to "kick the Vietnam syndrome," defined by Reaganite intellectual Norman Podhoretz as "the sickly inhibitions against the use of military force." He thought the disease was cured when we were "standing tall" after our astounding victory in Grenada. Perhaps that triumph of martial virtues was not enough, but now, at last, we have kicked these sickly inhibitions, the president exults. "Bush's leadership has transformed the Vietnam Syndrome into a Gulf Syndrome, where 'Out Now!' is a slogan directed at aggressors, not at us" (Thomas Oliphant); we were the injured party in Vietnam, defending ourselves from the Vietnamese aggressors—from "internal aggression," as Adlai Stevenson explained in 1964. Having overcome the Vietnam syndrome, we now observe "the worthy and demanding standard that aggression must be opposed, in exceptional cases by force," Oliphant continues—but, somehow, we are not to march on Jakarta, Tel Aviv, Damascus, Washington, Ankara, and a long series of other capitals.[14]

The ground had been well-prepared for overcoming this grave malady, including dedicated labors to ensure that the Vietnam War is properly understood—as a "noble cause," not a violent assault against South Vietnam, then all of Indochina. When the president proclaims that we will no longer fight with one hand tied behind our backs, respectable opinion asks only whether we were indeed too restrained in Indochina, or whether our defense of freedom was always a "lost cause" and a "mistake." It is "clear," the *New York Times* reports, that "the lesson of Vietnam was a sense of the limits of United States power"; in contrast, the lesson of Afghanistan is not a sense of the limits of Soviet power.

Reviewing the "heroic tale" of a Vietnamese collaborator with the French colonialists and their American successors, the *Times* describes the methods he devised in 1962 to destroy the "political organization" of the South Vietnamese revolutionaries. The most successful device was to send "counter-terror teams to track down and capture or kill recalcitrant Vietcong officials"—*counter-terror teams,* because it was the United States and its clients who were assassinating civilians to undermine an indigenous political organization that far surpassed anything the United States could construct, as fully conceded.[15]

So effectively has history been rewritten that an informed journalist at the left-liberal extreme can report that "the U.S. military's distrust of cease-fires seems to stem from the Vietnam War," when the Communist enemy—but not, apparently, the U.S. invaders—"used the opportunity [of a bombing pause] to recover and fight on" (Fred Kaplan). Near the dissident extreme of scholarship, the chairman of the Center for European Studies at Harvard can inform us that Nixon's Christmas bombing of Hanoi in 1972 "brought the North Vietnamese back to the conference table" (Stanley Hoffmann). Such fables, long ago demolished, are alive and well, as the propaganda system has elegantly recovered; no real problem among the educated classes, who had rarely strayed from the Party Line. Americans generally estimate Vietnamese deaths at about 100,000, a recent academic study reveals. Its authors ask what conclusions we would draw about the political culture of Germany if the public estimated Holocaust deaths at 300,000, while declaring their righteousness. A question we might ponder.[16]

Leader and his Teachings

George Bush's career as a "public servant" also has its lessons concerning the New World Order. He is the one head of state who stands condemned by the World Court for "the unlawful use of force"; in direct defiance of the Court, he persisted in the terror and illegal economic warfare against Nicaragua to prevent a free election in February 1990, then withheld aid from his chosen government because of its refusal to drop the World Court suit. The Court's call for reparations for these particular crimes (others are far beyond reach) was dismissed with contempt, while Bush and his sycophants solemnly demanded reparations from Iraq, rightly confident that respectable opinion would see no problem here.

Or in the fact that in March 1991, the administration once again contested World Court jurisdiction over claims resulting from its crimes; in this case, Iran's request that the Court order reparations for the downing of an Iranian civilian airliner in July 1988 by the U.S. warship *Vincennes,* part of the naval squadron sent by Reagan and Bush to support Iraq's aggression. The airbus was shot down in a commercial corridor off the coast of Iran with 290 people killed—out of "a need to prove the viability of Aegis," the warship's high-tech missile system, in the judgment of U.S. Navy commander David Carlson, who "wondered aloud in disbelief" as he monitored the events from his nearby vessel. Bush further sharpened our understanding of the sacred Rule of Law in April 1990, when he conferred the Legion of Merit award upon the commander of the *Vincennes* (along with the officer in charge of anti-air warfare) for "exceptionally meritorious conduct in the performance of outstanding service" in the Gulf and for the "calm and professional atmosphere" under his command during the period when the airliner was shot down. "The tragedy isn't mentioned in the texts of the citations," Associated Press reported. The media kept a dutiful silence—at home, that is. In the less disciplined Third World, the facts were reported in reviews of U.S. terrorism and "U.S. imperial policy" generally.[17]

As Third World observers commonly observe, the "ominous halo of hypocrisy" can rise beyond any imaginable level without posing a serious challenge for the guardians of political correctness in the West.

Bush opened the post-Cold War era with the murderous invasion of Panama, immediately after the fall of the Berlin Wall. Since Bush became United Nations Ambassador in 1971, the United States is far in the lead in vetoing Security Council resolutions and blocking the UN peacekeeping function, followed by Britain—"our lieutenant (the fashionable word is partner)," in the words of a senior Kennedy adviser.[18] Bush took part in the Reaganite campaign to undermine the UN, adding further blows during the Gulf crisis. With threats and bribery, the United States pressured the Security Council to wash its hands of the crisis, authorizing individual states to proceed as they wished, including the use of force (UN Resolution 678). The Council thus seriously violated the UN Charter, which bars any use of force until the Council determines that peaceful means have been exhausted (which, transparently, they had not, so no such determination was even considered), and requires further that the Security Council—not George Bush—will determine what further means may be necessary. Having once again subverted the UN, the United States compelled the Security Council to violate its rules by refusing repeated requests by members for meetings to deal with the mounting crisis, rules that the United States had angrily insisted were "mandatory" when it objected to brief delays in earlier years. In further contempt for the UN, the United States bombed Iraqi nuclear facilities, proudly announcing the triumph shortly after the General Assembly reaffirmed the long-standing ban against such attacks and called upon the Security Council "to act immediately" if such a violation occurs; the vote was 144-1, the United States in splendid isolation as usual (December 4, 1990).[19]

Bush was called to head the CIA in 1975, just in time to support near-genocide in East Timor, a policy that continues with critical U.S.-U.K. support for General Suharto, whose achievements dim even the lustre of Saddam Hussein. Meanwhile, exhibiting his refined taste for international law, Bush looks the other way as his Australian ally arranges with the Indonesian conqueror to exploit Timorese oil, rejecting Portugal's protest to the World Court on the grounds that "There is no binding legal obligation not to recognise the acquisition of territory that was acquired by force" (Foreign Minister Gareth Evans). Furthermore, Evans explains, "The world is a pretty unfair place, littered with examples of acquisition by force...," and in the same breath, following the U.S.-U.K. lead, he bans all official contacts with the PLO with proper indignation because of its "consistently defending and associating itself with Iraq's invasion of Kuwait." His colleague, Australian Prime Minister Hawke, meanwhile declared that "big countries cannot invade small neighbors and get away with it" (referring to Iraq and Kuwait), proclaiming that in the "new order" established by the virtuous Anglo-Americans, "would-be aggressors will think twice before invading smaller neighbours." The weak will "feel more secure because they know that they will not stand alone if they are threatened," now that, at last, "all nations should know that the rule of law must prevail over the rule of force in international relations." British Aerospace entered into new arrangements to sell Indonesia jet fighters and enter into co-production arrangements, in "what could turn out to be one of the largest arms packages any company has sold to an ASEAN [Association of Southeast Asian Nations] country," the *Far Eastern Economic Review* reported—while British political figures and leading intellectuals lectured with due gravity on the noble values of their traditional culture, now, at last, to be imposed by the righteous.[20]

The public has been protected from such undesirable facts, kept in the shadows along with a new Indonesian military offensive in Timor under the cover of the Gulf crisis, and the western-backed Indonesian operations that may wipe out a million tribal people in Irian Jaya, with thousands of victims of chemical weapons among the dead, according to human-rights activists and the few observers. The posturing about international law and the crime of aggression can therefore proceed, untroubled. The attention of the civilized West is to be focused, laser-like, on the crimes of the official enemy, not on those we could readily mitigate or eliminate without tens of thousands of tons of bombs.[21]

On becoming vice-president, Bush travelled to Manila to pay his respects to another fine killer and torturer, Ferdinand Marcos, praising him as a man "pledged to democracy" who had performed great "service to freedom," and adding that "we love your adherence to democratic principle and to the democratic processes." The Reagan-Bush administrations increased U.S. support for one of Africa's finest, the dictator Mobutu of Zaire, maintained in power by the United States and its Israeli ally, among other benefactors. To honor this world-class gangster and robber, President Bush chose him as the first African leader to be received at the White House, hailing him as "one of our most valued friends" and making no reference to human-rights violations, a practice that continued as terror and corruption mounted. Bush also showed his appreciation for Nicolae Ceausescu of Romania until shortly before his downfall, selecting him as the only "most favored" trading partner in Eastern Europe, as well as for the Chinese rulers after their achievements at Tiananmen Square. Bush also continued to block congressional condemnation of his friend Saddam Hussein as a "gross violator of internationally recognized human rights." The White House chose the occasion of the invasion of Panama to announce new high-technology sales to Beijing and plans to lift a ban on loans to Saddam Hussein, implemented shortly thereafter—all explained as good for American business.[22]

Bush also looked away while another friend, Turkish president Turgut Ozal, used the cover of the 1990-91 Gulf crisis to intensify Turkey's repression of Kurds—acting as "a protector of peace," in Bush's words, joining those who "stand up for civilized values around the world" against Saddam Hussein. While making some gestures towards his own Kurdish population, Ozal continues to preside over "the world's worst place to be Kurdish" (Vera Saeedpour, director of the New York-based program that monitors Kurdish human rights). Journalists, the Human Rights Association in the Kurdish regions, and lawyers report that this protector of civilized values made use of his new prestige to have his security forces expel 50,000 people from 300 villages, burning homes and possessions so that the people will not return, while continuing the torture that is standard procedure in all state-security cases. In late January, as U.S.-U.K. bombs demolished the civilian infrastructure in Iraq, the *Washington Post* briefly noted that the UN Disaster Relief Office (UNDRO) was preparing to care for 400,000 Iraqi refugees, citing Turkish press reports that 200,000 had fled to the Iraq-Turkey border. Two days earlier, the German press reported the destruction of towns along the Iraq-Turkey border by the Turkish airforce. The Frankfurt relief organization Medico International reported that hundreds of thousands of Kurds were in flight from cities near the Iraqi frontier, with women, children, and old people trying to survive the cold winter in holes in the ground or animal sheds while the government barred any help or provisions, the army destroyed fields with flame throwers, and jet planes bombed Kurdish villages. Human Rights Watch reports that in mid-August, Turkey officially suspended the European Convention on Human Rights for the Kurdish provinces, eliminating these marginal protections with no protest from any western government, while the army "stepped up the village burnings and deportations." Censorship is so extreme that the facts remain obscure, and lacking ideological utility, are of no interest in any event.[23]

Bush also lent his talents to the war against the Church and other deviants committed to "the preferential option for the poor" in Central America, now littered with tortured and mutilated bodies, perhaps devastated beyond recovery. In the Middle East, Bush supported Israel's harsh occupations, its murderous invasion of Lebanon, and its refusal to honor Security Council Resolution 425 calling for its immediate withdrawal from Lebanon (March 1978, one of several). The plea was renewed by the government of Lebanon in February 1991,[24] ignored as usual while the U.S. client terrorized the occupied region and bombed elsewhere at will, and the rest of Lebanon was taken over by Bush's new friend Hafez el-Assad, a clone of Saddam Hussein.

Plainly, we have here a man who can be expected to "breathe light" into the problems of the Middle East. Or, if we prefer, we may derive further conclusions about the New World Order.

The Background to the War

Prior to August 2, 1990, the United States and its allies found Saddam Hussein an attractive partner. In 1980, they helped prevent UN reaction to Iraq's attack on Iran, which they supported throughout. At the time, Iraq was a Soviet client, but Reagan, Thatcher, and Bush recognized Saddam Hussein as "our kind of guy" and induced him to switch sides. In 1982, Reagan removed Iraq from the list of states that sponsor terror, permitting it to receive enormous credits for the purchase of U.S. exports while the United States became a major market for its oil. By 1987, Iraq praised Washington for its "positive efforts" in the Gulf while expressing disappointment over Soviet refusal to join the tilt towards Iraq (Tariq Aziz). U.S. intervention was instrumental in enabling Iraq to gain the upper hand in the war. Western corporations took an active role in building up Iraq's military strength, notably its weapons of mass destruction. Reagan and Bush regularly intervened to block congressional censure of their friend's atrocious human-rights record, strenuously opposing any actions that might interfere with profits for U.S. corporations or with Iraq's military buildup.[25]

Britain was no different. When Saddam was reported to have gassed thousands of Kurds at Halabja, the White House intervened to block any serious congressional reaction, while in Britain, not one member of the governing Conservative Party was willing to join a left-labor condemnation in Parliament. Both governments now profess outrage over the crime, and denounce those who did protest for appeasing their former comrade, while basking in media praise for their high principle.[26]

The scale and character of U.S.-U.K. support began to leak after the war. An investigation by the London *Financial Times* and ABC News revealed the energetic intervention of the Bush administration to ensure a $1 billion loan guarantee to Iraq in November 1990, overruling objections by the Federal Reserve and the Treasury and Commerce Department along with ample evidence that Iraq was not creditworthy and that credits were being diverted to military procurement (including missile projects). The justification was Iraq's contribution to "stability in the region" and the "great trade opportunities for U.S. companies" (Undersecretary of State Robert Kimmitt, speaking for the president). High-level White House meetings continued to reject economic sanctions through June 1990. U.S. officials also revealed that U.S. ballistic-missile technology, shipped illegally to South Africa from 1984 to 1988 with the full knowledge of the CIA, was probably transmitted to Iraq, including equipment that could be used for nuclear-tipped missiles. This was part of an elaborate arms trafficking network involving the United States, South Africa, Iraq, Chile, and Israel, extended during the Reagan-Bush years. A congressional panel reported that from 1985 to the day of the August 2 invasion, the Reagan-Bush administrations approved 771 export licenses to Iraq, totaling $1.5 billion, for "dual-use items" that have military as well as commercial uses. These were specifically designated "for protection of the head of state" (Saddam), according to a State Department memo of December 6, 1988. Meanwhile, the British government was apparently exporting to Iraq raw materials for making mustard gas, shipping chemicals used in the manufacture of chemical weapons until August 1990. London authorized export of sensitive military equipment and radioactive materials "until three days after Iraq's invasion of Kuwait," the *Financial Times* reported.[27]

It was, of course, understood that Saddam Hussein was one of the world's most savage tyrants. But he was "our gangster," joining a club in which he could find congenial associates. Repeating a familiar formula, Geoffrey Kemp, head of the Middle East section in the National Security Council under Reagan, observed that "We weren't really that naive. We knew that he was an SOB, but he was our SOB." "Iraq was a natural ally of moderate Arab states," cooperating with U.S. regional goals, senior Reagan-Bush NSC official Peter Rodman comments in retrospect: "The fact that Saddam was a murderous thug did not change this." Reviewing post-war developments, *New York Times* chief diplomatic correspondent Thomas Friedman observes that Saddam's "iron fist...held Iraq together, much to the satisfaction of the American allies Turkey and Saudi Arabia," not to speak of the boss in Washington, who had no problem with the means employed.[28]

By mid-July 1990, our SOB was openly moving troops towards Kuwait and waving a fist at his neighbors. Relations with Washington remained warm. Bush intervened once again to block congressional efforts to deny loan guarantees to Iraq. On August 1, while intelligence warned of the impending invasion, Bush approved the sale of advanced data transmission equipment to his friendly SOB. In the preceding two weeks, licenses had been approved for $4.8 million in advanced technology products, including computers for the Ministry of Industry and Military Industrialization, for the Saad 16 research center that was later destroyed by bombing on grounds that it was developing rockets and poison gas, and for another plant that was repeatedly bombed as a chemical-weapons factory. The State Department indicated to Saddam that it had no serious objection to his rectifying border disputes with Kuwait, or intimidating other oil producers to raise the oil price to $25 a barrel or more. For reasons that remain unexplained, Kuwait's response to Iraqi pressures and initiatives was defiant and contemptuous.[29]

The available evidence can be read in various ways. The most conservative (and, in my view, most plausible) reading is that Saddam misunderstood the signals as a "green light" to take all of Kuwait, possibly as a bargaining chip to achieve narrower ends, possibly with broader goals. According to Bob Woodward's account, the Bush administration expected Saddam to set up a puppet government behind which he would keep effective power. He quotes George Bush in an August 4 meeting warning that Saudi Arabia might "bug out at the last minute and accept a puppet regime in Kuwait"—on the model of the United States in Panama and many other cases.[30]

None of this is acceptable. No independent force is permitted to gain significant influence over the world's major energy reserves, which are to be in the hands of the United States and its clients.[31]

Saddam's record was already so sordid that the conquest of Kuwait added little to it, but that act was a crime that matters: the crime of independence. Torture, tyranny, aggression, gassing, and slaughter of civilians are all acceptable by U.S.-U.K. standards, but not stepping on our toes.

Blocking the Diplomatic Track

Iraq's invasion of Kuwait fell within the range of many other recent atrocities. The regular response of the international community is condemnation, followed by sanctions and diplomatic efforts. These procedures rarely succeed, or even begin, because they are blocked by the great powers, in the past several decades, primarily the United States, with Britain second; these powers account for 80 percent of Security Council vetoes in the 20 years of George Bush's national prominence. Since the United States and U.K. happened to oppose Iraq's aggression, sanctions could be invoked, with unusually high prospects for success because of their unprecedented severity and the fact that the usual violators—the United States, U.K., and their allies—would, for once, adhere to them. The likelihood of success was stressed by virtually all witnesses at the Senate Hearings (including former Defense Secretaries and chairs of the Joint Chiefs), as well as by academic specialists on sanctions. The question may be idle; quite possibly sanctions already *had* worked by late December, perhaps mid-August. That seems a reasonable interpretation of the Iraqi withdrawal proposals confirmed or released by U.S. officials.

Washington moved resolutely to bar the success of peaceful means. Following the prescriptions of the National Security Policy Review, it ensured that this "much weaker enemy" would be punished by force. On August 22, Thomas Friedman outlined the Administration position in the *New York Times:* The "diplomatic track" must be blocked, or negotiations might "defuse the crisis" at the cost of "a few token gains" for Iraq, perhaps "a Kuwaiti island or minor border adjustments." A week later, Knut Royce revealed in *Newsday* that a proposal in just those terms had been offered by Iraq, but was dismissed by the Administration (and suppressed by the *Times,* as it quietly conceded). The proposal, regarded as "serious" and "negotiable" by a State Department Mideast expert, called for Iraqi withdrawal from Kuwait in exchange for access to the Gulf (meaning control over two uninhabited mudflats that had been assigned to Kuwait in the imperial settlement, leaving Iraq landlocked) and Iraqi control of the

Rumaila oil field, about 95 percent in Iraq, extending two miles into Kuwait over an unsettled border.

Investigative reporter Robert Parry added further information. The offer, relayed via Iraqi Deputy Foreign Minister Nizar Hamdoon, reached Washington on August 9. According to a confidential congressional summary, it represented the views of Saddam Hussein and other Iraqi leaders. On August 10, the proposal was brought to the National Security Council, which rejected it as "already moving against policy," according to the retired Army officer who arranged the meeting. Former CIA chief Richard Helms attempted to carry the initiative further, but got nowhere. Further efforts by Hamdoon, the Iraqi Embassy in Washington, and U.S. interlocutors elicited no response. "There was nothing in this [peace initiative] that interested the U.S. government," Helms said. A congressional summary, with an input from intelligence, concludes that a diplomatic solution might have been possible at that time. That we will never know. Washington feared that it was possible, and took no chances, for the reasons expressed through the *Times* diplomatic correspondent.

From the outset, the U.S. position was clear, unambiguous, and unequivocal: No outcome will be tolerated other than capitulation to force. Others continued to pursue diplomatic efforts. On January 2, U.S. officials disclosed an Iraqi proposal to withdraw in return for agreement of an unspecified nature on the Palestinian problem and weapons of mass destruction. U.S. officials described the offer as "interesting" because it mentioned no border issues, taking it to "signal Iraqi interest in a negotiated settlement." A State Department Mideast expert described it as a "serious prenegotiation position." The facts were again reported by Knut Royce of *Newsday*, who observed that Washington "immediately dismissed the proposal." A *Times* report the next day suggested that mere statement by the Security Council of an intention to deal with the two "linked" issues might have sufficed for complete Iraqi withdrawal from Kuwait. Again, the United States was taking no chances, and quashed the threat at once.[32]

The story continued. On the eve of the air war, the United States and U.K. announced that they would veto a French proposal for immediate Iraqi withdrawal in exchange for a meaningless Security Council statement on a possible future conference; Iraq then rejected the proposal as well. On February 15, Iraq offered to withdraw completely from Kuwait, stating that the withdrawal "should be linked" to Israeli withdrawal from the occupied territories and Lebanon, in accord with UN resolutions. The Iraqi Ambassador to the UN stated that the offer was unconditional, and that the terms cited were "issues" that should be addressed, not "conditions" involving "linkage." The State Department version, published in the *New York Times* and elsewhere, mistranslated the Iraqi offer, giving the wording: "Israel must withdraw..." Washington at once rejected the offer, and the Ambassador's comments, which were barely noted in the press, were ignored. The United States insisted that Iraqi withdrawal must *precede* a cease-fire; Iraqi forces must leave their bunkers and be smashed to pieces, after which the United States might consider a cease-fire. The media seemed to consider this quite reasonable.[33]

Washington's plan was to launch the ground operation on February 23. Problems arose when the Soviet Union, a day earlier, reached an agreement with Iraq to withdraw if UN resolutions would be cancelled. The President, "having concluded that the Soviet diplomacy was getting out of hand" (as the *Times* put it), brusquely dismissed the proposal. Again, the crucial difference between the two positions had to do with timing: Should Iraq withdraw one day after a cease-fire, as the Soviet-Iraqi proposal stated, or while the bombing continued, as the United States demanded.[34]

Throughout, the media went along, with scarcely a false note.

The record strongly supports the judgment of Reagan insider James Webb, former Navy Secretary, one of the few critics of the war to gain a public forum. In the *Wall Street Journal,* he wrote that "this Administration has dealt in extremes," favoring "brute force" over other means. Bush "relentlessly maneuvered our nation into a war" that was unnecessary. He chose to turn the country into "the world's Hessians," a mercenary state paid by others while "our society reels from internal problems" that the administration refuses to address.[35]

This record is, again, highly informative. The possibility of a negotiated settlement was excluded from the political and ideological systems with remarkable efficiency. When Republican National Committee Chairman Clayton Yeutter states that if a Democrat had been president, Kuwait would not be liberated today, few if any Democrats can respond by saying: If I had been President, Kuwait might well have been liberated long before, perhaps by August, without the disastrous consequences of your relentless drive for war. In the media, one will search far for a hint that diplomatic options might have been pursued, or even existed. The mainstream journals of opinion were no different. Those few who felt a need to justify their support for the slaughter carefully evaded these crucial issues, in Europe as well.

To evaluate the importance of this service to power, consider again the situation just before the air war began. On January 9, a national poll revealed that two-thirds of the U.S. population favored a conference on the Arab-Israeli conflict if that would lead to Iraqi withdrawal from

Kuwait. The question was framed to minimize a positive response, stressing that the Bush administration opposed the idea.[36] It is a fair guess that each person who nevertheless advocated such a settlement assumed that he or she was isolated in this opinion. Few if any had heard any public advocacy of their position; the media had been virtually uniform in following the Washington Party Line, dismissing "linkage" (i.e., diplomacy) as an unspeakable crime, in this unique case. It is hardly likely that respondents were aware that an Iraqi proposal calling for a settlement in these terms had been released a week earlier by U.S. officials, who found it reasonable; or that the Iraqi democratic forces, and most of the world, took the same stand.

Suppose that the crucial facts had been known and the issues honestly addressed. Then the two-thirds figure would doubtless have been far higher, and it might have been possible to avoid the huge slaughter preferred by the administration, with its useful consequences: The world learns that it is to be ruled by force, the dominant role of the United States in the Gulf and its control over Middle East oil are secured, and the population is diverted from the growing disaster around us. In brief, the educated classes and the media did their duty.

The "War"

The threat of peaceful settlement having been successfully deflected, the U.S.-U.K. coalition turned to the attack. There was, of course, nothing resembling a war, any more than there was when Iraq conquered Kuwait—at least, if a "war" is understood to involve two sides in combat, say, shooting at each other.

The U.S.-U.K. "war" had two targets: the Iraqi military forces, and the civilian population. The military component reduced to the slaughter of Iraqi soldiers, largely Shi'ite and Kurdish conscripts it appears, hiding in holes in the sand or fleeing for their lives—a picture quite remote from the Pentagon disinformation relayed by the press about colossal fortifications, artillery powerful beyond our imagining, vast stocks of chemical and biological weapons at the ready, and so on. The operation culminated in the "turkey shoot" described by U.S. forces, who borrowed the term used by their forebears slaughtering Filipinos at the turn of the century in operations described by a British observer as "not war" but "simply massacre and murderous butchery." The same terms apply to the desert massacre of demoralized and unwilling conscripts, along with Asian workers and Kuwaiti hostages, so BBC reported.[37]

In brief, the "war" followed the script laid out for confrontations with a "much weaker enemy." A ground war was avoided. U.S. combat casualties were on the scale of Grenada, while Iraqi military deaths are estimated by the U.S. military in the range of 100,000 (with a huge error factor), killed from a safe distance. The victors bulldozed corpses into mass graves, in violation of the Geneva Conventions to which they appeal when some interest is served. But the laws of war are as relevant as they were in earlier days, when the *New York Times* cheerily described how helicopter gunships would attack the "dazed and bleeding people" surrounding B-52 bomb craters in Vietnam and "put them out of their misery," honoring the law that soldiers unable to fight "shall in all circumstances be treated humanely."[38]

Several months later, U.S. Army officials released the information that ground forces had used plows mounted on tanks and earthmovers to bulldoze *live* Iraqi soldiers into trenches in the desert. This latest atrocity, "hidden from public view," was released in a major story by Patrick Sloyan of *Newsday,* reporting from Fort Riley, Kansas. The commander of one of the three brigades involved said that thousands of Iraqis might have been killed; the other two commanders refused estimates. "Not a single American was killed during the attack that made an Iraqi body count impossible," Sloyan continues. This "unprecedented tactic" revealed with stark clarity the understanding of the U.S. command that there would be no war, only "murderous butchery." The report elicited little interest or comment.[39]

The brief glimpse of the "ground war" horrified much of the world. The U.S. reaction was remarkable, sometimes passing beyond the macabre, as when one thoughtful commentator explained that it was not U.S. actions, but "the strange and horrifying immobility [of the Iraqis] that littered the desert with Iraqi corpses." This inexplicable "immobility" was a consequence of the cultural inferiority of Iraqi Baathists, who lack our orientation "toward natural reality" and therefore became "immobile" when torn to pieces by B-52 raids and cluster bombs or bulldozed into holes in the sand.[40] He did not go on to ponder the even more pathetic cultural inferiority of the Kurds, proven by their inability to resist even the primitive Baathists.

Many did express qualms about the savagery of the final slaughter, but a look at history should have relieved their surprise. When violence is cost-free, all bars are down. During the Indochina war, there were constraints on bombing of Hanoi and Haiphong, or dikes in North Vietnam, because of fear of a Chinese or Soviet reaction and the political cost elsewhere. But in the southern sectors of North Vietnam, or elsewhere in Indochina, no one important cared, and the practice was that "anything goes." The Pentagon Papers reveal extensive planning about the bombing of the North, because of potential costs to the United States; the far more devastating bombing of the South, begun years earlier and including major war crimes, is passed over with little attention.[41]

The same was true of World War II. At the end, Japan was defenseless, therefore demolished at will. Tokyo was removed from the list of atom-bomb targets because it was "practically rubble," so that an attack would not demonstrate the bomb's power. Many believe that the war ended with the atom bombs. Not so. In the official U.S. Air Force history, we read that General Arnold "wanted as big a finale as possible," and, with management skills that compare to Stormin' Norman's, assembled over 1,000 planes to bomb Japan after Nagasaki. Thousands were killed in this grand finale. Others survived to read the leaflets dropped with the bombs, saying "Your Government has surrendered. The war is over!" Truman announced Japan's surrender before the last planes returned. Japan was prostrate, so why not? As the Korean war ground on, the Air Force could locate no more targets. Therefore, as an official U.S. Air Force study records, it attacked North Korean dams, leading to such stirring sights as a "flash flood [that] scooped clean 27 miles of valley below," while 75 percent of the water supply for rice production was wiped out and the enemy suffered "the destruction of their chief sustenance—rice." "The Westerner can little conceive the awesome meaning which the loss of this staple food commodity has for the Asian," the study explains: "starvation and slow death,...more feared than the deadliest plague. Hence the show of rage, the flare of violent tempers, and the avowed threats of reprisals when bombs fell on five irrigation dams." The threats of reprisal were empty, and there were no political costs, so these war crimes joined the long list of others compiled with impunity by the powerful, who never fail to strike impressive poses as they call for war-crimes trials—for others.[42]

The second component of the U.S.-U.K. assault was an aerial attack on the civilian infrastructure, targeting power, sewage, and water systems; that is, a form of biological warfare, designed to ensure long-term suffering and death among civilians, mounting—possibly disastrously—after hostilities ended. The goal of the attack on the civilian society was made reasonably clear: to place the United States in a strong position to attain its political goals for the region by inducing some military officer to take over and wield the "iron fist" as Saddam himself had done with U.S. support before he stepped out of line. Recalling those happy days when Saddam's "iron fist...held Iraq together" before his single transgression on August 2 (see above), *Times* diplomatic correspondent Thomas Friedman explained current State Department reasoning: If Iraqi society suffers sufficient pain, Iraqi generals may topple Mr. Hussein, "and then Washington would have the best of all worlds: an iron-fisted Iraqi junta without Saddam Hussein."[43]

There was some concern that soft-hearted folk might balk at the sight of tens of thousands dying from starvation and disease while the United States holds the civilian population hostage. Hopes were expressed that Bush's ex-pal might help us out of this dilemma. The *Wall Street Journal* observed that Iraq's "clumsy attempt to hide nuclear-bomb-making equipment from the U.N. may be a blessing in disguise, U.S. officials say. It assures that the allies [read: United States and U.K.] can keep economic sanctions in place to squeeze Saddam Hussein without mounting calls to end the penalties for humanitarian reasons."[44] With luck, this huge exercise in state terrorism may proceed unhampered by the bleeding hearts.

Through February, the U.S.-U.K. forces were responsible for the direct attack on the civilian society. After the cease-fire, the task was turned over to the elite units of the Iraqi army, largely spared by the U.S. attack, who proceeded to slaughter first the Shi'ites of the South and then the Kurds of the North, with the authorization of the Commander-in-Chief.

Bush had openly encouraged uprisings against Saddam Hussein, and, according to intelligence sources, had authorized the CIA in January to aid rebels. But he stood by quietly as Saddam slaughtered Shi'ites and Kurds, tacitly approving the use of helicopter gunships to massacre civilians, refusing to impede the terror or even to provide humanitarian aid to the victims. Fleeing refugees bitterly asked journalists, "Where is George Bush?" probably not knowing the answer: he was fishing in Florida. Turkey was accused by Kurdish leaders of blocking food shipments to starving Kurds, at first closing its borders to most of those in flight. U.S. forces turned back people fleeing the terror in the South, and refused even to provide food and water to those who had escaped, Reuters reported, though individual soldiers did so. A senior Pentagon official said: "The bottom line here is, if you're suggesting we would stay purely for a purpose of protecting the refugees, we won't." "We are under no obligation to them," another added. Our job is to destroy, nothing more. The United States and Britain blocked efforts to have the UN Security Council condemn the massacre, let alone act in any way, until public pressures finally compelled a "rescue operation" for the Kurds (not the Shi'ites), well after the "iron fist" had done its work.[45]

So profound was Bush's commitment to the principle of noninterference that he also could lend no support to Kuwaiti democrats. His delicacy barred mention of the word "democracy" even in private communications to the Emir, officials explained. "You can't pick out one country to lean on over another," one said; never will you find the United States "leaning on" Nicaragua or Cuba, for example, or moving beyond the narrowest interpretation of international law and UN initiatives. As human-rights abuses mounted in postwar Kuwait, Bush became "the foremost apologist for the perpetrators," the director of Human Rights Watch, Aryeh Neier, observed, noting that Bush's apologetics for repression were featured on the front page of the Kuwait government daily under the headline: "Bush declares his understanding of Kuwaitis' attitude toward collaborators: 'We would be asking a lot if we asked them to show mercy,' he says."[46]

Again, no surprises here.

By the end of March, front-page stories reported that "President Bush has decided to let President Saddam Hussein put down rebellions in his country without American intervention rather than risk the splintering of Iraq"—meaning, the threat of democracy. "The prospects are pretty good for [Saddam's] being around for a long time," a senior Pentagon official observed, while senior administration officials concluded that his "grip on power is stronger today than before Iraqi forces invaded Kuwait."[47]

Returning from a March 1991 fact-finding mission, Senate Foreign Relations Committee staff member Peter Galbraith reported that the administration did not even respond to Saudi proposals to assist both Shi'ite and Kurdish rebels, and that the Iraqi military refrained from attacking the rebels until it had "a clear indication that the United States did not want the popular rebellion to succeed." A BBC investigation found that "several Iraqi generals made contact with the United States to sound out the likely American response if they took the highly dangerous step of planning a coup against Saddam." They received no support, concluding that "Washington had no interest in supporting revolution; that it would prefer Saddam Hussein to continue in office, rather than see groups of unknown insurgents take power." An Iraqi general who escaped to Saudi Arabia told the BBC that "he and his men had repeatedly asked the American forces for weapons, ammunition and food to help them carry on the fight against Saddam's forces." Each request was refused. As his forces fell back towards U.S.-U.K. positions, the Americans blew up an Iraqi arms dump to prevent them from obtaining arms, and then "disarmed the rebels" (John Simpson). Reporting from northern Iraq, ABC correspondent Charles Glass described how "Republican Guards, supported by regular army brigades, mercilessly shelled Kurdish-held areas with Katyusha multiple rocket launchers, helicopter gunships and heavy artillery," while journalists observing the slaughter listened to General Schwarzkopf bragging to his radio audience that "We had destroyed the

Republican Guard as a militarily effective force" and eliminated the military use of helicopters.[48]

This is not quite the stuff of which heroes are fashioned, so the story was finessed at home, though it could not be totally ignored, particularly the attack on the Kurds, with their Aryan features and origins; the Shi'ites, who appear to have suffered even worse atrocities right under the gaze of Stormin' Norman, raised fewer problems, being mere Arabs.

In the most careful analysis currently available, the Greenpeace International Military Research Group estimates total Kuwaiti casualties from August 1990 at 2 to 5,000; and Iraqi civilian casualties at 5 to 15,000 during the air attack, unknown during the ground attack; 20 to 40,000 during the civil conflict; perhaps another 50,000 civilian deaths from April through July; along with another 125,000 deaths among Shi'ite and Kurdish refugees. The truth will never be known, nor seriously investigated by the conquerors—the familiar norm.[49]

Had the diplomatic track that Washington feared been successfully pursued, Kuwait too would have been spared the war and the Iraqi terror, which, according to reports, rapidly increased in the final days. An environmental catastrophe would also have been averted. In the small print, the *Times* noted that according to Pentagon officials, "the burning of Kuwait's oil fields might have been a defensive action by Iraq, which appeared to be anticipating imminent attack by allied ground forces." While Iraq created the largest oil spill, the one that threatened the desalination plant at Safaniya in Saudi Arabia probably resulted from U.S. bombing, U.S. military officials said. A Pentagon official added that the Iraqi oil spill might have been aimed at the water sources for U.S. troops, in retaliation for U.S. destruction of Kuwait's major desalination plant just before. The prime responsibility for the Gulf tragedy lies on the shoulders of Saddam Hussein; but he is not without his partners in crime, nor are his crimes unique.[50]

Deterring Iraqi Democracy

Throughout these years, Iraqi democratic forces opposing Bush's comrade Saddam Hussein were rebuffed by the White House, once again in February 1990, when they sought support for a call for parliamentary democracy. In the same month, the British Foreign Office impeded their efforts to condemn Iraqi terror, for fear that they might harm Anglo-Iraqi relations. Two months later, after the execution of London *Observer* correspondent Farzad Bazoft and other Iraqi atrocities, Foreign Secretary

Douglas Hurd reiterated the need to maintain good relations with Iraq. Iraqi Kurds received the same treatment. In mid-August, Kurdish leader Jalal Talabani flew to Washington to seek support for guerrilla operations against Saddam's regime. Neither Pentagon nor State Department officials would speak to him, even though such operations would surely have weakened Iraq's forces in Kuwait; he was rebuffed again in March 1991. The reason, presumably, was concern over the sensibilities of the Turkish "defender of civilized values," who looked askance at Kurdish resistance.[51]

It is a very revealing fact that the Iraqi democratic opposition was not only ignored by Washington but also scrupulously excluded from the media, throughout the Gulf crisis. That is easily explained when we hear what they had to say.

On the eve of the air war, the German press published a statement of the "Iraqi Democratic Group," conservative in orientation ("liberal," in the European sense), reiterating its call for the overthrow of Saddam Hussein but also opposing "any foreign intervention in the Near East," criticizing U.S. "policies of aggression" in the Third World and its intention to control Middle East oil, and rejecting UN resolutions "that had as their goal the starvation of our people." The statement called for the withdrawal of U.S.-U.K. troops, withdrawal of Iraqi troops from Kuwait, self-determination for the Kuwaiti people, "a peaceful settlement of the Kuwait problem, democracy for Iraq, and autonomy for Iraq-Kurdistan." A similar stand was taken by the Teheran-based Supreme Assembly of the Islamic Revolution in Iraq (in a communiqué from Beirut); the Iraqi Communist Party; Mas'ud Barzani, the leader of the Kurdistan Democratic Party; and other prominent opponents of the Iraqi regime, many of whom had suffered bitterly from Saddam's atrocities. Falih 'Abd al-Jabbar, an Iraqi journalist in exile in London, commented: "Although the Iraqi opposition parties have neither given up their demand for an Iraqi withdrawal from Kuwait nor their hope of displacing Saddam some time in the future, they believe that they will lose the moral right to oppose the present regime if they do not side with Iraq against the war." They called for reliance on sanctions, which, they argued, would prove effective. "All the opposition parties are agreed in calling for an immediate withdrawal of Iraqi forces from Kuwait," British journalist Edward Mortimer reports, "but most are very unhappy about the military onslaught by the U.S.-led coalition" and prefer economic and political sanctions. They also condemned the murderous bombing.[52]

A delegation of the Kuwaiti democratic opposition in Amman in December 1990 had taken the same position, opposing any western assault against Iraq. On British television, anti-Saddam Arab intellectuals in London, including the prominent Kuwaiti opposition leader Dr. Ahmed al-Khatib, were unanimous in calling for a cease-fire and for serious consideration of Saddam's February 15 peace offer. In October 1990, Dr. al-Khatib had stated that Kuwaitis "do not want a military solution" with its enormous costs for Kuwait, and strenuously opposed any military action.[53]

The silence here was deafening, and most instructive. Unlike Bush and his associates, the peace movement and Iraqi democratic opposition had always opposed Saddam Hussein. But they also opposed the quick resort to violence to undercut a peaceful resolution of the conflict. Such an outcome would have avoided the slaughter of tens of thousands of people, the destruction of two countries, harsh reprisals, an environmental catastrophe, further slaughter by the Iraqi government, and the likely emergence of another murderous U.S.-backed tyranny there. But it would not have taught the crucial lessons, already reviewed.

With the mission accomplished, the U.S. disdain for Iraqi democrats continued unchanged. A European diplomat observed that "The Americans would prefer to have another Assad, or better yet, another Mubarak in Baghdad," referring to their "military-backed regimes" (dictatorships, that of Assad being particularly odious). A diplomat from the U.S.-run coalition said that "we will accept Saddam in Baghdad in order to have Iraq as one state." The Saudi Ministry of Information ordered editors to stop critizing Saddam and to limit coverage of the popular uprisings, while a State Department official told a European envoy that the United States would be satisfied with "an Iraqi Assad," "a reliable and predictable enemy."[54]

By mid-March, Iraqi opposition leaders could see the handwriting on the wall. Leith Kubba, head of the London-based Iraqi Democratic Reform Movement, alleged that the United States favors a military dictatorship, insisting that "changes in the regime must come from within, from people already in power." London-based banker Ahmed Chalabi, another prominent opposition activist, said that "the United States, covered by the fig leaf of non-interference in Iraqi affairs, is waiting for Saddam to butcher the insurgents in the hope that he can be overthrown later by a suitable officer," an attitude rooted in the U.S. policy of "supporting dictatorships to maintain stability." Official U.S. spokespeople confirmed that the Bush administration had not talked to any Iraqi opposition leaders and did not intend to: "We felt that political meetings with them…would not be appropriate for our policy at this time," State Department spokesperson Richard Boucher stated on March 14.[55]

"The Best of all Worlds"

Despite its substantial victory, Washington had not yet achieved "the best of all worlds," as Friedman observed, because no suitable clone of the Beast of Baghdad had emerged to serve the interests of the United States and its regional allies. To be sure, not everyone shares the Washington-media conception of "the best of all worlds." Well after the hostilities ended, the *Wall Street Journal,* to its credit, broke ranks and offered space to a spokesman for the Iraqi democratic opposition, Ahmed Chalabi. He saw the outcome as "the worst of all possible worlds" for the Iraqi people, whose tragedy is "awesome."[56] From the perspective of Iraqi democrats, remote from Washington and New York, restoration of the "iron fist" would not be "the best of all worlds."

The doctrinal system faced a certain problem as the Bush administration lent its support to Saddam's crushing of the internal opposition. The task was the usual one: To portray Washington's stance, no matter how atrocious, in a favorable light. That was not easy after months of ranting about George Bush's magnificent show of principle and supreme courage in facing down the Beast. But a formula was quickly found. True, few can approach our devotion to the most august principles and our moral purity. With our orientation "toward natural reality" we recognize the need for "pragmatism" and "stability," useful concepts that translate as "Doing what we choose."

In a typical example of the genre, *New York Times* Middle East correspondent Alan Cowell attributed the failure of the rebels to the fact that "very few people outside Iraq wanted them to win." Note that the concept "people" is used here in the conventional Orwellian sense, meaning "people who count"; many featherless bipeds wanted them to win, but the important people did not. The "allied campaign against President Hussein brought the United States and its Arab coalition partners to a strikingly unanimous view," Cowell continued. "Whatever the sins of the Iraqi leader, he offered the West and the region a better hope for his country's stability than did those who have suffered his repression."[57]

This version of the facts, the standard one, merits a few questions. To begin with, who are these "Arab coalition partners?" Answer: Six are family dictatorships, established by the Anglo-American settlement to manage Gulf oil riches in the interests of the foreign masters. The seventh is Syria's Hafez el-Assad, of whom no more need be said. The last of the coalition partners, Egypt, is the only one that could be called "a country." Though a tyranny, it has a degree of internal freedom.

We therefore naturally turn to the semi-official press in Egypt to verify the *Times* report of the "strikingly unanimous view." The report is datelined Damascus, April 10. The day before, Deputy Editor Salaheddin Hafez of Egypt's leading daily, *al-Ahram*, commented on Saddam's demolition of the rebels "under the umbrella of the Western alliance's forces." U.S. support for Saddam Hussein proved what Egypt had been saying all along, Hafez wrote. American rhetoric about "the savage beast, Saddam Hussein," was merely a cover for the true goals: to cut Iraq down to size and establish U.S. hegemony in the region. The West turned out to be in total agreement with the beast on the need to "block any progress and abort all hopes, however dim, for freedom or equality and for progress towards democracy," working in "collusion with Saddam himself" if necessary.[58]

The Egyptian reaction hardly comes as a surprise. Though one could learn little about the matter here, the "victory celebration" in Egypt had been "muted and totally official," correspondent Hani Shukrallah of the London *Mideast Mirror* reported from Cairo. Post-cease-fire developments "seem to have intensifed the [popular] feelings of anger against the leading members of the anti-Iraq coalition," inspired as well by the report of the Egyptian Organization of Human Rights that "at least 200 Egyptians have been arrested in Kuwait and that many have been subjected to torture on legally unsubstantiated charges of collaboration." The Egyptian press had also bitterly condemned the U.S. conditions imposed on Iraq, a transparent effort to ensure U.S.-Israeli military dominance, *al-Ahram* charged. "Cairenes are identifying more with the vanquished 'enemy' than the triumphant 'allies'," Shukrallah reported as the ground attack ended, particularly the poor and students, three of whom were killed by police in an anti-government demonstration. "Not in over a decade have Egyptians felt and expressed so intently their hostility to the U.S., Israel, and the West," political scientist Ahmad Abdallah observed.[59]

There was some regional support for the U.S. stance outside the friendly club of Arab tyrants. Turkish President Ozal doubtless approved, and in Israel, many commentators agreed with retiring Chief-of-Staff Dan Shomron that it is preferable for Saddam Hussein to remain in power in Iraq. "We are all with Saddam," one headline read, reporting the view of Labor dove Avraham Burg that "in the present circumstances Saddam Hussein is better than any alternative" and that "a Shi'ite empire" from Iran to the territories would be harmful to Israel. Another leading dove, Ran Cohen of the dovish Ratz Party, also "wants Saddam to continue to rule, so that perhaps the hope for any internal order will be buried" and the Americans will stay in the region and impose a "compromise." Suppression of the Kurds is a welcome development, an influential right-wing commentator explained in the *Jerusalem Post,* because of "the latent ambition of Iran and Syria to exploit the Kurds and create a territorial, military, contiguity between Teheran and Damascus—a contiguity which embodies danger for Israel" (Moshe Zak, senior editor of the mass-circulation daily *Ma'ariv).*[60]

None of this makes particularly good copy. Best to leave it in oblivion.

The "strikingly unanimous view" supporting U.S. "pragmatism," then, includes offices in Washington and New York and London, and U.S. clients in the region, but leaves out a few others—notably, Iraqi democrats in exile and most of the population of the Middle East, insofar as they have any voice in the U.S. client states. Respectable opinion in the United States could not care less, in keeping with the traditional disparagement of the culturally deprived lower orders.

Deterring U.S. Democracy

The academic study of attitudes and beliefs cited earlier revealed that the public overwhelmingly supports the use of force to reverse illegal occupation and serious human-rights abuses. But, like journalists and others who proudly proclaim this "worthy standard," they do not call for force in a host of cases that at once come to mind. They do not applaud Scud attacks on Tel Aviv, though Saddam's sordid arguments compare well enough to those of his fellow-criminal in Washington, if honestly considered; nor would they approve bombs in Washington, a missile attack on Jakarta, etc.[61] Why? Again, because of the triumphs of the ideological system. The facts having been consigned to their appropriate obscurity, the slogans can be trumpeted, unchallenged.

Such examples, readily extended, illustrate the success in suppressing democracy in the United States. The ideal, long sought by the business community and the political class, is that the general population should be marginalized, each person isolated, deprived of the kinds of associations that might lead to independent thought and political action. Each must sit alone in front of the tube, absorbing its doctrinal message: trust in the Leader; ape the images of the "good life" presented by the commercials and the sitcoms; be a spectator, a consumer, a passive worker who follows orders, but not a participant in the way the world works. To achieve this goal, it has been necessary to destroy unions and other popular organizations, restrict the political system to factions of the business party, and construct a grand edifice of lies to conceal every relevant issue, whether it be Indochina, Central America, the Middle East, terrorism, the Cold War, domestic policy, or whatever—so that the proper lessons are on the shelf, ready when needed.

The methods have been refined over many years. The first state propaganda agency was established by the Woodrow Wilson administration. Within a few months, a largely pacifist population had been turned into a mob of warmongers, raging to destroy everything German and later backing the Wilson repression that demolished unions and independent thought. The success impressed the business and intellectual communities, leading to the doctrines of "manufacture of consent" and the elaboration of methods to reduce the general public to its proper spectator role. When the threat of popular democracy and labor organizing arose again in the 1930s, business moved quickly to destroy the virus, with great success. Labor's last real legislative victory was in 1935, and the supporting culture has largely been swept away. "Scientific methods of strike-breaking" rallied community support against the disruptive elements that interfered with the "harmony" to which "we" are devoted—"we" being the corporate executive, the honest sober worker, the housewife, the people united in support of "Americanism."[62]

Huge media campaigns trumpeting vacuous slogans to dispel the danger of thought are now a staple of the ideological system. To derail concern over whether you should *support their policy,* the PR system focuses attention on whether you *support our troops*—meaningless words, as empty as the question of whether you support the people of Iowa. That, of course, is just the point: to reduce the population to gibbering idiots, mouthing empty phrases and patriotic slogans, waving ribbons, watching gladiatorial contests and the models designed for them by the PR industry, but, crucially, not thinking or acting. A few must be trained to think and act, if only to serve the needs of the powerful; but they must be kept within the rigid constraints of the ideological system. These are the tasks of the media, journals of opinion, schools, and universities.

They have been accomplished with much distinction. To approach any serious question, it is first necessary to clear away mountains of ideological rubble. But the triumph is far from complete, far less so than a generation ago. Outside elite circles, the indoctrination is thin, and often is cast aside with surprising ease if people have an opportunity to think. Skepticism and disbelief are barely below the surface. Where there are even fragments of organization, many have been able to defend themselves from the ideological onslaught. The famed "gender gap" is an example. The opportunities for association and independent thought offered by the women's movement have led to a dramatic shift in attitudes—or, perhaps, willingness to express long-held attitudes—over the past two decades. The same is true of church groups, solidarity organizations, and others.

U.S. political leadership and others who hail the martial virtues know well that the domestic base for intervention in the traditional mode has eroded: no more Marines chasing Sandino, or U.S. forces marauding for years in the Mekong Delta. Either proxy forces must be used, as in the international terror networks of the Reagan-Bush years, or victory must be "rapid and decisive." And a "much weaker enemy" can be attacked only if it is first demonized and built to awesome dimensions by vast propaganda campaigns. By the same token, those who hope to narrow the options for violence and state terror must find ways to clear away the rubble under which the reality of the world has been buried. It is not easy, but the task of raising consciousness never is, and it has been pursued effectively under circumstances that most of us can barely imagine.

The Political Culture

The published record tells us more about the political culture in the United States and the West generally. As noted, the possibility of a peaceful resolution was virtually banned from discussion. Whenever George Bush thundered that *There Will Be No Negotiations,* a hundred editorials and news reports would laud him for "going the last mile for peace" in "extraordinary efforts at diplomacy." Democratic forces in Iraq, with their unwanted message, were also successfully barred. Popular opposition to the war in most of the world was sporadically reported, but primarily as a problem: Can the friendly dictatorships control their populations while we gain our ends by force? Even among those who did not exalt the "martial values," the totalitarian commitments were scarcely below the surface.

In the United States, dissident voices were effectively excluded from the mainstream, as is the norm; and while the media in other industrial democracies were far more open, support for western state power on the part of the educated classes was so uniform, particularly after the bombs starting falling, that the effects were slight. Strikingly, there was no detectable concern over the glaringly obvious fact that *no official reason was ever offered for going to war*—no reason, that is, that could not be instantly refuted by a literate teenager. That is the very hallmark of a totalitarian political culture.

The matter merits a closer look. After various failed efforts, one single official reason was offered for war, repeated in a litany by George Bush and his acolytes: "There can be no reward for aggression. Nor will there be any negotiation. Principle cannot be compromised."[63] Accordingly, there can be no diplomacy, merely an ultimatum—capitulate or die—followed by the quick resort to violence.

Presented with this argument, the educated classes did not collapse in ridicule, but solemnly intoned the Party Line, expressing their awe and admiration for Bush's high principles. One would have to search far for the reaction that would be immediate on the part of any rational and minimally informed person: True, principle cannot be compromised, but since George Bush is a leading supporter of aggression and always has been, the principle invoked is not his, nor his government's, nor that of any other state. And it follows that no reason has been given at all for rejecting negotiations in favor of violence.

The specific words just quoted happen to be Bush's oblique response to the Iraqi withdrawal proposal released by U.S. officials on January 2. But the stance was maintained throughout. Intellectuals asked no questions, finding little to challenge in the farcical official pronouncements and the doctrine clearly implied: The world is to to be ruled by force.

The conclusion is brilliantly clear: No official reason was offered for the war, and the educated classes suppressed the fact with near unanimity. We must look elsewhere to find the reasons for the war—a question of great significance for any citizen, though not for the guardians of doctrinal purity, who must bar this quest.

The methods adopted were enlightening. Those who had the indecency to demolish the official justifications were accused of demanding "moral purity," opposing any response to Iraq's aggression by states that had been "inconsistent" in the past (in fact, they had consistently pursued their own interests, generally supporting aggression for this reason). Returning to the realm of rational discourse, these miscreants were pointing out that war without stated reason is a sign of totalitarian values, and citizens who reject these values will have to turn elsewhere to discover the real reasons. In the mainstream, they would find very little.

Outside official circles, the standard justification for war was that sanctions would not work and that it was unfair to allow the Kuwaitis to suffer on. Some held that debate over sanctions was a standoff, perhaps irresoluble. By the same logic, the bombing of numerous other countries can at once be justified by mere assertion that nothing else will put an end to aggression, annexation, and human-rights abuses. Transparently, all of this is nonsense, even if we ignore the evidence that sanctions had already worked. Indisputably, the burden of proof lies on those who call for the use of force, a heavy burden that was never met, nor even seriously faced.

One could not seriously argue that the suffering of the victims in this case was more extreme than in numerous others for which force has never been proposed. Nor is there any merit to the argument that this case was different because of the annexation: Putting aside the U.S.-U.K. response to other cases of annexation, no less horrifying, the drive towards war continued unchanged after Iraqi withdrawal offers that the United States did not risk pursuing. The claim that a peaceful settlement would not have destroyed Saddam's warmaking capacity is no more persuasive. Apart from the broader consequences of such an argument, if taken seriously, the obvious procedure for eliminating this capacity would have been to explore the possibilities for regional disarmament and security arrangements (proposed by Iraq, rejected by the United States, well before the invasion of Kuwait); and after his negotiated withdrawal from Kuwait, to refrain from providing Saddam with lavish high-technology military assistance, surely a possibility if the West could overcome its greed in this sole instance. Other arguments are equally weighty.

In one of the more serious efforts to address some of the questions, Timothy Garton Ash asserts in the *New York Review* that while sanctions were possible in dealing with South Africa or Communist East Europe, Saddam Hussein is different. That concludes the argument. We now understand why it was proper to pursue "quiet diplomacy" while our South African friends caused over $60 billion in damage and 1.5 million deaths from 1980 to 1988 in the neighboring states—putting aside South Africa and Namibia, and the preceding decade. They are basically decent folk, like us and the Communist tyrants. Why? No answer is offered here, but a partial one was suggested by Nelson Mandela, who condemned the hypocrisy and prejudice of the highly selective response to the crimes of the "brown-skinned" Iraqis. The same thought comes to mind when the *New York Times* assures us that "the world" is united against Saddam Hussein, the most hated man in "the world"—the world, that is, minus its darker faces.[64]

The emergence of western racism with such stunning clarity is worth notice. It is an understandable consequence of the end of the Cold War. For 70 years, it has been possible to disguise traditional practices as "defense against the Soviets," generally a sham, now lost as a pretext. We return, then, to earlier days when the New York press explained that "we must go on slaughtering the natives in English fashion, and taking what muddy glory lies in the wholesale killing 'til they have learned to respect our arms. The more difficult task of getting them to respect our intentions will follow."[65] In fact, deprived of the benefits of our form of civilization, they understood our intentions well enough, and still do.

"Two Triumphs"

The "peace process" aside, there is not a great deal that could be brought forth to illustrate U.S. achievements in the Gulf. This too is not much of a problem; as state priorities shift, respectable folk follow suit, turning to approved concerns. But it would have been too much to allow the August 2 anniversary to pass without notice. A last-ditch effort was therefore necessary to portray the outcome as a Grand Victory. Even with the journalistic achievements of the past year, it was no simple matter to chant the praises of our leader as we surveyed the scene of two countries devastated, hundreds of thousands of corpses with the toll still mounting, an ecological disaster, and the Beast of Baghdad firmly in power thanks to the tacit support of the Bush-Baker-Schwarzkopf team.

Even this onerous task was successfully faced. In its anniversary editorial, the *New York Times* editors dismissed the qualms of "the doubters," concluding that Mr. Bush had acted wisely. He "avoided the quagmire and preserved his two triumphs: the extraordinary cooperation among coalition members and the revived self-confidence of Americans," who "greeted the February 28 cease-fire with relief and pride—relief at the miraculously few U.S. casualties and pride in the brilliant performance of the allied forces."[66] Surely these triumphs far outweigh the "awesome tragedies" that trouble Iraqi democrats.

These are chilling words. One can readily understand the reaction of the non-people of the world.

The Contours of the New World Order

Despite basic continuities, there have been changes in the international system. By the 1970s, it was clear that the world economy was becoming "tripolar," a fact recognized in the "trilateralism" of the day and symbolized by Richard Nixon's dismantling of the Bretton Woods system, the foundation of the post-war economic order, in 1971. The collapse of Soviet tyranny adds new dimensions: much of Eastern Europe can be restored to its former status as a quasi-colonial dependency of the West; new pretexts are needed for intervention; there is no longer any deterrent to the use of military force by the United States. But the United States no longer has the economic base to impose "order and stability" (meaning, a proper respect for the masters) in the Third World. Therefore, as the business press has been advising, the United States must become a "mercenary state," paid for its services by German-led continental Europe and Japan, and relying on the flow of capital from Gulf oil production, which it will dominate. The same is true of its British lieutenant, also facing serious domestic problems, but with a "sturdy national character" and proper tradition. John Keegan, a prominent British military historian and defense commentator for the right-wing *Daily Telegraph,* outlines the common view succinctly: "The British are used to over 200 years of expeditionary forces going overseas, fighting the Africans, the Chinese, the Indians, the Arabs. It's just something the British take for granted," and the war in the Gulf "rings very, very familiar imperial bells with the British."[67]

The financial editor of the conservative *Chicago Tribune* has outlined these themes with particular clarity. We must be "willing mercenaries," paid for our ample services by our rivals, using our "monopoly power" in the "security market" to maintain "our control over the world economic system." We should run a global protection racket, selling "protection" to other wealthy powers who will pay us a "war premium." This is Chicago, where the words are understood: If someone bothers you, you call on the mafia to break their bones. And if you fall behind in your premium, your health may suffer too.[68]

The use of force to control the Third World is only a last resort. Economic weapons remain a more efficient instrument. Some of the newer mechanisms can be seen in the current GATT negotiations. Western powers call for liberalization when that is in their interest; and for enhanced protection of domestic economic actors when *that* is in their interest. One major U.S. concern is the "new themes": guarantees for "intellectual property rights," such as patents and software, that will enable TNCs to monopolize new technology; and removal of constraints on services and investment, which will undermine national development programs in the Third World and effectively place investment decisions in the hands of TNCs and the financial institutions of the North. These are "issues of greater magnitude" than the more publicized conflict over agricultural subsidies, according to William Brock, head of the Multilateral Trade Negotiations Coalition of major U.S. corporations.[69]

In general, the wealthy industrial powers advocate a mixture of liberalization and protectionism (such as the Multifiber Arrangement and its extensions, the U.S.-Japan semiconductor agreement, Voluntary Export Arrangements, etc.), designed for the interests of dominant domestic forces, and particularly for the TNCs that are to dominate the world economy. The effect of these measures would be to restrict Third World governments to a police function to control their working classes and superfluous population, while TNCs gain free access to their resources and monopolize new technology and global investment and production—and of course are granted the central planning, allocation, production, and distribution functions denied to governments, which suffer from the defect that they might fall under the baleful influence of the rabble. These facts have not been lost on Third World commentators, who have been protesting eloquently and mightily. But their voices are as welcome here as those of Iraqi democrats.

The United States is attempting to establish a regional bloc to enhance its competitive position. Canada's role is to provide resources and some services and skilled labor, as it is absorbed more fully into the U.S. economy with the reduction of the welfare system, labor rights, and cultural independence. The Canadian Labour Congress reports the loss of more than 225,000 jobs in the first two years of the Free Trade Agreement, along with a wave of takeovers of Canadian-based companies. Mexico and the Caribbean basin are to supply cheap labor for assembly plants, as in the *maquiladora* industries of northern Mexico, where horrendous working conditions and wages and the absence of environmental controls offer highly profitable conditions for investors. These regions are also to provide export crops and markets for U.S. agribusiness. Mexico and Venezuela are also to provide oil, with U.S. corporations granted the right to take part in production, reversing efforts at domestic control of natural resources. The press failed to give Bush sufficient credit for his achievements in his fall 1990 tour of Latin America. Mexico was induced to allow U.S. oil companies new access to its resources, a long-sought policy goal. U.S. companies will now be able "to help Mexico's nationalized oil company," as the *Wall Street Journal* prefers to construe the matter. Our fondest wish for many years has been to help our little brown brothers, and at last the ignorant peons will allow us to cater to their needs.[70]

Such policies are likely to be extended to Latin America generally. And, crucially, the United States will attempt to maintain its dominant influence over Gulf oil production and the profits that flow from it. Other economic powers, of course, have their own ideas, and there are many potential sources of conflict.

Considering these matters, a Latin America Strategy Development Workshop of academic specialists and others held at the Pentagon in September 1990 concluded that current relations with the Mexican dictatorship are "extraordinarily positive," untroubled by stolen elections, death squads, endemic torture, scandalous treatment of workers and peasants, and so forth. But there is a cloud on the horizon: "a 'democracy opening' in Mexico could test the special relationship by bringing into office a government more interested in challenging the United States on economic and nationalist grounds," the fundamental concern over many years, along with the threat of democracy, always lingering ominously in the background.[71]

The population at home must also be controlled, and diverted from growing domestic crises. The basic means have already been described, including periodic campaigns against "much weaker enemies." Cuba is a likely next target, perhaps in time for the next election, if economic warfare, terrorism, intimidation of others to bar normal relations, and other devices of the familiar arsenal can set the stage.

In the Middle East, the United States is now well placed to impose its will. The traditional strategic conception has been that the United States and its British lieutenant should maintain effective power but indirect control in the manner outlined by British imperial managers long ago: The cost-effective mechanism is an "Arab Facade," with "absorption" of the colonies "veiled by constitutional fictions as a protectorate, a sphere of influence, a buffer State, and so on" (Lord Curzon and the Eastern Committee, 1917-18). But we must never run the risk of "losing control," as John Foster Dulles and many others warned.[72] The local managers of Gulf oil riches are to be protected by regional enforcers, preferably non-Arab: Turkey, Israel, Pakistan, and Iran, which perhaps can be restored to the fold. Minority-based tyrants of the Hafez el-Assad variety may be allowed to take part, possibly even Egypt if it can be purchased, though the regime is not brutal enough to be reliable. U.S. and British force remain on call if needed, and can now be freely deployed, with the Soviet deterrent gone.

There has long been a tacit alliance between the "Arab Facade" and the regional gendarmes that help protect it from nationalist currents. It is now coming close to the surface, even receiving some media notice. In the *New York Times,* Thomas Friedman notes Saudi preference for Israel over the PLO or Jordan's Hussein "for controlling the progressive, potentially radical Palestinians," Israel being "a more efficient policeman."[73] With Arab nationalism having been dealt yet another crushing blow, thanks to the gangster who disobeyed orders and PLO tactics of more than the usual foolishness, the Arab rulers have less need than before to respond to popular pressures and to make pro-Palestinian gestures.

Accordingly, the prospects for U.S.-Israeli rejectionism advanced several notches, and the United States was able to move towards a conference satisfying the basic condition stressed by Henry Kissinger years ago: that Europe and Japan must be kept out of the diplomacy.[74] It would be helpful if the USSR could hang together long enough to join symbolically, so that the U.S.-run conference can be portrayed as "international."

The United States is, then, in a good position to move toward the solution outlined by James Baker well before the Gulf crisis:

I. There can be no "additional Palestinian state in the Gaza district and in the area between Israel and Jordan" (Jordan already being a "Palestinian state").

II. "There will be no change in the status of Judea, Samaria, and Gaza other than in accordance with the basic guidelines of the [Israeli] Government," which reject an "additional Palestinian state."

III. "Israel will not conduct negotiations with the PLO," though Israel may agree to speak to certain Palestinians other than their chosen political representatives.

IV. "Free elections" will be held under Israeli military control with much of the Palestinian leadership rotting in prison camps.

These are the terms of the Shamir Plan of May 1989, actually the joint Shamir-Peres plan of the Likud-Labor coalition government. As Baker had always made clear, "Our goal all along has been to try to assist in the implementation of the Shamir initiative. There is no other proposal or initiative that we are working with." Baker elaborated a five-point proposal in October 1989, the crucial one being the condition to be met by the Palestinian representatives—more accurately, by what Baker called the "satisfactory list of Palestinians" to be selected by their caretakers: Israel, Egypt, and the United States. This condition reads: "The United States further understands that Palestinians will come to the dialogue prepared to discuss elections and negotiations in accordance with Israel's initiative [i.e., the Shamir-Peres plan]. The United States understands, therefore, that Palestinians would be free to raise issues that relate to their opinions on how to make elections and negotiations succeed." In short, the "Palestinian delegation" will be free to express opinions on the technical modalities of Israel's proposal to bar any meaningful form of Palestinian self-determination—and even this right they will be accorded only if they convince Israel and its patron that they have no link to the chosen political representatives of the Palestinians.[75]

This is the essence of the Baker-Shamir-Peres plan, the official "peace process." Its terms have been effectively suppressed, masked behind such slogans as "territorial compromise" and "land for peace."

These Orwellisms are interpreted in accord with traditional Labor Party rejectionism, which has always been favored by the United States over the Likud variant: Israel will take what it wants in the territories, leaving the surplus population stateless or under Jordanian administration. Note that all of this was in place well before the failure of the Palestinians to line up behind the U.S. crusade in the Gulf, which allegedly disqualified them from the "peace process." In fact, the rejectionist framework goes back for many years, basically unmodified. The refusal to deal with the PLO has nothing to do with their alleged sins, but with the fact, always recognized quite openly by the Israeli leadership across the mainstream political spectrum, that authentic representatives of the Palestinians will call for self-determination, which Israel will not accept. Now, new excuses will be devised for old policies, which will be hailed as generous and forthcoming.[76]

Economic development for the Palestinians had always been barred, while their land and water were taken. The Labor Party leadership advised that the Palestinians should be given the message: "You shall continue to live like dogs, and whoever wishes, may leave" (Moshe Dayan, more pro-Palestinian than most).[77] The advice was followed, though the grim story has been largely suppressed here. Palestinians had been permitted to serve the Israeli economy as virtual slave labor, but this interlude is passing. The Gulf War curfew administered a further blow to the Palestinian economy. The victors can now proceed with the policy articulated in February 1989 by Yitzhak Rabin of the Labor Party, then Defense Secretary, when he informed Peace Now leaders of his satisfaction with the U.S.-PLO dialogue, meaningless discussions to divert attention while Israel suppresses the Intifada by force. The Palestinians "will be broken," Rabin promised, reiterating the prediction of Israeli Arabists 40 years earlier: The Palestinians will "be crushed," will die or "turn into human dust and the waste of society, and join the most impoverished classes in the Arab countries." Or they will leave, while Russian Jews, now barred from the United States by policies designed to deny them a free choice, flock to an expanded Israel, leaving the diplomatic issues moot, as the Baker-Shamir-Peres plan envisaged.[78]

For Washington's purposes, it is not of great importance that the "peace conference" succeed. If it does, the United States will have established its traditional rejectionism, having sucessfully rebuffed the near-unanimous world support for an authentic political settlement. If that comes about, it will be hailed as another triumph for our great leader, a renewed demonstration of our high-minded benevolence and virtue. If the "peace process" fails, we will read of "a classic cultural clash between American and Middle Eastern instincts," a conflict between Middle Eastern fanaticism and Baker's "quintessentially American view of the world: that with just a little bit of reasonableness these people should be able to see that they have a shared interest in peace that overrides their historical antipathies" (Thomas Friedman).[79] It's a win-win situation for U.S. power.

These are some of the contours of the planned New World Order that come into view as the beguiling rhetoric is lifted away.

Notes

1. Baker, Address to the Los Angeles World Affairs Council, October 29, 1990. Bush, February 1, cited by Robert Parry, *Nation,* April 15, 1991. Lewis, *New York Times,* March 15, 1991.
2. *Il Sabato,* March 2 (AP, February 26, 1991); Sommer, *Guardian* (London), April 13; *Proceso,* January 23, 1991.
3. *Times of India,* cited by William Dalrymple, *Spectator* (London), February 23, 1991; *Third World Resurgence* (Malaysia), No. 6, February; cover, No. 7, March 1991; *Folha de Sao Paulo,* Ken Silverstein, p.c.; *South,* February 1991.
4. Jansen, *Middle East International,* February 22, 1991; Lloyd, *Financial Times,* January 19-20, 1991; Iraqi democrats, see below; al-Khalil, *New York Review,* March 18, 1991; *South,* February 1991; *Mideast Mirror* (London), January 28, 1991.
   Sources in Syria estimated that 80 to 90 percent of the population opposed its participation in the war (Sarah Gauch, *Christian Science Monitor,* March 28, 1991). Much the same was reported elsewhere.
5. *La Epoca,* May 4, 1991.
6. Foreword, Thomas Fox, *Iraq* (Sheed & Ward, 1991), ix.
7. Paul Lewis, *New York Times,* January 12, 1991; UN Draft A/44/L.51, 6 December 1989.
8. Associated Press, April 13, 1990. Reuters, *Boston Globe,* April 14, 1990. *Financial Times,* March 9, 1991; Clyde Farnsworth, *New York Times,* March 18, 1991.
9. Robert Pear, *New York Times,* August 11, 1991; Tyler, *New York Times,* July 28, 1991.
10. *New York Times,* February 23, 1991.
11. Figures from Robert Reich, *Wall Street Journal,* January 30, 1991; Joshua Cohen, "Comments on the War," MIT, March 4, 1991; Erich Heinemann, *Christian Science Monitor,* April 2, 1991. Prison population, Maurice Briggs, *Chicago Sun-Times,* January 9; Tom Wicker, *New York Times,* January 9, 1991.
12. Maureen Dowd, *New York Times,* March 2, 1991.
13. E.J. Dionne, *Washington Post Weekly,* March 11, 1991; John Aloysius Farrell, *Boston Globe Magazine,* March 31, 1991; Martin Nolan, *Boston Globe,* March 10, 1991; Oliphant, *Boston Globe,* February 27, 1991. Roosevelt, see Chomsky, *Turning the Tide,* Boston: South End Press, 1985, pp. 61, 87.
14. Oliphant, op. cit.
15. Peter Applebome, *New York Times,* March 1, 1991; Terrence Maitland, *New York Times Book Review,* February 3, 1991 reviewing Zalin Grant, *Facing the Phoenix.*
16. Kaplan, *Boston Globe,* February 23, 1991; Hoffmann, *Boston Globe,* January 6, 1991. Sut Jhally, Justin Lewis, and Michael Morgan, *The Gulf War: A Study of the*

Media, Public Opinion, and Public Knowledge, Department of Communication, Amherst: University of Massachusetts.

17. *Chicago Tribune,* March 6, 1991; Carlson, *U.S. Naval Institute Proceedings,* September 1989; *Los Angeles Times,* September 3, 1989; AP, April 23, 1990; *Third World Resurgence,* October 1990.

18. Mike Mansfield, cited by Frank Costigliola, in Thomas Paterson, ed., *Kennedy's Quest for Victory,* Oxford University Press, 1989.

19. Michael Tomasky and Richard McKerrow, *Village Voice,* February 26, 1991.

20. Reuters, Canberra, February 24; Communiqué, International Court of Justice, February 22, 1991; *Daily Hansard* SENATE (Australia), 1 November, 1989, 2707; *Indonesia News Service,* November 1, 1990; Greenleft mideast.gulf.346, electronic communication, February 18, 1991; *Monthly Record,* Parliament (Australia), March 1991; *FEER,* 25 July 1991.

21. ABC (Australia) radio, "Background briefing; East Timor," February 17, 1991; Robin Osborne, *Indonesia's Secret Wars,* Allen & Unwin, 1985; George Monbiot, *Poisoned Arrows,* London: Abacus, 1989; Anti-Slavery Society, *West Papua,* London, 1990.

22. *State Department Bulletin* 81, August 1981, No. 30; *Harvard Human Rights Journal* 4, Spring 1991, 139ff., 107f.; Chomsky, *Deterring Democracy,* London and New York: Verso, 1991, p. 152.

23. Reuters, September 26, 1990; Saeedpour, Pacific News Service, March 11, 1991; John Murray Brown, *Financial Times,* February 12 and March 8, 1991; AP, March 20, 1991; Michael Gunter, *Kurdish Times,* Fall 1990; Ray Moseley, *Chicago Tribune,* February 6, 1991. *Washington Post,* January 30, 1991; *Die Tageszeitung,* 28 January 1991; Medico International, *Krieg und Flucht in Kurdistan,* Frankfurt, citing also *Frankfurter Rundschau,* January 25. *Human Rights Watch #1,* Winter, 1991.

24. *New York Times,* February 19, 1991.

25. See Chomsky, articles in *Z Magazine,* March and October 1990, February 1991, and *Deterring Democracy,* chapters 5, 6. For further reports (lacking sources, hence difficult to evaluate), see Pierre Salinger and Eric Laurent, *Guerre du Golfe,* Paris: Olivier Orban, 1991; Adel Darwish and Gregory Alexander, *Unholy Babylon,* New York: St. Martin's Press, 1991. Also Don Oberdorfer, Stuart Auerbach, *Washington Post Weekly,* March 18-24, 1991; Michael Massing, *New York Review of Books,* March 28, 1991; Helga Graham, *South,* February 1991.

26. Darwish and Alexander, 79; Tony Benn, et al., letter, *Manchester Guardian Weekly,* March 31, 1991.

27. Alan Friedman and Lionel Barber, *Financial Times,* May 3 and May 24, 1991; AP, *Boston Globe,* May 23, 1991; Ralph Atkins et al., *Financial Times,* July 29, 1991; James Adams and Nick Rufford, *Sunday Times* (London), July 28, 1991.

28. Kemp, Darwish and Alexander, 63; Rodman, *Financial Times,* May 3, 1991; Friedman, *New York Times,* July 7, 1991.

29. Auerbach, Salinger, Darwish, and Alexander. Also Michael Emery, *How Mr. Bush Got His War,* Open Magazine Pamphlet Series #9, Westfield NJ, 1991.

30. Woodward, *The Commanders,* New York: Simon & Schuster, 1991; *Washington Post-Boston Globe,* May 3, 1991.

31. On the U.S.-U.K. reaction to the Iraqi coup of 1958, which was the first break in the Anglo-American condominium, see the review of declassified documents in *Deterring Democracy,* 183f.

32. For details, see *Deterring Democracy;* Parry, *Nation,* April 15, 1991.

33. The translation by AP from Cyprus and by the BBC was accurate. AP, *Boston Globe,* February 16, 1991; BBC, *Financial Times,* February 16, 1991; State Department version, *New York Times,* February 16, 1991, *Time,* February 25,

1991. See also William Beeman, PNS, February 18, 1991. Original obtained by Edward Said. Iraqi Ambassador, *New York Times,* February 17, 1991, 100 words. John Cushman, "U.S. Insists Withdrawal Comes Before Cease-Fire," *New York Times,* February 16, 1991.

34. Thomas Friedman and Patrick Tyler, *New York Times,* March 3, 1991; Transcript of Moscow Peace Proposal and Bush-Fitzwater statements, *New York Times,* February 23, 1991; Patrick Tyler, *New York Times,* February 26, 1991.

35. Webb, *Wall Street Journal,* January 31, 1991.

36. *Washington Post,* January 11, 1991.

37. Luzviminda Francisco and Jonathan Fast, *Conspiracy for Empire,* Quezon City, 1985, pp. 302, 191. BBC-1 TV news, 9 PM, March 5; BBC radio, cited by Christopher Hitchens, *Nation,* April 8, 1991.

38. Patrick Tyler, *New York Times,* June 5, 1991; Walter S. Mossberg and David Rogers, *Wall Street Journal,* March 22, 1991; Holly Burkhalter, Washington director of Human Rights Watch, *Los Angeles Times,* March 12, 1991; *News,* Middle East Watch, March 7, 1991. Malcolm Browne, *New York Times,* May 6, 1972; see E.S. Herman and N. Chomsky, *Manufacturing Consent,* New York: Pantheon, 1988, p. 193, for longer quote and context.

39. Patrick Sloyan, "Buried Alive," *Newsday,* September 12, 1991, p. 1. The *Boston Globe* gave the story a few lines on p. 79 under "National Briefs," September 13. The *Times* ran a casual account a few days later: Eric Schmitt, *New York Times,* September 15, 1991.

40. Paul Berman, *New Republic,* May 27, 1991.

41. For a detailed review, see Chomsky, *For Reasons of State,* New York: Pantheon, 1973.

42. For details, see Chomsky, *American Power and the New Mandarins,* New York: Pantheon, 1969, pp. 210-1; *Towards a New Cold War,* New York: Pantheon, 1982, pp. 112-3. On Tokyo, see Barton Bernstein, *International Security,* Spring 1991.

43. Friedman, *New York Times,* July 7, 1991.

44. *Wall Street Journal,* July 5, 1991.

45. Jim Drinkard, AP, April 3, 1991; Geraldine Brooks, *Wall Street Journal,* April 3, 1991; Michael Kranish, *Boston Globe,* April 4, 1991; Walter Robinson, *Boston Globe,* March 21; Paul Taylor, Reuters, March 21, 1991; *Mideast Mirror,* March 21, 1991; *Los Angeles Times,* April 2, 1991; Christopher Marquis, *Boston Globe,* April 3, 1991; Paul Lewis, *New York Times,* April 3, 1991.

46. Andrew Rosenthal, *New York Times,* April 3, 1991; Neier, *Nation,* September 23, 1991.

47. Andrew Rosenthal, *New York Times,* March 27, 1991; Al Kamen and Ann Devroy, *Washington Post-Manchester Guardian Weekly,* April 28, 1991.

48. Galbraith, testimony excerpted in *New Combat,* Summer 1991; David Hoffman, *Washington Post,* May 3, 1991. Simpson, Glass, *Spectator,* London, August 10 and April 13, 1991.

49. Greenpeace press release, July 23, 1991; Environet.

50. Andrew Rosenthal, *New York Times,* February 23, 1991; AP, *Boston Globe,* February 9, 1991; Pamela Constable, *Boston Globe,* January 27, 1991.

51. Sources in London-based Iraqi democratic opposition; Darwish and Alexander; Talabani, Vera Saeedpour, *Toward Freedom,* Burlington, VT, March 1991; Stephen Hubbell, *Nation,* April 15, 1991.

52. Gruppe Irakischer Demokraten, "For a Peaceful Settlement," *Frankfurter Rundschau,* January 14, 1991; al-Jabbar, *Manchester Guardian Weekly,* February 3, 1991; Mortimer, *Financial Times,* January 21, 1991.

53. Lamis Andoni, *Financial Times,* December 6, 1990. David Pallister, *Guardian* (London), February 18, 1991. Khatib, *Middle East Report,* January/February 1991, cited by Mouin Rabbani, letter, *New Statesman,* March 22, 1991, replying to Fred Halliday. The quote is from Khatib's interview with Halliday, who advocated war, also claiming that it was supported by the populations of the region, which is untrue, as far as we know, and hardly relevant; no one, including Halliday, relies on regional attitudes to justify the use of force against Israel to remove it from Lebanon and the occupied territories.

54. Jane Friedman, *Christian Science Monitor,* March 20, 1991; Elaine Sciolino, *New York Times,* April 7, 1991.

55. *Mideast Mirror* (London), March 15, 1991.

56. *Wall Street Journal,* April 8, 1991.

57. *New York Times,* April 11, 1991.

58. *Al-Ahram,* April 9, 1991. *Mideast Mirror,* 10 April, 1991.

59. *Mideast Mirror,* 27 March, 26 March, 27 February, 1991.

60. Ron Ben-Yishai, interview with Shomron, *Ha'aretz,* March 29, 1991; Shalom Yerushalmi, "We are all with Saddam," *Kol Ha'ir,* April 4, 1991; *Jerusalem Post,* April 4, 1991.

61. See notes 16, 14.

62. See Alex Carey, "Managing Public Opinion," unpublished manuscript, New South Wales, 1986.

63. AP, January 14, 1991; George Bush's letter to Saddam Hussein, *New York Times,* January 13, 1991.

64. Ash, "The Gulf in Europe," *NYRB,* March 7, 1991. Inter-Agency Task Force, Africa Recovery Program/Economic Commission, *South African Destabilization: the Economic Cost of Frontline Resistance to Apartheid,* NY: United Nations, 1989, No. 13, cited by Merle Bowen, *Fletcher Forum,* Winter 1991. Mandela, AP, *New York Times,* November 8, 1990. Editorials, *New York Times,* February 23 and 27, 1991.

65. See *Turning the Tide,* p. 162.

66. Editorial, *New York Times,* August 2, 1991.

67. Richard Hudson, *Wall Street Journal,* February 5, 1991.

68. William Neikirk, *Chicago Tribune,* September 9, 1990 and January 27, 1991. Some feel that his columns are intended as ironic. I doubt it, but in the current phase of civilization, it is often hard to tell.

69. Quoted in Martin Khor Kok Peng, *The Uruguay Round and Third World Sovereignty,* Penang, 1990, p. 10. See also Chakravarthi Raghavan, *Recolonization: GATT, the Uruguay Round and the Third World,* Penang, 1990.

70. Virginia Galt, "226,000 jobs lost since pact, CLC says," *Toronto Globe & Mail,* December 15, 1990; John Maclean, "Venezuela reverses economic course," *Chicago Tribune,* May 27, 1991; *Wall Street Journal,* November 28, 1990.

71. *Latin America Strategy Development Workshop,* September 26 and 27, 1990, minutes, p. 3. Andrew Reding, "Mexico's Democratic Challenge," *World Policy Journal,* Spring 1991.

72. William Stivers, *Supremacy and Oil,* Cornell University Press, 1982, pp. 28, 34; *America's Confrontation with Revolutionary Change in the Middle East,* New York: St. Martin's Press, 1986, p. 20f.

73. Friedman, *New York Times,* July 28, 1991. On earlier stages of the "alliance," see Chomsky, *Towards a New Cold War,* New York: Pantheon, 1982; *Fateful Triangle,* Boston: South End, 1983; Andrew and Leslie Cockburn, *Dangerous Liaison,* New York: HarperCollins, 1991.

74. "Memorandum of Conversation," Meeting with Jewish Leaders, June 15, 1975; *Middle East Reports (MERIP),* May 1981. See Chomsky, *Towards a New Cold War,* p. 457.

75. Israeli Government Election Plan, Jerusalem, 14 May 1989, official text distributed by the Embassy of Israel in Washington, reprinted in the *Journal of Palestine Studies,* Autumn 1989; excerpts in *New Outlook* (Tel Aviv), August 1989. The Prime Minister's own four-point plan a month earlier, with somewhat different terms, was called "the Shamir plan" prior to the formulation of the government proposal. See "The Shamir Plan," *Jerusalem Post,* April 14, 1989. For discussion of this version, see Norman Finkelstein, in *Middle East Report (MERIP),* No. 158, May-June 1989. Baker, Thomas Friedman, *New York Times,* October 19; "Baker's Five Points," Daniel Williams, *Los Angeles Times,* October 29, 1989.

76. For background on these matters, including the remarkable record of media distortion, see *Fateful Triangle* and Chomsky, *Necessary Illusions,* Boston: South End Press, 1989.

77. Yossi Beilin, *Mehiro shel Ihud* (Revivim, 1985), reviewing internal cabinet records.

78. For references, see Chomsky, article in *Z Magazine,* January 1990 and October 1991, and *Deterring Democracy.*

79. *New York Times,* May 19 and 17, 1991.

CHAPTER 3

THE GENDERED GULF

Cynthia Enloe

Introduction

Most of us still are trying to make sense of the Gulf War. Its meanings
are as multilayered as a Mesopotamian archeological dig. For instance, I
realize now that I know nothing—nothing—about Kurdish women. This
means that I have an inherently faulty understanding of how Iraqi Kurdish
nationalism is being conceptualized; nor do I know how either the
Peshmerge guerrilla force or the non-combatant refugee communities are
organizing their lives. The three essays that follow, therefore, are best read
as incomplete, time-anchored attempts to bring a feminist sensibility to
bear on what was initially described as the "Gulf crisis" and later was
labeled the "Gulf War." The first attempt was written in mid-September
1990, only a few weeks after returning from my first visit to the South
Pacific.

I was in the Cook Islands when I heard the news of the Iraqi
military's invasion of Kuwait on the BBC World Service. The South Pacific
was teaching me to imagine this world in new and surprising ways. I was
seeing Australia as an emerging and militarizing regional power, New
Zealand as not only an anti-nuclear renegade but as a former colonizer;
small islands no bigger than pin pricks on a world map were turning out
to have dynamic and complex international relations they barely had the
resources to monitor, much less control; women's relationships to men
in each one of these small societies—Fiji, Vanuatu, the Cook Islands,

---

Parts I and II of this esssay were originally published in the *Village Voice,* September
25, 1990 and February 19, 1991, respectively.

Tahiti—were as much the stuff of political myths, alliances, and anxieties as they were in any other society. So when I heard the news of what was instantly called the Gulf crisis, I tried not to slip back into my natural world-as-seen-from-Boston mode. I tried, not always successfully, to sense what the invasion and its ripple effects meant for Cook Islanders, Australians, and Fijians: higher petrol and kerosene prices, drops in tourism, further rationales for expanding Australian military presence— each with its own distinctively gendered causes and consequences. Perhaps it was this mental aerobics exercise that pushed me a month later, now back on the American east coast, to set off on my trial run at analyzing the crisis by imagining it from the vantage point of one of its apparently least significant participants, a Filipina working as a maid in Kuwait City. Although I didn't have all the analytical ends neatly tied together, I had been taught by feminists over the last 20 years to be very wary of presuming that the political actors with the most power—and the most media coverage—were the most useful starting points when trying to figure out exactly how politics works. I might get back to George Bush, François Mitterand, King Fahd, and Saddam Hussein eventually, but coming to their ideological outlooks and uses of state power via particular groups of women, via the relationships of those women to each other, would prove, I had learned, far more fruitful than taking the lazy masculinist short cut of presuming that those men in and of themselves revealed the most about why this crisis had developed and why it was following its peculiar course.

The second essay in this trilogy was written almost five months later, in February 1991. The Bush administration and its allies—including Australia's Hawke administration—had launched their massive air bombardment of Iraq and were in the opening stages of what would be an alarmingly short ground war. I had been following the elite Saudi women's driving protest, watching for the consolidation of military prostitution policies which would rely on Third World women, and scanning the European press (more promising than the U.S.) for any signs that the feminist, pro-democracy Iraqi Women's League would be recognized in the exiled opposition coalitions. But in February, I felt compelled to turn my puzzlement directly toward women closer to home. Yellow ribbons were sprouting like dandelions in spring. They seemed to be spontaneous expressions, especially expressions by women; only later did the press and Washington officialdom make efforts to impose their own meanings on them.

To this day I am not at all sure I know what each woman who put a ribbon on her winter coat lapel or on her secretarial in-tray or on her hospital staff association noticeboard was saying. That is something we still had better be curious about. But in the midst of the ground war I felt that women suddenly had become invisible. At least during the tense months of the "pre war" autumn, women—as familiar wives, soldiers, girl friends, mothers, as alien veiled women—had served as valuable "human interest" stories. Now that the serious business of combat had begun, women had slid further off the page; only their yellow ribbons caught the public eye. Yet it seemed clear that the yellow ribbon phenomenon (which occurred to a lesser degree in Canada and Britain) was drawing U.S. women into the Bush administration's larger global scheme in ways we needed to understand—not just because any new or old world order would affect women, but, more radically, because any configuration of international relationships can only be fashioned by government leaders if they can devise ways to harness women's compliance.

The final essay was written in June 1991. The British and U.S. troops were being pulled out of northern Iraq, where they had been protecting Kurdish refugees.

The Bush and Major governments wanted the refugees to return to their homes in Iraq less because the Kurds were now secure than because a lingering American troop presence might remind voters back home of a Vietnam-like "quagmire." Also, if Iraqi Kurds stayed in southern Turkey they might destabilize that less-than-ethnically harmonious NATO partner. Oily smoke continued to hang over Kuwait City, though only the most committed of environmental investigators were charting the spills threatening Persian Gulf marine life or the after-effects of the bombing of Iraq's chemical plants. There was no date set, no list of invitees agreed upon for an Israeli-Palestinian peace conference, and meanwhile new Soviet Jewish immigrants were being settled on the disputed West Bank. Arms salesmen were doing a brisk business in the Middle East; disarmament seemed to have few genuine advocates. Yet, even with Saudi Arabia and Israel as showcases for its Patriot missiles, Raytheon was laying off hundreds of women and men in recession-hit Massachusetts. Wearing yellow ribbons and hosting the president back in February hadn't saved their jobs in June.

Yet with all these signals that the war—wars, actually—had not ended, most North Americans and Europeans were acting in early summer as though they were living in a "post-war" era. Those who had come, however reluctantly, as had a majority of women, to support the U.S.-led warmaking went to parades. Those who opposed the warmaking went to conferences. Post-war periods are dangerous times. They are times when lessons—often the wrong lessons, often lessons right for some but harmful to others—are hammered out. Post-war is a time for feminists to keep their eyes wide open, for it is now when masculinity and femininity will be reconsidered, and perhaps reconstructed, by warmakers and war resisters alike.

I. September, 1990: Womenandchildren

In the torrents of media coverage that accompany an international crisis women typically are made visible as symbols, victims, or dependents. "Womenandchildren" rolls so easily off network tongues because in network minds women are family members rather than independent actors, presumed to be almost childlike in their innocence about the realpolitik of international affairs. Rarely are women imagined to reveal any of the basic structures of a dangerous confrontation.

If there is an image that defines television's Gulf crisis, it's a disheveled white woman coming off a 747, an exhausted baby on her shoulder. States exist, this media story implies, to protect womenandchildren. U.S. intervention in the Gulf would be harder to justify if there were no feminized victim. The real diplomatic wives, the British and American women who in the last decade have created formidable lobbying organizations to press their interests, don't fit this scenario.

It follows that the Gulf crisis story must also ignore the female attaché at the U.S. embassy in Kuwait, negotiating with the Iraqis for the release of these very same womenandchildren. Passing over State Department women's organizing, which opened up the previously masculinized foreign service, the media treats her merely as an honorary man: capable, able to take care of herself—and others. Her existence is not allowed to disturb the womenandchildren-protected-by-statesmen scenario.

Though you don't see them on the evening news, there are an estimated 17,000 Filipino women today working as domestic servants in Saudi Arabia. Thousands of others have been cleaning, washing, and minding children in Kuwait and the United Arab Emirates. Together, there are over 29,000 Filipino domestic servants in the Middle East. Government officials not only in the Philippines but in Sri Lanka, Indonesia, Jamaica, and Ethiopia have been counting on the paychecks that maids send home to lessen their nations' imbalance of payments and to keep the lid on politically explosive unemployment.

These Asian women, now trapped in occupied Kuwait or crowded into Jordanian refugee camps, have been crucial players in reducing global tensions generated by international debt.

After the 1970s oil boom, Kuwaiti and Saudi women became employers in their homes. But their relationships with their Sri Lankan or

Filipino maids had to be devised in ways that met with their husbands' approval and kept the foreign workers at least minimally content. As stories have filtered back home of the abuse that some—not all—Asian domestic servants experienced, the Sri Lankan and Philippines governments have been pressed by their own women's advocates to take steps to protect their nationals working abroad. The regimes have acted ineffectually, in part because they have been afraid of offending Gulf states on whom they depend for oil, in part because they have rebellions and other worries closer to home diverting them, and in part because they have concluded that they need to satisfy the men from the International Monetary Fund (IMF) obsessed with balance-of-payments more than they need to win the support of their own domestic women's movements.

Caryl Murphy, the *Washington Post* reporter who sent out clandestine reports from Kuwait in the days following the Iraqi invasion, has described how some Filipino maids were taken by their Kuwaiti employers to the Philippines embassy so that they would have some modicum of protection. Other Kuwaitis, she reports, fled in front of the invading troops, leaving their Filipino employees to fend for themselves. Filipinas in Kuwait City told Murphy that they had heard stories of Iraqi soldiers raping other domestic workers. Rape in war is never simply random violence. It is structured by male soldiers' notions of their masculine privilege, by the strength of the military's lines of command and by class and ethnic inequalities among women. If you're a rich Kuwaiti woman you have less chance of being raped than if you are an Asian maid.

To make sense, then, of the Iraqi occupation of Kuwait we have to talk about soldiers' ideas of manliness, middle-class women's presumptions about housework, and the IMF's strategies for handling international debt. Debt, laundry, rape, and conquest are understandable only in relation to each other.

Though we have a hard time understanding it, to many Jordanians, Palestinians, and other Arabs Saddam Hussein is a potent symbol of nationalist aspirations, which are fueled by a resentment of European and U.S. attempts to impose their values and their priorities on the societies of the Middle East. To many Arab men, women are the people most vulnerable to Western corruption and exploitation. This conviction has infused debates over women's attire and women's education with political passion.

But Middle East women haven't been mere symbols. First, they are diverse, distinguished by ethnicity, ideology, class, and nationality. Second, since the turn of the century many have been active participants in their countries' freedom movements. Arab feminists have criticized many of their male compatriots for trying to fashion a nationalism that camouflages male privilege under the legitimizing mantle of "Arab tradition."

Being an Arab nationalist feminist is a risky enterprise (one might say that being a nationalist feminist in any community is a daunting project). A women's-rights advocate always is open to nervous men's double-barreled charge that she is succumbing to alien western bourgeois values, while splitting the nation at a time when it needs unity above all else. The current Gulf crisis, defined largely by massive U.S. military posturing, has radically complicated local feminists' task. Arab women activists walking a tightrope between male nationalists' patriarchy and Western policymakers' cultural imperialism have the most to lose when an international crisis polarizes internal debate. Western male officials who claim their policies are supporting "civilized" politics are, in fact, painting Arab women into an oppressive corner.

But many observers nonetheless are portraying wartime mobilization as good for women. Saddam Hussein, a secular not a religious nationalist, has made wide use of women in his military buildup. During the Iraq-Iran war, Saddam encouraged the Iraqi Women's Federation (an organization quite separate from the exiled Iraqi Women's League) to channel women into non-traditional jobs in order to free men to fight.

A Saudi feminist stationed with the United Nations in Baghdad during that war has even wondered aloud whether it didn't further Iraqi women's emancipation. The more devastating the war became, she recalled, the more Saddam's all-male Revolutionary Council called on women to lend their efforts to the nation (though never forsaking their primary responsibility of producing more children). Her puzzle would sound familiar to many U.S. feminists. The U.S. government followed the same course during World War II. Of course, the Iraqi cousins of "Rosie the Riveter" also discovered, once the war ended, male government officials—and their fathers and husbands—expected women to return to the more restricted domestic feminized roles that bolstered male egos and made space for the employment of demobilized male soldiers.

Today there is evidence that once again the Iraqi Women's Federation is being called upon to mobilize women, this time to put in place the consumer-rationing programs that will be the key to the Saddam regime's ability to withstand the UN embargo. It would not be surprising if many Iraqi women activists saw in the crisis yet another opportunity to use wartime mobilization to demonstrate their public capabilities. Now, however, in search of Muslim allies, Saddam is beginning to refer to his campaign as a holy cause. The more he couches his brand of Arab nationalism in religious terms, the less likely even the exigencies of wartime mobilization will produce long-term gains for Iraqi women.

There are reports out of Saudi Arabia this week that King Fahd has instructed his ministries to encourage Saudi women to volunteer for war-related jobs until now closed to them. Saudi women nurses who have been restricted to caring only for women patients are now to be permitted to attend male patients. Though the western media is heralding this announcement as evidence that the wartime mobilization may benefit "benighted" Saudi women, there has been scarce curiosity about the history or current thinking of those women.

In fact, U.S. coverage of the Gulf crisis has been framed by a contrast between the liberated American woman soldier and the veiled Arab woman. It is striking how consistent this current media preoccupation is with the western tradition of "Orientalism," that package of often-ambiguous ideas about the presumed backwardness, yet allure of Arab culture. The harem was at the center of western writers' preoccupation. In the past it was the daring Victorian lady traveller who posed the stark contrast with the secluded Arab woman. The former's presence served to reassure the self-satisfied western man that his society was the more "civilized" and thus within its natural rights in colonizing the Middle East. The European woman traveler also tempted many of her homebound sisters to imagine that they were a lot more emancipated than they really were: Even if they were denied the vote, couldn't control their own reproduction, and couldn't divorce a violent husband, at least they weren't pent up in a harem. The imperialist enterprise relied on both western women and men feeling superior to the patriarchal Arabs.

Today, many television and print journalists are substituting the U.S. woman soldier for the Victorian lady traveller, but the political intent remains much the same. By contrasting the allegedly liberated American woman tank mechanic with the Saudi woman deprived of a driver's license, U.S. reporters are implying that the United States is the advanced civilized country whose duty it is to take the lead in resolving the Persian Gulf crisis. Women of both countries are being turned into the currency with which men attempt to maintain the unequal relations between their societies.

Yet Arab women, even in the conservative societies of the Gulf, are more than passive victims of *purdah*. There are Saudi women who have university educations, who have founded women-only banks, who practice medicine in women-only hospitals, earn wages in newly established garment factories. One need not overstate the political and economic freedom of these women to argue nonetheless that Saudi women are diverse and have authentic analyses of their own.

There are Kuwaiti women who have organized neighborhood-level protests against the occupying Iraqi army. Susan Shuaib, a Kuwaiti-British feminist writing in the latest *New Statesman and Society,* puts this surprising news in the broader context of Kuwait's changing political relations between women and men. Just this July, according to Shuaib, women had become more visible as activists pressing for parliamentary government. They organized petition drives and took part in public rallies.

The second problem with the neo-Orientalist interpretation adopted by so many U.S. reporters is that it treats U.S. women soldiers' "advances" outside any consideration of militarism. There are daily stories now about women soldiers coping with life in the desert. Approximately 6 percent of all U.S. forces in Saudi Arabia are women, a little more than half their proportions in the military as a whole. In the U.S. and British media, the woman flying a giant C-141 transport plane is portrayed as the natural descendent of Susan B. Anthony.

It is true that many women in the military do see themselves as feminists, breaking down formidable sexist barriers. For them, the Persian Gulf operation is not part of Middle East political evolution, with its volatile mix of imperialism and nationalism. Rather, it is part of a political struggle that began with the American women in Vietnam, and was carried into the U.S. invasions of Grenada and Panama. Each U.S. military intervention has provided a chance for women to hone their bureaucratic skills, perfect end runs around chauvinist field commanders, and turn up the heat on Pentagon officials still dragging their feet in opening up military career opportunities to women soldiers.

If, however, winning "first-class citizenship" depends on American women gaining full acceptance in the military, what does that suggest about the very meaning of citizenship? In all the coverage of American women soldiers' advances, there is the implication that the military defines citizenship.

The always artificial categories of "combat," "near combat," and "non-combat" may indeed be crumbling in the desert. But few women are talking yet about what sorts of sexual harassment they are likely to experience as the weeks pass with male soldiers having none of their usual access overseas to foreign women. Which country will play host to the thousands of American soldiers on "R & R"? Not Saudi Arabia. Whichever government agrees to serve as a rest-and-recreation site will make agreements with the Pentagon to ensure that American male soldiers have direct access to local women without endangering the men's health. Buried in the fine print of government-to-government R & R agreements are stipulations about public health and police authority that directly affect local women's relations with GIs. According to the Pentagon's own recently released study, 64 percent of women in the military say they have been sexually harassed. A woman soldier who won't pay attention to a male colleague is always vulnerable to lesbian-baiting. But this is made doubly intimidating when the Pentagon persists in its policy of forcing suspected lesbians out of the service.

The Persian Gulf crisis has not been built out of relations between ungendered presidents, kings, foreign ministers, oil executives, and soldiers. If we pay attention to the experiences and ideas of the women involved, two realities come into sharper focus. First, this international confrontation, like others before it, is played out in part by governments attempting to confine women to roles that, even when they briefly shake conventional social norms, nonetheless serve those governments' interests. Second, those government attempts are not always successful. Third, men's sense of their own masculinity, often tenuous, is as much a factor in international politics as the flows of oil, cables, and military hardware.

II. February, 1991: Tie a Yellow Ribbon Around The New World Order

On the eve of the Gulf War, polls revealed a startling gender gap: American women were far less likely than American men to support going to war with Iraq. As recently as one week before the fighting began, the ABC News/ *Washington Post* poll showed that only 58 percent of women surveyed, compared with 82 percent of men, thought war was the best way for the U.S. government to respond to Saddam Hussein. For pollsters, a 24-point spread is a gender gap of monumental proportions. Then on January 16, U.S. bombs began falling on Baghdad. As the bombs rained, the gender gap began to shrink. It wasn't men who were changing their minds. It was women. By January 20, the gender gap had shrunk to a mere 10 points, 71 percent to 81 percent.

George Bush has justified using force against the Iraqis to protect a "New World Order." Whereas under the old order, East was pitted against West, in the new post-1989 order, North is pitted against a South personified by Saddam Hussein. Yet this allegedly "new" order remains stuck in the old presumption that military power must be the principal tool for wielding international influence.

Bush's world order depends on its own kind of gender gap: George Bush, Colin Powell, John Major, Saddam Hussein, Yitzhak Shamir, the Iraqi Republican Guards, and British Tornado and American B-52 pilots remain state elites, their masculinities unquestioned. The wives of each of these men, as well M-16-toting American women soldiers and Saudi women driving protesters, are of course discussed as women, but consequently treated as trivial. Yet, as feminists have revealed in the last decade, every public power arrangement has depended on the control of femininity as an idea and of women as workers, carers, and sexual partners. We cannot make sense of any government's hoped-for world order in a gender vacuum. The post-August U.S. gender gap, and its recent dramatic shrinkage, must be explained precisely because the not-so-new militarized Pax Americana won't work unless women cooperate.

The current world order is "orderly" only if national-security officials can imagine their responsibilities to be manly, if diplomats can be served by unpaid diplomatic wives, if nationalist men can count on their women to pay homage to the nation's gendered culture, if multinational corporations can feminize and thereby cheapen labor, if indebted governments can send maids overseas to mail home remittances, and if technocrats can celebrate supermoms as models of modernity.

A militarized world order needs women to find rewards in a militarized femininity. Wives who refuse to behave like self-sacrificing "military wives," mothers who reject military service as their sons' avenue to manhood, young women who will not see enlisting as a guarantor of "first-class citizenship" jeopardize Bush's global design. For the United States to wage a war successfully in the Gulf, the gender gap had to be closed. A lot of women had to be persuaded to move across the opinion divide, without throwing overboard their notions of femininity.

Turning U.S. soldiers into "our troops" seems to have been the key. It was when U.S. soldiers in the Gulf were subjected to the dangers of actual combat that the gender gap collapsed. In tying a yellow ribbon 'round an old oak tree—or car antenna, porch pillar, or shop sign—most women probably do not see themselves as endorsing something as grandiose as a new world order. They probably see themselves as providing moral support to particular sons, daughters, neighbors, and friends. But, for the U.S. national security elite, they are voluntarily constructing a feminized "homefront" to complement—thousands of American women soldiers notwithstanding—a masculinized battlefront. As well-meaning and as profoundly humane as every ribbon-tying gesture may be, each one makes it harder than ever to preserve that earlier distinction between caring for particular soldiers on the one hand and objecting to the Bush policy on the other.

Patriotism always has been an arena into which it's especially difficult for women to enter. It has always been easier for an Oliver North to gain entrance than for a Betsy North. For many women, the only path is through the narrow doorways marked "mother" and "wife." If a woman cannot become a recognized patriot on her own merits, then she may try to become one by becoming a patriotic mother or a patriotic wife—real or vicarious. Governments encourage women to imagine that being a loyal female member of a family is synonymous with being a patriot. For women in wartime, the nation becomes a family.

The Gulf War makes this myth of the wartime family even more potent. The U.S. military today has daughters as well as sons, husband-soldiers married to wife-soldiers, single parents. Yet the spiritual soul of the institution, male-only "combat," remains intact. So long as the allies continue to rely on air war, the image of American global power will be of male top guns, not female ground mechanics.

At the same time, the military's reliance on 200,000 women in uniform has given the U.S. military a new cloak of legitimacy. The institution doesn't seem such an anachronism. It even can claim to be a means for women to achieve full political status as people who can "die for their country." To many American women, whether or not they themselves are considering signing up, today's military is no longer the "Other." The military looks every day more like General Hospital. That makes it all the better an instrument for building and entrenching a U.S.-designed not-so-new world order.

Not only American society, but Saudi, Egyptian, Kuwaiti, Israeli, Iraqi, British, Japanese, and German societies are waging this war at a sexually specific historical moment. For instance, this war has sparked new debates amongst Saudi men about just what constitutes Saudi nationalism: can Saudi nationhood withstand dependence on other countries' men to fight its battles? Thus news of a Saudi fighter pilot's first victories in the air has consequences for women. The wartime coalition between American senior partners and Saudi junior partners may create a new, more militarized form of Saudi nationalist masculinity. In post-war Saudi Arabia will Saudi women, just now reaching out for political rights, be faced with not only religiously sanctified patriarchal barriers, but militarily blessed ones as well?

Likewise Americans have named the gender gap only during the past two decades—as women have developed their own perspectives on many public policies, have become more organized in articulating those perspectives, and have voted into office more women willing to give authoritative voice to those perspectives. Furthermore, this war has been launched by a president who nervously wielded masculinity in his 1988 electoral campaign at a time when U.S. collective manliness appeared to be jeopardized by the country's slide in global economic competitiveness.

The Gulf War furthermore is being waged by Americans still living in the shadow of the sexual politics of another war. The Vietnam War has left a cultural legacy of gendered guilt: the betrayed male vet. He has taken 15 years and a lot of celluloid and paper to create, but today he is a potent figure inspiring complex emotions. While there are at least 7,500 female American Vietnam veterans, it is the unappreciated, alienated male Vietnam vet whose image looms over the present war. It is for him as much as for the soldiers actually in the Gulf that many women seem to be tying yellow ribbons around their trees and antennas. This war is about masculinity, just as all wars have been; but it is a historically and socially specific masculinity. Without the feelings of guilt inspired by the image of the betrayed Vietnam male vet, without a public discourse that permitted the stories of male soldiers to blot out discussions of government policy errors, perhaps it would have been much harder to convert January 15th women against a war into January 20th women supporting it.

III. "Post-War" Patriarchy

As I walked home yesterday in the 100-degree heat of a Somerville, Massachusetts, June afternoon, I noticed yellow ribbons still tacked up on my neighbors' front porches. They drooped now in the heat, their color almost drained by months of rain and wind. Most of the houses that had proudly flown American flags had taken them in, but somehow the yellow ribbons seemed best left to age naturally in the New England elements.

We are now officially in the "post-war era." Though the fate of Iraq's Kurdish minority hangs precariously undecided and wartime embargos are causing, medical experts report, scores of infant deaths among other Iraqi communities, we have adopted a post-war emotional and political stance. We are thinking retrospectively. We are generating lessons.

The Gulf War lasted less than a year, but this post-war period is as fraught as that following on the heels of longer conflicts. Just as atheism is defined by reference to a god, so any post-war era is marked by its relationship to the war it succeeds. In that sense this is a militarized time, not a time of peace. And thus it is a time for vigilance, not just introspection. Many of those horrified by their inability to have prevented the massive use of military power, or perhaps even by their inability to withstand the seductive attractions of technological wizardry and post-Vietnam patriotism, will use these post-war months to take a close look at the failings of their country's peace movement. But it is at least as crucial that we watch how other players in the Gulf War are using this post-war era to fashion "lessons." For what lessons are presumed to have been taught by the war against Iraq will become the basis for militarizing the next international conflict. Many of those lessons are specifically about the relationships between women and men.

After every war, governments—on the losing, as well as winning side—take stock of how gender served or undermined their war efforts. The Crimean War offers a striking example of the post-war politics of gender. Every government involved in this mid-nineteenth-century conflict came away unhappy about its performance. The British military command and its parliamentary masters, for instance, were convinced that British soldiers had been ill-equipped to fight in the Crimea. Just like military strategists today, they devoted their post-war energies to pinpointing what ensured that male soldiers had high morale and optimum physical well-being. And just like their counterparts today in Washington, London, Riyadh, and Baghdad, they paid special attention to masculinity—and to the ways different groups of women might be controlled so that they could not jeopardize the sort of manliness deemed best suited for waging the government's military campaigns. In practice, this meant that British officials sparked two fierce debates: 1) over whether rank-and-file men should be allowed to marry (Were women as wives a drag on the military as long supposed or were they a potential insurance against venereal disease and debt?) and 2) over whether the rampaging venereal disease among male soldiers was controllable (Was it more effective and honorable to impose police restrictions on women in British garrison towns than to humiliate military men by making them undergo compulsory genital examinations?). Britain's first women's national political campaign—the Anti-Contagious Diseases Acts Campaign—was prompted by the nineteenth-century post-war lessons devised by worried military planners.

Marriage, morale, sexuality, discipline—these are the arenas for lesson-forging that still produce post-war attempts to refine the relations of women to the government's mostly male soldiery .

The first post-Gulf War attempt to change the American military's relationship to mothering already has been concluded: The military won. Representative Barbara Boxer, a progressive California Democrat, was dismayed by the stories published during the war of dual-military families having both parents called up and deployed far from their very young children. For several weeks the media had been full of pictures of infants being tearfully left behind with relatives while their mothers and fathers donned their fatigues and headed for the Gulf. No one should have been surprised. The military during the past decade had been relying more and more on the reserves in their global planning. The Pentagon deliberately had been using women to compensate for the decline in the pool of eligible (high-school graduate, drug-free, non-felon) young men; and, after an initial reluctance, it had come to see dual-career military couples as promoting re-enlistment and deepening whole families' loyalty to military service. But for the media, much of the public, and Congress it came as a rude shock to see this military-personnel strategic formula being translated into the apparent abandonment of infants.

Barbara Boxer thus saw as one lesson of the Gulf War the need to put limits on military deployment: Parenting of very young American children must take priority over the Pentagon's need for soldiers. Yet her bill barely survived its initial hearings. Defense Department officials, not surprisingly, raised immediate objections. In the Bush administration's vision of the New World Order, the U.S. military would have fewer overseas bases and reduced numbers of soldiers in its active-duty force while continuing to carry global responsibilities. In personnel terms, this combination will be possible only if the military can have absolutely free rein in calling up reserves and moving those reserves and active-duty soldiers anywhere any time at a moment's notice. Mobility: It always has been the *sine qua non* of an effective military. And it always has required military commanders to have control over some women as service workers, as wives, as mothers, and as girlfriends. Bush's conception of the New World Order makes this need for control over women (so that they will in no way slow down mobilization) acute.

Barbara Boxer's bill was a very real threat to optimum mobility. But in the 1990s U.S. political scene the politics of parenting—especially of mothering—are at least as potent as the strategic imperative for a mobile military. So why did the Boxer bill never get off the ground? It would appear that it was killed not just by the Pentagon's opposition, but by the cool reception it received from many women military careerists. They, perhaps rightly, feared that while the bill sought to restrict deployment of "parents" of young children, if passed, it would be used to restrict the deployment of mothers in uniform. The Boxer bill, many canny military women lobbyists predicted, would create a militarized "mommy track."

"Women in combat" achieved an even higher post-war profile than military mothering. What lessons did the Gulf War generate about women's capacity to engage in combat and militaries' willingness to use them for combat? The Canadians had carried on this debate for several years before their government sent women and men to fight Iraq: As the result of a court case brought by women's-rights advocates under the country's new Charter of Rights, women soldiers as a class no longer could be excluded from combat. But neither they nor Dutch women, also theoretically eligible for combat, actually served in officially designated combat roles during the Gulf conflict. The British and Australian forces ban women from whatever they deem to be "combat" (the definitions are arbitrary in any military). But observers in both of these countries watched as the much larger and more visible U.S. contingent became the site for this latest in a long series of debates over femininity, masculinity, and the changing landscape of high-technology warfare.

Again, it was women members of the House of Representatives who took the lead in raising this post-war issue. Patricia Schroeder, Democrat of Colorado, and Beverly Byron, Democrat of Maryland, interpreted the Gulf War as proving that the nature of contemporary warfare made the conceptual divide between combat and non-combat irrelevant. Despite the U.S. ban on women in combat, 13 U.S. women soldiers were killed in Gulf action and two were taken prisoner by the Iraqi forces. "Women returning in body bags" turned out not to have seriously undercut the legitimacy of the Bush administration's war policy. The Pentagon itself was divided over the political and logistical wisdom of ending the combat ban. According to astute Pentagon watcher Linda Grant De Pauw, editor of the journal *Minerva*, older military professionals didn't conclude that the Gulf operations had proved that allowing women access to combat roles would not jeopardize the fighting morale of men in the now masculinized infantry, armor, fighter plane and bomber units. Morale always has been the sticking point. A military cannot afford to take any step that undermines the morale of its mainly male force; and morale among men is dependent to a large measure on esteem derived from their sense of manliness.

But a younger generation of Pentagon officials, civilian and uniformed, had come of age professionally since 1973, the start of the military's deliberate efforts to compensate for the end of the male draft by recruiting large numbers of women. These officials were willing to let the post-war lessons be honed by public representatives. If the U.S. public would legitimate women in combat, the military would have even more flexibility in deploying personnel according to its own needs. Women officers who made their views known backed the Schroeder and Byron legislative initiatives. They had become convinced that the combat ban was a major stumbling block on their path towards senior promotions.

According to Linda Grant De Pauw, however, the actors most notable for their silence in this post-war debate were organized feminists. When the legislation reached the Senate in May 1991 (sponsored by Bill Roth, R-Delaware), no feminist organization submitted testimony. Although during the war, the National Organization for Women had issued a declaration calling simultaneously for support of women in the Middle East and an end to all forms of sexism in the U.S. military, they, like other women who had spent years working for the Equal Rights Amendment, still remembered how anti-ERA forces had wielded women-in-combat anxieties to defeat the amendment. As in the past, too, many U.S. feminists, even those who adopt a liberal-feminist approach which assigns priority to equal opportunity, were profoundly ambivalent about making women's access to combat jobs a political priority. The debate, coming as it did in the wake of a war that frustrated many women whose feminist activism had been devoted to unsuccessful peace campaigning, seemed to leave no space for a more complicated dialogue about women's relationship to a militarized state.

So it was without an active civilian feminist organized presence that on May 22, 1991 the overwhelmingly male House of Representatives passed the 1992/93 Defense Authorization Bill as amended by Byron and Schroeder to permit for the first time the civilian secretaries of Navy and Air Force to assign women soldiers to fly combat aircraft. The amendment—which formally repeals the combat-exclusion Section 512 (the Army's combat-exclusion policy is not dictated by law but by the service's administrative policy)—is expected to pass the Senate later this year.

At the same time, further away from the floors of Congress and from the public limelight, Defense Department officials were assessing how well they did in ensuring that military wives and girlfriends stayed supportive not only of their men in uniform but of the military cause at large. This war provided the department with a chance to try out their revised family strategies. Since the early 1970s, in part in response to increasingly vocal military wives, the military had taken a far more activist and interventionist role in military-family affairs. The once-autonomous Military Family Resource Center, run by the YMCA, was integrated into the Pentagon. Child abuse and wife abuse became issues to be discussed administratively inside the Defense Department. Men's anti-violence groups reported being asked to come on bases to give training sessions to men returning from Operation Desert Storm, men likely to have inflated expectations of wifely homecomings, men likely to be too quick to resort to physical abuse when confronted with the messier realities of ordinary domestic life. Military social workers and military spouses learned that, if they could show that dysfunctional families threatened "military readiness," they could get even Under Secretaries to sit up and take notice. During the Gulf War, the Pentagon authorized the creation of family support groups for girlfriends and parents as well as spouses. Despite officers' wives during the 1980s becoming more resistent to pressures to perform unpaid labor on military bases, many of these groups relied on women married to senior male officers to serve as the hub of supportive networks. While many family members found the authorized groups helpful in everything from sharing fears to figuring out how to deal with creditors, others who took part said the groups seemed to be intent upon ensuring that women stayed supportive of the Bush policy and that they poured their energies into reducing soldiers' worries, not their own.

Even further from public attention, Allied militaries thought about the lessons of a war fought without prostitutes. The Saudi regime of King Fahd had made a no-brothels policy a stipulation of his acceptance of foreign forces. As his harsh suppression of the apparently modest women's-driving protest later revealed, the regime was being challenged by male Islamic fundamentalists. Each group of men—the monarchy's supporters and the emergent opposition—used its respective abilities to control Saudi women as the litmus test of political legitimacy. We still know almost nothing about what the consequences of this prohibition were for militarized masculine sexuality. In Central America, Vietnam, the Philippines, South Korea, Japan, Puerto Rico, mainland United States, Germany, and Italy the Pentagon has operated as if prostitution were a necessary and integral part of U.S. military operations. It has not always, it is true, been easy to control that prostitution: It has been connected to the spread of AIDS; it has produced marriages not wanted by the military; it has caused friction between local police and military police; it has exacerbated tensions between Black and white soldiers; it has threatened the morale of American women in the services. But not until this war did the U.S. Defense Department believe it could sustain the masculine morale needed to ensure motivated, disciplined soldiering without prostitution. Perhaps the intensity and brevity of the Gulf conflict will make the absence of prostitution merely an anomaly, generating no institutional policy revisions. Or perhaps there have been delayed negative results, male sexual behaviors only known to awaiting girlfriends and wives back home or to Thai women working as prostitutes who greeted some of the first U.S. ships returning from the Gulf to Japan. We don't know yet. What we do know, based on years of experience, is that somewhere in the military someone is trying to figure out whether this war provided lessons for a better way to control sexuality for the sake of more effective warmaking.

Women's relationship to their government's military remains one not fashioned primarily by broadly based women's organizations in large part because that relationship sows such confusion. Is the military chiefly a public institution that distributes valuable benefits (pride, skills, salaries, influence, independence)? Or is the military best understood as a vehicle for state violence? What should feminists' stand be if it has become *both?* The hanging of yellow ribbons and the push to end the exclusion of women in combat seem to be intimately connected in the United States of the 1990s.

Women inside and outside the country's military are insisting that they have their own thoughts, their own aspirations. But long as women have so little control over the terms of debate, even their genuine efforts to voice those ideas and press for those aspirations are likely to produce short-term gains (more media coverage, more military promotions) without changing the basic ways in which public power is used. For their part, many men working in peace movements have barely conceded that the issue of women's relationship to state power, confusing as it is, is worthy of serious political attention. Few men asked women exactly what thoughts they were expressing when they put a ribbon on their secretarial in-tray; few monitored with genuine concern the congressional debate over women in combat. In this sense, many male peace activists have yet to recognize that militarization cannot be reversed until the politics of femininity's relationship to both masculinity and to the state are taken seriously.

It may be that the U.S. military—and other NATO militaries—has learned how to absorb just enough of the changes in women's expectations and influence to permit it to use women without drastically altering its own political mission. Maybe the U.S. military has come out of the Gulf War more thoroughly integrated into the social structure than it ever has been in the last two centuries. If so, the end of the Cold War will not mean the end of the militarization of women's lives.

CHAPTER 4

DID YOU MEASURE UP?

The Role of Race and Sexuality in the Gulf War

Abouali Farmanfarmaian

Introduction

In its preparation as well as in its conduct, the flash war in the Gulf functioned as a machine realizing a national fantasy, with all its fears, anxieties, desires, and excitements. This national fantasy, insofar as it was related to the identity formation of America, circulated primarily in the sphere of sexuality and consequently of race. For the history of imperial and colonial ventures—and the Gulf War was one—has dictated a racial connection wherever sexuality appears. In America, where racial identities have been formed internally, in the back yard so to speak, the connection is much stronger and less subliminal than in Europe, where identities were formed in relation to a racial Other that existed geograph-

An earlier version of this article appeared in *Genders,* Number 13, Spring 1992. Reprinted by permission of *Genders.*

AUTHOR'S NOTE: Although I am aware of the problems inherent in the use of "America" when speaking of the United States, I am using the term because of its particular connotations. A specific rhetoric is attached to "being American" which cannot be captured by any other term. Since I view this construct of "America" as tightly linked to other notions in the essay—such as "family," "Whiteness," "Nationhood"—I judged its use to be appropriate here.

ically apart. What becomes striking in the analysis of a fantasy machine in this war is not so much the differences but the broad similarities and connections between European and American constructs that have at different historical moments justified and determined these nations' respective agendas of control over Others.

I examine the role of sexuality in the Gulf War not as a metaphor, but as a determinant. Recent reviews of historical information increasingly reveal how the evolution of Empire from conquest to today's indirect control has, both structurally and discursively, been intertwined with concerns of sexuality, mainly around the issues of miscegenation, family, and manhood.[1] Notions of family in the West have developed along strongly defined racial boundaries that are in turn reflected and reproduced in the larger construct of the Nation. The development and definition of these constructs formed the identities of the European populace in the nineteenth century. The United States had its own internal definitions of race, sexuality, and family, but what is often ignored in historical analyses is the way in which the United States, too, functioned as an imperial power-creating similarities (though not total uniformity) between the sexual and imperial conduct of Americans around the world and the sexual attitude of European colonizers. Furthermore, many of the imperial constructs that were active in forming consciousness and identity were not only propagated and uniformalized in Europe, but were widely disseminated and well-accepted in the United States from the end of the nineteenth century onwards.

Concerns about Iraq and the desirability of war were mediated through notions of family and sexuality—always with a racial link that implicitly emphasized western values—and only thereby managed to generate a unanimity in outrage against an outside evil, Iraq. Much of the national American attitude towards the Gulf War (probably more uniform in the United States than anywhere else) was concerned with family: the families of the GIs, the families inside the army, the families of hostages, even the family of peace-loving nations. The unity of the nation was kept through the use of the family, first as a notion embodying everything good and American in opposition to the projected Iraqi embodiment of anti-family values; and then the family as a real unit watching the war together on television in contrast with the Iraqis being watched on television. Unity was also a concern in the Gulf War's debate over the Vietnam War and the specter of national failure it raised: Sexual anxieties associated with racial fears take on a more potent charge in war, and, as I will show, the fear of Vietnam functioned very much as castration anxiety for an emasculated American manhood that could only be soothed by an open and overwhelming display of prowess in the Gulf. In short, the war took place not with Iraq but with the self, with America itself, with the tensions, insecurities, and images constructed historically in the American consciousness and accumulated to form a fantasy.

The Appeal

When George Bush and the United Nations issued the January 15 deadline many were still not convinced that a war would take place. In fact, many inside as well as outside Congress expressed a measured level of disapproval. Yet, by the end of December the United States showed overwhelming support for the war, to such an extent that a February issue of *The Village Voice* reported that a surprising number of activists and peaceniks sympathized with the choice of war.[2]

The appeal to the American people to accept the choice of war was made primarily on the level of morality rather than reason. By positioning the United States as the righteous protector of the world and Iraq as an evil destructive force, George Bush managed to rally and unite public opinion in favor of a military strike. In his choice of words and speeches there was nothing that was intended to hide this project of morality under a veil of reason: In a speech on November 30, 1990, a day after the UN ultimatum was ratified, Bush justified the likelihood of war by speaking directly on "the immorality of the invasion" of Kuwait by Iraq. The campaign to paint immorality on Iraq and moral righteousness on the United States started around the same time with a sudden and massive infusion of reports on Iraqi violations, focusing particularly on *sexual* atrocities.

The images and concomitant fears of rape were present from the outset. The first freed western men and women shown coming out of Kuwait breathlessly reported danger for wives and daughters. But such accounts really hit the front pages a month before the deadline. As Bush desired American outrage to escalate, the "violation of Kuwait's sovereignty" became increasingly tied to *sexual* atrocities committed by the Iraqis, and infanticide, rape, and torture became the main focus of attention. Thus, repeatedly the concepts of sovereignty and violation in the international arena were linked to sexual counterparts of integrity and rape.

A cursory glance at the *Boston Globe* around mid-December would reveal something like the following: one of Bush's many speeches quoted on the front page saying, "Looting, torture, and rape" are an assault "on the soul of a nation"; or an escaping American commenting on "...'barbaric Iraqi soldiers' who 'pillaged and raped their way through the country,'" followed immediately by "God bless America"; or hearsay reports without examples or confirmations that "Americans also heard reports of rape, torture..."

The New York Times ran a report on its front page with this lead: "More than four months after Iraq's invasion, Kuwaitis are being subjected to looting, rape, torture..." *The Times* also quoted an "unidentified senior U.S. official" who identified Middle Eastern culture as "the culture of rape." Note that the exact series of words used by George Bush in the *Boston Globe* quote appears in the *New York Times* article. If this general and stereotypical depiction was not a concerted and manipulated effort, then it only goes to show how easily and naturally certain constructs get lined up and emphasized across the national consciousness.

On December 19 Amnesty International issued a document on reported events in Kuwait. The main story that emerged from that document was a reported "infanticide" in a Kuwaiti hospital, where Iraqi soldiers allegedly took babies out of incubators and watched them die. Bush used that report (he actually waved it) in outrage to point to an intrinsic, sadistic evil residing in Iraqi soldiers. It turned out that the incubator story was a myth,[3] but it was unquestioningly devoured by an American population more than ready to digest such suggestions. The false report also propagated two signifiers that were never negated thereafter: The evocation of "infanticide" posed a threat to the notion of family, since it represents the discontinuation of family; and it confirmed the Iraqis as the epitome of moral evil (on par with Hitler)—on the opposing pole of all good morality as contained principally within the boundaries of the family.

From mid-December to early January, the media were inundated with such reports. Their sources were unimportant and their validity equally irrelevant. They were extremely successful, though, in shifting national consensus in favor of war. And women were the segment of the population that underwent the most significant change as a result of this evoked threat. Early on in the crisis, 53 percent of women were against war, but by January 71 percent of women favored war (races unspecified in poll).[4] Hiroshima-on-the-Tigris was endorsed as "just" and indeed "necessary" because the Other side could be perceived as rapist and barbaric.

Here I am trying to show that the frame of rape was indeed constructed around the justification for war and that it had a discernible impact on national consciousness. The fears and reactions that the constructs generated have a history, which I will examine later. For now I merely want to suggest that many of the emotions, fears, and images justifying war rose out of this history and were completely internal to the American identity. When President Bush consistently spoke of "the rape of Kuwait" or when a book entitled *The Rape of Kuwait* was written and sold over 200,000 copies, it was not merely fiery rhetoric: Rather, these moved the issue of war outside the realm of real causal threats and appealed to notions and anxieties that are an intricate and integral part of American consciousness: the image of an Other and the boundaries set against that Other in favor of the Self. The war took place against that image, against the representation of Iraq, not Iraq itself.

I do not want to imply that the terrors unleashed mainly on migrant female workers in Kuwait by the Iraqi army were imaginary events. From the moment the Iraqi army entered Kuwait City, defenseless migrant workers, mainly Filipino and South Asian, were subjected to various forms of typical military violence; and, indeed, migrant women workers did become targets of frequent rape attacks. However, to imagine that rape is not one of the facets of military life everywhere in the world is an illusion. The difference lies in people's perceptions and their willingness to react. Whereas rapes by Iraqi soldiers elicited a massive retaliation, American rapes are dismissed. Whether in the Philippines today, in Vietnam two decades ago, or in World War II Europe, American soldiers certainly demonstrated no sexual restraint—for example leaving behind 500,000 (!) Vietnamese working as prostitutes;[5] and encouraging a mushrooming prostitution industry in Manila, where the number of prostitutes has reached 100,000, up from from 8,000 in 1945. And, despite ample evidence of abuse, no U.S. soldier has even been prosecuted for sexual harassment.[6]

Locating danger and deviancy in distinct groups of Others allows for an exonerating and coherent, though false and illusory, conception of self.[7] It also molds a "will to disbelief," refusing to admit rape as endemic to white, in this case American, men. So, for example, when after the landing of U.S. soldiers in France "rape and looting" became a widespread problem and complaints passed from the French population to De Gaulle to Eisenhower, little action was taken, though the debate made it to Congress (but not to history books). Reports coming in to De Gaulle and Eisenhower resembled this one: "Women no longer dare to go milk a cow without being accompanied by a man...In the Manche, a priest has been killed trying to protect two young girls attacked by American soldiers. These young girls were raped..." Members of Congress, then like now, were more prepared to see *widespread* rape as, say, a Black problem than to accept any possibility of it residing in white-American[8] soldiers. Congress proved entirely *unwilling* to accept that "decent American boys" could turn into "rapists."[9]

Such is the *international division of attributes:* The label of rape only sticks to the racial Other. Europe and America must display themselves as, and hence believe themselves to be, paragons of respectability and order. Chaos, irrationality, and violence are the constructed realm of the racial Other—the "Orient," Africa, but, significantly, not the ex-arch enemy the "Russians," whose constructed identity as European significantly erased the Muslim and Asian populations of the Soviet republics and did not carry the labels of irrational or rapist but merely represented an abstract and quite recent ideological evil called communism. The international division of attributes rose out of the dynamics of colonialism, and with the development and domination of mass media and western information networks it has taken on a central role in the present international dynamics. The divisions remain unquestioningly accepted. That is why it proved so easy to build a case around Iraqi immorality and atrocity, equally easy to spoon-feed it to the nation, and then go on to annihilate Basra without the blink of an eye.

Whiteness, Colonialism, and Identity

To understand how and why the above consensus took shape so easily in the United States we need to examine the historic construct of race, with particular attention to the Middle East as a uniformalized Other.

In starting with European colonialism the intention is not to suggest a uniformity among colonizers, including the United States. Nor is it to suggest that colonialism took the same shape in relation to every colony. However, there exist similarities in the patterns of policy and action as well as in certain constructs that shaped a common European and American vision of an Other. Such generalizations, though at times problematic, are particularly useful in explaining some of the more striking linkages that would otherwise pass unexamined. At the same time, due to the structure of information networks, peoples in the United States and Europe end up bound by similar bodies of knowledge creating similar consciousnesses. This is a phenomenon that saw its most popular and visible manifestation in the great exhibitions of the previous century which travelled between European and North American cities carrying the same constructs (literally) of the rest of the world; it continues to flow through the sharing of literary and academic texts such as Baudelaire and Flaubert, Shelley and Kipling, Durkheim and Weber; and beginning in the 20s, it has had an immovable place in the realm of cinema, which seems to be accomplishing its dissemination on a worldwide scale.

In the period of pioneering and conquest, only white people, mostly men, participated in colonization. Usually, white women were barred from travel to the colonies. In the same period concubinage and miscegenation were quite common practices, with many early colonial officials erecting their own harem of 13 or 14 wives.[10] In most places, in fact, acquiring concubines, or *petites epouses* for the French, was actively encouraged because it provided a foothold in the local economy, thereby giving Europeans access to trade and land—through women. It was, literally, a means of penetrating the whole territory. For colonials in Malaya concubinage meant profit and hence prestige, rather than poverty; and officials of the Royal African Company as well as the Hudson Bay Company were encouraged to "form connections with the principal families immediately on their arrival."[11] Misperceptions of race and an obsession with non-white peoples' sexuality existed prior to conquest and continued well into the period of pioneering. And although established power differentials accompanied racist obsessions during this period, the physical and mental boundaries between colonizer and colonized, European and Other, had still not concretized.[12] If exploitative, the process was at least interactive.

Later, when strict and defined boundaries were installed, legitimate interaction disappeared, physically and mentally. A well-defined outline of a Self was drawn against projected notions of the Other—and actions, motivations, and decisions emerged in relation to safeguarding that definition and maintaining its boundaries. The turning point occurred as each colonial holding shifted out of a mode of exploration into one of administration, as government overtook commerce in the priorities of empire. Around this time white women started migrating to the colonies, shifting the racial-sexual dynamics to a location that would serve to determine, formalize, and ideologically fix the boundaries between ruler and ruled in empire. To what extent these two events—the advent of white women and the shift from commerce to government—were related can be debated, but their aggregate effect on the development of a White consciousness can be more easily outlined.

Together these events ushered forth a Europeanization of towns and cities along with an overwhelming concern over separation. Boundaries were set up around families and towns, both of which gradually took bourgeois European shapes with White parameters, keeping natives outside their borders.[13] Studies of colonial cities reveal an interesting fact in connection with the development of boundaries. Where urban centers pre-dated the colonial encounter, such as in Dakar, Algiers, or Saigon, separation between white and native had to be almost immediate; in those places where towns and cities developed along with empire, the racial separation came once large white settlements formed and often after slavery was abolished.[14] This confirms the contention that although dynamics may have differed locally, the overriding concern for the government of empire, whether Dutch, British, or French, eventually became the drawing of absolute racial boundaries in an attempt at self-definition. From then on, the violation—perceived or real—of any of these mental-social boundaries would be cause enough for violent retribution.

In the period of administration, rigid physical and mental boundaries of Whiteness also developed within notions of family. Unlike the preceding period, the formation of white families was encouraged and strongly protected as such. In Southwest Africa the Germans passed a law (1905) that prohibited interracial marriages; in India the Cornwallis reforms prescribing "appropriate behavior," along with distance and Victorian morals, put a virtual end to the taking of the *bibi*, or Indian mistress.[15] Elsewhere such boundaries were strictly kept, and although there may not have been official laws against interracial marriages, other laws served to underline the sanctity of white families and in particular white women. The White Women's Protection Ordinance in Papua (1926), the Southern Rhodesia Immorality Act (1903), and militias monitoring and punishing native men approaching white women in Kenya in the 1930s all served to strictly separate the ruling race from the ruled, and in particular white women from native men.

While boundaries were drawn along racial lines, the terrain on which they were drawn was sexuality. If empire as a system of government were to survive it had to reinforce its boundaries in such a way as to ensure the continued separation between Self and Other, ruler and ruled. The colonial administrator was obsessed with self-reproduction; he had to reproduce the white colonial family.[16] He, therefore, attempted to control White womanhood by sanctifying it and thereby justifying its protection from impurity, evil intent, lasciviousness, rape—all these being qualities and motivations attributed to non-whites. Miscegenation and concubinage were restricted; they could no longer be tolerated because that would leave a nation of mestizos and mulattos to inherit empire. Exactly this fear was openly voiced in the U.S. Congress in 1790 and echoed in the words of such American forefathers as Thomas Jefferson and Benjamin Franklin: If Negroes married whites, it was said, "then the white race would be extinct, and the American people would be all of the mulatto breed."[17] Consequently, the sexuality of the colonized became a threat and instead of miscegenation, white families and settlements began to be encouraged. As the means of reproduction, White womanhood became responsible for the reproduction of colonial community and empire. In this transformation white women were turned into sacred and idealized figures to fit the constructs of Whiteness. As Ann Stoler argues, "European women were essential to the colonial enterprise and the solidification of racial boundaries in ways that repeatedly tied their supportive and subordinate posture to community cohesion and colonial peace."[18] The protection laws and rape scares that permeated empire were not in relation to a real threat.[19] But it was precisely the fabrication of a threat that served to define the boundaries of Whiteness. White womanhood could only be, and indeed was, sanctified in contrast to a transgressive Other, namely, the native rapist and the promiscuous native woman. If the myth of the Other Rapist fades, White womanhood as an ideal collapses, and vice-versa. The construct of the White Self and the construct of Other cannot be evoked without each other. Therefore, racial engagements with the Other have rarely been more than internal battles in the definition of self. America's evocation of the Other Rapist in the Gulf War by definition involved the ideal of White womanhood, and functioned to reinforce the construct of the American self at a time when the American economy, quality of life, and values were being globally and internally questioned.

American whites developed boundaries with respect to their race at a quicker pace than Europeans in the colonies. Because the mentality of the "American" colonial centered on settlement from early on, it was essential to rapidly ensure self-reproduction as a system. After the early and initial period of commerce with, and later annihilation of, Native Americans in the "new world," settlers in America quickly established clear racial boundaries between imported slaves and themselves. In Georgia, for instance, settlers came with the purpose and vision of setting up a "white utopian community of virtuous, hard-working, small farmers." They had a law banning Black slaves from their territory, and only in 1752, after a political battle, did they admit Black slaves for labor.[20] American anti-miscegenation laws which explicitly mentioned "Negroes" were already passed in 1664, though, predictably, they assumed stricter terms as the slave population grew.[21]

The direct contact with Black people brought about by an increase in slavery in America necessitated stronger physical and psychological boundaries that could maintain and carry hierarchy through the high-contact life on the plantation as well as in later northern urban interaction between mistress and domestic. As in European projects of empire, America erected the sanctity of White womanhood to define its own boundaries. Beauty, delicacy, and perfection—attributed to white women in contrast to Black women[22]—defined function and position in society as much as assigned chores. For white males, the ideal of White womanhood assumed such an important role that it was thereafter constantly evoked in the passing of laws, events, and conflicts. In fact, reinforced after emancipation, the sanctity of White womanhood—over and above notions of white superiority—became the main underlying argument against integration.[23] As an ideal that ensured continuity and secured the definition of home, family, and nation, White womanhood was inviolable. Any perceived threat to its sanctity could lead, in America as well as in the colonies, to an unleashing of violence. Harry Stack Sullivan claims, "The occasions of great violence towards the Negro arise in connection with the master taboo of the society, the prohibition of any intimacy between a Negro male and a white female."[24] By the time of the urban race riots of the 20s, the protection of White womanhood from "rapist Black men" occupied the principal platform in the justification of attacks on and lynching of Black men: In Washington riots started with unfounded rumors of assault on seven white women, and in Chicago and St. Louis rumors of assault on white women became the focus of the riots.[25]

Historically, then, "rape" as such has been constituted as a threat only in relation to white women. The word itself does not, in common consciousness and usage, signify the rape of non-white women, since such rapes have never been made the center of attention; on the contrary, the rape of Black women has consistently been condoned, denied, or disregarded. Thus, in the context of the Gulf War—particularly so soon after the New York jogger trials—the word rape, without any specific referents, triggered fears that could only be connected to the constructs of Black rapist/white woman. Calculated or not, it was, as was shown above, the concentration on this particular fear that mobilized the American public behind the war effort. If in the 20s the evocation of "rape" would lead to mass vigilantism and participation in violent lynching rituals, in 1991 the majority of the American people participated by voting for, and then watching, live on the networks, the exercise of military violence.

Although for white Americans the occasion for the expression of violence has come principally in relation to African Americans, constructs of superiority and White womanhood have been upheld against other peoples too. Otherwise, the Gulf War would not have been so popular and as easily condoned. In world fairs, which gained massive popularity at the end of the nineteenth century, the American imagination fed on images of European colonies, and developed its own notions of expansionism. Starting in Philadelphia in 1876, these fairs were consciously designed to celebrate " the white man's…creation of societies modelled on European lines."[26] Installations in the exhibit were arranged according to race in such a way as to "show the advancement of man" with Europeans and Americans at its pinnacle.[27]

The significance of these fairs to the present context lies in two

Grand Finale of the Stupendous Spectacular Success, "Uncle Sam's Show."

Cartoon from Prints and Photographs Division, Library of Congress.

aspects. First, these fairs were literal constructs, designed unabashedly, that exposed their agendas without sublimation of intent. Looking back, therefore, we see that the fairs openly claimed to "offer living proof of the onward march of *imperial* civilization" (emphasis added), while at the same time were designed by Congress as something that "should illustrate the function and administrative faculty of the government in time of peace and its resources as a war power..."[28] Thus the American imperialist agenda was openly and fully conveyed in the content and intent of the fairs. Not only was imperialism condoned and encouraged, but it was made an agenda that continued to occupy a place in the American consciousness until today. Today it is the "onward march of the American way"—but Congress' words remain applicable without a change of rhetoric. Indeed, a cartoon dating to the Chicago world's fair of 1893 presents the best depiction yet of the current American role in the international arena. Entitled "Grand finale of Uncle Sam's show," the cartoon shows a large Uncle Sam leading caricatured representatives of Africa, East Asia, Europe, Russia, etc., in a group dance. The chorus at the bottom could as easily apply to the spectacle America put on in the Gulf War:

Uncle Sam: It's done, It's done! The show and fun
We've had for six months past;

I've made the world stare
At my wonderful fair...
Chorus of All Nations: For he's a jolly good fellow...

The linkage between spectacle and empire, perfectly achieved in the fairs, constitutes the second important aspect of these fairs. Connecting the control of images to the control of peoples, the fairs marked a turn in the project of empire that reached its strident and logical conclusion in the use of television as a weapon in the Gulf War. Laws reserved for societal arrangements began to infiltrate regulations regarding popular culture. Anti-miscegenation laws, for example, were implemented in the control of cinematic images in the 20s. Rules and regulations prohibited the depiction of "white men in a state of degradation amidst native surroundings" and forbade "equivocal situations between white girls and men of other races." Similarly, small publications for youth that gained increased circulation at the beginning of the twentieth century condemned miscegenation.[29] Simulation of reality in visual forms led to the production and control of reality via the same medium, with powerful results, since vision seems to be the most credible of senses: "I won't believe it 'til I see it." The White consciousness, by and large, moved in and out of these images.

The impact of these fairs on the American psyche, particularly with regard to the international situation, should not be underestimated. According to Robert Rydell, the exhibits "certainly were among the most authoritative" sources in the shaping of popular beliefs. High attendance testifies in support of Rydell: One-fifth of the U.S. population passed through the first American exhibit in Philadelphia. Figures were as high for European exhibits: The 1924 exhibit in Wembley drew a crowd of 27 million, and the Paris exhibit of 1900 drew 48 million.[30] At the same time, these exhibits travelled carrying the same displays between European and American countries. The famous "Cairo Street," for instance, passed from city to city—Chicago in 1893, Antwerp 1894, Wembley 1899, Paris 1900, St. Louis 1904. In other words, there was the common dissemination of information through these fairs, as later through cinema and television. "Cairo Street" was shown everywhere in the White world, and everywhere in the White world the Middle East was seen in "Cairo Street.'

Beyond the overriding intention of justifying empire through the visual display of colonies, the fairs served to uniformalize racist notions of the Other and spread these constructs between Europe and America. Within the first few years, fairs raised their racial message as their main banner. Both Chicago and Wembley had fairs whose main building was called the Great White City, projecting "a little ideal world...some far away time when the earth should be as pure, as beautiful, and as joyous as the

White City itself."[31] In a separate building, contrasted to the White City and right next to the (white) women's building sat the Midway building, in which the rest of the world was on exhibit. The dynamics and relations of structures had to reflect the imagination of empire and thereby reproduce those same dynamics and relations in popular consciousness. These juxtapositions (common in all the fairs) were quite intentional and the result equally successful, for as the following passage from one visitor shows, Whiteness and White womanhood were inscribed as interdependent oppositions to "other races" in the consciousness of visitors:

> In Midway it's some dirty and all barbaric...the worst folks in there are avaricious and bad...and when you're feeling bewildered with the smells and sounds and sights...you come out and all of a sudden you are in a great beautiful silence. The angels on the women's building smile down and bless you...you've passed out o' darkness and into light.[32]

What this visitor called "barbaric" (echoed by the words of Americans describing Iraqis [see above]) was a lumping together of anthropological objects, settings, and peoples from all over the world in one uniformalizing image of Otherness.[33] Displays like those in Midway would contain, say, 174 Africans from different tribes in four constructed villages, then a display of Bushmen and baboons along with two Malay families, Swazis and Boers, a Native American exhibit, and an exotified street of Cairo complete with camels, donkeys, and so on.[34] This meant that despite details of difference in the depiction and construction of racial Others, a certain uniformity was imposed through the lumping together of "other races." Since for white Americans and Europeans, in their own words, "...colonial solidarity and the obligations that it entails allies all the peoples of white races,"[35] the center—that is, Whiteness—in this construction of difference was what mattered; the rest merely formed varying and by definition peripheral formulations of Otherness.

The tags for the region of the Middle East—the "Orient"—varied in detail from those for Africa, African Americans, Java, Malaya and so on. The "Orient's" main particularity appeared in the image of the "Oriental despot" that not only permeated the travelogues, booklets, and films, but had found a firm place in western sociology through the likes of Marx and Weber. A continuous line gets drawn between those conceptions of a bloodthirsty despot cutting off the heads of courtiers as well as citizens and today's media depictions of Saddam Hussein. "Barbaric" is another construct attached largely to that region and used extensively by President Reagan to describe Arabs at the height of hostage-takings in the mid-80s. Over the past decade and a half, starting with Palestinians and moving onto other Arabs and finally covering all Islamic peoples, the options of political struggle in the region of the Middle East have been depicted as inherently "barbaric" and "uncivilized" in accord with the conceptions of that region passed down from the nineteenth century. In all other capacities, peoples of that region are absent from the machinery of public knowledge, so that when a threat appears, the steadfast notions of two centuries past reappear in White consciousness. During periods in which the focus is not on the Middle East these labels may be dormant, but they remain ready for use at will.

In terms of sexuality and race, White consciousness of the Middle East took shape in the nineteenth century primarily around the idea of licentiousness and "endless sexual gratification."[36] However, the threat to white women so prominent in other parts of empire figures less in the otherwise sexualized white obsession with the East. This could be attributed to a lack of large-scale white settlement in the area, and hence the lack of white families. Only recently, with widespread travelling, and books such as Betty Mahmoody's best-selling *Not Without My Daughter* and Linda Blanford's *Oil Sheiks,* has a somewhat consistent threat to white women been articulated in relation to the region. More than anything, the Middle East of the past century figured as an open territory for white males to escape the limitations of their Victorian surroundings and indulge in the perceived sexual permissiveness of the "Orient."[37] Still, a different kind of sexualization painted the Middle Eastern male as a rapist prototype. In the White mind, sexuality in the "Orient" inevitably appeared laced with violence: the despot cutting off the head of his lover, the exchange of women slaves for arms, and so on. These "Baroque instance[s] of sexual violence,"[38] as Rana Kabbani calls them, positioned the Middle Eastern man not only as licentious (like the Middle Eastern female) but also violent in his sexuality. Thus, despite the absence of settlement and the absence of a need to protect white women, the basic mythology of rapist survived through other projected ideas precisely because that mythology had already been erected in relation to other Others in empire.

In the dualistic construct of the Western imagination and its mind-body split, all non-European peoples constituted that vast body of Otherness known as the "Savage," who is a creature of instinct and thus uncontrolled sexuality. Differences and hierarchies (based on color and culture) existed such that Africans were held in the greatest contempt, but all Others received their share of denigration.[39] Within the bounds of the larger constructs the varying details matter much less; the consciousness of the White American turned into one big exhibit space reserved for racial Others, where baboons and bushmen lurk around the corner from camels and belly dancers. Looking back at the construction by Americans of Iraqi violations as intimately related to their sexually violent impulses, it becomes obvious that constructs can be transposed and circulated as long as the larger boundaries of Otherness are the same. Thus, for the consciousness that white-washed the Stuart case in Boston or fixated on the New York jogger case with perverse hype, it proved to be only a small jump from Central Park to Kuwait City. The ability of the American consciousness to move fluidly and ignorantly between its racial and sexual constructs is illustrated by a Los Angeles Police Department officer who, in the aftermath of the Rodney King beating by the LAPD, smoothly lumped together two looming threats: "Saddam Hussein scared the shit out of us with chemical weapons and even though...he didn't use the gas, we still made him pay the price. Same with Rodney King."[40] A Black man in LA and an Arab ruler several thousand miles away differ only in terms of the weapons they use and the weapons used against them; the threat they represent is similar.

Thus, in contrast to rigid definitions of self, the lack of boundaries between constructs of Otherness—their uniformalization—positioned all non-whites as part of the same mass of flesh constituting the subjects of empire; hence, the sexual constructs of African Americans can evoke and be evoked within the sexual construct of the "Orient." This fluidity was partly responsible for the facility with which consensus was built prior to war.

Leading into the Gulf

As most studies of colonial constructs correctly point out,[41] the myths and portrayals of the racial Other had much more to do with those who created them than with those who were its objects. This would help explain, for example, the use of genital mutilation after the ritual of lynching in American culture. If the penis is cut off—and, as happened occasionally, stuffed in the victim's mouth—after the lynching, then clearly the ritual had little to do with the actual use of the penis or the person attached to it; it had much more to do with the concerns of white men who were in charge of the rituals.[42] By castrating the racial Other, they proved their virility and momentarily escaped the castration anxiety produced, ironically, by the force of White constructs of non-White men as sexually aggressive. It is interesting to note that although most lynchings did not even involve the charge of rape,[43] the most popular and valid explanation of lynchings became and continues to be the sexual one: Regardless of the real circumstances surrounding the event, the sexualized construct has gripped the American imagination.

On occasions like the Gulf War, when the threat of rape is evoked, it is inevitably accompanied by a similar sexual anxiety which necessitates a display of virility. Rape, as was discussed, suggests a threat unique to White womanhood and automatically reawakens underlying fears of White impotence. In this respect the timing of the Gulf War was also significant since it immediately followed the nationally covered Central Park jogger trials. These anxieties are indisputably products of the White consciousness and the constructs that have fed its imagination. The conflicts are not with a real foe, but with erected opponents who fit within the boundaries of White consciousness. Whether it be lynching, court verdicts, or war the anxieties and the national reaction rise out of the same history: a threat to the constructed boundaries of White manhood. Aside from the castration anxiety produced inside U.S. borders mostly in relation to constructs and boundaries erected around African Americans, American virility had for some time been ridiculed in the international arena too.

The adamancy with which the Gulf War was pursued over a five-month period marked it as a *desire,* not merely a necessary *option.* The desire was to restore a lost potency to a nation that, despite its massive and well-advertised prowess, was saturated in public humiliation. In the international arena, America's military machine had been frustrated continuously. Despite extensive military prowess it had not been able to display its power since World War II. This was the fear of impotence that permeated the whole nation, the fear brought on by possessing the largest military machine of the world in theory, but remaining unsure of its ability to rise to the occasion.

America's largest overt colonial endeavor—Vietnam—ended not merely in a military defeat but in national humiliation. The sentiment was not hidden either. From a male perspective, Michael Hutchison analyzed it as such: "The fact remained that America, which had never lost a war, had been humiliated by a bunch of skinny little Orientals in black pajamas."[44] One woman described the images of Vietnam as follows: "…dying men, reeking with mud and foul green-stained bandages, shrieking and writhing in a grotesque travesty of *manhood...*" (emphasis added).[45] The Vietnam War—inherited from a colonial conflict, it should be added—was the largest symbol of impotence for a relatively new White colonial power, during which America had watched the "spilling of a quota of blood" but had seen the wrong color.

The "recovery" from Vietnam has been slow. Castration anxiety lived on in "the ghost of Vietnam," haunting America until the Gulf War. America's *forte* in the post-Vietnam War era has been covert operations. But these can not serve the purpose of restoring national virility. National virility, as perfectly illustrated by the era of colonial exhibits up to 1930, requires a public display. Furthermore, the military embodies the virility of a nation. According to testimonies from World War II, for instance, 90 percent of what soldiers talked about was proving their virility by bragging in public "about intimate details of their sexual conquests"[46]—an aspect of the military that is known by everyone everywhere. Thus, the military as the virile microcosm of the nation must be the vehicle through which national virility in an international arena is reconquered. Covert wars can not fulfill this purpose, for the military's achievements are by definition out of public view; their images, their discourse, and their knowledge are also covert.

From Vietnam, America moved to the hostage crisis of the 80s and again witnessed "a travesty of its manhood" paraded across the globe. The 1979 hostage drama left America impotent, unable to wield its might. The small, confused, rather desperate attempt at freeing the hostages led to a humiliating catastrophe in the desert near Tabas, Iran. While the U.S. army was looking pitiful in the sand, white American masculinity—since all African-American and white-women hostages were released by the Iranian captors—was gagged, tied, and put on display for the world to see. Meanwhile, at the head of this nation was a man perceived as weak: Forever the anti-macho, Jimmy Carter would even have a heart attack jogging. The saga of hostages continued until recently, with various images of white western—including European—men tied up or blindfolded with guns at their heads. America, and to some extent Europe, stood obsessed but paralyzed watching the humiliation of their male citizens. That these most recent evocations of American impotence arose out of the Middle East in part explains the national enthusiasm for the military lynching ceremony we witnessed in the Gulf War. Indeed, the Gulf War started precisely with such a panic over captured, humiliated citizens. It reached a hysterical climax with the airing of images of bruised prisoners of war, and caused a traumatic self-doubt when news of women prisoners and casualties hit the air.

During the years prior to and in the months leading up to the Gulf War, the fear of impotence was "a consciously held fear,"[47] in part because of the historically unique role castration has played in the American consciousness. As Winthrop Jordan has pointed out, America was the only country that used castration as a legal punishment, and only in relation to Black men. It was mostly ordered for alleged or attempted attacks on white women, but sometimes appeared as punishment for basic threats to White manhood such as striking a white person.[48] So castration, and hence castration fear, began as a conscious and actualized theme in American minds. Impotence was even an issue in the presidential elections, first in all the talk about Ronald Reagan's age and white hair, then over Bush's "wimp" image. But the flood of macho international-relations movies in the 80s made up the largest and most open manifestation of the desire to overcome this fear, particularly in an international arena.

Leading up to the war, America defined itself as ailing, "suicidal" as *The New York Post* put it, with "an odor of collapse and doom."[49] As the debate over the Gulf War went public, one of the main articulated fears was a fear of humiliation à la Vietnam. Immediately Dover Air Force base, where dead bodies rolled in from Vietnam and, through TVs, into American living rooms, was closed to the media. From the outset, the words that rang loudest were the emphatic negation of a Vietnam-style castration: "This will not be another Vietnam" became a favorite phrase of American leaders and their public.

The military movement toward war and the behavior during the war bear out the above points. The effort to restore potency to the United States probably began with Grenada. The invasion of Grenada was the first small but successful military operation engaged in by the U.S. military. Although there was no direct media coverage, its victory chant permeated the media and fed American consciousness. Then came Panama, a larger, more ambitious operation, and again a successfully executed one. Finally, it seemed, the American military machine was coming through. Grenada and Panama were calculated, sequential, and escalatory reclaimings of virility; post-Vietnam power was cautiously pulled out of the closet and put on display.

This movement climaxed in the Gulf War. The first week's outburst of virility, the explosion of military images onto the world's television screens, constituted the most impressive collection ever of "surgical strikes" flawlessly delivered. In a sense the first week of war was the most important week for the American psyche: "Intimate details" of bombs going down chimneys, breaking open doors and exploding into bunkers was the display—"the show and fun" Uncle Sam had prepared "for six months past" and "made the world stare." A new and improved world fair. A new and improved manhood. The missiles that missed, we never saw. American casualties, we never saw. This was not to be another image of failure; it had to be an undefeatable machine, not another Vietnam.

Meanwhile, a white brotherhood formed at the helm, pressing onto the American consciousness the notion of a male community, impenetrable, inviolable, and virile. In press briefings and meetings with ambassadors, Bush never appeared without his top aides, the same faces lined up protectively on his side. Once the speeches were over, it was not Bush that walked off, but the group, the brotherhood. Sununu, Cheney, Baker, and Bush formed a privileged and inviolable chain. The weak link of Danforth Quayle was noticeably absent, and General Powell rarely figured within the chain, at most appearing on the sides. General Powell's significance, despite a relatively low profile, didn't escape anyone. For the first time a Black man was, at least symbolically if not in actuality, at the head of the nation's military. But we are precisely concerned with the symbols, for in the progression towards a reclaimed American virility would he not signify borrowed virility to aid the nation's recovery?

Press briefings from the front conveyed much the same images. From maverick director of operations, father-figure for all soldiers, and father-hero for the nation, Norman Schwarzkopf, to Brigadier General Richard Neal, there was an exchange, an exclusive flirtatious dance around information (held back, emphasized, circumvented, hinted at) and a constant switching of partners, spokespersons, and experts, which included Saudi officials. An impenetrable unity took shape, not because of secretiveness or misinformation, but by virtue of the dance itself, the tireless deference of passing the microphone to the next expert, the next officer, even of waving a question, confidently, to a Saudi official—all of which strengthened the brotherhood.

Occasionally, too, we caught glimpses of soldiers' collective virility in their group rituals, with one in particular outlining a clear link to territorial penetration. Cameramen filmed a group of Black and white GIs demonstrating their war chant. Like all war chants, it was to give the soldiers a sense of camaraderie and invincibility. The ritual involved the usual chanting, but this time with each of their hands tightly gripped on their crotches which were then thrust forward from their waists in a motion of penetration (towards Iraq?). A World War II testimony of a soldier's feelings during war offers something of an explanation: "The tank...It protrudes shafts of cold metal with which to fuck a landscape and, by fucking, raze it..."[50] The important difference in the Gulf soldiers' fucking of a landscape lies in its collectivity—the same manifestation of brotherhood as in the press briefings; the use of a collective phallus with which to penetrate.

A look at the discourse of war only confirms the overwhelming castration anxiety that had beset the nation. Under various quite transparent guises "virility" and "impotence" were openly expressed as central issues. Starting with the end: In an interview with Barbara Walters on March 22, 1991, Stormin' Norman Schwarzkopf admitted his main concern as the top military planner:

> NS:...you want desperately to measure up!
> BW (seductively): Did you measure up?[51]

He did measure up, but this war was much more about "staying power" than about size. The two key terms leading up to war were "staying power" and "withdrawal." Withdrawal was the first and only condition set forth by the coalition. Use of this term may seem either natural or coincidental, but the common consciousness of its double entendre was demonstrated by the oft-heard joke told about both Saddam and Bush: "Withdraw, like your father should've." The term becomes more striking when contrasted with its opposing one: If Bush asked Iraq to withdraw, he asked America to have "staying power." Only staying power could win the war. "Staying power" as a term appears much less natural or coincidental than "withdrawal" for it is a term rarely used outside the context of virility. In fact, Bush, too, may have heard it in this context, possibly from a one-time friend, General Manuel Noriega, who contended that "virility is proved by staying power."[52]

Fighting for the Ideal

To paint the Gulf War as principally a war concerned with a recovery of lost virility (whether all wars are this is an entirely different matter), means to see it as a war of desire, a desire rising out of a sense of lack. Historically, castration anxiety emerged out of constructs that defined racial and sexual boundaries, embodied by and contained in the same boundaries that defined the ideal of White womanhood. Consequently, threats to those boundaries that call up sexual fears will also evoke those ideals around which the fears originated. This war was no exception and in it White womanhood played a defining role in America's consciousness.

Here I limit my arguments to the ideal of White womanhood as it relates to this war and as it has emerged out of the above-mentioned historical forces. The endless number of t-shirts and posters picturing over-sexualized, exclusively blond women over the inscription "Desert Storm" point to a generalized connection in the American imagination between sex, race, and war. The main message, confirmed in other places too, seems to be that running parallel to the fighting, to the war itself, is a sexual fantasy based on a racial ideal, as in those idealized poster images. The contents of the fantasy come as no surprise, for their racial and sexual history were outlined above. The idealized figure—whether in the over-sexualized time of today or the overprotective Victorian days—has been signaled by all that White womanhood signifies. The question here, then, is not whether, why, or how white women appear as a fantasy linked to a colonial endeavour, but how does this fantasy actually function in the context of the Gulf War?

Mithers' main point, made in relation to the Vietnam war, that women have a role in war as incarnations of all that men must fight to protect[53] (a common explanation of the male's perception of women during war), misses the mark on two points. First, she fails to mention that the woman referred to must be white, as amply shown on the posters. Second, she fails to position that imagined woman as a fantasy, a longing, an ideal that is internal to manhood itself and thus renders the battle an internal one: A fantasy to fight for and not merely fight to protect, it embeds itself as a permanent motivation rather than a contextual one. In specific contexts, such as war, the fantasy only takes on greater and more emphasized proportions. Theweleit, unlike Mithers, incorporates both aspects in his analysis of the male fantasy of women in war. He specifically refers to the projected ideals as "white" women and "white nurses;" and he grants that ideal "a preeminent role in the psychic security system of men" which provides "the principal mainstays of [men's] freedom."[54] In other words, as much as men are fighting for constructed ideals of democracy and freedom, they are also fighting for that other fantasy— note, too, that both constructs, "freedom" and "White womanhood," are exclusively contained within the boundaries of the West. The governing logic is internal to the fantasy and not merely a symbolic link between the fantasy and the war. Another testimony from World War II, this time about a battle with the Japanese, clarifies the point: As the battle raged, a female apparition hoisted her skirt and invited the soldier towards the enemy lines; then a shell exploded nearby, "but my yearning for sexual release remained. I unfastened my dungarees and touched myself. I came in less than five seconds."[55] The fighting is itself a fantasy, a longing for an ideal, and so its excitement escalates (five seconds) and gets channelled through images and fetishes that are disseminated as desirable in that society.

As fantasies, however, White women, like the reified notions of freedom, cannot be more than images, words, apparitions, possibly passing encounters. "The moment she [becomes] real, all of those beautiful fictions would have to die."[56] That is why the circulated fantasies of women during war have always been "perfect" yet unattainable, represented yet fantastical. The British had "Jane" during World War II. A sexualized cartoon figure, in rough times Jane "always kept up morale by keeping her clothes off."[57] For the Americans there was the pin-up, plastered over almost every piece of military equipment.

The American troops, despite all the talk about Saudi censorship, imported their share of idealized white women to fight for. Pin-ups, pictures, and posters, along with entertainment like Brooke Shields, supplied the iconographic representation of the White fantasy. Dolly Parton's image, the same idealized blond oversexualized figure seen on posters and t-shirts, was reportedly painted on a number of planes.[58] A jeans-clad pin-up of a white woman also became extremely popular in the Gulf, so much so that a spokesman for the Navy said "Most every marine seems to be aware of the poster."[59] These were the centers of fantasy, the psychological aphrodisiacs of war. Accompanying them were, no doubt, actual sexual aphrodisiacs, for by any calculation pornography had to be readily available.[60] One report said that "...pilots aboard the USS John F. Kennedy told AP that they'd been watching porn movies before bombing missions."[61] Both in the case of pin-ups and the porn movies, the internal dynamics of fantasy and war surface. Porn movies play the same role as the female apparition did for the soldier in World War II—war and fantasy interlocked.

As for pin-ups, there is no need for interpretation since testimonies articulate the point directly. An American soldier in World War II saying "pin-ups...give us a good idea of what we are fighting for," found an equally honest and revealing echo in a Gulf War soldier who commented on the denim-clad pin-up, "We are in a country where women are treated different than in the States, and are not as beautiful. Your picture is a constant reminder why we are here."[62] "Why we are here" can all too easily confuse "freedom" and "White womanhood'—and eventually "freedom [of access] to White womanhood." The ideals of America, the ideals to fight for, were summarized in the body and the circulation of that pin-up. And the racial contrast could not be underlined in a clearer fashion, for the statement's internal logic dictates that as there are no beautiful women here to American liking, so there is no freedom in accord with American standards. Both must be fought for. *Vanity Fair* confirmed the racial clarity of that testimony when it ran a cover story on Dolly Parton and her visit to the troops. The full-page color pictures, emphasizing the blond, had Black and white American soldiers holding her up, even stretching their hands towards her as if, standing in front of a giant American flag, she were, like everything the flag stands for, unattainable unless fought for. She and the flag, she and America, were not separately identifiable. As the article pointed out, the airmen seemed "more nervous about confronting a blonde bombshell than an enemy one."[63]

Finally, in keeping with the renewed concern over the family markedly emphasized in this war, one major innovation came about in the presentation of fantasy to the American troops: Fantasy found its way inside the boundaries of the family—so that now, unlike in the repressive Victorian age when European colonialism developed, fantasy no longer needs a displaced space. The "Sally Jesse Raphael Show" managed to convey the same logical mix of ideal beauty, protection, and war, but within a family context. Airing photos of servicemen's wives with new "beautiful" hairdos, she had this exchange with one named Amy:

SJR:....There are not a lot of men who have...women as beautiful as you.
Amy: They pampered us a lot.[64]

At the same time a Massachussetts photographer invented the new pin-up: a family version. In "Operation Desert Cheer," he photographed soldiers' wives half nude, lace-clad, and sent the pictures to the husbands in the gulf. For a military more than ever made up of family people, this can uphold fantasies without leaving the parameters of the family. Even family men need a "constant reminder of why [they] are here."

The participation of women in the war does little to overturn arguments centering on virility. In connecting the nation, manhood and family, the much-lauded participation of women, rather than castrating the army, appeared as the much-needed link that would familialize the military. With (white) women demanding a share of everything, "a militarized world order needs women to find rewards in a militarized femininity."[65] The military needs to become a family in order for the nation to remain one. Thus, not only is the military no longer dominated by single men, but more than ever we saw images of wives and husbands as soldiers.

Conclusion

Any project linking sexuality and imperial enterprises in a concrete, rather than merely symbolic, fashion, suffers from lack of information. Sexuality is hidden and often censored. For instance, the reports on sexuality in the U.S. Army during World War II that Costello used in his book were censored for 40 years. Moreover, the sexual atrocities of the victors remain hidden, outside of any network that could create and disseminate constructs: The Associated Press report on porn videos was censored, for example. At the same time, only recently with the advent of feminist theories has an interest in the link been awakened, and most of these works are related to the past. For contemporary occurrences, the connections are more difficult to establish because the moral stance of the feminist and anti-racist struggles have pushed many revealing and persistent sentiments out of public view and into more subliminal spaces. We would have to know what sexual fantasies emerged in U.S. homes or in soldiers' discussions, what was the actual sexual conduct of the troops (there were rumors, for example, of imported prostitutes) and even what Bush, Baker, and Cheney were joking about over the summer. What, for example, did George tell Barbara when he appointed Colin Powell? Was there anything in his words that might have pointed to the question of virility? These would be the needed testimonies.

In their absence History assumes an eminently important role, for by tracing constructs, events, images, and words to a connected accumulation in which sexuality, race and imperialism form a coherent system, we provide ourselves with an interpretive tool. Without tracing and identifying the ideal of White womanhood, its protection and its link to empire, the conversation in the "Sally Jesse Raphael Show" would have no dimensions beyond a fleeting exchange on a television.

Historical analysis also situates the war and its interpretation in a multi-dimensional sphere. The arguments over the development of boundaries and families, seen as a development in the realm of sex and race, provide layers of insight into other events, putting the Gulf War within a larger trend: In the absence of frontier, of conquest, boundaries of identity concretize further, the holes are filled, and the checkpoints are increased. Suburbs are an example of racially, sexually (family), and physically distinct communities attempting to solidify their borders. More rigidly cordoned-off communities are emerging, however, since suburbs are not closed enough to America's "teeming" Black and Hispanic masses. Gated and planned communities, fenced-off spaces with rigid rules, containing everything from the corporation you work for to shopping complexes, are growing in popularity.[66] Europe 1992 reflects exactly the same phenomenon on a continental scale. While making travel easier for its citizens, it has made its shell virtually impenetrable by concentrated border-control programs.[67] It is meanwhile banishing its version of the teeming masses: France deporting plane loads of Malians, and Germany deporting anyone from the Third World.

The physical participation of African Americans in the army does not automatically overturn the arguments about White boundaries and fantasies of White consciousness. Physical integration does not mean a change of constructs or signifiers. Even with a Black general or Black CEOs, the association of rape to Blackness will not and has not disappeared—that would mean the dissolution of the White self which relies on such associations to define itself. In fact, participation merely means acceptance of those boundaries. This war, unlike Vietnam which took place at a time of worldwide decolonization, coincided with an unprecedented era of American hegemony. The ultimate patriarch with the ultimate machine led, in President Bush's own words, "the family of nations." Into this glory, some African Americans were assimilated. Unconditionally. Although a majority of African Americans still opposed the war,[68] a large percentage endorsed it and some soldiers in the front even used the term "sand niggers" in reference to Iraqis and possibly to all Arabs since sand has a geological presence in the whole region. This is the final stamp of participation in the project of nation, for when African Americans, too, begin to define themselves by the same constructs and against the Other "rapists," "deviants," and "barbarians," they can join the nation; they can enter its boundaries as long as they bury their own past.

Bush himself encouraged the act of "forgetting" in his victory speech by claiming that the "the ghost of Vietnam" was purged and "national self-doubt" eliminated. We might see an end to the ceaseless flow of Vietnam movies, but that will be it. Irrespective of the number of victories, irrespective of any real events, as long as the described constructs and their psychological boundaries are kept alive, the associated anxieties and ideals will also continue to live. Since the very boundaries that define Whiteness depend on the construct of the Other, and since the roots of the anxieties and ideals lie in those constructs, White consciousness will continue this internal battle through engagements with the Other until it understands, faces, and radically redefines its own historical identity. "Forgetting" or "purging" will do nothing towards this understanding and redefinition. They are merely pre-conditions to joining an entity, such as the nation, which will continue to reproduce those same patterns of identity, fantasy, and violence. As Renan said almost a century ago, "Forgetting...is a crucial factor in the creation of a nation."[69] To join the nation you must forget the violence done unto you, much as joining the family requires forgetting the possible violence of abuse, incest, and neglect.

Notes

1. F. Cooper and A. Stoler, "Introduction: Tensions of Empire," *American Ethnologist* (November 1989).
2. See commentaries from different writers in "Fighting Words," *The Village Voice,* February 19, 1991.
3. Alexander Cockburn, "Beat the Devil," *The Nation,* February 4, 1991. Also see letters in *The Nation,* April 8. 1991.
4. From CBS/*NYT* poll December 14, 1990 and Cynthia Enloe, "Tie a Yellow Ribbon 'Round the World Order," *The Village Voice,* February 19, 1991.
5. Cynthia Enloe, "A Feminist Perspective on Foreign Military Bases," in J. Gerson and B. Brichards, eds., *The Sun Never Sets* (Boston: South End Press 1991). The dimension of rape is more difficult to establish but a Northwestern University study uncovered that over half of *American* nurses serving in Vietnam had been sexually harassed by U.S. soldiers themselves. C. L. Mithers, "Missing in Action: Women Warriors in Vietnam," *Cultural Critique,* No. 3, Spring 1986.
6. Cynthia Enloe, "A Feminist Perspective": 101; John Costello, *Love, Sex and War, 1939-1945,* (New York: Pan Books, 1985): 146; Robert Nussbaum, "Une Histoire de Survie," *Femina (Magazine De La Tribune de Geneve),* (23 Aout 1991): 13. Just around Subic Naval Base in Olongapo City there are a reported 20,000 prostitutes, many below the legal age.

7. Outside the scope of this paper but related to it, one can also argue that this conception is a phallocratic project. Leslie Wahler Rabine, "A Feminist Politics of Non-Identity," *Feminist Studies,* Spring 1988.
8. Where I use "white" with a small "w" it functions as an adjective referring to particular individuals or groups. Used with a capital "W" it denotes the construct of Whiteness in which racially non-white individuals may participate. Thus, "White consciousness" does not refer exclusively to the consciousness of white-skinned populations, but also to those of other races who accept and develop the same notions that have been built around Whiteness and at some point may have been meant for white people only. I opted for the term White rather than the alternative of Western because the constructs and rhetoric of Whiteness/Westernism revolve so much around the issue of race. The use of "white" as a definition of a people was current in the colonial period and disappeared sometime after the first World War. Its sublimation erases some key issues in the cultural politics of the Western world.
9. Costello, op. cit., 143.
10. Hyam speaks for example, of Sir David Ochterlony, a resident of Delhi, 1803-25, and Col. James Skinner having 13 and 14 mistresses/wives respectively. Ronald Hyam, "Empire and Sexual Opportunity," *Journal of Imperial and Commonwealth History* (Vol. 14, No. 2 1986): 38.
   The linking of empire's stages to sexuality is better, though not satisfactorily, expressed in two texts, Amirah Inglis, *The White Woman's Protection Ordinance: Sexual Anxiety and Politics in Papua* (London: Chatto and Windus for Sussex University Press, 1975) and Ann Stoler, "Making Empire Respectable: the Politics of Race and Sexual Morality in Twentieth Century Colonial Cultures," *American Ethnologist* (November 1989).
11. Stoler, "Making Empire:" 639; Hyam, "Empire and Sexual Opportunity:" 56. Stoler does make the point, though, that in certain places like Java, concubinage was considered at the root of White poverty and thus discouraged. Stoler, ibid., 639. By the end of the seventeenth century the East India Company made payments to mothers who bore Eurasian children, but only "upon the day the child be christened," Kenneth Ballhatchet, *Race, Sex and Class under the Raj* (London: Wiedenfeld and Nicolson 1980): 96.
12. See, for instance, the analysis and quotes in Winthrop D. Jordan, *White Over Black: American Attitudes Toward the Negro, 1550-1812* (New York: W. W. Norton and Company), Chapter 1.
13. A well-documented instance of this for a town is Port Moresby in Papua, as described by Inglis, op. cit., 46. Similar changes took place everywhere from Indochina to Africa.
14. Robert Ross and G. J. Telkamp, eds., *Colonial Cities: Essays on Urbanism in a Colonial Context* (Boston: Martinus Nijhoff Publishers, 1985). In particular see essays by Robert Ross, J. L. Miege, Mary Karasch, and Colin Clarke.
15. Maria Mies, *Patriarchy and Accumulation on a World Scale: Women in the International Division of Labour* (London: Zed Press 1987): 97-8; Ballhatchet, op. cit., 144.
16. See Irvin Cemil Schick, "Representing Middle Eastern Women: Feminism and Colonial Discourse," *Feminist Studies* (Summer 1990): 359-60.
17. William Loughton Smith in the congressional debates of 1790 as quoted in Jordan, op. cit., 470. Jefferson wanted the "Negro" "to be removed beyond the reach of mixture" so as not to stain "the blood of his master," Jordan, ibid., 546.
18. Stoler, "Making Empire:" 643. White women were not merely instruments or symbols in the service of empire. Their participation ("supportive posture" in Stoler's words) in the matters of empire was in collusion with White men. See

Caroline Oliver, *Western Women in Colonial Africa*, (Westport, CT: Greenwood Press 1982), for a celebration of five White women colonialists in Africa. For a view on White women's violence directed at Black women slaves see Jacqueline Jones, *Labor of Love, Labor of Sorrow: Black Women, Work and the Family from Slavery to the Present* (New York: Basic Books 1985): 26.

19. Inglis, op. cit., 57; Stoler, "Making Empire:" 641-2.

20. D. D. Wax, "Georgia and the Negro Before the American Revolution," in B. A. Galsrud and A. M. Smith, eds., *Race Relations in British North America, 1607-1783* (Chicago: Nelson Hall 1982): 191.

21. John L. Alpert, "The Origin of Slavery in the United States—The Maryland Precedent," in B. A. Glasrud and A. M. Smith, eds., ibid., 131-4.

22. bell hooks, *Ain't I a Woman*, (Boston: South End Press 1981); Patricia Hill Collins, *Black Feminist Thought: Knowledge, Consciousness and the Politics of Empowerment*, (Boston: Unwin Hyman 1990): Chapter 4.

23. This is shown in a review of testimonies of that period by Charles Herbert Stauber, *Sexual Racism, The Emotional Barrier to an Integrated Society*, (New York: Elsevier 1976): Chapter 2.

24. Harry Stack Sullivan, "Memorandum on a Psychiatric Reconnaissance," Appendix in Charles S. Johnson, *Growing Up in the Black Belt*, (New York: Schocken 1967): 328-33.

25. Chicago Commission on Race Relations, *The Negro in Chicago: a Study of Race Relations and a Race Riot*, (Chicago: University of Chicago Press 1923.). For comments and studies on cities other than Chicago: 582+.

26. John A. MacKenzie, *Propaganda and Empire*, (Manchester: Manchester University Press 1984): 101.

27. Robert Rydell, *All the World's a Fair, Visions of Empire at American International Expositions* (Chicago: University of Chicago Press 1984): 56.

28. MacKenzie, ibid., 114; Rydell, ibid., 3.

29. MacKenzie, ibid., 78-9, 202-15.

30. Rydell, ibid., 6, 10; MacKenzie, ibid., 101.

31. Rydell, ibid., 39.

32. Rydell, ibid., 67.

33. It is quite clear that differences in various peoples were noticed. African Americans were compared to Africans, Indians compared to South Africans, etc. However, these were in terms of relative savagery. For example, it was said that "Unlike the Indian, the South African is a restless active savage." MacKenzie, ibid., 104.

34. Rydell, ibid., 60+; MacKenzie, ibid., 104+; Timothy Mitchell, *Colonising Egypt* (Cambridge: Cambridge University Press 1988): Chapter 1.

35. A French colonial as quoted in Stoler, op. cit., 645.

36. Rana Kabbani, *Europe's Myths of the Orient* (London: MacMillan 1986); Schick, "Representing."

37. Kabbani, ibid., 2. Edward Said, *Orientalism* (New York: Vintage Books 1979): 207, calls it a "male power fantasy."

38. Kabbani, ibid., 76.

39. Kabbani, ibid., 59-63.

40. In Marc Cooper, "Dum da Dum-Dum: LA Beware the Mother of All Police Departments is Here to Serve and Protect," *The Village Voice*, April 16, 1991.

41. For the construct of the Orient see Kabbani, op. cit; Said, op. cit.; Mitchell, op. cit; Malek Alloula, *The Colonial Harem* (Minneapolis: University of Minnesota Press 1986).

42. Two things are of note here. First that there appeared to be a widespread fascination with the penis of a Black man and on occasion the possession of

one(!): "It is generally said that the penis in the Negro is very large. And this assertion is so far borne out by the remarkable genitory apparatus of an Aethiopian which I have in my anatomical collection," from a German anthropologist quoted in Jordan, op. cit., 158. The second point, shown by the nationality of this anthropologist, is the way these ideas filtered back from the colonies to mainland Europe.

43. According to a study of lynching, between 1889 and 1929 only some 23 percent of lynch victims were charged with rape or attempted rape, quoted in Angela Davis, *Women, Race and Class* (New York: Vintage, 1983): 189. After Frederick Douglass and Ida B. Wells, Angela Davis argues that lynching did not start as an act of sexual retribution, but gained enormous propaganda value once the cry of rape and the protection of white women was attached to the event.

44. Michael Hutchinson, *The Anatomy of Sex and Power* (New York: William Morrow and Co. 1990): 58.

45. From Vera Brittani in her book entitled *Testament of Youth* as quoted in Mithers, "Missing in Action."

46. Costello, op. cit., 124.

47. Theweleit, *Male Fantasies, Vol. 1* (Minneapolis: University of Minnesota Press, 1987): 89.

48. Jordan, op. cit., 154-5.

49. In Lloyd DeMause, "The Gulf War as Mental Disorder," *The Nation*, March 11, 1991.

50. Costello, op. cit., 140. I use testimonies of World War II because of their honesty and availability as collected in Costello's book.

51. Television interview, *20/20*, March 22, 1991.

52. Quoted in Hutchinson, op. cit., 186.

53. Mithers, "Missing in Action."

54. Theweleit, *Vol. 1:* 125, 129. Theweleit makes the distinction of white women in contrast to "red" women, but the racial connotations remain consciously present.

55. Costello, op. cit., 139.

56. Theweleit, *Vol. 1:* 139.

57. Costello, op. cit., 193-4.

58. Kevin Sessums, "Good Golly, Miss Dolly," *Vanity Fair,* June 1991, 108.

59. Robert Reinhold, "Policewoman in Denim is Betty Grable of Gulf," *The New York Times,* Feb 15, 1991, A16.

60. See *Penthouse Magazine,* January 1991, on illicit sex in Saudi Arabia; also pornographic videos were reportedly available for soldiers, see note 61.

61. J. Ledbetter, "Deadline in the Sand," *The Village Voice,* Feb. 5, 1991.

62. Costello, op. cit., 62; Reinhold, "Policewoman."

63. Sessums, "Good Golly," 108.

64. Quoted in Margaret Spillane, "MUSH," *The Nation,* February 25, 1991.

65. Cynthia Enloe, "Tie a Yellow Ribbon 'Round the New World Order," *Village Voice,* February 19, 1991.

66. I. Peterson, "Planned Communities are Multiplying," *The New York Times,* April 21, 1991, section 10.

67. See *Race and Class* (Vol. 32, No. 3), special issue on Europe 1992.

68. CBS/*New York Times* poll, December 14, 1990.

69. E. Renan, "What is a Nation?" in Homi K. Bhabha, ed., *Nation and Narration* (London: Routledge 1990): 11.

CHAPTER 5

WHY THE EMPEROR CAN'T AFFORD NEW CLOTHES

International Change and Fiscal Disorder in the United States

Arthur MacEwan

I

This past year, one of my daughters was a member of the swim team at our local public high school. When I went to watch a meet, however, I had trouble telling which team was winning which race because not all the members of my daughter's team wore the same kind of swim suit. There were, I learned later, insufficient funds in the school budget to provide the girls' swim team with a full set of suits.

Now, this may seem a minor problem, far removed from the grand issues of international affairs, economic competition among nations, and

---

questions of war and peace. Moreover, the lack of suits may simply have reflected the low status given to *girls'* sports; I never have learned whether or not the boys' team had a full set of suits. Nonetheless, this "minor problem" provides a window onto the "grand issues."

At the beginning of 1991, we were given a less metaphoric window on the "grand issues" by the nightly television news, where, over and over again, we were faced with the awe-inspiring contrast between what the U.S. government spends on its military machine and what it spends on social services. The news first brought us pictures of the massive U.S. military operation in the Persian Gulf, with its daily explosions of millions upon millions of dollars of resources, and then presented us with images of the cutbacks in domestic services from around the nation, where resources are sadly wanting for everything from prenatal care for poverty-stricken mothers to reconstruction of bridges, sewers, and subway lines in our urban centers.

The United States is in many senses the most powerful nation in the world. The government and business of the United States jointly dominate affairs of politics and economics around the globe with an imperial power perhaps unmatched in history. Yet within the United States we are gripped with a sense of things falling apart. Homelessness, drugs, and high infant-mortality rates capture the headlines, while local social services seem to be deteriorating all over the country. The case of my daughter's team's swim suits is one tiny and mundane example of a very widespread phenomenon, namely that local governments are increasingly unable to pay for education and a broad range of social needs.

It is beginning to appear as though the emperor can't afford new clothes. Why not? Why do we find the United States in a situation of increasing fiscal disorder, in which government is increasingly unable to provide social services that the populace has long taken for granted? What is the connection between imperial operations and declining public services at home?

Answers to these questions lie in the story of the changing position of the United States in world affairs. However powerful the United States is today, it does not have the same degree of relative power among capitalist nations that it held in the 25 years following World War II. U.S. hegemony in the capitalist world during that period was an important factor accounting for the relatively rapid growth of the international and U.S. economies, and that rapid growth, combined with a relative decline in military spending, laid the basis for considerable expansion of government spending on domestic programs.

As U.S. hegemony declined, we entered a period of relative stagnation that has generated fiscal crisis. On the one hand, largely because relative stagnation has given rise to greater inequality and instability, it has increased the social demand for public services. On the other hand, relative stagnation has undermined the fiscal dividend with which government can pay for services; slower growth cuts tax revenues. Slower growth has also contributed to the rise of popular opposition to taxes. While this opposition has limited any general increase in taxes, the very rich have achieved considerable success in reducing their taxes and shifting the burden onto the poor. Moreover, while this combination of economic and political forces has limited the fiscal dividend, military spending has been re-expanded, and thus expenditures on other public services have been further squeezed. Consequently, the United States is faced with an increasingly severe fiscal crisis, having its manifestations at all levels of government.

The reassertion of U.S. power abroad through military action, as exemplified by the war in the Persian Gulf and the earlier interventions in Grenada and Panama, is a part of a strategy for regaining lost power. Many people in U.S. ruling groups, including George Bush and those around him, believe that, if U.S. international power is firmly re-established, many of the economic and social ills that plague the country can be solved. Also, they see U.S. international power as an essential condition for the operation of world capitalism and for U.S.-based firms to work their will and obtain their profits around the globe. To accomplish their goals, the people who sit at the center of power in the United States are willing to wreak havoc on peoples in the Third World, both through the everyday course of economic affairs and the cataclysms of military interventions. In this regard, in the brutality it imposes, U.S. imperialism in the 1990s is no different from U.S. imperialism in earlier eras.

Yet in another important way, U.S. imperialism in the current period is different. In the era after World War II, U.S. imperialism worked. Of course it did not "work" for the people who were its victims. Yet, in its own terms, from the perspective of the United States, it worked, providing a flow of resources from the rest of the world and establishing a basis for stable economic expansion. In a certain sense, a large part of the U.S. population shared the benefits of this situation. However, for some time now, U.S. imperialism has not been working even in its own terms. The current military strategy is an effort to get it working again. In all probability, however, this strategy is likely to fail, worsening the situation at home and providing no basis for stability internationally.

The purpose of this essay is to tell the story, as I have suggested it above, about the change that has taken place in U.S. imperialism. By focusing on the connections between the troubles of the empire and the fiscal crisis at home, I hope to shed some light on how the system is continually creating problems for itself and opportunities for those of us in opposition. Our opposition to U.S. imperialism would be the same whether (in its own terms) it worked or failed to work. The way we organize and make our opposition effective, however, does depend on how we see U.S. imperialism changing.

II

After World War II, the military victory by the Allied powers was combined with a great economic victory by the United States. This country stood alone, not only relatively unharmed by the war but with its economic capacity extended to new heights. The size and development of the domestic economy along with military supremacy allowed the U.S. government and U.S. business to wield great power in the capitalist world. This power was a pillar of economic expansion, providing the stability essential for growth and giving the United States vital access to foreign markets and resources. Stability involved both political and economic arrangements. In Europe, Japan, and the Third World, U.S. power assured the rise of governments that would cooperate with Washington's international political and economic policies and secure a friendly climate for U.S. business operations—if not as participants in a free-trade regime, then as friendly hosts to foreign investors. Militant labor organizations and radical political opposition were undermined through U.S. overt and covert actions, which were certainly not inhibited by the rhetoric of democracy and freedom. Through the post-World War II years, domestic strength supported international strength and vice-versa.

One important component of the era's economic stability was the financial system that the United States had imposed at the 1944 Bretton Woods conference. The Bretton Woods arrangements, by providing both stable monetary relations and sufficient liquidity, allowed the tremendous expansion of world trade that led economic growth. These arrangements, not coincidentally, also gave special advantages to U.S. businesses, providing them with an overvalued dollar, which, in turn, was a key to the massive expansion of foreign investment and the penetration and control, through that investment, of foreign markets. Relatively secure business-friendly governments and effective financial arrangements were indispensable components of capitalist expansion; they provided a favorable investment climate on a world scale.

It is difficult to gauge the quantitative impact of the post-war order on economic growth, either in the international capitalist economy generally or in the United States. From the point of view of the United States, it is worth noting that profits from foreign investment as a share of after-tax profits of nonfinancial corporations rose from about 10 percent in 1950 to more than 20 percent in 1965.[1] Moreover, even while U.S. firms were rapidly expanding their direct investments abroad, they were continually returning more funds home from profits on previous investments, on net a process which contributed to the expansion of investable funds, and therefore to growth, within the United States.

Beyond the gains from these flows of funds, there were other substantial advantages for the United States from its position of international power. Of considerable importance were the low price of oil and the high oil profits for U.S. oil companies, a joint set of benefits that could come only with the maintenance of pliable regimes in the oil-rich parts of the world. Similar advantages existed in the cases of other mineral resources—for example, copper and bauxite. In addition to the profits they garnered directly from their foreign operations, the growth and power of U.S. firms in world markets enhanced their positions at home. They could reap huge economies of scale in finance, marketing, research and development, and political influence—as well as increased power over their domestic labor force, which has taken on greater significance in more recent years.[2]

There were surely other factors that contributed to the rapid growth of the U.S. economy during the 1950s and 1960s—relatively peaceful relations between large firms and organized labor, stimulation from government fiscal and monetary policy, and the particular conditions generated by World War II itself (e.g., the backlog of consumer demand and the technological spin-offs). Furthermore, because these other factors enhanced the economic strength of the United States, they enhanced U.S. imperial power. Likewise, in Europe, Japan, and elsewhere in the world economy, numerous other forces contributed to the unusually rapid economic expansion of the post-World War II era. Yet, all of these other factors and forces operated within the framework of the imperial power of the United States, and it is hard to conceive of their having had anything like the impact that we saw without the general stability and special conditions provided by that imperial power.

III

Rapid economic growth is not always accompanied by general improvements in living standards. In the United States during the 1950s and 1960s, however, most indicators—per-capita incomes, real wages, educational levels, health standards—demonstrate a wide improvement in living conditions, affecting virtually all segments of the population. Consistent with what we can see through the various particular indicators, there was a significant, although neither large nor rapid, reduction in income inequality, measured either across the population as a whole or by the standard of the relative incomes of whites and minorities.

One important basis for the improvement in living standards between the end of World War II and the early 1970s was the increase of government spending on domestic programs (federal, state, and local combined) shown in Figure 1. Measured as a percentage of gross national product (GNP), spending on domestic programs almost doubled between the early 1950s and the mid-1970s—from less than 14 percent to more than 26 percent.[3] Some of this increase was tied to demographic change,

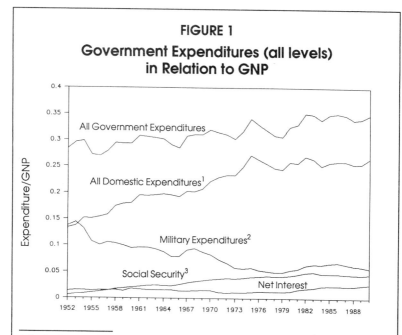

FIGURE 1

Government Expenditures (all levels) in Relation to GNP

1. Includes everything except military (and international affairs) expenditures and net interest payment. 2. Includes international affairs as well as national defense. 3. Social Security is a part of all domestic expenditures.

SOURCES: *Historical Statistics of the United States, Colonial Times to 1970* and various editions of the *Economic Report of the President.*

for as "baby boomers" moved through the school system, expenditures on education rose. Also, rising social-security payments constituted a significant portion of the increase. Such points, however, do not diminish the fact that, along with the expansion of the economy in this era, U.S. society was devoting an increasing share of its resources to a variety of social-welfare and other domestic programs.

Broadly speaking, this rapid expansion of government's domestic spending was a successful response to needs generated by the growth process itself. From the perspective of capital, growth presents ever increasing costs, and businesses' ability to obtain profits—and therefore the viability of the growth process itself—depends on their success in socializing those costs. A classic example of this socialization of costs is government's development of physical infrastructure, and in the 1950s and 1960s this meant primarily expenditures on roads. In the 1950s government spending on roads rose rapidly as a share of GNP, and then was maintained through the next decade. Educational spending, though it serves diverse functions, in significant part is a socialization of business costs, providing both training and screening of the work force. In the post-war era, spending on education expanded dramatically, rising continuously from about 3 percent of GNP in the early 1950s to more than 5 percent of GNP at the end of the 1960s. [4]

Government spending during an era of rapid growth, however, is far more than simply a socialization of business costs. As well as creating costs for business, growth imposes extensive social costs upon the general populace. The market tends to cause dislocation and instability, and, especially as it draws a larger percentage of the population into the wage-labor force, the market tends to raise inequality and insecurity. The very dynamism of the capitalist growth process, the "creative destruction" that Joseph Schumpeter saw at the center of capitalist development, has severe negative impacts on workers, on farmers, and, indeed, on many capitalists, even as the system expands and average levels of income (and of other social indicators) rise.

Government intervention in the economy has been a means by which these negative impacts *and* their political consequences have been attenuated. As a society, we have come to expect government to provide a "social safety net" for those most harmed as growth proceeds. The increases of spending on social welfare, education, housing, health, and old-age pension funds have all been responses to this general need. Also, if growth is to continue with minimal political disruption, government must spend to legitimize the system, to give it at least the appearance of fairness; expenditures on public education provide a prime example. (Of course, the rise of spending on the police and prisons is also a response to these same demands of the growth process.)

Ironically, a period of relative prosperity can bring forth strong political demands and the potentially disruptive actions that, in turn, call forth the growth of government spending. An example is provided by the rise of the civil rights movement and then the riots in African-American communities during the 1960s. While these phenomena had long and complex histories, they were in part products of the country's economic success. African-Americans, who had been so long and thoroughly excluded from the benefits of U.S. capitalism, saw this success and would no longer be denied a share. Legal adjustments came in the Civil Rights Act of 1964 and a spending response came in the War on Poverty and in other areas of social spending. (Note in Figure 1, after the flat period of the early 1960s, the rapid rise in "all domestic expenditures" even as military expenditures jumped upward with the Vietnam War.) Of course, it is not only an era of success that creates the political conflict that forces an increase in government spending. Social security grew out of the broad social struggles of the 1930s. With Social Security, however, the impacts on spending were not immediate, appearing with increasing weight on the government ledger only in the post-war era. The important general point to be drawn out of the various experiences with expansion of spending on social programs is that they were responses to action—changes forced, not simply changes chosen.

In addition to serving particular needs, the high level of government spending during the post-World War II decades served as an aggregate stimulus to economic expansion. Regardless of ideological reservations in many business and political circles, big government became an accepted engine of growth. As long as the prosperity continued, Keynesian arguments held sway; government spending could be the key to economic success, and social demands for expanding programs found no barrier in aggregate considerations.

If the economic success of the post-war era gave rise to a social demand for rising government expenditure, even more did it create a context in which these demands could be met. Rising wages and rising family incomes were the bedrock upon which an expansion of government could take place. In the 1950s and 1960s, popular resistance to taxes was minimal because taxes were not perceived as interfering with the extension of private affluence. Even with historically high levels of taxation and government spending, average take-home wages rose throughout the era. Growth, in effect, created a fiscal dividend because with growth rising taxes could be part of the general prosperity.

Moreover, the major increases in overall government spending, and thus the major increases in taxes, were originally undertaken to finance military programs rather than domestic programs. With the demobilization after the war, total government spending began to return to a level commensurate with the status quo before the war. Then the government, backed by virtually all segments of business and the media, undertook a major campaign to re-raise spending on the military. During the Korean War, military spending leaped upward—from 6.3 percent of GNP in 1950 to 14.4 percent in 1953—and exceeded all government spending (federal, state, and local) on domestic programs. Then, after Korea, even while the Cold War continued full force, military spending began a long decline in relation to GNP. Overall government spending did not fall in relation to GNP, however, as domestic programs expanded to make up for the decline in military spending. (All these phenomena are evident in Figure 1.)

From the early 1950s up to the 1970s, domestic programs benefited from a *de facto* "peace dividend." As military spending declined in relative terms, it was not necessary to raise tax rates appreciably in order to pay for the expansion of domestic programs. Even the military buildups of the early 1960s and the Vietnam War did not seriously alter this basic phenomenon. Thus the "peace dividend" combined with general rising wages and incomes to create the fiscal dividend for domestic programs in the United States.

IV

In the early 1970s, the end of U.S. hegemony in the capitalist world was marked by several international events, including particularly the U.S. defeat in Vietnam, the success of OPEC in pushing up oil prices, the appearance of a U.S. foreign-trade deficit, and the demise of the Bretton Woods arrangements. These events revealed longer-term trends in world power relations. The relative economic success of Japan and Western Europe was especially important and, not incidentally, was a necessary product of the system created by U.S. hegemony. The rising power of Third World interests, both in the form of liberation movements such as that in Vietnam and nationalist elites such as those in the OPEC countries, played a significant role. Also, the growing relative military capacity of the Soviet Union (a matter of special importance when considering the implications of all this at the beginning of the 1990s) served to constrain U.S. power.

In short, by the middle of the 1970s things had changed dramatically. The United States was still extremely powerful in world affairs, more powerful than any other nation by all reasonable measures. Yet its ability to dictate the terms of economic relations, to set the rules of international finance and trade, to intervene militarily and control events in the Third World—all this had changed.

So too had the condition of the U.S. economy changed. Beginning with the developments of the early 1970s and most evident after the world recession at the middle of the decade, the U.S. economy and the economies of the other advanced capitalist countries entered a period of slower economic growth. (The degree of decline in growth rates was greater in Europe and Japan than in the United States, but only because those other countries' economies had been expanding so much more rapidly than the U.S. economy in the post-World War II era.) Relative stagnation continued through the 1980s, and at the beginning of that decade the advanced countries were joined by much of the Third World, which had maintained growth during the 1970s only on the basis of a massive infusion of foreign loans.

Just as we can attribute much of the economic success of the previous era to the conditions provided by U.S. hegemony in the capitalist world, we can explain much of the relative stagnation of the 1970s and 1980s in terms of the international situation of these more recent decades. Oil events provide the most striking example of the connection between international power relations and the instability of the U.S. economy. It is widely recognized that the "oil shock" of 1973 precipitated the recession of 1974 and 1975, that the second jump in oil prices at the end of the decade contributed to the even more severe downturn that marked the early 1980s, and that the general instability of oil prices has been a major contributor to long-term economic uncertainty, weakening investment and growth. Of course the oil-price changes, having their origin in the formation of OPEC, were one of clearest manifestations of international power shifts.

Oil, however, has only been one part—though a very important part—of the instability that has plagued the international and U.S. economies since the early 1970s. There have also been rapid movements in exchange rates, sharp shifts in trade balances, a huge expansion of international debt, and, along with all this, frequent and extreme shifts in government fiscal and monetary policies. Furthermore, the economic policies adopted by different nations' governments have often been inconsistent with one another, exacerbating instability of exchange rates, trade, and capital movements. Without either U.S. power or some new mechanism to impose common policies and regulate the operation of markets, these sorts of instabilities became the hallmark of the new era.

Paradoxically, these instabilities were all the more serious because the preceding era of expansion had been so successful. One of the great accomplishments of the post-World War II era—its major economic legacy perhaps—was the extensive interdependence established among the world's capitalist economies, a phenomenon of special note for the United States, which previously had been more self-sufficient than the other advanced capitalist countries. More highly dependent on the world economy than it had been before the rapid expansion and integration of the 1950s and 1960s, the United States was also more sensitive to the instabilities of the international system.

The U.S. economy slowed during the 1970s and 1980s, with GNP growing about 3 percent a year as compared to about 4 percent in the 1950s and 1960s. This slowdown was sufficient to undermine the expansion of the fiscal dividend and halt the relative expansion of government spending on domestic programs.

With slower growth since the early 1970s, unemployment rates have been significantly higher than in the preceding decades and average wages have stagnated. Indeed, after the impacts of the mid-1970s recession and the recession of the early 1980s, it was only toward the end of the decade that average real wages came up to their 1973 peak (and surely the 1991 recession has forced them back down again). The relative stagnation of the period undercut labor's bargaining power.

The problems were particularly severe because the stagnation was combined with a more thorough integration of the world economy. With the more highly integrated world economy, where capital is very mobile and labor is relatively immobile, the negative impacts in the United States were especially severe for low-wage workers and workers in many manufacturing industries where production had been highly routinized and de-skilled. International integration placed these workers in direct competition with more-poorly-paid workers elsewhere in the world.

In addition to the poor performance of real wage, the new conditions of the era show up in figures on income distribution, with rising inequality first appearing in the mid-1970s and then developing more substantially in the 1980s. Between 1973 and 1987, as average family cash income for the poorest one-fifth of families actually *dropped* by 7.3 percent, the richest one-fifth attained a 14.1 percent *increase* in their real average incomes.[5]

While relatively rapid economic expansion in the 1950s and 1960s generated demands for greater government expenditures on domestic programs, relative stagnation in subsequent years did anything but reduce those demands. It is one of the paradoxes of capitalist development that when the system is working well in its own terms it engenders social misery for many people and widespread economic disruptions, *and* then when the system works poorly the same is true—even more so. Most obviously, in the 1970s and 1980s higher unemployment rates and the rising level of poverty that appeared with greater income inequality engendered a growing need for social-welfare expenditures. Many of the social problems of economic decline—and thus a greater need for funds—have been thrust upon the educational system, making it more difficult for the schools to fulfill even their traditional functions as they have been expected to provide solutions to everything from drugs and crime to teenage pregnancy and AIDS. Moreover, taken as a whole, domestic programs hardly found any relief in demographic change, for as the population aged the need for spending on the elderly rose substantially.

Likewise, business demands upon the government have not been attenuated by slower growth—just the opposite. Business continually expects the educational system to provide a work force that can allow it to operate effectively in a more competitive international environment, and business also demands that government, through one mechanism or another, ease its way in world markets. Most dramatic in recent years, government has gone to great lengths to protect business from the costs of failure that go with slower growth and greater instability. The savings-and-loan debacle is the largest and most blatant example, but government actions in other financial fiascos—from the rescue operations for some of the large commercial banks to the huge loans provided to Third World governments—illustrate the same point.

However, while the relative stagnation of recent decades has driven up the need for government domestic spending, it has also set the stage for a general resistance to any tax increases that would finance that spending. With wages stagnating, incomes maintained only by more people working, greater insecurity, and—through a self-reinforcing circularity—a growing need to replace government services with private services (education is the foremost example), is it any wonder that people are not willing to pay more taxes?[6] There is no mechanism by which people can vote for higher wages or less inflation, the elimination of the business cycle, or lasting security. They can, however, vote against taxes. Voting for lower taxes and thus higher incomes is the one response that the political system allows to a deteriorating economic situation.

Popular opposition to taxes, however, is only part of the story. Government revenues have been limited as the very rich have obtained cuts in their taxes. It is difficult to measure the actual tax rates that various groups pay (because many taxes are paid indirectly), but the most authoritative study of recent years comes to an unequivocal conclusion: Considering federal, state, and local taxes altogether, between 1966 and 1985 effective tax rates for the rich fell substantially. The overall effective tax rate for the richest 1 percent of taxpayers fell by at least 27 percent, and perhaps by as much as 36 percent; for the richest 10 percent, the decline was somewhere between 10 percent and 16 percent. (These tax-rate reductions for the rich were combined with substantial increases for the poorest 20 percent of taxpayers and relatively stable rates for most groups in between.) While robbing from the poor to give to the rich virtually became official policy during the Reagan administration, the trend of moving the tax burden from the rich to the poor appears to have been well established long before Reagan's ascendancy. For example, the share of all federal, state, and local taxes that are social insurance taxes—and fall at a much higher rate on the poor than on the rich—rose from 11 percent in 1950 to 20 percent in 1970, and then to 25 percent in 1980 and 28 percent in 1989. At the same time, the taxes on corporate profits fell from 25 percent of all taxes in 1950 to 11 percent in 1970; policies of the Reagan era could only reduce these taxes from 10 percent of all taxes in 1980 to 8 percent in 1989. When direct tax rates on the rich were reduced in the 1980s, it was only a continuation of process that had been going on somewhat indirectly for years.[7]

While slower economic growth and tax politics have limited the funds available for government spending, since the late 1970s there also has been a new expansion of military spending. As declining military expenditures (in relation to GNP) of the earlier era created a "peace dividend" that allowed the expansion of spending on domestic programs, the more recent rise in military expenditures has reduced government's fiscal capacity for domestic programs. Throughout the 1980s, then, spending on domestic programs has been caught between the pincers of rising political resistance to taxes and rising military spending. Just as the tax resistance was a response to relative stagnation, as I shall argue shortly, the rising military spending can also be interpreted as a response to economic weakness.

It is of some significance that, in spite of these downward pressures, actual spending on domestic programs did not show a great decline during the 1980s. Spending was maintained, of course, by large budgetary deficits. Those deficits combined with stagnation of spending (relative to GNP) on domestic programs—in spite of rising needs—have provided the accounting of the fiscal crisis. In effect, political authorities have attempted to perform a juggling act, responding to both the demand for lower taxes and at least some of the demand for public services. The result has been to shift political attention away from the basic problem of stagnation and its impact on living standards, and to focus popular ire instead on the budgetary problems of the public sector. The deficits and waste in government are seen by many as the principal economic problem of the era, when they are, in reality, symptoms of the general economic weakness.

V

Powerful business and government groups in the United States have devoted considerable attention to the question of how to reestablish an order in world affairs that would facilitate a new era of economic expansion. There have been those who accept the U.S. decline from its extreme power of the post-World War II era, recognizing that conditions of that period were due to singular historical circumstances. This segment of the business and political elite have become known as "trilateralists" because they advocate a policy of cooperation among the United States, Western Europe, and Japan as the basis for recreating an orderly system of international affairs. These people also generally advocate that the government focus its attention on the economic strength of the country, seeing economic strength as the foundation for a secure and stable international position, economically and politically. A secure and stable international position for the United States would, in turn, feed back and support economic success domestically as it had in the post-World War II era. The trilateral strategy, while accepting a partnership with other advanced capitalist nations, contains no suggestion of increasing international equality between advanced countries and the Third World. And within the United States, it is quite clearly a strategy for corporate power, abjuring any moves toward equality or democracy.

Trilateralism gained prominence in the mid-1970s, when several business and political figures—most notably the financier David Rockefeller—formed the Trilateral Commission to develop and push their positions. President Jimmy Carter was himself a member of the Trilateral Commission, and his administration gave prominent positions to several other members, including National Security Advisor Zbigniew Brzezinski and Secretary of State Cyrus Vance. Today, the trilateralist position is represented in the editorial stance of *Business Week* (which, not coincidentally, was reticent about George Bush's march toward war in the Persian Gulf). In giving emphasis to the importance of the government focusing its attention on domestic economic strength, several business-based groups espouse the outlook of trilateralism; a good example is the influential Committee for Economic Development.

Despite their moment in the sun during the late 1970s, the trilateralists failed to establish any stable mode of cooperation among the leading capitalist powers or any popular political appeal at home. While they by no means departed the scene, the trilateralists lost the policy debate. Since the ascendancy of Ronald Reagan to the presidency in 1980, a very different position has dominated U.S. politics. This different position, which finds its clearest public expression in the editorial outlook of the *Wall Street Journal*, shares one important premise with trilateralism, namely that a secure and stable international position for the United States is an essential element for economic success.

However, Ronald Reagan, George Bush, and those around them have acted as though a secure and stable international position for the United States is, *in itself,* sufficient foundation for economic success. They have abjured an active role for the government in building the economic strength of the country, professing a faith that business operating within "free markets" is all that is necessary.

Moreover, Reagan, Bush, and their supporters have largely followed a unilateralist and militarist approach to foreign affairs. They have built their policies on the belief that U.S. preeminence in world affairs could be reestablished, and that it could be reestablished on the basis of military strength. Accordingly, since 1980, the U.S. government has followed a dual policy of expanding military spending and pursuing an aggressive international political strategy. From a low point at less than 5 percent of GNP in 1978 and 1979, military expenditures rose to almost 7 percent of GNP in 1986, while the government pursued military and political "roll back" in the Third World and rhetorical confrontation with the Soviet Union.[8]

This "militarist" policy reached a high point in 1991. The great changes taking place within the Soviet Union and the apparent end of the Cold War eliminated a crucial constraint on the U.S. government's military pursuit of its international strategy. When Iraq invaded Kuwait it created the opportunity for U.S. action. (The opportunity was not completely fortuitous. The United States had both supported the development of the Iraqi government's strength and given at least tacit encouragement for the invasion of Kuwait.) The subsequent war in the Gulf, which was so successful militarily for the United States, was defined by George Bush as an important step toward a "new world order."

However much the advocates of this "new world order" may clothe their policies in a rhetoric of "collective security," no one doubts that the war was a U.S. show and that the victory for the "coalition" was a victory for U.S. power in world affairs. Furthermore, the war in the Persian Gulf clearly demonstrated that the U.S. government is bent on following the same sorts of policies toward the Third World in this era that it followed in the period of U.S. hegemony after World War II. The slaughter of thousands of Iraqi soldiers, the lack of press attention given to the impact of the war on people in Iraq (and elsewhere in the Middle East), and the jingoism that has prevailed since the war all underscore a politics of continuity between the earlier and current eras. Similarly, in building its policies around the anti-democratic, reactionary regimes in Saudi Arabia and Kuwait, the Bush administration has followed the time-honored tradition of U.S. imperialism. However much the administration may profess a support for democracy when its favored dictators are forced from power—as in the Philippines and Haiti, for example—its preference for elitist, authoritarian, but stable regimes in the Middle East is uncompromising. Thus the "new world order" would appear very similar to the world order that prevailed in the post-World War II years.

Appearances, however, can be deceptive. While there can be little doubt about the military supremacy of the United States, it is not at all clear that in the "new world order" this military strength can be the foundation of an economic stability and prosperity like that existing in the 1950s and 1960s, especially for the United States itself. Leaving aside the international political problems that may occur because of or in spite of U.S. military success in the Gulf (for example, the possibility of civil strife in much of the Middle East and continuing instability in the Soviet Union and Eastern Europe), one can cite numerous continuing international economic problems that U.S. military power and the victory in the Gulf War do not resolve. Consider the following:

- Military strength is not likely to allow the U.S. government to impose the economic policies it desires upon the other leading capitalist nations. Among the most pressing difficulties in this area are the trade negotiations, under the General Agreement on Tariffs and Trade, which broke down in late 1990. A particular sticking point was the U.S. government's insistence that the European Community (EC) greatly reduce its barriers to the import of U.S. agricultural goods. More generally, the negotiations are stalled because each government (or set of governments, as in the EC) is unwilling to sacrifice its economic interests, and there is no single power—no hegemonic nation—that can impose agreement. Lacking a complementary economic capacity, U.S. military strength will not yield a resolution to these trade conflicts when negotiations resume.

- Military strength is not likely to recreate a stability in world financial markets that is particularly favorable to U.S. interests. In recent years economic stability has been undermined by the failure of central banks to adopt common and cooperative interest-rate policies. The U.S. government, for example, would have the German government lower interest rates by pursuing a more expansionary monetary policy, while the Germans (and others) have argued that the problem of high interest rates has its roots in the U.S. fiscal deficit. Without stable interest rates, currency speculators—including the treasurers of large multinational firms—move large sums of money quickly from one currency to another, undermining governments' abilities to enact effective economic policies. Moreover, stability in world financial markets is elusive as long as several large Third World countries continue to have severe debt problems, which could quickly become defaults with widely spreading repercussions. The "smart bombs" of the Persian Gulf offer no solutions to these financial difficulties.

- Military strength is not likely to eliminate the U.S. trade deficit and the continuing growth of U.S. reliance on foreign capital. U.S. trade and debt problems are partly results of the lack of competitiveness of U.S. goods in many important markets. Partly they are results of the U.S. government's macroeconomic policies that have, generally, kept the value of the dollar high, encouraging imports and discouraging exports. (Since the excess of imports over exports can only be paid for by obtaining funds from abroad, a large and continuing trade deficit necessitates a growing reliance on foreign capital.) There is no reason to believe that military strength will either make consumers suddenly prefer more expensive U.S. electronics to East Asian products or make the government alter its macroeconomic policies, by balancing the federal budget, for example. Indeed, insofar as military strength depends upon higher and higher levels of spending, it will contribute to the macroeconomic disorder.

- Military strength is not likely to enhance the position of U.S. multinational firms in their competition with Japanese, German, and other rivals. Japanese auto firms and German chemical companies have made inroads in the United States and elsewhere because of superior technology, more effective management, and more aggressive marketing—not because they are backed by their governments' military capacities. Japanese banks have become the largest in the world because the tremendous economic success of that country has provided them with a huge quantity of funds. Neither the industrial nor the financial firms from Japan and Germany, or anywhere else, are likely to change their practices simply because of U.S. victory in the Persian Gulf.

Of course there are some economic advantages which will accrue to the United States as a result of military success. International oil markets, most obviously, are now more than ever securely in the hands of U.S. firms and cooperative governments. This is no minor matter, and surely provided a major motivation for the U.S. decision to go to war. (However, it is most likely that the oil gains, as well as the removal of Iraq from Kuwait, could have been accomplished without war. It was the general aim of a "new world order," rather than any of these particular goals, that necessitated war.) Also, the war will give a boost to U.S. arms producers, and, in the very short run, U.S. firms will have advantages in obtaining contracts for reconstruction and new activity in Kuwait and Saudi Arabia.

Overall, however, there is little reason to believe that the success of the U.S. military strategy will recreate the economic "golden age" of the post-World War II era.[9] If this conclusion is correct, then the fiscal crisis is more likely to be exacerbated than eased by the "new world order."

As I have already suggested, laying the foundation for the new world order through the 1980s—that is the rapid expansion of military spending—contributed significantly to fiscal disorder in the United States, in the form of both large budget deficits and a failure to provide for a broad set of domestic needs. Surely maintaining the new world order will require continued reliance on heavy military spending. If there is no substantial payoff in terms of economic growth, then following this military strategy will have a doubly negative impact on domestic spending. In the first place, there will be no growth dividend. The lack of rapid economic growth will both exacerbate needs for public programs and reduce the willingness of the populace to pay for those programs. Secondly, there will be no peace dividend, as a high level of military spending continues to drain the public coffers.

This is hardly a prognosis of lasting success for the new world order that has been thrust upon us at the beginning of the 1990s. My daughter's swim team is not likely to have a full set of swim suits in the foreseeable future. This lack will probably go unrecorded in the pages of history, but the larger issue cannot be ignored. Failure to spend on domestic programs will both undercut business in the United States and contribute to social conflict. There is little reason to think that current policies of the U.S. government will restore either domestic or international economic stability. Thus, U.S. imperialism is not likely to work as it worked so effectively in earlier years. An imperialism that does not work is no less nasty than an imperialism that does work. In fact, great powers in decline may be especially vicious and dangerous. Yet when an imperial system does not work, there are greater opportunities for blocking it, changing it, and eliminating it.

Notes

1. See Table XLI in Harry Magdoff, *The Age of Imperialism* (New York: Monthly Review Press, 1969), p. 183. These profits from foreign operations were highly concentrated in the very largest firms. For example, in 1965, 13 industrial corporations, all among the top 25 on the *Fortune 500* list, accounted for 41.2 percent of foreign earnings; see Thomas E. Weisskopf, "United States Foreign Investment: An Empirical Survey," in R.C. Edwards, M. Reich, and T.E. Weisskopf, eds., *The Capitalist System* (Englewood Cliffs, N.J.: Prentice-Hall, 1972), p. 433.
2. Aside from the substantial theoretical problems in computing the extent of many of these gains—e.g., how would we determine what the price of oil would have been in the absence of U.S. international power? Or how would we determine the gains to Ford Motors in the domestic market that were possible only because of its great size, a function in part of its international operations?—there is also the problem that the internal pricing arrangements of the large firms (transfer pricing) make it virtually impossible to identify the geographic origins of a multinational firm's profits.
3. The general pattern—rising from the early 1950s through the mid-1970s and then roughly flat through the 1980s—is the same whether one makes the calculation for all domestic spending or just the "social" programs. Removing Social Security spending—included in the "all domestic spending" category of Figure 1—would not alter the pattern. The sharpest fall in spending on domestic programs relative to GNP came in the 1976 to 1979 period, pre-dating the Reagan presidency.
4. These and other data on government spending for the pre-1970 period are from *Historical Statistics of the United States, Colonial Times to 1970* (Washington: U.S. Bureau of the Census, 1975), Vol. 2, pp. 1120-21. Similar data for later years are from various issues of the *Economic Report of the President.*
5. United States Congress, House Committee on Ways and Means, *Background Material and Data on Programs Within the Jurisdiction of the Committee on Ways and Means,* 1989 edition, Washington, March 15, 1989. Measured in 1987 dollars, average family cash income for those in the bottom one-fifth was $5,507 in 1973, $5,439 in 1979, and $5,107 in 1987. For the richest one-fifth, the figures for the three years were $60,299 in 1973, $61,917 in 1979, and $68,775 in 1987.
6. The growing replacement of public services by private services appears to be a phenomenon of considerable significance. In addition to private educational services, private security services are growing especially rapidly. The implication of such developments is that while the actual supply of these services may not be decreasing substantially, there is a sharp change in the distribution of such services—away from society in general, the poor in particular, and toward the wealthy. Of course, as the process proceeds, the constituency to support public services shrinks, and people are forced to spend a larger share of their income providing themselves with the services privately. It is a rather nasty downward spiral.

7. The study of changing tax rates for different groups is Joseph A. Pechman's, *Who Paid the Taxes, 1966-85?* (Washington: The Brookings Institute, 1985). The problem in estimating who pays taxes is illustrated by the corporate-profits tax, which most people believe is a tax on the wealthy, assuming that it reduces dividends or the value of equity. However, there is evidence that the corporate-profits tax may be paid partly by workers, as companies offset their tax costs with lower wages, and partly out of consumers' pockets, as companies pass on the tax in higher prices. Pechman estimates tax rates using a variety of assumptions about how the burden of a particular tax falls on different groups—e.g., about the extent to which the corporate-profits tax affects dividends, wages, and prices. Using his most progressive set of assumptions (those that imply the most progressive tax structure), he finds that the tax rate on the richest 1 percent of taxpayers fell from 39.6 percent in 1966 to 25.4 percent in 1985, and that the rate on the richest 10 percent fell from 30.1 percent to 25.3 percent. At the same time, under this set of assumptions, the tax rate on the poorest 10 percent rose from 16.8 percent to 21.9 percent. Using the least progressive set of assumptions, Pechman found that the tax rate on the top 1 percent fell from 28.9 percent to 21.2 percent and from 25.9 percent to 23.3 percent for the richest 10 percent. Under this least progressive set of assumptions, the tax rate for the poorest 10 percent rose from 27.5 percent to 28.2 percent. While Pechman's results for these two ends of the population are relatively dramatic, the changes he finds for middle income groups are small and are sensitive to the particular set of assumptions he employs. The data on the shares of taxes that are social-insurance payments and corporate-profits taxes are from the *Economic Report of the President, 1991.*

8. Even this substantial increase in military spending relative to GNP does not cause a major shift in the long-run relative decline of military spending that appears in Figure 1, and the increase may appear surprisingly small to many. After all, between 1979 and 1986, military spending increased from $123.8 billion to $287.5 billion. This increase of $163.7 billion seems to be almost twice as large as the total of $83.9 billion spent on the military in 1968, at the height of the Vietnam War. However, these oft-cited figures are misleading, for they involve no correction for inflation. When we allow for inflation and recalculate all the numbers in terms of 1982 purchasing power, we obtain the following: an increase from $157.5 billion in 1979 to $252.6 billion in 1986, making for an increase of $95.1 billion; this increase is less than half of the adjusted 1968 figure of $222.5 billion. The growth of military spending between 1979 and 1986 was very substantial, involving an annual increase of roughly 7 percent per year in real terms while GNP grew at only a bit more than 2 percent a year, but it was nowhere near as large as the crude, unadjusted figures would lead one to believe.

9. Indeed, it is likely that military might will be particularly ineffective in forging unity among the advanced capitalist nations. During the 1950s and 1960s, U.S. military strength was an important unifier because of the threat, real or imagined, of the Soviet Union. The Cold War served as the glue that held the system together under U.S. domination, with other advanced nations embracing U.S. military protection. Without the glue, that military protection will hardly be so welcome. However effectively "narcoterrorists" and dictators of small countries may serve in the U.S. media as replacements for the "Soviet menace," they are not likely to serve the same function among political authorities elsewhere in the world.

PART III

THE WAR ABROAD

CHAPTER 6

WHY WAR?

Joe Stork and Ann M. Lesch

Why did the United States go to war against Iraq? The Bush administration asserts that the issues were straightforward: aggression and self-determination. But the scale and timing of the U.S. military intervention submerged the important issue of Iraqi aggression and Kuwaiti sovereignty within the larger issue of Arab self-determination against Washington's efforts to impose its hegemony over the Gulf region and the Arab world.

What was at stake, in the view of many people in the Middle East, were four intersecting issues: (1) the legitimacy of the existing political and economic order in the region, which the United States is striving to maintain and which Iraq appeared to be challenging; (2) control of the region's resources, especially oil, and distribution of the proceeds; (3) the resolution of longstanding grievances, particularly the conflict between Israel, the Palestinians, and the Arab states; and (4) rivalry among Middle Eastern states for dominance.

Iraq, Kuwait, and the Legacy of Colonialism

Baghdad claimed that Kuwait is part of Iraq. Did this claim have any basis in fact? Is Kuwait an artificial construction of British imperialism? After World War I, which saw the defeat of the Ottoman Empire, the European powers drew up most of the borders in the Middle East to suit

---

Most of this essay originally appeared in Middle East Report #167 (November-December 1990). It was updated by Joe Stork in September 1991 and includes material from his essay, "The Gulf War and the Arab World," World Policy Journal, Spring 1991.

their own competing political and commercial interests, only loosely basing them on existing Ottoman administrative divisions. This is true of Iraq as well, particularly Britain's addition of the oil-rich and heavily Kurdish-populated province of Mosul to Iraq in 1926. Yet none of those who assert Iraq's claim to Kuwait advocate that Mosul become part of Turkey or Syria, or an independent Kurdistan.

What is now southern Iraq and Kuwait had been under the nominal sovereignty of the Ottoman Empire based in Istanbul. After 1981 Kuwait town became part of the province of Basra, but Ottoman authorities exercised little or no real authority throughout the province. Britain took advantage of this Ottoman weakness to extend its political and commercial influence throughout the Persian Gulf region, including Iran.

Kuwait had been much like other essentially tribal enclaves along the shores of the Persian Gulf. Out of the constant migrations in search of water and trading locations, mainly from the Najd region of what is today the north central part of Saudi Arabia, a group of tribes had settled the town of Kuwait in the early 1700s. By the end of that century, the Sabahs had emerged as the leading family. The continuity of Sabah rule over two centuries distinguishes Kuwait from other such settlements, where political authority was more fluid.[1]

European intrusion had been a feature of the Gulf during this period, mainly a consequence of Britain's colonization of India. In 1899, the leading Sabah sheikh, Mubarak, agreed not to cede, lease, or sell territory to any other power without British consent, in return for 15,000 rupees. The British were motivated by growing commercial and political rivalry from Germany and Russia; the Sabahs were interested in using British power to counterbalance the Ottomans on the one hand and the aggressive expansion of the al-Sauds in the Arabian Peninsula on the other.

Kuwait's status as a British protectorate continued after Baghdad and Basra provinces became the League of Nations mandate territory of Iraq in the early 1920s, under British control, and Ibn Saud consolidated his family's control of most of the Arabian Peninsula. In 1922, Britain's proconsul in the Gulf, Sir Percy Cox, unilaterally set the boundaries between Kuwait, Saudi Arabia, and Iraq, placing some territory claimed by the al-Sauds within Iraq and adding to Saudi territory a sizable piece of what Kuwaitis considered their territory. Cox's borders deliberately limited Iraq's access to the Gulf.

Iraq became formally independent in 1932, but British influence remained dominant until the nationalist revolution of July 1958.[2] In the late 1930s, the Iraqi monarchy launched an unsuccessful campaign to "restore" Kuwait to Iraqi rule. When Kuwait became formally independent in June 1961, Iraq's nationalist leader Abd al-Karim Qassim renewed the Iraqi claim in a curious way, by appointing the sheikh of Kuwait as governor of the province of Basra. Britain responded by dispatching troops based in Kenya, which were soon replaced by an Arab League peacekeeping force. In 1963, Iraq again attended meetings of the Arab League and the Organization of Petroleum Exporting Countries (OPEC), which it had boycotted for seating Kuwait, and in October of that year Baghdad recognized Kuwaiti independence.

Iraq only revived its claim to all of Kuwait following the invasion of August 1990. Prior to this, though, Iraq had never agreed to finalize any border demarcation that did not give it access to two uninhabited islands off Kuwait, Bubiyan and Warba, thus enhancing Iraqi access to the Gulf. In the early 1970s, Baghdad embarked on a major expansion of its oil production and export capacity and wanted to build up the port of Umm Qasr as an alternative to the Shatt al-Arab exit to the Gulf which it shared with its major adversary, Iran. Iraq's claims on the islands led to some brief border skirmishes in the spring of 1973.

Iraq demanded to lease the two islands during the course of the 1980-88 war with Iran. Kuwait rejected the request, but did allow Iraq to set up artillery observation posts on Warba during critical battles in 1986 and 1988. Kuwait provided Iraq considerable economic assistance in the course of the war, and Kuwait itself functioned as Iraq's major port once Basra was shut down by the fighting.

Following the cease-fire with Iran of August 1988, Iraq once again stepped up efforts to improve port facilities at Umm Qasr. In the period leading up to the invasion of August 1990, Iraq's insistence on gaining a more secure outlet to the Gulf became tied up with a larger set of economic grievances against Kuwait—repayment of wartime debt, pumping from the Rumaila oil field that extends beneath their common border, and Kuwait's excess oil production leading to weak international prices and falling revenues.

Oil and the Legacy of Imperialism

Iraq's claim to all of Kuwait was not the reason Baghdad invaded in August 1990. Rather, it served as a justification after the fact. What gives the Iraqi argument currency in the Arab world is less the merits of this territorial claim than the powerful sense that the political and economic order prevailing in the region as a whole has been constructed and maintained primarily for the benefit of the western powers. Behind this perception is oil. Many of the political arrangements that characterize the region—borders, ruling families, economic structures, and more—exist and persist because of the importance of oil for western industrialized countries.

The discovery of oil in the Persian Gulf region predates World War II, but only in the 1950s did the region emerge as a major producer. The seven giant American and European oil companies (the "Seven Sisters"), which dominated the oil industry in the United States and the rest of the world, had gained exclusive control of Middle East oil through a system of interlocking concessions. The appeal of Middle East oil for the companies lay in its very low production costs—between 5 and 15 cents a barrel. The world market price (around $2.25 per barrel in the mid-1950s), then set by these same companies on the basis of production costs in the United States and elsewhere (upwards of $2 per barrel at the time), made for bonanza profits in the Middle East.[3]

The emergence of the Middle East as a major oil-producing region coincided with two critical political transitions: the rise of nationalist movements and the end of direct European colonial control, and the eclipse of British and French power in the region by the United States.

Nationalist challenges to foreign control included the oil industries. When Iran's parliament nationalized British Petroleum's interests in 1951, the western embargo of Iranian oil played a key role in setting the stage for the 1953 CIA-led coup that restored the shah to power. Britain and the United States and their oil companies used Iraqi and Kuwaiti production to replace Iranian supplies. A decade later, when Iraq was leading the nationalist challenge to western control, the companies used Iran and Kuwait to supply their markets, punishing Iraq by keeping its production, and hence revenues, low. Kuwait's role was the same in both instances: Between 1953 and the mid-1960s, Kuwait, with a population of around half a million, was the largest single oil-producing state in the Middle East.

The agenda of economic nationalism, set first by Iran and later by Iraq, Libya, Algeria, and other countries, has redefined the oil industry over the last 20 years. Despite these changes, Iraq's complaints in 1990 about Kuwaiti overproduction sound all too plausible in a region where people have an acute memory of the manipulative role of the western companies and governments, usually with the eager compliance of the local beneficiary regime.

Politics and Society: Kuwait

Oil restructured politics and society in all the producing countries. Before oil, Kuwait's economy had been based on trade and pearl diving.

A small merchant elite controlled the labor force and revenues, structurally linked with but independent of the ruling family. The major social cleavages were between the wealthy and the less privileged, the majority Sunnis and minority Shi'a, and the sedentary population of the towns and predominantly nomadic tribal families.

Oil revenues freed the ruling family from its historic alliance with the merchant elite. The wealthy trading families were the main beneficiaries of various schemes to redistribute revenues, but in the process surrendered a major political role. The power of the ruling family increased substantially, while the major social cleavage became that between those possessing Kuwaiti citizenship and the growing majority of "guest" residents. Kuwait drew on other Arabs—especially Palestinians—and people from Asia and the Indian subcontinent not only as physical laborers but as essential technicians and professionals such as doctors, teachers, lawyers, and engineers.

Non-citizens comprised about half the population at the time of independence in 1961. Citizenship was restricted to families resident in Kuwait since 1920, and only 50 persons per year could be eligible for naturalization. Non-citizens could be, and frequently were, deported when economic demand slackened or political crises threatened. By the 1980s, non-citizens accounted for about two-thirds of the population and about 80 percent of the workforce.

While medical and some educational benefits were extended to non-citizens in the mid-1960s, the social and economic gap between Kuwaitis and others remained profound. Only citizens were eligible to participate in the various revenue-distribution schemes. The circumstances of non-citizens, even those who became prosperous and have spent most of their lives in Kuwait, were precarious. Non-citizens—two-thirds of the population—could not own property; 51 percent of any company had to be Kuwaiti-owned. Wages and income for non-citizens were a fraction of those of Kuwaitis.

Non-citizens had no political rights, though Kuwaitis enjoyed few themselves. Voting was restricted to male citizens over 21—about 3.5 percent of the population—and the last parliament, elected in 1985, was dissolved a year later. The 1980s saw a reversal of an earlier trend to open up the political system—cabinet and other high posts, for instance—to Kuwaitis not related to the Sabah family. In the spring of 1990, Kuwaiti opposition forces held militant demonstrations demanding elections and reconstitution of the parliament. They boycotted June elections for the partially appointed National Assembly that the government offered as a substitute.

Politics and Society: Iraq

Iraq, a land about the size of California, is the Arab society perhaps most traumatized by the transformations wrought by oil. Its political revolution in 1958 prefigured in some respects the revolution in Iran 20 years later.

Iraq in the first half of this century was very largely a rural society. Nearly one quarter of the population are Kurds; some two-thirds of the Arabs are Shi'i Muslims, and one-third Sunnis. Land and wealth were extremely concentrated, and development projects and government expenditures financed by oil revenues benefited the wealthy few. The disruption of Iraqi society was expressed most graphically in the tremendous movement of impoverished peasants from the countryside to urban shantytowns, where they comprised the shock troops for the nationalist and communist forces competing to overthrow the British-installed monarchy.

The decade after the 1958 revolution was characterized by great instability. Different groupings contended for state power. There was a shift in the distribution of income from large landowners and merchants to the salaried middle class and, to a lesser degree, wage earners and small farmers. When the Ba'th seized power in July 1968 (there had been a brief and bloody Ba'thi reign from February to November 1963), it embodied a relatively homogeneous faction of the lower middle class who, broadly speaking, were the primary beneficiaries of the 1958 revolution—sons of small shopkeepers, petty officials, and graduates of teacher-training schools, the law school, and the military academies.

As in Kuwait, oil revenues financed the growth of the state. Because of Iraq's considerably larger population, and many social, ethnic, and sectarian cleavages, the repressive as well as the distributive organs of the state were most highly developed. In 1977, the Ministry of Interior alone, with its security and intelligence functions, employed almost as many persons—137,000—as all large private and public manufacturing firms combined.

Saddam Hussein, a master of putschist politics, is the only survivor among those who seized power in 1968. Vice-President until 1979, he took over the top post when Ahmad Hasan al-Bakr resigned that year. All other political forces besides the Ba'th, notably the Communist Party, the Kurdish Democratic Party and the (Shi'i) Dawa Party have been crushed, and political rivals within the Ba'th have been eliminated. Much of the cohesiveness of Saddam's regime is owed to the fact that most key members come from the region of Takrit, Saddam's hometown northwest of Baghdad, and many are kin.

Economic Crisis

There has been an underlying material dimension to the political crises that have punctuated the post-World War II history of the Middle East, involving contested control over oil production and revenues and, more broadly, the allocation and distribution of resources. The Gulf War of 1990-91 exhibits this economic dimension to a particularly high degree. Iraq emerged from its war with Iran economically exhausted, militarily the strongest state in the region by far, and with an unsated ambition to be the dominant political force in the Gulf. Saddam Hussein cited Kuwait's "economic warfare" against Iraq as a primary reason for Iraq's invasion. That invasion, unintentionally perhaps, raised issues of equity and social justice on a regional scale. And patterns of wealth, economic linkage, and dependency partly determined the alignment of Arab states in the ensuing confrontation.

The specifics of Baghdad's economic grievances against Kuwait are reasonably well known, but the extent of the Iraqi state's fiscal crisis may not be. Even following the 1988 cease-fire halting the war with Iran, budget deficits amounted to between a third and a half of total domestic product, inflation was running at an estimated 40 percent, and the regime was importing some $3 billion in military goods each year. Financial support from Saudi Arabia and Kuwait had ceased, and Baghdad frequently had to reschedule repayment of western debts amounting to more than $20 billion (out of total debts of $50-$60 billion).[4] By 1989 Baghdad's only source of western commercial bank credit was several billion dollars worth of unauthorized loans by the Atlanta branch of Banca Nazionale del Lavoro (BNL).

The costs of waging war and maintaining social peace (through subsidies on basic goods and services) had left Iraq's economy stagnant and nearly completely dependent on oil revenues for its financing. While Iraq planned to build its oil-export capacity to 6 million barrels per day by 1995, immediate possibilities for increasing revenues depended almost entirely on increasing or at the very least maintaining the price of crude oil. This price is what Kuwait's persistent overproduction undermined. (By way of further aggravating Baghdad, Kuwait repeatedly declined to "forgive" some $17 billion worth of loans it had made during the war with Iran.)

Beyond Iraq's economic motives on August 2, this confrontation reflects aspects of a larger crisis, one that has eroded the economic basis of the Arab state system which evolved out of the crises of 1967 and 1973.

The June 1967 war had produced a sort of political compact between the conservative oil monarchies of the Arabian Peninsula and the chastened radical-nationalist regimes in Egypt and Syria: The radicals would cease trying to subvert the monarchies; those monarchies would pay for this good behavior with financial aid and investments and allow the nationalists to buy a modicum of social peace at home. The October 1973 war, intersecting with and augmenting the ability of the Organization of Petroleum Exporting Countries (OPEC) to raise oil prices, provided the financing that allowed the 1967 pact to survive and flourish for another decade. To the flow of aid and investment capital was now added a much more significant flow of remittances, as hundreds of thousands and eventually millions of workers—from manual laborers to skilled professionals—migrated from Egypt, Jordan, Lebanon, and occupied Palestine to the rich but sparsely populated states of the peninsula to build and staff virtually every sector of those economies. In the aftermath of Kuwait's liberation one European ambassador remarked that "the reason things are going very slowly now is that when a Kuwaiti minister pushes the button on his desk, the Palestinian aide is not there to respond. It's not easy to operate the first floor when the ground floor is missing."[5]

Despite a second spike in oil prices and revenues at the end of the 1970s, thanks to Iran's revolution, these Eldorado times drew to a close in the 1980s. A restructured world energy market, drawing on non-OPEC sources such as the North Sea, Alaska, and Mexico, led to a sharp drop in OPEC's share of global sales. Oil prices dropped in the 1980s, and virtually collapsed by 1985-86. Even Saudi Arabia, the largest exporter, has run a budget deficit of between $9 billion and $20 billion per year since then.

Kuwait responded to this emerging crisis essentially by bailing out of the Arab state system.[6] Building on an existing strategy of overseas investment, the emirate built up its assets abroad, in the industrialized countries rather than in the region, buying stakes in leading industrial corporations and real estate firms. These investments included oil production, marketing, and petrochemicals. By the second half of the 1980s, Kuwait was earning more from official overseas investments, stock portfolios, and real-estate holdings than it was from the sale of Kuwaiti oil. These official investments may have totalled as much as $100 billion by 1990, and private Kuwaiti investments, including those of the ruling family, may be double this amount. In many important ways, Kuwait's rulers and economic elite shared the interests of western firms and governments in lower rather than higher oil prices. With its sizable outlets in Europe (marketed under the brand name Q8), Kuwait, like the vertically integrated giant oil companies, could shift its profit-taking to the refining or marketing end when crude prices were low, an option that was not open to most other oil-producing countries.

In its aid and investment policies in the Arab world, Kuwait was perhaps the most enlightened and generous of the rich oil states. In some years it gave as much as 7 percent of its GNP in aid—a level not approached by any other country. Nevertheless, as the Gulf confrontation revealed, Kuwait was seen by vast numbers of poorer Arabs as an integral part of an unfair and imposed structure that had separated Arab people from Arab resources for the benefit of western corporations and consumers and local ruling classes.

This sense of grievance was heightened by the decline in aid and investments to poorer Arab states that followed the mid-1980s slump in oil revenues. As revenues declined and major construction projects were finished, workers returned home and the flow of remittances which tied the non-oil producing states into the "Arab oil economy" slackened as well. By the time the Gulf crisis erupted in the summer of 1990, incomes and living standards in many countries had stopped rising and in many countries actually declined. Algerian per-capita income dropped from $2,234 in 1980 to $2,096 in 1988 (adjusted for inflation); in Syria the decline over that period was from $1,484 to $1,256.[7] The oil-producing states experienced declines in absolute and per-capita income as well. Egypt was the only country to experience a notable gain in per-capita GNP over this period. The last several years had seen sharp outbreaks of unrest, provoked by economic crisis, in Jordan, Algeria, Morocco, and Tunisia, and economic deterioration played no small part in fueling the Palestinian Intifada. A generalized resentment at the concentrations of wealth in the small oil sheikhdoms of the Gulf was now heightened by a strong sense that a historic opportunity for regional development had been squandered by the regimes (including Iraq), an opportunity that would not come again.

From One Invasion to the Next

Certainly Saddam's previous foreign aggression, the invasion of Iran in September 1980, was seen in the region as one of the most egregious instances of squandering vast human and material resources. More carefully calculated than the 1990 move against Kuwait, that invasion was intended to overthrow the new Islamic republic in Teheran and establish

Iraq's position as the paramount power in the Gulf, and had the tacit encouragement of the United States.

Saddam's army quickly bogged down, though, and by March 1982 was on the defensive. The threat of an Iranian victory produced an unusual alliance of regional and international powers who shared the goal of preventing Iraq's collapse. Kuwait and Saudi Arabia provided massive financing; France and the Soviet Union were the largest of scores of arms suppliers; Egypt and Jordan provided weapons and military advisers. The United States provided credits, some "non-military" aircraft, and considerable political support. Kuwait's request for U.S. protection against Iranian attacks on its oil tankers provided the entree for U.S. naval intervention in the Persian Gulf in 1987-88. Washington led the effort in the UN Security Council to produce a cease-fire resolution tailored to Iraq's needs.

Saddam views the Persian Gulf as Iraq's "natural" sphere of influence. After the cease-fire with Iran, though, Iraq signalled a clear intent to play a role in the wider Arab world. Baghdad aided far-off Mauritania in its conflict with Senegal, and assisted the merger of North and South Yemen. Saddam's excursions of solidarity were not hampered by any requirements of ideological consistency: Baghdad provided arms to the isolated Islamist junta in Sudan and General Michel Aoun's Maronite Christian rebellion in Lebanon.[8]

Among the most important Iraqi alliances to take shape in this period was with the Palestine Liberation Organization (PLO) and Jordan. The PLO had been feeling physically and politically insecure in Tunis since the Israeli air raid in October 1985 and the assassination of Abu Jihad in April 1988, and had moved substantial sections of its administrative and military operations to Baghdad. This also reduced the PLO's diplomatic dependence on Egypt, and rendered moot any improvement in PLO-Syrian relations.

Iraqi leaders articulated a perspective that attracted the beleaguered Palestinians. Iraq argued that so long as the Arabs remained economically and militarily weak, they would not be able to dislodge Israel from the occupied territories and establish a Palestinian state. An Arab approach to peace, Iraq maintained, must be coupled with a pan-Arab military and material buildup. Oil revenues must be invested in the Arab world rather than abroad; wealthy Arab governments must aid poor ones, and special pan-Arab funds should be set up to help the Palestinian Intifada.

This was the thrust behind Saddam's speech on April 1, 1990. In that speech he declared, first, that Iraq would retaliate with chemical weapons to any Israeli nuclear attack, and second, that "If aggression is committed against an Arab and that Arab seeks our assistance from afar, we won't fail to come to his assistance." In the subsequent international clamor over Saddam's speech, two additional elements were lost: his reminder that Israel, not Iraq, had introduced nuclear and chemical weapons into the region; and his proposal for establishing a nuclear, chemical, and biological weapons-free zone in all of the Middle East.

Saddam's speech was welcomed by Palestinians and Jordanians. Palestinians had watched their peace initiative being frittered away when Israeli Prime Minister Yitzhak Shamir blocked even preliminary Israeli-Palestinian meetings. The PLO-U.S. dialogue, initiated in December 1988, lacked substance. Saddam seemed to offer the tough backing essential for negotiations.

To Jordanians, Ariel Sharon's slogan "Jordan is Palestine" implied the expulsion of thousands of Palestinians from the West Bank to Jordan and the forcible transformation of King Hussein's regime. The influx of Soviet Jews to Israel made this threat all the more imminent. Jordanians also worried about the vulnerability of their long border with Israel. Most of Jordan's economic resources are located in a 10-mile-wide strip along that border: the irrigated agriculture in the Jordan Valley, the minerals of the Dead Sea, and Aqaba port. Iraq was attractive as a strategic rear, able to respond if Israel attacked.

Conspiracies

The shrill tone of Saddam's April 1 speech, replete with talk of foreign conspiracies against Iraq, came on the heels of Iraq's execution of Iranian-born British journalist Farhad Barzoft on charges of spying. Soon afterward, British authorities intercepted alleged parts for nuclear devices en route to Baghdad. Saddam spoke of being encircled by Western enemies operating to prevent Iraq from achieving strategic parity with Israel. Talk of conspiracies helped arouse popular Arab support.

Saddam appeared at the peak of his popularity at the emergency Arab summit conference convened in Baghdad in late May 1990, where he called for a united front against aggression, the pooling of resources, and the need to match rhetoric with deeds. His own rhetoric stressed heightened Arab coordination and accelerated aid to the Intifada and to Jordan.

But contrary to his image of a united front led by Baghdad, signs emerged that other Arab governments would challenge Saddam's claim to leadership. Even in the Gulf region itself, Iraq felt its influence slipping. The small emirates of the Gulf Cooperation Council (GCC) were moving to normalize relations with Iran with unseemly haste. Kuwait, for example, resumed direct air flights to Iran and signed agreements on shipping and joint investment. Iraq complained that Kuwait had dragged its feet on initialing Iraqi-Kuwaiti joint projects and would not allow flights to Iraq to cross its air space, thus preventing Basra from functioning as an international airport. Iraq feared that the Gulf states were cultivating Iran as a counterweight, so that they could remain outside Iraq's sphere of influence. Overproduction of oil by Kuwait and the United Arab Emirates (UAE) provided further evidence of that deliberate distancing.

Saddam was particularly concerned that Syria no longer appeared isolated in the Arab world. After the Gulf War ended, Saudi Arabia and Egypt renewed efforts to draw Syria back into the Arab fold. Baghdad and Damascus represented rival wings of the Ba'th Party, but also had objective differences. Syria had sided with Iran during its war with Iraq; Baghdad was determined to thwart any resolution of the Lebanese civil war, such as the Saudi-sponsored Taif Accord, that left Syria as the power broker in that country; and they adopted divergent positions on the role of the PLO in peace negotiations. For the first time in years, Damascus hinted that it was prepared for serious negotiations over the Golan Heights. Such negotiations would further isolate the PLO and weaken any potential Iraqi-led Arab front. The Syrian-Egyptian reconciliation in December 1989 shocked Baghdad. A new axis seemed to be emerging, one that provided a counterweight to Iraq.

Egypt was Saddam's key concern. But Mubarak was also on the defensive: His efforts to broker an Israeli-Palestinian settlement had not achieved results. Saddam's critique of attempting to negotiate with Israel in the absence of strategic credibility must have stung the Egyptian officials. At the Baghdad summit, Mubarak joined Saddam in acclaiming the importance of pan-Arab solidarity in order to achieve a comprehensive peace. But he also implicitly chastised the Iraqi president. Arab leaders must know how to address the outside world, Mubarak said: "The Arab message should be humane, logical, realistic and free of exaggeration and intimidation. The fate of peoples cannot be determined through one-upmanship and self-deception."

Mubarak also distanced himself in tangible ways from Iraq. Once Egypt was readmitted to the Arab League in May 1989, he won support for returning the League's headquarters to Cairo. Mubarak restored relations with Syria and with Libya, and he suggested creating a Red Sea security zone. In a short time, Egypt had regained its regional weight and dimmed Saddam's vision of uncontested leadership.

When the Iraqi-Kuwaiti crisis mounted in late July, the lines of the subsequent schism were already evident. An Egyptian-Syrian-Saudi axis was emerging as a counterweight to Baghdad; the Gulf states were trying to reestablish an Iraq-Iran equilibrium; and even Libya was edging toward Egypt. In contrast, Jordan and the PLO were embracing Iraq, and newly-united Yemen welcomed Baghdad's Arab-nationalist assertions and its criticism of the wealthy Gulf regimes.

Saddam began to see himself encircled not only by international forces but also by regional powers. In January 1990, Turkey halted and afterwards severely restricted the flow of water past the new Ataturk Dam on the Euphrates River into Syria and Iraq. By July, Saddam said publicly that a third of Iraq's population was directly affected by the water shortage. Saddam placed the Turkish actions in the context of his hypoth-esized international conspiracy against Iraq, since Turkey is a member of NATO, has diplomatic relations with Israel, and has even offered to sell water to Israel. Imperialist powers in league with Israel, he asserted, were using Turkey to block Iraqi economic development and prevent its emergence as the leading regional power.

With Iran, Egypt, and Turkey each three times Iraq's size in popu-lation and stronger industrially, Saddam's strategic strength appeared to elude him—while his ambition remained intact. Iraq's internal economic situation, furthermore, was precarious, with clear implications for Saddam's ability to match word and deed. In late 1989 the government announced industrialization plans and a debt-repayment schedule based on the expectation of raising the $18-per-barrel oil price OPEC had just set. Instead, oil prices dropped precipitously in early 1990. At an extraor-dinary meeting of OPEC ministers in Geneva on May 1, the Iraqi oil minister called on members to adhere to the agreed-upon production quotas.

Soon after, Foreign Minister Tariq Aziz warned other oil producers of unspecified "consequences" of flooding the oil market. And at a closed session of the Baghdad May summit, Saddam declared that deliberate efforts to lower the price constitute war by economic means and warned: "We have reached a point where we can no longer withstand pressure."

The oil market remained in disarray. Iraq's vice president visited Saudi Arabia, Kuwait, and the UAE in late June. But the UAE delayed agreeing to observe the OPEC quota until July 12 and Kuwait held off until Tariq Aziz sent a harshly worded letter to the Arab League on July 15, 1990, accusing Kuwait of "systematically, deliberately" harming Iraq and undertaking economic "aggression that is not less effective than military aggression." Every $1 drop in the price of a barrel of oil, Aziz said, caused a $1 billion drop in Iraq's annual revenues, and Kuwait's actions had triggered an acute financial crisis in Baghdad. He also complained of Kuwait's refusal to cancel the billions of dollars of debts that Iraq had accrued during the war with Iran. Kuwait, he charged, had violated the pan-Arab principle that "everyone should benefit from the wealth" of the Arab nation.

Despite last-minute efforts to accommodate Iraq's demands, Saddam continued to denounce "certain rulers of the Gulf states" who have "thrust their poisoned dagger in our back." In that speech on July 17, he again linked the actions of Kuwait and the UAE to an international conspiracy. He asserted that the "premeditated" damage to Iraq's economy was encouraged by Washington.

There was a striking contrast between Saddam's claims of invulnerability and his sense of encirclement; his belief in Iraq's centrality to pan-Arab security and identity and his fear of being undermined by regional rivals; and his aspirations for economic power and the reality of limited resources. Those contrasts fed Saddam's focus on Kuwait: the richest of the oil sheikhdoms, flaunting its wealth, resisting his embrace, and flirting with outside powers. Saddam appears to have thought that he could quickly absorb Kuwait and present a *fait accompli* to the world. Kuwaiti oil would significantly enhance his resources and improve his international financial leverage. Kuwaiti territory would expand his access to the Gulf and extend his international military reach. His regional authority would be consolidated and his global leverage increased.

Saddam miscalculated drastically.

Political Faultlines

Iraq's approach to resolving its economic quarrel with Kuwait was to send its tanks rolling. At the next stage, some of the regime alliances that quickly developed were at least in some part expressions of economic dependency. Egypt's indebtedness to the United States, and to the international capital markets through the IMF and the World Bank, along with Saudi subventions, certainly helped persuade Cairo that it was making the only possible decision in aligning itself with Riyadh and Washington. Monetary calculations may not have been uppermost in the mind of Syria's Hafez el-Assad, but the billion or so dollars that were quickly transferred to Damascus accounts from the Gulf must have been a most welcome token of mutual esteem in the wake of cutbacks of Soviet aid. The monarchical affection of Morocco's King Hassan for his brothers in the Gulf had been nurtured over the years by Saudi grants and subsidies for Morocco's military campaign to occupy and annex the Western Sahara and Moroccan mercenary engagements against the forces of world communism in Zaire and Angola.

On the other side, Amman's response to the crisis had its economic dimension as well. Jordan, as a "front-line state" in the Arab states' alignment against Israel, had become used to some $2 billion in aid per year in the early 1980s, and depended heavily on worker remittances as well. By the end of the decade, Jordanians and Palestinians were returning from the Gulf without jobs; Palestinians withdrew more than a quarter-of-a-million dollars from Jordanian banks in 1988 and 1989. Transfers from the richer Gulf states had plummeted; Saudi aid, for instance, dropped from $1.25 billion in 1981 to $400 million in 1989. Over this same period, Jordan developed extensive economic links with Iraq. Baghdad provided several hundred million dollars in loans to Jordan to develop the port of Aqaba, though these sums were dwarfed by Jordanian export credits—Iraq still owed some $835 million to Jordanian firms in the fall of 1989. Aqaba had become, along with Kuwait city, Iraq's main port in the years of war with Iran. By the end of the decade, Iraq had become Jordan's single most important trading partner, and by one estimate some three-fourths of Jordan's industry was geared to export to Iraq.[9] King Hussein's principled opposition to U.S. policy, therefore, happened to coincide not just with the patriotic sentiments of the Palestinian and Jordanian masses but with the material stake of the country's bourgeoisie in Iraq's survival and economic prosperity.

Material Reality

The material factors that lay behind the crisis and war are relevant not just for understanding the dynamics that led to confrontation and war. They also suggest some of the difficulties that lie ahead. There was considerable pollyannaish blather in Washington, notably from the secretary of state and the president, about "closing the book of war" and "opening the book of peace," and how this plunge into the abyss of war has awakened the powerful and the privileged to the need for a more "equitable" approach to the allocation of Arab wealth.

There are grounds for skepticism that these homilies have any practical implications. After all, the structural separation of people and resources that underlies the colonial cartography of the region is one thing Washington went to war in order to preserve. Around 1950 or so, the U.S. government persuaded the giant oil companies that they should improve the longevity of the ruling families in the oil states by providing them a greater share of oil profits, and the U.S. Treasury obliged by allowing the companies to deduct these payments from their U.S. tax bills. Advisers from the U.S. government and from banks like Chase Manhattan were employed by the Saudi Arabian Monetary Agency and equivalent bodies in the the smaller sheikhdoms to recommend blue-chip investments in the West over riskier ventures in the Middle East region. In the mid-1970s, with the explosion of oil revenues, U.S. officials and financiers made a point of making sure that the largest share of those revenues got spent on American goods and services (military and otherwise), and that any sums left over be "recycled" through U.S. banks and investment houses.

Even if there is a will, is there a way? The generalized notion of a "rich" Arab world ignore the fact that "surplus" oil rents—revenues that regularly exceed the capacity to absorb imports and local investment—*were* pretty much the exclusive province of Kuwait, Saudi Arabia and the United Arab Emirates. The past tense is relevant. It seems safe to say that there will be less money in the Middle East in 1991 available for investing, lending, or sharing than there was in 1989. Kuwait and Saudi Arabia have already spent billions of dollars to finance the exile of rulers and citizens and to pay the hefty liberation invoices submitted by the U.S. secretary of state. Those bills and commitments have more than gobbled up the "windfall" revenues from briefly higher oil prices and increased Saudi exports. The Saudis have already gone to international capital markets, via J.P. Morgan, to raise $3.5 billion. The Kuwaitis are planning to do the same to finance the reconstruction of their devastated economy and society; the figure being mentioned at the low end is $20 billion.

It has always been something of an error to regard the Arab world as "rich." Some countries were very cash "liquid"; most were not. Today the "liquidity" of even the Saudis and the Kuwaitis is much reduced. Their capacity, not to mention their inclination, to provide funds to other states and societies in the region is very much in doubt. Somehow it seems unlikely that we'll see a bill for a sizable U.S. donation to the Arab world move very quickly through Congress.

As for private investment from outside the region, the war and its aftermath have surely done nothing positive for the risk-assessment ratings of any countries in the region. Some $15 billion in local private capital fled the peninsula as the crisis unfolded in August, and it is unlikely that even this will return any time soon as middle-class Arabs emulate the rich by moving their assets "offshore."[10] (At annual fees of 1 percent, the new western guardians of this money will be making about $150 million.) In the view of one London-based Arab banker, "Arab banks are never going to be able to operate in confidence again from the Gulf...the situation is hardly reversible for probably the next decade."[11] And this was before the crash of the Abu Dhabi-based Bank of International Credit and Commerce (BCCI).

The Arab world, despite western stereotypes, is not a rich area. Such wealth as does exist is extremely concentrated. Figures for income distribution within countries, if they exist, are considered state secrets. It is easy, though, to see the disparities as reflected in official national-income accounts. Yemen's ambassador to the UN, Abdallah al-Ashtal, has observed that the region contains six of the richest (i.e., most cash-liquid) countries in the world and six of the poorest.[12] Rami Khoury, the respected former editor of the *Jordan Times*, calculates that per-capita income in the Arab world, using 1986 figures, "ranged from $9,600 among the 15 million people of the oil-producing states, to $2,000 among the 60 million people of the middle-income Arab countries, to just $500 among the 113 million people of the low-income states."[13]

For every country, those sums are less today, though the discrepancies of income distribution remain at least as acute. For the period ahead, the situation is likely to be dire in a number of states. Worker remittances have been disrupted severely, and may never recover for countries like Yemen and Jordan. Yemen can look to modest earnings from oil exports to help cushion this loss. Jordan, though, has seen its trade and export links severed not just with Iraq but with Saudi Arabia, and the important tourism sector has been hit badly. UNICEF estimates that the proportion of Jordanians living below the poverty line has risen from 20 percent to 30 percent since the Gulf crisis began.[14]

The Arab states allied with Washington and Riyadh, notably Egypt and Syria, have seen their immediate losses covered by grants and debt forgiveness from the oil states and the West. The Saudis earmarked more than 600,000 work permits for Egyptians to replace the Yemenis, Palestinians and others who have been forced to leave the kingdom, but as yet there has been no significant shift of Egyptian labor to the peninsula.[15] The $15-billion fund that the Arab allies were considering to cover "strategic rent" for Egyptian and Syrian troops in a post-war Gulf security system has been abandoned in favor of direct military arrangements between the Gulf states and the United States and U.K. In any event, unlike worker remittances that accrue to individuals, families, villages, and neighborhoods, most of these replacement monies accrue directly to the state, and their distribution and allocation will no doubt follow the paths of established power.

Remittances, tourist receipts, and financial aid will decline. Military spending and capital flight will increase. To the extent that the region's already heavy debt burden does not grow, it will be because credit is not available.

Washington and its allies, though, will not be able blithely to ignore the economic troubles of contentious neighbors. Washington is already putting in a good word for Egypt with the IMF, an extension of Cairo's enhanced stature, but it seems unlikely that this will do more than postpone the unravelling of Egypt's still state-heavy economy. We are already starting to see the Washington-guided rehabilitation of King Hussein, whose services in maintaining law and order in Jordan cannot be dispensed with, but this is unlikely to bring with it a restoration of the prosperity that allowed the kingdom to absorb political shocks from Israeli repression in the occupied territories or economic shocks from the oil states.

The Storm Ahead

The Iraqi military force that invaded Kuwait in August 1990 had been built by the coalition of regional and international powers now aligned against Iraq. It seems probable that Iraq did not intend to pose a fundamental challenge to the prevailing order, and thus did not anticipate the alliance against it. The United States had given Saddam Hussein no reason to think it would oppose such a move. What the alliance against Iraq must confront, however, is something more frightening than Saddam's military power—namely, the extent of popular support that his aggression has tapped in the Arab world.

That support was less an endorsement of Saddam Hussein and his regime than an enthusiasm for any serious challenge to a political order widely regarded as illegitimate. The fact that the challenge to the prevailing order has come from a despot rather than from the forces of the Left made the political equation more difficult for progressives to assess. Iraq has squandered its resources and hundreds of thousands of lives by war and repression. Iraq under Saddam has subverted and done grievous harm to the Palestinian cause. The Baghdad regime's bloody suppression of popular uprisings in the Arab south and Kurdish north of the country following the military defeat at the hands of the United States resulted in tens of thousands of Iraqi dead and maimed.[16]

For many Arabs, though, ambivalence about Saddam Hussein took second place to unambiguous hostility to a state system that permits a handful of ruling families to monopolize the region's resources while millions of Arabs live impoverished. Alongside this class question, there is the irresolution of the Palestine-Israel conflict, and the transparent hypocrisy of the United States in its very selective opposition to aggression. Saddam's challenge appropriated its political strength from the Palestinian and broader Arab resentment against the apparent collusion of the United States, the West, and most of the Arab regimes to maintain a political and economic status quo which, for millions, has become intolerable.

Washington's latest imperial adventure in the Gulf, therefore, is likely to exhibit the tendency of past instances of intervention to exact unforeseen costs and to breed the tensions that create the next crisis, generating further intervention. During his mid-March 1991 tour of the region, Secretary of State Baker piously wished that Desert Storm "be the last great battle in the Middle East."[17] The prospects are not promising. There is a wellspring of political rage against what many Arabs see as just the latest installment of colonial intent, in which no price is too high to pay for victory, especially if the currency is Arab lives. This view is not confined to Palestinians and Algerians and other opponents of the U.S. project. Even a pro-American Saudi businessman complains that "the ugly defeat of the Iraqis has put a dent in the heart and mind of every Arab. It's a psychological defeat for all of us. It goes beyond that a regime is bad and it gets what it deserves."[18]

Not just Iraqi lives and Arab psyches have been shattered by this U.S.-led war. What poses the most serious threat of further upheaval and potential foreign intervention in the region is the intersection of this political polarization with a growing economic crisis directly affecting most Arab societies. This economic crisis forms the backdrop to Iraq's invasion. It partly explains the faultlines along which Arab states divided in response to the Iraqi-American confrontation. Baker and other U.S. policymakers claim to be sensitive to the issues of rich and poor, haves and have-nots, and are proposing special funds and development banks to address questions of basic equity. But the Arab world in the wake of Desert Storm is going to have less money, not more. The Eldorado years of petrodollar surpluses were a moment in history.

This discussion followed the usual convention of dealing with geopolitical identities—states and countries. The benefits of this war will accrue less to this or that nation than to certain classes and strata. The rich—people, not countries—will likely get richer. In a country like Egypt, for instance, the medium and large landowners and manufacturer-exporters are likely to strengthen their positions. The state—in Egypt, in Turkey, in Iran, in the United States—has strengthened itself against social forces struggling against the status quo. Economically the main winners will be where capital is located: on Wall Street and in The City. The House of

Morgan is doing well enough, having already handled the first Saudi state loan in a generation to finance the war. The economic benefits of this war will go first and foremost to the coupon clippers, whatever their race, color, or creed. And let us not forget the company of Bechtel: Thanks to a timely warning from George Shultz, the company bailed out of its participation in an Iraqi chemical-plant contract and is now heading up the Kuwaiti oil-sector reconstruction effort. Already compared to the Marshall Plan in dollar terms, this will enable the Bechtel board to amass the slush funds that will finance Republican political campaigns for the rest of the decade in the manner to which George Bush has become accustomed.

Notes

1. For an excellent account of the history and political economy of the Kuwaiti regime, see Jill Crystal, *Oil and Politics in the Gulf: Rulers and Merchants in Kuwait and Qatar,* Cambridge University Press, 1990.
2. On Iraq, see Hanna Batatu, *The Oil Social Classes and the Revolutionary Movements in Iraq,* Princeton University Press, 1978; Peter Sluglett, *Britain in Iraq 1914-1932,* Ithaca Press, 1976; Stuart A. Cohen, *British Policy in Mesopotamia 1903-1914,* Ithaca Press, 1976; Joe Stork, "Iraq and the Gulf War," *Middle East (MERIP) Reports* No. 97, September 1981.
3. Joe Stork, *Middle East Oil and the Energy Crisis,* New York, Monthly Review Press, 1975.
4. Kiren Chaudhry, "On the Way to Market: Economic Liberalization and Iraq's Invasion of Kuwait," *Middle East (MERIP) Report* No. 170, May/June 1991.
5. *New York Times,* March 14, 1991.
6. See Yahya Sadowski, "Revolution, Reform, or Retrogression? Arab Political Options in the 1990 Gulf Crisis," *The Brookings Review,* Winter 1990/91.
7. Calculated from *World Tables 1989-90* published by the World Bank.
8. On Sudan see *Middle East (MERIP) Report* No. 172, September-October 1991; on Lebanon see *Middle East (MERIP) Report* No. 162, January-February 1990.
9. Amatzia Baram, "Baathi Iraq and Hashimite Jordan: From Hostility to Alignment," *Middle East Journal* 45:1, Winter 1991, p.58.
10. *Euromoney,* September 1990.
11. *Annual Meeting News* of the IMF/World Bank meetings in Washington, September 1990.
12. *Middle East Report,* March-April 1991.
13. "The Post-War Middle East," in *The Link,* January-March 1991.
14. *Guardian* (London), March 4, 1991.
15. Yahya Sadowski, "Power, Poverty and Petrodollars: Arab Economies After the Gulf War," *Middle East (MERIP) Report* No. 170, May-June 1991; Eric Hooglund, "The Other Face of War," *Middle East (MERIP) Report* No. 171, July-August 1991.
16. Hooglund, "The Other Face of War."
17. *Washington Post,* March 13, 1991.
18. *Washington Post,* March 13, 1991.

CHAPTER 7

THE OTHER FACE OF WAR

Eric Hooglund

The human toll of the Persian Gulf War—as many as 100,000 deaths, five million displaced persons, and more than $200 billion in property damage—ranks this conflict as the single most devastating event in the Middle East since World War I.

At least three times as many people were killed during both the eight-year Iran-Iraq War and the 13-year civil war in Afghanistan, but the loss of life in those conflicts was spread over many years. In contrast, the majority of deaths in the most recent war occurred in a six-week period, commencing with the start of the U.S.-led bombing campaign in mid-January 1991 and ending with the 100-hour-long ground offensive in late February. A further period of massive bloodletting followed as the Iraqi army crushed popular rebellions in the south and north of the country.

It is also true that the continuing strife in Afghanistan has caused about five million people to flee their country, but their flight was spaced over years, allowing Iran and Pakistan, the principal host countries, to provide minimally adequate refugee assistance. In the Arabian Peninsula and Iraq, the confrontation uprooted millions of people in two large tidal waves, August-September 1990 and March-April 1991, catching both governments and international refugee-relief agencies woefully unprepared to cope with even the most basic needs of the displaced populations.

"The Other Face of War" by Eric Hooglund is reprinted from *Middle East Report* #171, July-August 1991, pp. 3-7, 10-12. Reprinted with permission by MERIP/Middle East Report, 1500 Massachusetts Ave., NW, #119, Washington, D.C. 20005

Finally, the destruction of Iraq's and Kuwait's industrial and transport infrastructure was on a scale comparable to the devastation of central and eastern Europe during World War II. The consequences of this death, displacement, and destruction, in a period of less than nine months, have seriously disrupted countries and societies throughout the Middle East and South Asia for years to come.

Death

The one irreversible consequence of war is death. In this war there may never be an accurate account of the number of people who lost their lives. During the occupation of Kuwait reports circulated that the Iraqis had killed at least 4,000 civilians suspected of participating in the resistance movement.[1] After Iraq was driven out of Kuwait, concerted efforts by human-rights organizations to document the killings determined that the earlier estimates had been greatly exaggerated. Middle East Watch has ascertained that 300 of the 7,000-9,500 Kuwaitis taken out of Kuwait by Iraqi forces during the course of the occupation have been killed. This number may rise if some of the 2,000-2,500 persons still unaccounted for have in fact been killed. There are also reports of 28 civilian deaths in Kuwait during the allied bombing campaign; at least 30 foreign nationals murdered by Iraqi soldiers, apparently to cover up crimes such as robbery and rape; and up to 100 Iraqi soldiers assassinated by Kuwaiti resistance operatives.[2]

There are very precise statistics on the number of U.S. casualties— 144 killed and 479 wounded. Two deaths in Israel were directly attributable to Iraqi missile attacks; another dozen Israelis died of heart attacks or suffocated under their gas masks, while at least eight Palestinians died in the occupied territories because the Israeli-imposed curfew prevented them from getting medical treatment in time.[3]

There are no reliable data at all on Iraqi casualties. The United States, along with Saudi Arabia, assumed *de facto* responsibility for burying many of the Iraqi dead. The United States unofficially estimates the number of Iraqi soldiers killed as a direct consequence of the air and ground war in January and February 1991 to be 75,000 to 105,000. Senior U.S. military officials have said that 60,000 to 80,000 Iraqis died in bunkers during the air assaults and an additional 15,000 to 25,000 were killed during the ground offensive. (An Iraqi doctor working in the Basra area told relief workers in Iraq that he estimated between 60,000 and 70,000 Iraqi soldiers were killed in the withdrawal, and that half of these could have been saved had medical facilities and supplies been available.)[4] Chairman of the Joint Chiefs of Staff General Colin Powell said that Washington does know how many Iraqi soldiers the Allies buried, but so far he has declined to make that figure public. Iraq, whose commanders were cut off from their troops on the battlefield due to the effectiveness of the Allies' bombing campaign, silently acquiesces in these U.S. estimates.[5]

The dead represent only part of the total casualties. Thousands more were maimed. There are no reliable estimates of the number wounded. The rule-of-thumb ratio of three wounded to each death, which dates back to World War I, suggests that as many as 300,000 Iraqis may have been wounded during the six-week campaign. Since the cease-fire, an unknown number of Iraqis and Kuwaitis have been killed and badly injured by mines and other unexploded ordnance.[6]

The Allied bombing campaign dropped many thousands of tons of explosive materials on Iraq and Kuwait. The U.S. military's reference to civilian casualties as "collateral damage" camouflaged the impact of the air assaults on the noncombatant population. The Iraqi government has cited a figure of 7,000 civilians killed in the air raids, most of whom perished in Baghdad, Basra, Falluja, and Nasiriyya. Subsequent eyewitness reports do suggest that civilian deaths as a direct result of bombing were probably in this range.[7]

The end of the war did not stop the killing. During March, thousands of Iraqi civilians and some troops and officials died in the unsuccessful popular uprisings against the government of Saddam Hussein. The estimates of those killed in southern Iraq start at 6,000.[8] Reports of political killings in the south continue in late May 1991. The estimates of the number killed during the fighting in the northern Kurdish region are lower, beginning at 2,000. Since the fighting ended, however, an estimated 20,000, mostly children, have died from disease and exposure in the overcrowded, squalid refugee encampments along Iraq's borders with Iran and Turkey.[9]

Altogether, at least 100,000 and possibly as many as 200,000 Iraqis, civilian and military, perished as a consequence of the U.S.-led military campaign and subsequent civil strife.

Displacement Before the War

Once the dead have been buried, the survivors try to get on with their lives. This will be tremendously difficult for millions of people directly displaced as a result of the war.

In attempting to determine the number of refugees, one again encounters the problem of inadequate data. During the initial phase of the confrontation (August 2-January 17), more than 2.6 million persons were displaced. This figure includes at least 1.6 million refugees who fled Kuwait during the Iraqi occupation, as many as 700,000 Yemenis forced to leave Saudi Arabia, and as many as 400,000 foreign nationals, mostly Egyptians, who managed to leave Iraq before the allied bombing campaign began.

The first refugees came out of Kuwait. Iraq's occupation policies, combined with international financial measures such as freezing Kuwaiti assets, prompted 1.6 million people to flee the country. These refugees included Kuwaiti citizens and foreign nationals working there.

The experience of each group was very different. When Iraq invaded, the emirate's resident population of approximately 2 million included less than 700,000 citizens. The remaining 1.3 million—65 percent of the total—were expatriate workers and their dependents. An estimated 125,000 Kuwaitis had been outside the country on August 2, most on summer holidays, and chose not to return home.[10] They were joined in exile by nearly 300,000 more fellow citizens. These 400,000 exiles obviously were generally spared the privations normally associated with refugee status, because the Kuwaiti government-in-exile provided monthly stipends of $1,000 to $4,000 per family.[11] Following Kuwait's liberation, the extent of devastation compelled authorities to discourage these refugees from returning immediately, but by mid-May most basic services such as piped water, sewerage, and electricity had been restored to some degree and restrictions on the refugees' return were lifted.[12]

Kuwait's foreign nationals fared considerably worse, losing their jobs, their homes, and their life savings. Some one million people, most of them breadwinners, saw their lives destroyed by Iraq's invasion. Their losses amounted to far more than simple personal misfortunes: Hundreds of thousands of families throughout the Middle East and South Asia, financially dependent on the remittances sent home by these workers, were suddenly deprived of a primary source of income. There is no precise tally of the number of expatriates in Kuwait at the time of the invasion, since many foreign nationals were undocumented. Official government estimates for 1989 included 625,000 Arabs, 600,000 Asians, 60,000 Iranians, 3,000 Turks, and 11,700 Westerners.[13]

The largest group of expatriates were an estimated 350,000 Palestinians. After the Kuwaitis and Westerners, who held the most prestigious jobs, the Palestinians generally held the emirate's better-paying, professional jobs. Most of the Palestinians sent regular remittances to families living in Jordan, Lebanon, and the Israeli-occupied territories, many in refugee camps. About 200,000 Palestinian residents, including as many as 30,000 who were outside the country at the time of the invasion, fled Kuwait during August and September. The next largest group of Arab workers was an estimated 150,000 Egyptians, who sent home $500 million annually; approximately 90 percent of them fled Kuwait after the invasion. Together, Palestinians and Egyptians accounted for 80 percent of Arab expatriates in Kuwait. The remaining 125,000 Arabs included Jordanians, Lebanese, Yemenis, Moroccans, Sudanese, and Tunisians; at least 80,000 of these Arab nationals also fled.

Kuwait's 600,000 Asian workers principally came from the Indian subcontinent. The largest group were Sri Lankans, estimated at 200,000 and including several thousand Sri Lankan women who worked as maids in Kuwaiti homes. Other subcontinent expatriates included 172,000 Indians, 90,000 Pakistanis, and 78,000 Bangladeshis. From beyond the Indian subcontinent were an estimated 45,000 nationals from the Philippines, including several thousand women who worked as nurses in hospitals and maids in homes. The remaining 15,000 Asian workers were from Thailand, China, Indonesia, Taiwan, South Korea, Japan, Hong Kong, and Malaysia. More than 500,000 Asian workers fled Kuwait in the initial 10 weeks following the Iraqi invasion.

In addition, an estimated 100,000 to 150,000 Asians, 90 percent of them from the Indian subcontinent, were working in Iraq on August 2. The overwhelming majority of these workers were repatriated between August and November.[14]

The remittances of Asian workers in Kuwait and Iraq not only sustained large families back home but also constituted an important source of hard currency for governments. The most severe impact was in Bangladesh. According to the United Nations Conference on Trade and Development (UNCTAD), 78,000 Bangladeshi workers in Kuwait lost an estimated $1.4 billion in wages, savings, and personal property when they fled.[15] Thousands of destitute Bangladeshis were stranded at refugee camps in Jordan during August and September because Dacca said it did not have sufficient foreign currency to pay for their air fares home. Eventually Saudi Arabia footed the bill to fly them and thousands of other Asians home.[16]

The flight of expatriate workers and their dependents included 65,000 who fled to Turkey (3,000 of them Turks), 60,000 to Syria (apparently including a large number of Iraqi deserters), and some 100,000 to Iran.[17] The country most immediately affected was Jordan. Out of some 2.5 million foreign nationals in Kuwait and Iraq at the onset of the crisis, more than one million transited through Jordan. Most refugees were destitute and endured a grueling trek through the desert to the Iraq-Jordan border. Jordan was unprepared for such a flood of refugees, and received virtually no international assistance to deal with the problem. Thousands of Asians were stranded for weeks in the desert refugee camps where dehydration, diarrhea, scorpion bites, and other ailments reached epidemic proportions.[18] Eventually the Asians were repatriated. About 250,000 refugees, including at least 200,000 Palestinians, were citizens of Jordan and remained there. Their remittances, estimated at $400 million per year just from Kuwait, had been one of the country's major sources of income and foreign exchange.

Dealing with the refugee crisis was only the beginning of Jordan's woes. As a result of developments related to the situation in the Gulf, Jordan suffered several devastating and simultaneous economic blows: (1) the loss of more than half its annual $800 million in remittances; (2) the task of absorbing thousands of working-age refugees when the country already was burdened with high unemployment; (3) the end of transit fees and the closure of export markets in Iraq, its primary trade partner, Kuwait, on account of UN-mandated sanctions, and Saudi Arabia, which restricted Jordanian imports as a form of punishment for King Hussein's reluctance to join the anti-Iraq coalition; (4) the termination of low-priced oil imports from Iraq (because of the UN embargo) and Saudi Arabia (again, as a punishment); and (5) the retaliatory cutoff of $500 million in grants—supplying one-third of the state budget—from its main foreign benefactors, Kuwait and Saudi Arabia, who were displeased with Jordan's perceived sympathy for Saddam Hussein.[19]

Jordan's economic difficulties spilled over into the Israeli-occupied territories. An unknown number of Palestinians possessing Jordanian passports actually resided in the West Bank. According to Palestinian economist Samir Hleileh, fewer than than 1,000 Palestinian wage-earners from the Gulf were able to return to the occupied territories. The economies of the West Bank and Gaza Strip depended heavily on remittances from the Gulf and wages earned by 120,000 workers who commuted daily to jobs in Israel. The Intifada had already reduced remittances, estimated at $300-$500 million annually in 1987, to only $50 million per year by August 1990.[20] Now even this amount was eliminated.

From the start of the crisis, Israel severely restricted the movement of Palestinian laborers who normally worked in Israel. During the six-week air war, when occupation authorities enforced curfews on the West Bank and Gaza an average of 21 hours per day, fewer than 20 percent of those Palestinians who had jobs in Israel were able to reach their workplaces on any given day, resulting in lost wages estimated at $2 million daily.[21]

The displacement suffered by Palestinians is likely to continue. Those 150,000 who remained in Kuwait experienced along with Kuwaitis the brutality of the seven-month Iraqi occupation, and a few of them even participated in resistance activities. Nevertheless, the Kuwaiti mood has been directed not at showing appreciation to those who cooperated with the resistance, but rather at harassing virtually all young Palestinians because a few did collaborate with the Iraqis. Amnesty International reported that as of early April, of the some 600 Palestinians in prison, scores had been summarily executed, and at least seven more had died as a result of torture during interrogation.[22]

About 1.2 million foreign nationals, including one million Egyptians, were employed in Iraq when that country invaded and occupied Kuwait. The freezing of Iraq's assets and the international embargo on its trade led to widespread lay-offs that affected thousands of workers. After Cairo joined the coalition allied against Iraq, Egyptian workers were often harassed, prompting many of them to obtain the requisite visas to depart Iraq—a bureaucratic headache in the best of times.[23] At least 350,000 Egyptians managed to get out of Iraq by mid-January. Including the estimated 135,000 Egyptian workers who returned from Kuwait, this meant approximately one-half million extra workers looking for jobs in an Egyptian economy already plagued with high levels of unemployment, and the loss of hard-currency remittances estimated at over $1 billion per year.[24]

Egypt was able to weather this economic crisis far better than Jordan or the countries of South Asia. Because it had joined what Jordanian commentator Rami Khoury calls the "cash register coalition," Kuwait, Saudi Arabia, Qatar, and the UAE rewarded Egypt financially by providing outright cash grants, forgiving more than $6 billion in accrued debts, and extending new low-interest loans. The United States wrote off more than $7 billion in Egyptian military debt, and the Paris Club of western creditor governments wrote off another $10 billion in late May.[25] Nevertheless, the expatriate workers who returned home as refugees benefited little from this state-to-state largesse. The promise of hundreds of thousands of jobs for Egyptian workers in Saudi Arabia and Kuwait has yet to materialize.

At least 700,000 Yemeni nationals—out of more than a million living and working in Saudi Arabia—were forced out of the kingdom between September and December 1990 in retaliation for Sana'a's refusal to join the U.S.-led coalition. Riyadh also cut off aid, loans, trade, and preferential oil shipments.[26] Most of the Yemenis were able to take some savings and possessions with them, which helped cushion the blow of unexpected displacement. When personal savings are exhausted, these returned workers may become an economic burden and a source of political instability for the newly-unified country.[27]

Thousands of other workers were also displaced. Virtually all of Kuwait's estimated 60,000 Iranian expatriates, most of them descendants of immigrants who had settled in Kuwait between 1935 and 1955, fled to Iran, leaving behind businesses and property worth up to $10 billion.[28] According to private voluntary aid agencies, more than 35,000 Sudanese worked in Iraq and Kuwait before the crisis; they remitted an estimated $2.7 million per year back to one of Africa's most impoverished countries. According to Khartoum, Sudan also lost $3.4 billion in project loans because the Bashir regime failed to join the anti-Iraq coalition.[29]

Displacement: The Civil War

The difficult situation for the Gulf's expatriate work force pales in comparison to the refugee situation that developed after the war as a result of the unsuccessful uprisings in southern and northern Iraq. During March and April, as many as 2.5 million Iraqis—14 percent of the country's total population—became refugees, fleeing from the soldiers of the Baghdad regime.

These uprisings seem to have begun spontaneously in the cities and towns of both southern and northern Iraq following the country's sudden and humiliating military defeat at the end of February. In the predominantly Shi'a south, hastily organized resistance groups attacked party headquarters, offices of the secret police, and other symbols of repression in all the major cities, and destroyed many key government installations. Because Iraq's population is up to 55 percent Shi'a, senior U.S. officials expressed concern that the Shi'a of southern Iraq were rebelling against the government in Baghdad because it was Sunni, and aimed to set up an Islamic republic allied to Iran.[30] More likely, the people of southern Iraq disdained the Ba'th government, whose officials are of both Shi'a and Sunni origins, for the same reasons as their fellow Iraqis in the central and northern part of the country: They were tired of living in a police state, and weary from the two devastating wars this regime had started.

The people of southern Iraq felt emboldened after February 27 because they witnessed first-hand the disorganized retreat of the Iraqi military as the Allied forces moved into the region. It is significant that the rebellion started in al-Zubair, a mainly Sunni town on the outskirts of Basra and the first town that soldiers retreating from Kuwait passed through. Many frustrated army conscripts were prepared to use their weapons against the government they believed was responsible for the debacle, and it was they who sparked the uprising. The rebels captured virtually all cities and towns in the Tigris-Euphrates river valley, from al-Zubair north to Karbala, and took grisly reprisal against local Ba'th party functionaries, government officials, and suspected secret police informers.[31] Their victories, however, were short-lived. Although Iraqi troops completely lacked the morale that would have enabled them to put up a fight against the well-organized and technologically superior U.S.-led coalition, the regime's Republican Guard units did have considerable experience in suppressing poorly armed civilians and disgruntled draftees. Using brute force, they crushed the disturbances in the south within two weeks.

Estimates of the number killed during the civil strife in the south range around 6,000. Shi'as who participated in the rebellion claim the toll is as high as 100,000. Most nonpartisan observers accept the lower figure. Joost Hiltermann, an editor of *Middle East Report,* toured the cities of southern Iraq in April, and concluded that "a few thousand deaths," rather than tens of thousands, likely occurred during the civil war in the south. Another 10,000 to 20,000 persons may have been wounded. Damage in residential neighborhoods was very extensive, especially in the cities of Najaf, Hilla, Karbala, and Kufa, where entire blocs of houses were demolished.[32]

As the army crushed the uprising, more than 100,000 civilians fled. An estimated 40,000 sought refuge behind the U.S. ceasefire lines in Iraq, and some 70,000 crossed into Iran. The status of these refugees, most of whom seem afraid to return to their homes, has been difficult to resolve. Both Iran and Saudi Arabia—but not Kuwait—have agreed to maintain refugee camps indefinitely.

The fighting in the Kurdish areas of the north was far less intense than in the south. The refugee situation that developed out of the collapse of the Kurdish rebellion, though, was horrendous. Iraq's Kurds number more than 3.5 million, more than 20 percent of Iraq's total population, and live predominantly in the mountainous north. They took over the main towns of Iraqi Kurdistan almost without a fight, and held them for two to three weeks. When the Iraqi army turned its attention from the south to the north at the end of March, the badly organized Kurdish fighters abandoned the towns for the mountains. Once the Kurdish population realized they were defenseless, they panicked and fled, literally overnight. In all, at least 2.3 million people, mostly Kurds but including some Iraqi Turkoman and Christian Chaldeans and Assyrians, headed towards the Iranian, Turkish, and Syrian borders. More than one million refugees had entered Iran by mid-April, and an estimated 450,000 more were camped on the roads leading to Iranian border checkpoints.

At least 500,000 fled into Turkey, and an estimated 350,000 more were in the mountains overlooking the Iraqi-Turkish border.

Why did so many Kurds flee? The one-word explanation of a Kurdish teacher—"Halabja"—may be the most plausible explanation. Halabja is the town in Iraqi Kurdistan that Saddam Hussein ordered bombed with chemical weapons in March 1988 during the final stages of the Iran-Iraq War. An estimated 5,000 Kurds, mostly women and children, died in that attack. This was followed five months later by the chemical bombardment of Kurdish guerrilla bases and the panicked flight of over 100,000 Kurds into Turkey and Iran. During the 1980s, Kurds had already watched Iraqi military forces destroy an estimated 3,000 Kurdish villages and disperse their inhabitants. Since Halabja, virtually all Kurds are convinced that the Baghdad regime would exterminate them if given an opportunity. (According to reliable Iraqi opposition sources, Tariq Aziz acknowledged that the army had used a non-toxic gas to frighten the population in this latest campaign.) This is the kind of fear that drives millions of people to flee for their lives and to refuse to return despite regime assurances of their safety.

The sheer number of refugees overwhelmed the ability of local and international relief agencies to care for them, leading to appalling camp conditions. Diseases swept the camps, claiming the lives of thousands of infants and children.[33] The United States, which maintained throughout March that it would not get involved in Iraq's internal affairs, finally felt compelled to join its European allies in the establishment of a "safe-haven" zone in the north. By the end of May, the presence of U.S. and European troops in a few small towns of northern Iraq had encouraged 350,000 Kurds to return to their homes or to resettle in special refugee camps, but the majority remained wary of returning to Iraq.

The uprisings and their consequences in southern and northern Iraq overshadowed the dislocations that had directly resulted from the allied war of January and February. According to the United Nations, which dispatched a special mission to Iraq to assess the humanitarian needs of the country in the aftermath of the war, as many as 72,000 people were left homeless by the war.[34] Saudi Arabia evacuated several thousand civilians out of the Khafji area before it became a battle zone. Finally, there are three additional categories of displaced persons being handled by the International Committee for the Red Cross (ICRC). These include an estimated 16,000 Iraqi prisoners of war who refuse to be repatriated and remain in limbo at a POW camp in Saudi Arabia, up to 4,000 Kuwaitis still missing and believed to be in Iraq, and several thousand stateless persons—*bidun*—mostly tribespeople of Iraqi and Iranian origin who had lived in Kuwait for decades without citizenship and whom the Kuwaiti government will not permit to return.[35]

Devastation

It remains to be seen if the Kurdish refugee problem can be resolved through repatriation and/or resettlement. At that point Iraq can get on with rebuilding its shattered economy. Authorities estimate that the destruction of bridges, roads, rail lines, port facilities, homes, shops, hospitals, factories, and oil installations amounts to $170 billion. It is unclear whether this figure includes the considerable damage in both southern and northern Iraq inflicted during the post-war uprisings. Southern cities such as Karbala and Najaf, which were spared during the allied bombing campaign, were particularly hard hit during the anti-Saddam uprising, and whole neighborhoods were demolished by tanks.[36] More immediately serious has been the destruction of infrastructure directly related to the health of the population: water purification plants, sewerage lines, and electric generating stations. By one estimate, 80 percent of the country's electric power generating stations were destroyed.[37] A 10-member Harvard University medical team visited Iraq in early May and reported that 18 out of Iraq's 20 generating plants were incapacitated or destroyed. In the three months after the cease-fire, Iraq has raised its generating capacity from 4 percent to 22 percent of prewar capacity. The inability to provide sanitary water, especially in the urban areas of southern Iraq, makes it difficult to contain potentially deadly communicable diseases such as gastrointestinal infections, typhoid fever, and cholera, all of which had appeared in the Basra area by April. The Harvard team's report stressed a direct correlation between this destruction and the subsequent breakdown in public health, and forecast that in the next year a minimum of 170,000 additional children under the age of five would die from infectious diseases as a result.[38]

The damage in Kuwait was at least as extensive. Authorities have estimated that it will cost at least $20 billion to repair the damage to infrastructure, including streets, roads, electrical grids, medical facilities, the airport, harbors, and oil installations. It is expected to take as long as five years to restore the country to its status before the invasion. Even then, Kuwait may not be as well off as before this catastrophe. The 600 oil wells that Iraqi forces set afire as they left the country were burning away around two million barrels of oil per day—more than Kuwait used to produce. As of late May, less than a quarter of those fires had been extinguished.

Kuwait's burning oil wells are causing unprecedented environmental damage and affecting the health of millions of people in the area. The smoke darkens the skies over Kuwait, southern Iraq, and southwestern Iran for the greater part of the daylight hours. It also pollutes the air with gases such as sulphur, nitrogen oxide, and hydrocarbons that interfere with breathing, especially in persons with respiratory ailments and young children. These noxious pollutants are equivalent to 10 times the average daily emissions from all U.S. industrial and utility plants.[39] The soot and gases from the oil fires mix with atmospheric moisture to form acid rain. This blackish and oily rain has damaged crops in both Iraq and Iran, raising concern for this year's grain harvests. The acid rain has spread as far as southern Turkey and western Pakistan.[40]

The acid rain also seeps into ground-water supplies, contaminating drinking water with chemicals such as lead and cadmium. World Health Organization Director-General Hiroshi Nakajima reported in April that samples of drinking water from southwestern Iran contained levels of lead that were up to six times higher than what was considered medically safe. Regular ingestion of even small amounts of lead can cause mental retardation in children. Since the area of highest water lead levels, the flat plain extending from the Shatt al-Arab, borders southern Iraq, it is likely that Iraq's ground water supplies also are contaminated. As Kuwait's burning oil-well fires are extinguished, the health risks from the toxic smoke and acid rain will diminish, but oil-industry experts predict that it will take at least a year to put out all of the fires—a long enough period to build up unhealthy accumulations of dangerous chemicals in soils and water sources.

The several million gallons of Kuwaiti oil that the Iraqis spilled into the Persian Gulf in January will have long-term environmental consequences for the region. The largest oil slick, estimated to contain at least 3.3 million gallons of oil, continues to endanger the unique marine life of the Gulf: coral reefs, sea turtles, sea cows, shrimp beds, special fish species, and various local and migratory birds. The slick has remained in the northern Gulf. The slicks are beginning to take their toll on the fishing industry. In southern Iran, where fish constitutes an important source of dietary protein, complaints that fish smells oily and sometimes is inedible have sharply reduced the market for fresh fish, idling many fishermen.

This war has been an unmitigated disaster for millions of people in the Middle East and beyond. The many tens of thousands killed, the billions of dollars of property destruction, the millions of displaced persons and disrupted lives, the uncounted thousands with permanent physical and psychological scars, and the badly damaged economies are far more devastating than anything that has happened in the region in this century. Living conditions in Iraq, Kuwait, and throughout the Middle East and South Asia are deteriorating badly as a direct consequence of this war, which has shattered the morale of millions of people. In Iraq and Kuwait, and even in nearby Iran, disease from contaminated water and polluted air will be killing and maiming innocent people for years to come. According to UNICEF, the war will result in deprivation for some 5 million children in Kuwait, Iraq, Jordan, Yemen, and the occupied Palestinian territories. "We can speak with alarming, grave assurance of a lost generation," says UNICEF's Middle East Regional Director Richard Reid.[41] The policial, social, and economic consequences of the U.S. assault on Iraq, and the Iraqi regime's consequent assault on its own people, will afflict the region and the world well into the next century.

Notes

1. See for example George Joffe, "Kuwait: Systematic Terror," *Middle East International,* October 12, 1990.
2. Telephone interview with Aziz Abu Hamad of Middle East Watch, May 28, 1991; *New York Times,* April 2, 1991.
3. A total of 343 allied soldiers died during the six-month confrontation, including 266 U.S. deaths (122 of them non-combatant accidents); other fatalities included 44 British, two French, one Italian, 29 Saudis, nine Egyptian, and six from the United Arab Emirates. See William Arkin, et al., *On Impact: Modern Warfare and the Environment, a Case Study of the Gulf War,* Washington: Greenpeace, May 29, 1991. Information on Palestinian deaths collected by Joost Hiltermann, an editor of *Middle East Report,* from the Union of Palestinian Medical Relief Committees and Maqassed Hospital in Jerusalem, during a trip to the West Bank and Gaza, April 22-May 7, 1991, on behalf of Physicians for Human Rights.
4. The "official" unofficial estimate is in the *New York Times,* April 9, 1991. The Iraqi doctor's estimate is from Joost Hiltermann, who visited Iraq from March 23 to April 10, 1991 on behalf of Physicians for Human Rights.
5. For a sobering survey of the munitions used by U.S. and European forces in the war, see Michael T. Klare, "High-Death Weapons of the Gulf War," *The Nation,* June 3, 1991. The estimated 100,000 battle deaths comes on top of eight years of war with Iran that resulted in at least 100,000 Iraqi deaths, although the Iraqi govenment has yet to publish any reliable figures on its casualties during the war with Iran. For a brief discussion of the problems with casualty data see Joseph Kechichian, "National Security," in Helen C. Metz, ed., *Iraq, A Country Study,* Washington: Library of Congress, 1990, p. 245.
6. Iraq's population was 17.5 million in the 1987 census, and is growing at a rate of more than 3 percent per year. 100,000 battle deaths is equivalent to the United States losing more than 1.4 million in the war, and 300,000 wounded is equivalent to about 4.25 million non-fatal casualties.

7. Interview with Joost Hiltermann. For an early discussion of civilian casualties, see Hiltermann, "Calculating 'Collateral Damage'," *Middle East Report*, March-April 1991, p. 3.
8. *Washington Post*, April 9, 1991.
9. There are no accurate data on the number of refugees who died during April and May due to the lack of proper medical care. The UN, relying upon information provided by various international voluntary agencies, reports that as many as 2,000 persons per day were dying in the Iranian camps during the height of the health emergency in late April. See further: *New York Times*, April 28, 1991.
10. *Middle East International*, August 31, 1990, p. 10.
11. *Washington Post*, May 2, 1991.
12. *New York Times*, May 11, 1991. The U.S. Army Corps of Engineers was responsible for most of the restoration of services which had occurred.
13. See *Middle East International*, August 31, 1990, p. 15; Martha Wenger, "Who Are the Refugees," *Middle East Report*, January-February 1991, p. 32; and *Washington Post*, March 30, 1991.
14. Estimates on Asian workers in Kuwait and Iraq are adapted from *Middle East International*, August 31, 1990, p. 15; *The Independent* (London), August 30, 1991; *Washington Post*, March 30, 1991; and United Nations Disaster Relief Coordinator (UNDRC), "Tentative Numbers of Displaced Persons in Jordan," March 12, 1991.
15. For further statistics on the impact of the war on Bangladesh and other Asian countries see UNCTAD, "Report on the Economic Consequences of the Gulf Crisis on Low-Income Countries," New York: United Nations, March 1991.
16. *Middle East International*, September 14, 1990, pp. 12-13; and Yahya Sadowski, "Arab Economies After the Gulf War: Power, Poverty, and Petrodollars," *Middle East Report*, May-June 1991, p. 5.
17. See the U.S. Government Accounting Office (GAO) Report to the Chair of the Subcommittee on Europe and the Middle East, Committee on Foreign Affairs, House of Representatives, *Persian Gulf Crisis: Humanitarian Relief Provided to Evacuees from Kuwait and Iraq*, March 1991 (GAO/NSIAD-91-160). The information on those fleeing to Syria comes from Iraqi sources in Damascus.
18. UNDRC, "Tentative Numbers…" See also *New York Times*, September 4 and 7, 1990; and *Financial Times* (London), September 4, 1990.
19. Sadowski, p. 10; United Nations Children's Fund (UNICEF), *Jordanian Children in the Eye of the Storm*, Amman, February 1991.
20. Hleileh provided his estimate to Joost Hiltermann in early May 1991. See also Daoud Kuttab, "The Palestinian Economy and the Gulf Crisis," *Middle East International*, September 14, 1990, p. 16.
21. For more on the problems in the occupied territories as a result of the war, see *The Middle East*, March 1991, pp. 36-7; Penny Johnson, "Letter from the Curfew Zone," *Middle East Report*, May-June 1991, pp. 38-39; and *The Palestinians and the War in the Gulf*, Washington, D.C.: Center for Policy Analysis on Palestine, February 1991.
22. "Kuwait: Amnesty International calls on Emir to intervene over continuing torture and killings," AI Press Release, April 18, 1991.
23. On the problems of Egyptian workers in Iraq see *Middle East International*, February 22, 1991, p. 6.
24. Sadowski, p. 10.
25. Sadowski, p. 5; *New York Times*, May 27, 1991.
26. Sheila Carapico, "Yemen: Unification and the Gulf War," *Middle East Report*, May-June 1991, p. 26.

27. Conversation with Prof. Robert Burrowes of the University of Washington, Seattle. For a more optimistic assessment of Yemen's adjustment in the aftermath of the war, see *Middle East International,* April 19, 1991, p. 25.

28. See *Iran Times,* September 7 and 14, 1990.

29. "The Economic Impact of the Gulf Crisis on Third World Countries," memo to the Foreign Affairs Select Committee [of the British House of Commons] by Oxfam, World Development Movement, Save the Children, et al., March 1991, p. 6; the figure on remittances and project aid is from *Al-Majalla,* January 16-22, 1991, provided by Khalid Medeni. Doug Henwood also provided valuable assistance in compiling displacement figures.

30. This view was conveyed at several off-the-record press briefings at both the Pentagon and State Department in late February and early March 1991.

31. *Washington Post,* April 9, 1991. See also Joost Hiltermann, "Bomb Now, Die Later," *Mother Jones,* July-August 1991.

32. Interview, Joost Hiltermann, May 18, 1991.

33. For a detailed and graphic description of medical conditions in refugee camps along the Iraq-Turkey border see transcript of the radio interview with Dr. Joanie Guptil of Medicins Sans Frontiers, "As It Happens," Canadian Broadcasting Corporation, May 3, 1991.

34. "Report to the Secretary-General on humanitarian needs in Kuwait and Iraq in the immediate post-crisis environment," New York: United Nations S/22366, March 20, 1991, p. 11.

35. Interview with ICRC spokeswoman Yetta Sorenson, on "As it Happens," Canadian Broadcasting Corporation, May 3, 1991. See also *Los Angeles Times,* May 20, 1991.

36. Interview, Joost Hiltermann, May 18, 1991.

37. Ahmad Chalabi, an Iraqi banker and exile opposition figure, provides this estimate in the *Washington Post,* April 9, 1991.

38. See accounts in the *Los Angeles Times,* May 21, 1991, and the *New York Times* and *Washington Post,* May 22, 1991.

39. *New York Times,* April 28, 1991. On environmental damage from the Gulf War, see also: *Gulf War Environmental Information Service, Impact on the Land and Atmosphere,* Cambridge, U.K.: World Conservation Monitoring Centre; *Potential Environmental and Public Health Effects from Attacks on Petrochemical Facilities,* Washington, D.C.: Friends of the Earth; *The Hidden Casualties: The Environmental Consequences of the Gulf Conflict: Interview by John M. Miller,* San Francisco: Arms Control Research Center; *The Long-Term Impact of Oil Spills, Chemical Weapons in the Persian Gulf,* and *On Impact: Modern Warfare and the Environment, a Case Study of the Gulf War,* Washington, D.C.: Greenpeace; and *War in the Gulf: an Environmental Perspective,* San Francisco: Political Ecology Group.

40. *Iran Times,* March 1, 1991.

41. *The Guardian* (London), March 28, 1991.

CHAPTER 8

OPERATION DESERT DISASTER

Environmental Costs of the War

Joni Seager

As I write this in June 1991, the outlines of an enormous Gulf-region environmental disaster are slowly emerging from the fog of disinterest and misinformation that has characterized western official and media representations of the war over the past eight months. Following on the heels of the official end of the war, a UN observer team describes conditions in Iraq as "apocalyptic"; a spokesperson for the returning Kuwaiti government speaks of an ecological catastrophe unparalleled in global history; the Saudi Arabian government has issued no public assessments of the state of their environment, groaning under the weight of one of the largest and fastest military mobilizations in recent history, but there is every indication that their country, too, will bear ecological scars of this conflict for decades to come.

The saddest and most damning fact about this environmental disaster was its predictability. In fact, the environmental costs of the war were predicted both by environmentalists and military spokespeople alike in the early days of the military buildup in the Gulf.[1] The predictability of the disaster derives in part from our larger understanding of militarized

An earlier version of this article appeared in Haim Bresheeth and Nira Yuval-Davis, eds., *Radical Perspectives on the Gulf War*, London: Zed Books, 1991.

environmental destruction, and from lessons drawn from other parts of the world, and in part from an understanding of the geography and the war-waging specific to the Gulf.

Militaries are the most destructive environmental institutions in the modern world; they have the technology and the global reach to destroy and poison entire regions and vast ecosystems. The environmental damage that is always left in the wake of military conflict continues to kill people and maim economies long after the guns have been rolled away. In this context, the Gulf region is merely the latest addition to a global roll-call of military environmental casualties. Central America is teetering on the brink of widespread ecological disaster as a result of decades of militarized activities there. Entire islands and archipelagoes in the South Pacific are contaminated forever, and some have entirely disappeared, "vaporized" in military lingo, as a result of nuclear testing and chemical dumping by the French, British, and U.S. militaries. Large regions of Afghanistan are virtually uninhabitable as a result of the USSR military incursion there. Thousands of towns across the United States, and tens of thousands of communities around the world, are poisoned and threatened by local military environmental violations.

Vietnam offers perhaps the most vivid example of the power of militarized environmental destruction. Large parts of that country are permanently damaged as a result of military activities during the war in Southeast Asia. Over the course of the war, the United States dropped more than 25 million bombs on Vietnam. Almost half the forests in the southern half of the country were soaked with defoliants. Over half of the country's coastal mangrove swamps were destroyed, and nearly 5 million acres of forests—almost 17 percent of the entire country—were damaged, many irreparably so. The ecological catastrophe wrought by the war has snowballed as a war-numbed people try to eke out a living in a poisoned land. Lacking forest cover, soil quality has deteriorated. Flooding has increased dramatically. Farmers, trying to grow food on degraded land, have turned to heavy pesticide use to try to boost production; as a consequence, chemical run-off from agricultural pesticides is now poisoning much of Vietnam's water supply. The health of Vietnamese women, more so than men, has suffered from the poisoning of their land. Many of the chemicals used by militaries cause reproductive disorders, and many are teratogenic (deformation-causing); Vietnamese women today have the highest rate of spontaneous abortion in the world and cervical cancer rates among the highest.

In the United States in the fall of 1990, there was considerable media interest in comparing and contrasting the looming Gulf War with the

Vietnam War. In point of fact, operational parallels turned out to not be particularly valid, but the environmental lessons are stark.

Geography

Before August 1990, most North Americans barely knew where to look for Kuwait on a map; many still can't tell the Red Sea from the Persian Gulf. Eurocentric images of the peninsular Middle East are largely shaped by myth and misinformation, and unfortunately the recent frenzy of reporting from and on the region only reinforced some of the worst preconceptions. For example, western media coverage of the region where the coalition forces were amassing in Saudi Arabia relied heavily on descriptors such as "sterile," "empty," "wasteland," and "barren." Reporting was typically accompanied by photographs of columns of soldiers half-obscured by rolling dust storms as they trooped across sandy plains. The north and northeast of Saudi Arabia was portrayed as little more than a wasteland, a representation that is untrue and, worse, that supports a smug carelessness about the ecological impact of a half-million strong army setting up base in a fragile, arid land environment.

The designation of land as "wasteland" is usually tinged with racist presumptions and the term carries with it colonial overtones; "wasteland" is a culturally-constructed notion, not one rooted in ecological or geographical sense. There is virtually no part of this planet that does not sustain a complex and rich ecological web. In some ecosystems, including deserts and polar regions, biotic processes may be slowed and operate at a repressed rate, but that does not mean that they are any less viable or valuable than environments that appear more vibrant and full. In fact, what it means is that they are even more fragile and vulnerable to disruption than are other ecosystems.

Desert environments in particular take a long time to recover from damage, largely as a result of the lack of regenerative moisture. The north and northeast region of Saudi Arabia is correctly portrayed as a desert, but incorrectly portrayed as a wasteland; it is one of three large ecosystems in the Gulf War "theater" that have suffered tremendous environmental damage as a result of the military buildup and the war.

The vast riverine/estuarine system in Iraq is the second of the regional ecosystems to bear the brunt of the war damage. The geography of Iraq is dominated by the Tigris and the Euphrates rivers, which converge just north of Basra. The confluence region marks the ancient land of Mesopotamia, known popularly as the "cradle of civilization." The contemporary geography of Iraq is still very much defined by the rivers, which are major corridors of transportation and provide most of the country's water for irrigation as well as drinking. The city of Baghdad, for example, takes 95 percent of its drinking water from the Tigris River. The Tigris is the main population corridor in Iraq, and the major urban and industrial centers of the country follow its course. The fact that these centers are river-based is especially important in assessing the damage from coalition bombing: chemical contamination from bombed factories, for example, will be flushed into the river, and eventually into the Persian Gulf itself.

The Tigris empties into the Persian Gulf through a network of marshes and wetlands at the river's mouth. These wetlands are of hemispheric significance, both for marine life and international bird migrations. The Gulf is already a highly stressed marine environment—it contains more oil than any other body of water in the world, for example. Nonetheless, it is a highly productive marine environment, home to thriving populations of turtles, dolphins, whales, birds, and dugongs (manatee-like mammals), as well as coral reef communities and major fisheries. For many of these species, the Gulf is a critical habitat: Gulf islands are primary nesting grounds for green turtles; the Gulf represents the extreme western range of the dugongs, and supports a population of about 7,000. The Gulf is the third ecosystem to bear in mind in considering the environmental impact of the war.

The Military Presence

The ecosystems of Kuwait and Iraq appear to have suffered the most severe battle damage. But the environments of Saudi Arabia, and to a lesser extent the Gulf rim states of Oman, the United Arab Emirates, and Bahrain, were all significantly degraded by the sheer weight and nature of the military presence in the region.

The north and northeast of Saudi Arabia, where most of the coalition troops amassed along the border, is thinly populated with few permanent settlements of any size. Within a period of five months, this region experienced a population boom of unprecedented scale. Between late August 1990 and early January 1991, more than 20 governments poured hundreds of thousands of soldiers (70 percent of them American) and thousands of tanks, fighting vehicles, and assorted heavy equipment, along with thousands of tons of support equipment and arms, into these fragile arid lands. The total imported military population tipped over a half million. This is a substantial population, equivalent to a mid-sized city in the United States.

A population of this size generates a tremendous amount of waste, both sewage and solid (garbage). A sewage expert at the U.S. Environmental Protection Agency (EPA) reports that an "expected, conservative" average of sewage production in the United States is 60 to 70 gallons per day per person; actual figures from cities around the country put the number closer to 115 gallons of sewage waste per person per day. Even if we halve the conservative EPA estimate, allowing for the limited support infrastructure for the troops in Saudi Arabia, and assuming a tight control on water use, this still means that the force of half a million was producing a minimum of between 15 and 20 million gallons of sewage a day.

The amount of garbage piling up in Saudi Arabia is also staggering. Inhabitants of most industrialized countries produce an average of 2.5 to 4 pounds of garbage a day. To the "normal" quantities of garbage that one can expect to be produced by the troops in Saudi Arabia, huge quantities of heavy-duty packaging materials must be added: every item of food, support, and equipment for the troops was flown or shipped in, most in bulk crates and cartons. Plastic waste may be a particular problem—the ubiquitous disposable water bottles that we saw soldiers clutching in every press photo have to go somewhere.

In response to my inquiries, the Pentagon said that "disposal of solid and sewage waste is, by agreement, the responsibility of the host country." So, in addition to the other logistical and political responsibilities of hosting a huge multinational force, it appears that the Saudis now must also dispose of the wastes from an added population that is almost equal in size to their largest city. Even if every attempt was made to dispose of these wastes in the most environmentally responsible manner, Saudi facilities would be overwhelmed. But in fact, most of the troops were and are located in a region with few permanent settlements and no nearby disposal facilities. So, the actual means of waste disposal is most likely just a big hole in the desert—or, rather, several big holes.

Garbage and human waste take a long time to degrade in the desert. With little moisture to promote biological degradation, the waste that is being dumped in the desert today will sit undisturbed and undegraded literally for decades. We may be witnessing the creation of a true "wasteland."

In humid climates, hazardous substances from garbage dumped in open pits or landfills leach into water supplies. Such leaching is unlikely to be a problem in the desert. However, liquid sewage will migrate through sandy soils, and there is always the possibility that the underground aquifer water supply in Saudi Arabia could be contaminated by raw human waste. This threat escalates as large numbers of soldiers are left sitting in concentrated pockets for long periods of time—as was the case before and after battle deployment. The effects of aquifer contamination may not be detected for several months—especially if environmental assessment analysts, already coping with one of the world's largest ecological catastrophes, turn their attention and resources to problems that seem more pressing.

A more likely and dangerous threat to both the underground Saudi Arabian water system as well as the local ecology is the astounding array of toxic substances that accompany all military maneuvers. The U.S. military is this country's largest polluter, and the largest producer of toxic substances. Because of its size, the U.S. military ranks among the world's largest generators of hazardous waste, producing, according to a recent article in *Nuclear Times,* nearly a ton of toxic pollutants every minute.[2] Militaries in most other industrialized countries hold lesser, but similar, records of toxic distinction. Not only do they manufacture and consume vast quantities of chemicals of all description, solvents, paints, PCBs, cyanides, acids, radioactive materials, and poisons, but most militaries are protected polluters. Using "national security" as a shield, their flagrant polluting practices have gone unchecked for decades. Public scrutiny and outrage are piercing this veil of protection, and military facilities in the United States are now subject to all major environmental regulations, but armies remain environmentally dangerous forces. By the Pentagon's own estimates, it has at least 14,000 toxic sites at more than 1,500 military facilities across the United States, almost 100 of which have been placed on the federal Superfund priority clean-up list. The total bill for cleaning up military facilities in the United States will cost at least $20 billion and could easily reach $200 billion.

Even if environmental regulations are zealously applied to U.S. military facilities, which has generally not been the case, regulation still stops at the border. U.S. military facilities and activities located overseas are not subject to U.S. environmental laws. Basing agreements often exempt foreign armies from local environmental laws. Even in the cases where bases do technically fall under the environmental jurisdiction of the host government, it has never been clear that environmental regulators of the foreign host have the authority to enter or inspect U.S. military facilities, let alone penalize them in the event of violations. In practice, host regulation of foreign military forces is really no regulation. The Pentagon has successfully suppressed reports on its foreign bases operations, but a *Los Angeles Times* investigation this past summer concluded that U.S. militaries in foreign lands, "operating in secret and far outside the reach of American environmental regulation [have] left a quagmire of chemical contamination around the globe that will cost billions of dollars to correct and will damage American foreign-policy interests for years to come."[3]

The Saudi Arabian government has a relatively recent but strong commitment to improving and protecting its environment. However, environmental issues are always placed on the back burner when a larger threat—in this case the Iraqis—is perceived. There is no evidence that the Saudis have raised environmental issues with the foreign military forces, nor can the Pentagon confirm whether they have signed a memorandum of environmental understanding (a frequent practice when U.S. forces operate overseas) with the Saudis.

The forces in the Gulf are using a wide array of highly toxic paints for recamouflaging all their equipment, solvents for cleaning equipment, oil for fuel and machinery maintenance, and decontaminating chemicals. They brought with them more than 1,000 tactical nuclear weapons, and quite possibly even small arms containing radioactive materials; they were certainly using weapons that contain explosive chemicals and heavy metals.

The thousands of gallons of used oils and solvents generated by the daily use and maintenance of thousands of vehicles over several months will produce high levels of chronic pollution unless there are proper safeguards against leaks, as well as provisions for safe disposal. In addition to this low-level continuous pollution, high-volume spills and accidental leakages of stored fuels and chemicals are an omnipresent threat in a military operation of this size. Pentagon officials would not provide information on responsibility for treatment and disposal of hazardous wastes in the Gulf "theater."

As a general rule, underground water supplies are especially vulnerable to chemical, solvent, and oil contamination. Water is one of the scarcest resources in the Middle East. In recent years the Saudis have undertaken massive agricultural expansion, based entirely on irrigation, to diversify their economy and reduce their dependence on imported food. The scheme has been a success in that Saudi farmers now produce 35 percent of the country's food, up from 15 percent in 1984. But the environmental costs have been high. The agricultural sector consumes an estimated 90 percent of all water used in Saudi Arabia, the largest share of which comes from virtually nonrenewable underground aquifers.

Outside observers suggest that the Saudis are depleting their underground water supply at an alarming rate. Chemical contamination of the scarce, and diminishing, water will pose a serious threat to the country's agriculture and would throw the economy into chaos. Ironically, because the aquifers are partially depleted, the water table has dropped measurably in recent years; as a result, surface contaminants are less likely to migrate into underground supplies. Nonetheless, the implications of chemical contamination of water supplies are so severe that the threat must be taken seriously.

The north and northeast of Saudi Arabia is physiographically a combination of sand desert and low-lying plain. It is, in the judgment of a Saudi wildlife specialist, an already much-abused and much-degraded environment—and thus in an especially precarious state. It sustains a wildlife population of small mammals (including jackals, hares, and sand cats), both domestic and feral camels, and insects, reptiles, and birds; larger mammals such as oryx and gazelles were hunted out within the last 20 to 30 years. Parts of the desert have a surprisingly heavy vegetation base; press photos show a consistent ground cover of brushes, grasses, and shrubs across much of the landscape.

Arid lands such as these are very susceptible to long-lasting surface disturbances. General Patton used the Mojave Desert in California for tank training in World War II; his army's tracks are still there, almost as legible as the day they were made. Large parts of North Africa still bear the clear markings of World War II military maneuvers. The 1973 war between Egypt, Israel, and Syria wrought severe changes in the configuration of the desert in the North Sinai.[4]

As we saw every night on our TV screens, thousands of tanks, heavy equipment, and track vehicles of all shapes and sizes have ranged freely for several months over the Saudi desert. Their activities have placed enormous stress on an already strained environment. In Kuwait, similarly, the invading Iraqi troops and then the pursuing coalition forces have caused enormous damage to the desert topography and ecology. Further, the coalition forces built an extremely complex infrastructure in the deserts of Saudi Arabia—laying down roads, paving runways, building semi-permanent housing and support buildings, and cutting holes in the desert surface. These activities have breached the desert's natural shield cover, destroyed vegetation, damaged wildlife habitats, and disrupted surface-water patterns.

The extent to which deserts can survive such pounding depends, in great measure, on the extent to which the perennial and annual vegetation cover survives. Large-scale heavy-equipment maneuvers and large-scale infrastructure construction have apparently destroyed the perennial cover over much of Saudi Arabia and Kuwait. And what the heavy equipment doesn't crush, soldiers and refugees will no doubt strip for kindling. The seed bank for annual vegetation will also have been destroyed. Deserts are "pulse" environments. They go through seasonal cycles of very low biotic activity, interspersed with enormous bursts of energy: when the rains come, seeds that lie dormant on or just below the desert surface for much of the year spark into life. This dormant annual seed bank has undoubtedly been destroyed by heavy traffic (both foot and vehicle) that pulverizes seeds or buries them at a depth at which they cannot germinate.

We do not yet have an assessment of desert-ecology damage in the war zone. However, if any significant portion of both the annual and perennial desert vegetation has been destroyed, the consequences will ripple throughout the entire ecosystem. For example, just the loss of vegetation could have dramatic long-term consequences for regional ecology. With reduced plant cover, solar radiation from the desert surface will increase; the combination of reduced plant cover and increased reflectivity has the potential to affect local rainfall. A number of atmospheric scientists, working from evidence gathered in the African Sahara and deserts in Rajasthan, India, posit that a combination of vegetation removal, surface disturbance, and increased dust concentration in the atmosphere can reinforce dry spells or droughts and increase the tendency to aridity. Disruption of rainfall, when there's so little of it, can tip the ecological balance into irreversible decline.

The breaching of the desert surface in Kuwait, northeast Saudi Arabia, and southern Iraq will destabilize the desert topography. The first result will be a substantial increase in sand and dust storms. Perhaps more seriously there will be increased soil erosion and instability in sand surfaces which will result in the formation of new, moving fields of sand dunes that could threaten to engulf agricultural lands, settlements, roads, and surface water systems.

Much of the desert in both Saudi Arabia and Kuwait is used by herders and nomads as a seasonal grazing ground; the movement of people through the region is synchronized with the environmental pulse. With 500,000 soldiers in their grazing range, not to mention months of almost continuous live ammunition fire and then the war, this cycle will be disrupted: The Bedouins with their herds, this year at least, won't move. This in turn means that they will be grazing more intensively and continuously in the regions they migrate from. If the desert ecology is tipped out of balance over a longer period of time, grazing patterns throughout the region will shift and could place extreme pressure on parts of the country far from the arena of "Operation Desert Shield."

Throughout the buildup to war, there were constant reports in the media of "live fire" exercises in the desert. On average, 5 percent of all shells do not explode when fired, yet they remain potentially explosive for years—sometimes decades. When ordnance does explode, it releases chemicals, heavy metals, and, depending on the weapons, radioactive materials. Many areas of the world that have been subject to massive bombardments in target practice or war are now permanently uninhabitable.

In addition, both the Iraqis and the anti-Iraq forces laid mines along the Iraq-Saudi Arabia border and throughout Kuwait. Large parts of Saudi Arabia, Kuwait, and Iraq are now strewn with shells, unexploded ordnance, and miles of live mines. Despite bravado American claims that they will force Iraq to identify and remove their mine fields, this possibility is at best illusory, particularly now that the Iraqi military has been reduced to shambles.[5] For its part, the American military has not publicly discussed its plans for removal of its own mines and ordnance. The litter of tens of thousands of rounds of unexploded ordnance and thousands of live mines will render large parts of Iraq, Saudi Arabia, and Kuwait "off limits" for years to come; human and animal populations in the area will be at risk for decades. The notion of national environmental "sacrifice zones" is unpopular here in the United States; there is no reason to expect that it will be any more popular in Saudi Arabia or "liberated" Kuwait.

While most eyes were fixed on the land-based buildup of troops, a sizeable naval force assembled in the Gulf. There is no information available on the disposal of wastes (hazardous, sewage, or solid) from these ships, but it is not unduly cynical to expect a massive pollution trail from the naval presence. Amphibious-landing exercises on the coasts of the Gulf states, especially in Oman, Kuwait, and Saudi Arabia, have wreaked havoc with coastal ecology: Wildlife habitats have been destroyed, ordnance and mines litter the beaches and coastal waters, abandoned vehicles and fortifications constructed from military "junk" blockade access to the sea, and coastal archaeological sites have been totally demolished. Even seemingly minor and mundane "operational procedures" leave their mark on the marine habitat: For example, it is a standard safety procedure for jets to dump their excess fuel before landing on carrier ships. Each of the tens of thousands of jet "sorties" carries an environmental price.

All of the environmental effects outlined so far are consequences merely of the military presence in the Gulf region: even if the forces on both sides had only occupied territory for several months and then withdrawn without coming to war, their presence would leave an indelible mark on the ecology of the region. But it is, of course, the escalation of military presence into military conflict that may well have pushed the environment of the Gulf to the breaking point.

War

In the last months of 1990, western newspapers regularly featured maps of Iraq identifying probable target sites for the anticipated coalition bombing: nuclear facilities, chemical-weapons production facilities, industrial sites, urban centers. The dots of targets on the maps snaked north and west throughout the country, following the course of the Tigris River. These facilities were attacked early in the war, and repeatedly. By late January, the U.S. military reported that over 500 "sorties" had been flown against 31 Iraqi chemical and nuclear plants; they reported that several of these facilities had been "reduced to rubble," and that all targeted facilities had been seriously disabled. (It should be noted that this bombing is in direct contravention of a UN Resolution of December 4, 1990 that specifically prohibits attacks on nuclear facilities.) Despite the damage caused to these facilities, of which the U.S. military was unduly proud, Pentagon spokesmen hastened to add that they are "99 percent" confident that no chemical or radiation contamination resulted. On the face of it, this seems an implausible claim, and it serves us well to remember that the U.S. military is not entirely forthcoming when it comes to bomb-damage information, nor is the military a reliable narrator in environmental matters.

Independent observers suggest that there is considerable danger of chemical and nuclear contamination when working nuclear and chemical plants and storage facilities are destroyed. The Iraqi military is presumed to have had stockpiles of chemical weapons including mustard gas, hydrogen cyanide, nerve gases such as tabun, sarin, and phosgene, and biological agents such as anthrax, botulism, and plague organisms. Iraq reportedly had the capacity to produce as much as 700 tons of chemical-warfare agents annually, and it has reportedly stockpiled literally thousands of tons of mustard gas and unknown quantities of other chemical substances. Many of these gases are stored in liquid form; the intense heat from a bomb explosion on storage facilities would vaporize the liquid, releasing clouds of contaminants that would create acute local poisoning, and perhaps spread over several dozen miles.

The incineration of materials stores at Iraqi installations may well have generated a variety of toxins, including cyanide, dioxin, and PCBs. The use of water to put out fires caused by the bombing of chemical facilities would leach the chemicals deep into the soil, or wash them into rivers. Moreover, while substances such as nerve gas dissipate quickly, other substances such as mustard gas and anthrax remain carcinogenic and toxic for years. Anthrax contamination, in particular, would create 'dead zones' that will be uninhabitable for decades. As in Vietnam and Bhopal, one would expect that among civilians, women will suffer health damage first and longest from any widespread chemical contamination. Chemical, radioactive, and biological releases are immediately life-threatening; but they also threaten riverine and underground water supplies, agricultural lands, and food stocks, posing a long-lasting health and environmental threat.

In the absence of reliable information about the current state of affairs in Iraq, there are only gleanings of information about possible chemical contamination. Several members of the multinational Peace Camp on the Saudi/Iraq border, who relocated to Baghdad for several days after the disbanding of the Camp in late January, report fleeing acrid chemical clouds wafting through a residential section of the city. In early February, a spokesman for the Patriotic Union of Kurdistan, an Iraqi opposition group, asserted that Allied attacks against chemical and ammunition plants had led to widespread contamination of water resources.[6]

In the coming months, as the horrors of devastation inflicted on Iraq come to light, we should expect reports to be corroborated of possibly severe chemical and biological contamination of areas in the vicinity of bombed factories and storage facilities. The effects of such contamination, however, might be difficult to distinguish from the generalized environmental havoc that will kill tens of thousands of people in Iraq. Similarly, if chemical contamination has travelled through the river system into the Gulf, it may never be clear whether marine animal die-offs in the Gulf were caused by the massive oil spills or by chemical agents masked by the oil.

The oil spills in the Gulf caused an international stir. But despite a massive press presence in the Gulf region, news reports on the environmental effects of the Gulf War were as murky as the oil slick itself—what is clear is that there was more to the spilling of oil than meets the eye. On January 24, 1991, Baghdad Radio announced that the U.S.-led forces had bombed two oil tankers in the Kuwaiti harbor, releasing large quantities of oil. American military spokespeople dismissed these claims, describing the tankers as strategic targets. Then, two days later, the Americans announced that Iraqi forces had opened the spigots on one or more oil pipelines, pouring oil directly into the Gulf. Cries of outrage and of "environmental terrorism" filled the press, and pictures of panicked, wide-eyed, dying oil-slicked cormorants splashed across every front page. Several days later, in a minor briefing note, the Americans admitted that the Iraqi-caused oil slick had not yet hit land, and that the oil that was killing the birds on the beaches was in fact a slick released from earlier oil-installation attacks, including the U.S. bombing of the tankers. Further, reading behind the smug headlines that U.S. "surgical" bombing had stopped the oil spilling from pipelines into the Gulf, it appears that this bombing only stopped the release of oil at the Gulf outlet—it didn't stop the oil flow itself. From all reports, oil was still flowing from the damaged pipeline several days after the "surgical" bombing, (and it may still be), spilling on land instead of sea. From an ecological point of view, this is not a substantial improvement.

Military actions that result in the intentional or predictable releases of large quantities of oil into the environment might well indeed be described as "environmental terrorism," but terrorism, like so many other things, often starts at home.

Regardless of which military force caused the oil spills (although I do not think this is an incidental question), the fact is that there are several very large spills now circulating throughout the Gulf, trailing absolute devastation in their wake. Estimated at more than 3 million barrels by the Saudi Meteorology and Environmental Protection Administration, the Gulf spill roughly equals the largest in history—the Ixtoc-well blowout in the Gulf of Mexico in 1979—and is 10 times the size of the Exxon Valdez accident. Grassbeds are coated with oil, beaches are fouled, wetlands are destroyed, and mousse-like slicks several miles wide threaten the entire coastal ecology of the Gulf from Kuwait to Oman. Fragile coral-reef systems are threatened. The fishing industry in the Gulf, which provides a crucial source of food protein for residents of Gulf-rim countries, was all but closed down by late January. The Saudi shrimp industry, for example, has been wiped out and is considered unlikely to recover before the end of the decade.

Early in the war, wildlife specialists in the region predicted a massive die-off of marine animals. The "body count" of dead marine animals as of January 29, according to a reporter based in Jordan, at that time included 500 turtles, 32 dugongs, and 15,000 sea snakes. These were at best preliminary and uncertain counts, but they point to the makings of a significant wildlife disaster. The Gulf is a critical nesting ground for the endangered green-turtle population, and for dugongs the Gulf is, according to Saudi wildlife experts, "the most important habitat in the western part of its range."

Birds, especially cormorants, grebes, and herons, were particularly hard-hit by the oil pollution. Saudi officials estimate that at least 14,000 birds were killed along the Saudi shore alone. The wetlands of the Gulf are absolutely crucial to the international migration of birds—this region is a major flyway for birds between Africa and Euro-Asia. One to two million birds, representing 125 species, winter in the Gulf wetlands; another 113 species use them for passage migration. Given this crucial role played by the Gulf, widespread contamination there will disrupt hemispheric bird and wildlife patterns.

The poisoning of the Gulf, and the animal kills, may not just be due to oil releases. During the Iran-Iraq war, a major oil spill in 1983 appeared to be the cause of massive marine-animal kills. Scientists now believe, however, that tankers and oil companies took advantage of the spill to dump wastes and chemicals, which are significantly more toxic than oil. One United Nations Environment Programme representative said, "It was later surmised that the oil spill was used as a cover by some oil companies and operators to dump chemicals they had on hand and didn't want."[7] It is entirely possible that damage from oil in this latest war will again be used as a dumping smokescreen.

It is all but impossible to clean up a marine oil spill of this size and nature. Even under the best of circumstances, oil-industry specialists estimate that a 15-percent cleanup is all that can be expected. By way of comparison, for all the massive cleanup effort of the Exxon Valdez spill in Alaska, analysts now report that only 8 percent of that spill was retrieved. In the midst of the Gulf War, oil-cleanup efforts were at best halfhearted and largely illusory. The bill for long-term cleanup could run to $5 billion, a cost that no country appears willing to bear. It is unclear who, if anyone, will take the initiative, or who bears responsibility, for cleaning up the Persian Gulf, a body of water shared by a half-dozen countries and damaged in a war that involved the armed forces of more than 20 governments.

One of the puzzling and damning facts about the Gulf oil spills was the absolute lack of spill preparedness. In the fall of 1990, U.S. military spokespeople were persistently warning that Saddam Hussein would use oil as a literal weapon of war—it was part of the total picture that they were painting of him as an evil and ruthless man. We were told that there would be massive oil spills—and conflagrations; the public knew it, the military knew it; it was discussed at length. And yet, when the oil spills began, the U.S. military spokespeople were found to be sputtering around like chickens without their heads. They expressed horror, dismay, disbelief, and, chiefly, paralysis. There was a sudden flurry of rounding up international oil-spill experts, and a months-long folly of trying to collect oil containment and abatement equipment from around the world. With six months to prepare for the war, and absolute foreknowledge that oil would figure largely as a weapon of war, it is inexplicable and unforgivable that no plans were made to respond to this certain environmental disaster.

Oil fires—as many as 600—are raging, mostly in Kuwait; an estimated 6 million barrels of oil are going up in flames every day. Again, it is not clear that Iraqi sabotage caused all—even, perhaps, most—of these fires. Coalition bombing certainly accounts for some portion of the conflagration. The best estimates are that it will take years to extinguish all the fires.

These fires are creating a massive "pollution incident," on a scale that the world has not previously seen. Spewing smoke, soot, carcinogenic gases, and particulate matter over hundreds of miles, these fires will take a staggering toll. The Environmental Protection Agency estimated in March 1991 that roughly 10 times as much air pollution was being emitted in Kuwait as by all U.S. industrial and power-generating plants combined.[8] Medical workers in Kuwait report dramatic rates of serious respiratory diseases, especially among the elderly and children, populations at particular health risk. Soot acts as an ozone scavenger, and localized holes in the ozone layer will persist for months after the fires are extinguished. The skies over Kuwait are darkened by smoke, and temperatures in the region have already dropped by an average of 10 degrees; if this condition is prolonged, there is a strong possibility of "nuclear winter" effects. The fires—a massive burn-off of fossil fuels—may well escalate global warming. Wind-borne oily particulate matter and soot are settling on agricultural lands throughout the Gulf, polluting water supplies as well as food stocks. More than 1 million tons of sulphur dioxide and approximately 100,000 tons of nitrogen oxides are released each month. These releases will produce acid-rain fallout and dry-acid deposition up to 1200 miles away, again threatening food and water supplies.

Beyond these grim indicators, at this point, no one actually knows what will be the local, regional, or global effects of 600 oil fires burning: It is an unprecedented catastrophe, and, with few predictive tools at our disposal and virtually no ameliorative tools, we will all witness the tragedy unfold. However, "we"—the global community—will not suffer the consequences equally, if at all. The peoples of the Gulf region are global guinea pigs in this environmental catastrophe, a fact that may explain the relative complacency in western coalition countries about the war "victory" and the startling lack of curiosity among western media and government representatives about the larger environmental state of affairs in the Gulf. As with the oil spills, the oil fires—and the resulting climatic catastrophe—were predicted. At the second World Climate Conference in Geneva in November 1990, King Hussein of Jordan outlined very clearly the conflagration disaster that would ensue if the conflict escalated into open war.

The scorched-earth policy inflicted by the Iraqi army on the environment of Kuwait is a massive tragedy that will cost hundreds of lives and untold billions of dollars. It may push complex, once-thriving ecosystems over the edge of sustainability. Unbelievable as it seems, though, the enormity of the damage in Kuwait appears to be far surpassed by the damage to Iraq. As I write this in June 1991, reporting out of Iraq is still spotty and chaotic, but the few independent observers who have issued reports—including a UN task force—paint a picture of a country teetering on the brink of an apocalypse. Coalition bombing destroyed water supplies, electrical-supply systems, fuel supplies, food stocks, sewage systems, transportation systems, garbage-disposal systems, and public-health systems in every major settlement in the country. The urban infrastructure of the country is in tatters; tens of thousands of people— 72,000 by one estimate—have been left homeless from bomb damage to private homes. Trees in cities are being felled for fuelwood. With raw sewage running in the streets of most cities, water systems fouled, and health facilities debilitated, epidemics are sweeping the country. Mass starvation is, by all accounts, is likely.

Just as the Iraqis have fled Kuwait, taking no responsibility for reconstruction of that country, so the United States has washed its hands of the devastation it has wrought in Iraq. President Bush has pledged that "not one American dollar will go to reconstruct Iraq," while at the same time reminding us that "America has no argument with the Iraqi people— only with Saddam Hussein"—a comment that makes one wryly wonder what would happen to a people that the U.S. government *did* have an argument with. Even the most hawkish of the U.S. press corps have wondered aloud whether the premeditated destruction of Iraq didn't overstep the coalition mandate to push Iraqi troops out of Kuwait. Indeed, the report from the UN task force that visited Baghdad in mid-March suggests that the bulk of the damage to civilian support structures in Iraq was neither coincidental nor accidental, but rather the consequence of a successful and intentional air campaign to destroy Iraq's war machine by attacking its urban and industrial base. Despite brave talk of "smart bombs" and precision-guided missiles, much of the damage to Iraq was inflicted by a purposeful policy of random and indiscriminate saturation bombing. Even the U.S. Air Force admits that 70 percent of the bombs dropped in the war missed their intended targets.

While most of Iraq and Kuwait are in shambles, the burden of war damage, and especially war-related environmental damage, is never borne evenly. Women bear a disproportionate responsibility for maintaining family life—providing food, water, and essentials for their families. When the resource base is poisoned or damaged, these demands on women do not go away; rather, their work becomes harder. Women in both Kuwait and Iraq—even urban women unaccustomed to fashioning family provisions from raw materials—have become the hewers of wood and carriers of water. A brief report from the UN observation team comments that women and children are spending large parts of their day searching out food, fuel, and water, often carrying these supplies for miles.

As women cook, wash clothes and dishes, and draw water from sewage-poisoned rivers, they will be the first and most seriously affected by water-borne diseases. Worldwide patterns indicate that, under conditions of food scarcity, adult women and girl children typically eat last and least. The patterns of malnutrition that emerge over the next year or so will most likely reflect this cultural pecking order. In regions suffering chemical contamination, women's reproductive capacities will be impaired, and elevated rates of reproductive failures and gynecological diseases will most likely be evidenced in Iraq, and perhaps Kuwait, over the next few years. Women comprise a staggeringly high proportion of the war refugees (including former "guest workers" in Kuwait, now no longer wanted), who are suffering unimaginable conditions in border camps.

Indigenous peoples, too, pay a particular price of militarized environmental damage. The lands of the Bedouins have been devastated; the desert ecosystem on which they rely has been mined, bombed, poisoned, and debased by the military presence in Saudi Arabia and the war in Iraq and Kuwait. Several reports out of Jordan in late January brought news of attacks on Bedouin camps in Iraq; British newspapers reported that "it is believed that the attacks took place either by accident or because pilots mistook their tents for missile-launcher sites."[9] Large numbers of camels have been killed throughout the region, victims of bored soldiers on desert duty taking target practice, or of mistaken identity: In one particularly bloody scene of camel carnage, U.S. military spokespeople said that they mistook the thermal patterns of herds of camels on their infrared screens for tanks, and bombed without verification. Military activity, pollution, and oil spills have dislocated the Marsh Arabs, a little-known population that lives in the wetlands and marshes of the Persian Gulf.

And at Home

There were no bombs dropped on Boston, no Scud missiles over London, no missiles flying over Toronto. And yet, the Gulf War will have a dramatic effect on the environmental state of affairs on the "home fronts" of countries far removed from the battlefront. In the first instance, the increased budgetary and resource commitments to the military will inevitably take away money and staffing from non-military domestic programs, including—and perhaps especially—environmental efforts.

Environmental-protection programs always slip down the priority scale when budgetary hard times hit. As military budgets swell, others shrink. For example, the Canadian government, the very week following the official end of the war, announced increases in military spending and concomitant decreases in foreign-aid expenditures and domestic environmental budgets. The dollar cost of the war itself is staggering, and in each country the money allocated to support the war meant that there was less money for other priorities. Some comparisons make this stark point: the cost of the 23 Patriot missiles fired by January 22 would buy 12 months of clothes, seeds, pots, and storage facilities for 2 million people in Mozambique (a current Oxfam appeal); the cost of the 216 Tomahawk missiles fired by January 19 would provide total food aid for Ethiopia for six months; the cost of one bomb on a B-52 would run a health clinic in Bangladesh for one month.[10]

But more than this, in countries that participated in the coalition, the sense of national priorities may well shift. In the United States, rather than stimulating the search for non-oil and renewable energy sources, the current U.S. military commitment to defending and securing "our" oil seems to be hindering the formulation of a sane energy policy. Environmentalist Barry Commoner has noted that the "victory" over Iraq will solidify the U.S. commitment to a petroleum-based economy. The current prominence of military activities, and the fact that so many non-military men and women now seem to have an increased stake in the military, will privilege military priorities at home. Environmentalists have been fighting for the past decade to expose the environmental cost—in health and dollars—of that military privilege, but the renewed commitment to military priorities will be a setback to efforts to contain and control environmental violations by the military.

There are already disquieting signs of this shift in the United States. The day after the Iraqi invasion of Kuwait, a U.S. senator introduced legislation that targeted the Arctic National Wildlife Refuge, and other protected areas, for an aggressive program of oil exploration and recovery; the defense bill was passed the same day. President Bush repeated this refuge-exploitation priority in his 1991 energy policy statement, which also proposes deregulation in the nuclear industry and increased reliance on oil, while rejecting strong conservation measures.

Even more startling, the National Toxic Campaign Fund disclosed in January that an agreement was signed between the Pentagon and the White House in August 1990 to waive the National Environmental Protection Act (NEPA). This agreement exempts the military from the requirement to produce an environmental-impact report on all proposed domestic activities, a process that NEPA requires to be open to public review. The military establishment is likely to use the waiver to gain advantage in long-running ecological disputes involving military sites across the country. A Pentagon spokesman admitted that the waiver could be the first in a wider program seeking suspension of other federal environmental statutes, possibly including the Clean Water Act, the Clean Air Act, and the Endangered Species Act.

The Iraqi devastation of Kuwait and the coalition devastation of Iraq are mirror images. Despite the sweeping distinctions that Western officials and the media like to portray between the military behavior of "us" and "them," the similarities are more striking than the differences. There are several grim environmental lessons that we can take from this war. Militaries everywhere, whether at peace or at war, are egregious environmental destroyers. Military strategy is shaped by common assumptions about the use of the physical environment as a stage for the exercise of male power. Militaries share a contempt for civilian environmental regulation, placing themselves and their "national security" priorities above the law. They use secrecy to deflect attention from even their most flagrant environmental violations. When pressed to account for their environmental destruction, they evoke notions of a "greater good." Militaries increasingly share a fascination with high technology that sanitizes killing and keeps environmental catastrophe at arms length. When they wreak their destruction abroad, militaries can walk away from the devastation they leave behind.

War inflicts the most devastating environmental damage; as the weapons of war become more powerful, the environmental damage they cause escalates. In the aftermath of the Gulf "victory," the international arms trade is flourishing; as more and more governments rush to buy more and more powerful weaponry, there can be no doubt that we will witness an escalation in environmental damage caused by any future conflicts, regional or global.

Ours is a small and much abused planet. Militaries are at the very top of the list of the most violent environmental abusers. We need to engage in serious discussion, at all levels of public discourse, about whether we—and the planet—can afford the destruction offered in the name of military "protection." We need to re-examine notions of national and global security. We need to understand the gendered workings of power within militaries, and the way that that power is exercised on the environment. Witnessing the horrific damage done to the Gulf ecosystems—land, riverine, and marine—environmental concerns should figure strongly in the chorus of voices urging restraint and caution before committing ever again to military action.

The people of the Gulf are now most directly bearing the environmental brunt of military adventurism. Many of the environmental impacts may not be immediately obvious. Only over the coming months and years will the full ecological cost of this Gulf War become more apparent. As global citizens, the larger lesson of this war is that the terrible environmental cost of maintaining militarized states is extraordinarily high—indeed, it may cost us the earth.

Notes

1. See, for example, Joni Seager, "Tigris, Tigris Burning Bright," *Village Voice,* December 25, 1990.
2. Seth Shulman, "Toxic Travels: Inside the Military's Environmental Nightmare," *Nuclear Times,* Autumn 1990.
3. John Broder, "U.S. Military Leaves Toxic Trail Overseas," *Los Angeles Times,* June 18, 1990.
4. Constance Holden, "Kuwait's Unjust Desserts: Damage to its Desert," *Science,* March 8, 1991.
5. It is also stunningly hypocritical since the U.S. military refused—as it still does—to identify or decommission its minefields in Vietnam laid during the war, and even today, 15 years after the official end of the U.S./Vietnam War, Vietnamese people die every day from exploding mines.
6. As cited in Michael Renner, "Military Victory, Ecological Defeat," *Worldwatch Magazine,* July/August 1991.
7. Cited in "Oil Spill," *Boston Globe,* February 4, 1991.
8. Michael Renner, "Military Victory, Ecological Defeat," *Worldwatch Magazine,* July/August 1991.
9. "Bedouins claim allied jets attacked camps in Iraq," *The Guardian,* January 25, 1991, p. 22.
10. *The Guardian* (London), January 25, 1991.

CHAPTER 9

WEAPONS OF MASS DESTRUCTION IN OPERATION DESERT STORM

The Non-Nuclear Equivalent of Hiroshima and Nagasaki

Michael T. Klare

Long after the particulars of the Persian Gulf conflict are forgotten, Operation Desert Storm will be remembered as the decisive moment when high-technology conventional weapons secured their place as the dominant instrument of modern combat. Using highly-accurate "smart" bombs and a variety of wide-area munitions—some designed to mimic the explosive impact of small atomic bombs—the United States crushed the Iraqi military in 42 days of high-intensity combat. But while viewed as a virtual marvel by many observers, the widespread use of these new non-nuclear munitions raises important questions about the morality of employing near-nuclear conventional weapons against virtually defenseless soldiers and civilians.

An estimated 85,000 tons of conventional bombs were dropped on Iraq and Kuwait during five weeks of around-the-clock air attacks,[1] or the equivalent (in destructive power) of five Hiroshima-sized bombs. Comparable quantities of rockets, missiles, and artillery shells were also fired at Iraqi positions during the course of the war, making this the most firepower-intensive conflict since World War II. Many of these munitions, originally designed for use against Soviet forces in Europe, were first used in combat during Operation Desert Storm. And, while the non-nuclear weapons used in the Gulf did not produce any of the radiation effects associated with nuclear weapons, their use against water, electricity, and transportation systems has resulted in extensive death, disease, and hunger.[2]

To inflict these damages on Iraq, the United States and its allies used a vast array of non-nuclear weapons, ranging from highly-touted "smart" weapons like the Tomahawk and Patriot missiles to ordinary "dumb" bombs of the sort used in Korea and Vietnam. What made the Gulf War so distinctive, however, was the widespread (and often experimental) use of a new breed of munitions designed to duplicate the destructive effects of America's smallest tactical nuclear weapons. These munitions—fuel-air explosives, penetration bombs, and scatterable mines—were used in great profusion to destroy Iraqi fortifications, disable tanks and vehicles, and kill or maim frontline soldiers. Many casualties were also produced by so-called "collateral damage"—bombs or missiles that missed their intended targets and exploded among civilians instead.

Although the full impact of these attacks may never be fully calculated, a frightening impression is provided by the report of a United Nations observation team that visited Baghdad shortly after the end of the war. "Nothing that we had seen or read quite prepared us for the particular form of devastation which has now befallen the country," the team reported on March 21. "The recent conflict has wrought near-apocalypti-cal results on the infrastructure of what had been, until January 1991, a rather highly urbanized and mechanized society. Now, most means of modern life support have been destroyed or rendered tenuous."[3]

Nor was Baghdad the main target for U.S. air, missile, and artillery attacks—far heavier loads of ordnance were dropped on Iraqi troop positions in Kuwait and along the Saudi border. Most of the heavy bombing by B-52 bombers and other combat planes was directed against these positions, as well as all of the artillery and rocket attacks conducted by U.S. warships and ground forces. In the final hours of the war, U.S. aircraft repeatedly struck a 30-mile column of Iraqi tanks and vehicles on the "highway of death" from Kuwait City to Basra in southeastern Iraq. Many thousands of Iraqis are believed to have perished in this attack, either incinerated within their burning vehicles or eviscerated by piercing shrapnel from anti-personnel cluster bombs. "It was close to Armageddon," was the verdict of one U.S. officer who witnessed these attacks.[4]

We may never know how many Iraqi soldiers died in the 42 days of Desert Storm—U.S. officials ordered the immediate burial of enemy dead in mass graves—but estimates of 100,000 to 150,000 killed in action do not seem excessive. As noted by General H. Norman Schwarzkopf, the Desert Storm commander, "There were a very, very large number of dead in these [frontline combat] units. A very, very large number of dead."[5]

This carnage was necessary, U.S. officials argued, to force Iraqi forces out of Kuwait and to satisfy other conditions set by the UN Security Council. As the death toll mounted, however, it became apparent that U.S. war policy was driven by other considerations than the mere withdrawal of Iraqi troops from Kuwait. At a very early stage in the conflict, President Bush and his senior advisers concluded that Iraqi forces must be physically *destroyed* as well as driven from Kuwait, and that Iraq itself be so thoroughly devastated that it would never again be capable of assuming a major military role in the area.[6] Furthermore, to ensure that these tasks be completed quickly and without producing significant U.S. casualties, senior White House officials authorized the use of massive firepower to stun, smash, and pound Iraq into submission.

The *destruction* (as distinct from *defeat*) of Iraqi military capabilities was considered necessary by U.S. officials in order to prevent Baghdad from ever again pursuing a hegemonic role in the Persian Gulf area—a region considered far too important in geostrategic terms to be allowed to fall under the sway of a hostile power. "Clearly, our national security is at stake here in the Gulf," Bush told U.S. soldiers on Thanksgiving Day—at stake "not just from the threat of force, but from the potential economic blackmail of a Gulf dominated by a power-hungry Iraq."[7] Concern over Iraq's long-term intentions was all the more acute in Washington because Saddam Hussein was thought to be transforming his nation into a major military powerhouse equipped with modern conventional weapons and a nascent nuclear capability. Hence, Washington's determination to destroy not only Hussein's *existing* military capabilities but also all scientific and industrial capabilities that could conceivably contribute to Iraqi strength *in the future*. "It's far better for us to deal with [Hussein] now," Defense Secretary Dick Cheney explained in December 1990, "than it will be for us to deal with him five or ten years from now when the members of the coalition have gone their disparate ways and when Saddam has become an even better armed and more threatening regional superpower than he is at present."[8]

By January 1991, this desire to prevent Iraq from becoming a "regional superpower" had become the driving force behind U.S. military policy, far exceeding the administration's professed concern over Kuwait. "We are determined to knock out Saddam Hussein's nuclear bomb potential," Bush affirmed on January 16, in the first public announcement of the air campaign. "We will also destroy his chemical-weapons facilities. Much of Saddam's artillery and tanks will be destroyed."[9]

In accordance with this edict, U.S. and allied forces conducted a systematic bombing campaign against military installations, munitions plants, and research laboratories in Iraq. Also attacked were facilities that would be needed to rebuild Iraqi military capabilities *after* the war: electric-power plants, highways, factories, and oil refineries. And, of course, the human element of the Iraqi war machine was targeted for destruction: the hundreds of thousands of troops—most of them conscripts and reservists—who willingly or not were obliged to serve in Saddam Hussein's armies.

Had this been Europe during the early Cold War period, and our adversary been the USSR, the United States would in all probability have conducted this campaign with tactical nuclear weapons—that, after all, is what those weapons were designed to do. But the use of nuclear weapons against a Third World country in 1991, in the absence of a demonstrated nuclear threat, would have produced such international revulsion as to have defeated U.S. objectives elsewhere. Hence, the decision by the Bush administration to eschew nuclear weapons in the Gulf and to rely on non-nuclear weapons to achieve America's strategic objectives.[10] The fact that U.S. forces were equipped with conventional weapons with near-nuclear destructive capabilities made it far easier, of course, for President Bush to order the ban on nuclear weapons.

The uninhibited use of near-nuclear conventional weapons against Iraq had another major attraction for the Bush administration: It would demonstrate to *other* aspiring Third World powers that they could expect comparable levels of punishment if they dared to challenge vital U.S. interests in key geostrategic areas. As suggested by Bush on January 29, the destruction of Iraq will send "an enduring warning to any dictator or despot, present or future, who contemplates outlaw aggression."[11]

It is in this sense, more than any other, that the bombing of Iraq represents the modern-day, non-nuclear equivalent of Hiroshima and Nagasaki. By August 1945, when President Truman authorized the use of atomic weapons against Japan, enemy forces were already badly beaten and their will to resist further U.S. military pressure was virtually nonexistent. Hence, the attacks on Hiroshima and Nagasaki were intended as much to intimidate *future* adversaries, especially the USSR, as they were designed to inflict further damage on Japan. Similarly, the systematic destruction of Iraq—coming as it did *after* Hussein had agreed to the

Gorbachev peace plan—was intended as much to intimidate future Third World challengers as it was designed to liberate Kuwait.

Once the war began, moreover, this emphasis on the display of firepower was given further impetus by another major strategic concern—the administration's fear of a resurgence of domestic anti-war sentiment of the sort occasioned by the Vietnam conflict. In this sense, the relentless pounding of Iraq was motivated as much by a desire to nullify the "Vietnam syndrome" as by any calculation of operational military requirements.

For many Americans, the Vietnam syndrome reflects a belief that the U.S. defeat in Vietnam was the product of poor strategic judgment coupled with a reckless inclination to intervene in an essentially unwinnable civil conflict. For U.S. military leaders, however, the U.S. failure was caused not by grand strategic miscalculations but rather by the slow and cautious buildup of U.S. strength, and the failure to use superior firepower in a more aggressive and concentrated fashion. Hence, the Bush administration's determination to settle the Gulf War quickly through the overwhelming application of superior firepower.

"This will not be another Vietnam," Bush affirmed on November 30, 1990, "this will not be a protracted, drawn-out war." If war was to occur, "we will not permit our troops to have their hands tied behind their backs, and there will not be any murky ending. If one American soldier has to go into battle, that soldier will have enough force behind him to win.... I will never, ever agree to a halfway effort."[12]

In line with this outlook, General Schwarzkopf and his associates were instructed to employ whatever force was needed to produce a rapid and conclusive victory. And while the use of nuclear arms was excluded, Schwarzkopf was empowered to use any other weapons in the U.S. arsenal, including powerful new munitions designed for an all-out war with the Soviet Union. If ordered into combat, Schwarzkopf observed in September 1990, U.S. forces "would be using capabilities that are far more lethal, far more accurate, and far more effective than anything we have ever used."[13]

The existence of such weapons in the U.S. arsenal can be traced back to decisions made in the early 1970s, when U.S. and NATO officials sought to overcome a critical paradox that had emerged in western defense policy. This paradox stemmed from the fact that neither European nor U.S. voters were willing to shoulder the immense costs of enlarging the NATO ground forces in order to match improvements in Warsaw Pact capabilities, while at the same time these same voters were calling for a diminished reliance on the nuclear weapons that had long constititued the West's counterweight to superior numbers of Pact forces. This paradox left U.S. military planners with but one choice, as they saw it—to develop extremely powerful and accurate conventional arms that could be used in place of tactical nuclear weapons in attacks on high-value Soviet and Warsaw Pact targets.

Such weapons were especially needed, in the military's view, to attack "high-value" targets in the enemy's rear—such facilities as command-and-control centers, radar stations, air bases, river crossings, and tank formations. To destroy these capabilities, NATO officials called for the development of two types of advanced munitions: first, highly-accurate "smart" bombs and missiles capable of striking critical "point" targets (radar masts, underground bunkers, bridges, and so on) with immense precision; and second, wide-area munitions capable of engulfing large facilities (airfields, vehicle parks, railroad yards) with deadly shrapnel and explosives.

At a time when European and U.S. public opinion was turning more and more strongly against NATO's reliance on nuclear weapons, the introduction of such weapons was seen as a major priority. "A series of conventional initiatives resulting from U.S. investment in research and development offers the opportunity to reduce reliance on nuclear weapons," the House Armed Services Committee affirmed in 1983. "These initiatives, based upon newly-developed technologies, provide the capability to engage military targets with conventional weapons that *previously could be effectively engaged only with nuclear weapons.*"[14] (Emphasis added.)

By Janunary 1990, when Desert Storm commenced, U.S. and Allied forces were able to draw on an impressive arsenal of potent conventional weapons developed or improved for NATO operations against the Soviet Union. Some of these weapons, never before used in combat and still considered experimental, were rushed to the Gulf in order to be tested under "real-world" battle conditions. Designed primarily for use against Soviet and Warsaw Pact forces in Europe, these weapons proved remarkably effective when used against the less-capable Soviet-style forces of Iraq.

As a result of Operation Desert Storm, these new and improved non-nuclear munitions will be viewed as the super-weapons of the 1990s. Because they are likely to play a key role in any future U.S. or Allied military operations abroad, it is important to identify them in greater detail.

The Weapons of Desert Storm

- **Multiple-Launch Rocket System (MLRS):** Introduced in 1983 and first used in battle in the Persian Gulf, the MLRS is a tracked box-like container that can fire a dozen rockets armed with hundreds of individual "submunitions" or "bomblets" (small explosive cannisters) at distances of up to 20 miles. According to the Department of Defense, "A single launcher can fire its load of 12 rockets in less than a minute, covering an area the size of six football fields with approximately 7,700 grenade-like submunitions effective against both personnel and lightly-armored targets."[15] During Operation Desert Storm, dozens of these launchers were often used simultaneously, spewing a lethal shower of explosive bomblets—dubbed "steel rain" by U.S. soldiers—over city-sized areas.[16] First produced in the United States, MLRS is now being "co-produced" in France, Germany, Italy, and the United Kingdom.

- **Army Tactical Missile Systems (ATACMS):** Developed by the Army in the 1980s to provide front-line NATO forces with a surface-to-surface missile capable of striking Warsaw Pact bases and facilities deep inside enemy territory. Designed to be fired from an MLRS launch cannister, ATACMS has a range of approximately 65 miles and carries a payload of some 950 anti-personnel bomblets. Although still in the final test and evaluation phase in late 1990, the missile was rushed to the Persian Gulf and used for strikes against rear-area Iraqi forces and installations.[17]

- **Tomahawk:** One of the most highly publicized weapons to make its combat debut during the Persian Gulf conflict, Tomahawk is a sea-launched cruise missile designed for attacks on ships and high-value inland targets. The land-attack version of Tomahawk that was used in the Gulf has a range of about 700 nautical miles, carries a 1,000-pound warhead, and can be fired from surface ships and submarines.[18] According to the Defense Department, approximately 240 Tomahawks were fired at Iraq during the first two weeks of the war, representing one-fourth of the total U.S. inventory of these missiles. Although described as highly effective in strikes against highly defended "point" targets such as nuclear reactors, power stations, and military headquarters, several of the Tomahawks reportedly missed their targets and struck civilian structures in populated areas.

- **Standoff Land-Attack Missile (SLAM):** A derivative of the Harpoon anti-ship missile, SLAM is an aircraft-fired missile with a range of 60 nautical miles and a 500-pound warhead. It carries a Walleye video data link in its nose-cone, allowing a pilot to maneuver the missile directly toward its target while remaining at "standoff" distances beyond the range of enemy air-defense systems. Like ATACMS, SLAM was still in its final test-and-evaluation phase when Desert Storm commenced; rushed to the Gulf, SLAM was used early in the conflict for strikes against Iraqi naval bases and power stations.[19]

- **Laser-guided bombs (LGBs):** Made familiar to millions of Americans through extensive television coverage of its effects, the GBU-10 "Paveway-II" laser-guided bomb was used extensively during Operation Desert Storm to attack Iraqi military bases and facilities—including some in downtown Baghdad. The 2,000-pound bomb carries a "laser seeker" that homes in on a laser beam directed at the target by a crewmember on the launching aircraft or an accompanying plane. Although widely celebrated by U.S. officials for their pinpoint accuracy, the GBU-10 and other LGBs (GBU-12, -24, and -27) reportedly missed their intended target as much as 40 percent of the time—often striking nearby structures and producing thereby many of the civilian casualties reported by Iraqi officials.[20]

- **Fuel-air explosives (FAEs):** One of the most potent weapons used in the Persian Gulf conflict, fuel-air explosives have come to replace tactical nuclear munitions as the weapon-of-choice in attacks on underground bunkers and heavy fortifications.[21] Essentially, FAEs are large bombs filled with highly volatile fuels (ethylene oxide, propylene oxide, butane, and propane, among others) and an explosive charge. When dropped over the target area, the fuel is released in a cloud of flammable vapor that covers the area; when detonated, the vapor cloud explodes in a massive fireball that engulfs everything within several hundred square yards.[22]

  An impression of the awesome potential of FAEs is provided by a recent CIA report on unconventional munitions: "When detonation occurs, an overpressure is created that can reach 420 pounds per square inch [sufficient to crush fortified bunkers and underground shelters] in the cloud's center. As the explosive wave burns toward its fringes, it is accompanied by a supersonic pressure front that moves at up to 1,825 meters per second—about six times the speed of sound.... When the fuel is burned, the wave front travels on, creating overpressures of enormous destructive potential over considerable distances. *The pressure effects of FAEs approach those produced by low-yield nuclear weapons at short ranges."*[23] (Emphasis added.)

  Several FAEs are known to be in the U.S. arsenal, including the 500-pound CBU-55/B bomb (equipped with three ethylene-oxide-filled BLU-73/B cannisters) and the CBU-72 bomb. An even more potent weapon is the BLU-82/B "daisy cutter," a 15,000-pound monster filled with an aqueous mixture of ammonium nitrate, aluminum powder, and polystyrene soap as a binder.[24] Too heavy to be carried by conventional aircraft, the BLU-82/B (also known as "Big Blue 82") was dropped on Iraqi positions by specially-fitted C-130 aircraft flown by Special Operations personnel.[25]

- **Cluster-bomb units (CBUs):** Other than plain high-explosive iron bombs, the most widely used air-delivered weapons in Operation Desert Storm were cluster bomb units of various types and nationalities. Typically, a CBU consists of a large bomb-like metal casing that splits opens over the target, spewing out dozens or hundreds of anti-armor and/or anti-personnel bomblets or submunitions. By releasing these bomblets in a controlled manner, a single CBU can inundate a very large area (several football fields in size) with a lethal deluge of metal fragments. Those humans unfortunate enough to be caught out in the open when such a volley strikes are literally cut to pieces by the torrent of shrapnel.[26]

  During Desert Storm, many thousands of CBUs were dropped on Iraqi positions by U.S. and allied aircraft. U.S. munitions of this type used in the Gulf include the CBU-52/B, CBU-71/B, CBU-87/B, and CBU-89/B cluster bombs, most of which fire a combination of anti-armor and antipersonnel submunitions.[27] According to one Air Force official, the CBU-87/B was the "weapon of choice" for use in B-52 strikes against dug-in Republican Guard units, because its BLU-97/B submunition (202 of which are carried by the CBU-87) contains an explosive charge for use against tanks as well as metal fragments and an incendiary device for use against personnel.[28] Cluster bombs were also used in strikes against fleeing Iraqi vehicles on the "highway of death" leading from Kuwait and the Iraqi border, causing thousands of casualties.

  Similar weapons were used by other members of the anti-Iraq coalition. The most common British CBU is the Hunting Engineering BL-755 cluster bomb, which fires 147 submunitions—each of which produces some 2,000 high-velocity anti-personnel steel fragments. French CBUs include the Thompson-Brandt BM-400 (which can inundate an area of 60,000 square meters with lethal steel fragments), and the smaller BLG-66 Belouga.[29] Also worthy of note is the British JP-233 runway-attack CBU system, widely used in air strikes against Iraqi airfields.[30]

- **Penetration Bombs:** In an effort to cripple enemy defenses, U.S. forces attempted the "decapitation" of the Iraqi military—that is, they sought to kill senior Iraqi military officers through bombing and missile attacks on underground "command and control" centers in Baghdad. Such attacks are warranted, Lt. Gen. Thomas Kelly explained at a

February 13 Pentagon briefing, because "That's the head. That's the brain. That's where the missions come from."[31] To conduct these attacks, the United States employed a family of specialized weapons known as "penetration bombs" because of their ability to punch through thick layers of earth and concrete before exploding.

At least two new bombs of this type were used in the Gulf War: the 2,000-pound GBU-27 and the 4,700-pound GBU-28. The GBU-27 is composed of a Paveway-III laser-guidance unit and an I-2000 penetrator warhead; designed specifically for the F-117 "stealth" bomber, it was used in the fateful February 13 attack on an underground bunker in Baghdad in which hundreds of civilians are believed to have died.[32] The heavier GBU-28, made up of 8-inch howitzer tubes, was developed during the course of the war and rushed to the Gulf in the final days of combat; carried by the FB-111, it was used in attacks on an underground command center on the outskirts of Baghdad.[33]

When used together and in great profusion, as occurred during Operation Desert Storm, these weapons clearly have a devastating effect on any forces not equipped with adequate defenses. As a result of the Persian Gulf experience, many countries—including the Soviet Union and China—have begun to rethink their military policies and to seek new high-tech weapons of the sort used by U.S. and Allied forces. Thus, just as the (technically) successful use of atomic weapons at Hiroshima and Nagasaki ignited a nuclear quest among those nations seeking great-power status in the post-World War II era, so the successful use of high-tech conventional weapons against Iraq and Kuwait will spur a new non-nuclear arms race among current and aspiring powers in the current period.

For those nations with access to the critical technology—the United States, Britain, France, and Germany—a conventional arms race of this sort may not appear particularly burdensome because of their presumed success in such a contest. As the technology spreads to other countries, however, as it surely will, the proliferation of high-tech conventional weapons will pose significant risks to global security given the relative freedom with which potential users are likely to consider their employment (as contrasted with the strong inhibitions against the use of nuclear and chemical weapons). Clearly, any future wars fought between comparably-equipped high-tech forces are likely to result in terrifying levels of death and destruction on all sides, *irrespective of the final outcome of the conflict.*

A conventional arms race will also prove extremely costly for all parties involved, given the high price of sophisticated technology. As demonstrated by the cost overruns experienced in developing many of the weapons used in Desert Storm, each new advance in technical sophistication is likely to be obtained through an exponential increase in R&D (research and development) spending. Hence, all of the savings that might accrue from the end of the Cold War in Europe could be wiped out if the United States and its allies seek to replace existing non-nuclear weapons with even more capable and sophisticated variants.

Even more important to consider are the ethical and moral issues raised by the unrestrained use of the new munitions. While the world has adopted strong moral inhibitions against the use of nuclear and chemical weapons, no such restraints govern the use of non-nuclear weapons. Yet, as demonstrated by the Gulf conflict, the concentrated use of high-tech conventional munitions can produce levels of death and destruction comparable to those wreaked by low-yield tactical nuclear weapons. Foreseeing this potential in a 1983 article on the new NATO strategy, British historian John Keegan wrote that: "A high-intensity conventional war and a low-intensity nuclear war might inflict very much the same level of damage on any given piece of inhabited landscape."[34]

What are the moral implications of this new reality? Surely, if the world community considers it unethical to use nuclear or chemical weapons of mass destruction against forces that do not use such weapons first, some moral qualms should arise from the similar use of conventional weapons of mass destruction. Even greater concern should arise when such weapons are used against civilians, or, as occurred in the Gulf conflict, when they are used against military targets in highly populated areas.

Although some U.S. and European leaders have expressed discomfort over the one-sided nature of the slaughter in the Gulf, most Americans approved the use of high-tech conventional weapons against Iraq—and seem willing to support the continued development and procurement of such munitions. However, if we are to confront the moral issues raised by the introduction of high-tech conventional weapons and their use in defense of a "new world order," it is essential that they be stripped of their "gee-whiz" appeal and be seen as what they truly are—highly effective killing instruments that are designed to produce nuclear-like levels of destruction without arousing excessive public apprehensiveness.

Notes

1. *The Washington Post,* March 16, 1991.
2. See the UN report of March 21, 1991, as reproduced in *The New York Times* of March 23, 1991.

228 COLLATERAL DAMAGE

3. Cited in *The New York Times*, March 23, 1991.
4. Quoted in *The New York Times*, February 27, 1991. See also: *The Washington Post*, February 27, 1991.
5. Press briefing in Riyadh, February 27, 1991, as reproduced in *The Washington Post*, February 28, 1991.
6. See the retrospective analysis by Thomas Friedman and Patrick Tyler in *The New York Times*, March 3, 1991.
7. Presidential address, Dhahran, Saudi Arabia, November 22, 1990, as transcribed in *U.S. Department of State Dispatch*, November 26, 1990, p. 279.
8. Testimony before the Senate Armed Services Committee, Washington, D.C., December 3, 1990, from the transcript in *The New York Times*, December 4, 1990.
9. Television address from the White House, January 16, 1991, as transcribed in *The New York Times*, January 17, 1991.
10. This decision is disclosed in *The Washington Post*, January 7, 1991.
11. State of the Union Address, January 29, 1991, from the transcript in *The New York Times*, January 30, 1991.
12. White House press conference, from the transcript in *The New York Times*, December 1, 1990.
13. Quoted in *The Wall Street Journal*, September 6, 1990.
14. U.S. Congress, House Committee on Armed Services, *Improved Conventional Force Capability: Raising the Nuclear Threshold*, Staff Study, 98th Congress, 1st Session, 1983 (published 1984 by U.S. Government. Printing Office).
15. *Department of Defense Annual Report*, Fiscal Year 1988, p. 160.
16. "Steel rain" citation, multiple-salvo firings from *The Washington Post*, February 22, 1991.
17. *Defense News*, February 11, 1991, pp. 4, 36.
18. *Aviation Week & Space Technology*, January 21, 1991, p. 61; January 28, 1991, p. 29.
19. *Aviation Week & Space Technology*, January 28, 1991, pp. 31-32.
20. Fred Kaplan in *Boston Globe*, January 29, 1991; also *The Washington Post*, February 22, 1991.
21. For reports of FAE use in the Gulf War: *The New York Times*, March 4, 1991; *Los Angeles Times*, March 1, 1991.
22. *The Washington Post*, February 16, 1991; Gervasi, *America's War Machine*, p. 253; U.S. Central Intelligence Agency, *Conventional Weapons Producing Chemical-Warfrae-Agent-Like Injuries*, February 1990, pp. 6-7.
23. CIA report, op. cit., pp. 6-7.
24. Gervasi, op. cit., p. 253.
25. *Baltimore Sun*, February 12, 1991; *The New York Times*, March 1, 1991.
26. Gervasi, op. cit., pp. 250-51.
27. "Modern Bombs in the Gulf," *Jane's Defence Weekly*, February 9, 1991, p. 178.
28. Air Force quote in *The Washington Post*, January 23, 1991; information on CBU-87 from *Jane's Defence Weekly*, February 9, 1991, p. 178.
29. Paul Rogers and Malcolm Dando, *NBC-90: The Directory of Nuclear, Biological and Chemical Arms and Disarmament 1990*, London: Tri-Service Press, 1990, pp. 77-78.
30. *The Washington Post*, January 27, 1991.
31. *The Washington Post*, February 14, 1991.
32. *The Washington Post*, February 14, 1991.
33. *Los Angeles Times*, May 4, 1991.
34. John Keegan, "The Specter of Conventional War," *Harper's*, July 1983, p. 10.

PART IV

THE WAR AT HOME

CHAPTER 10

THE STRUGGLE CONTINUES AT HOME AND ABROAD

Randolph N. Stone

As a criminal-defense lawyer, a Public Defender, an African American and a human being, I rarely find myself agreeing with President Bush. However, I recall that President Bush stated at some point during the conflict that a soldier in Kuwait was in less danger of being killed than a person on the streets of some of our American cities. As it turned out, he was correct. Ironically, his statement tells us more about our criminal-justice system and violence in America than it does about the war in the Persian Gulf.

Of course what he should have said more specifically was a *U.S.* soldier in Kuwait versus an *African American* in our inner cities. As it now appears, as many as 150,000 Iraqis may have been killed in the war. And we all know that the number-one cause of death for Black men between the ages of 15 and 34 is murder, most often at the hands of another Black man. A Black male today is at least six times more likely to be murdered than a white male here in the United States. Tough odds.

The chronology of events surrounding the Persian Gulf crisis was quite astounding: the U.S.-backed Kuwaiti attempt to syphon Iraqi oil; the Iraqi invasion of Kuwait; the pillaging of Kuwait; the burning of the oil wells; the intransigence of Hussein and Bush; the massive saturation bombing of Iraq; the ultimate U.S. military triumph against Iraq; the

---

This is an excerpt of a speech delivered to the National Lawyers Guild Midwest Regional Conference in Chicago on April 6, 1991.

231

fervent patriotism engendered in the United States; the display of yellow ribbons; the 500,000-plus Americans engaged directly in the war effort in the Middle East, the tens of billions of dollars spent by the United States; the widespread suffering, chaos, and instability in Iraq; the billions and billions of dollars' worth of profits coming to U.S. corporations to "rebuild" Kuwait; and the likely establishment of a permanent United States military base in the Middle East. How quickly things change on the world's stage and on the other hand, how some things never change.

The United States, a country of 250 million people, committed over one-half million troops, and millions of other Americans engaged in support activities to wage a three-month war against a country of 17 million in order to reinstate a feudal monarch with deposits of hundreds of billions of dollars in banks all over the world. Some estimates suggest that the war cost us about $500 million a day. Each air sortie cost a million dollars. One hundred Patriot missiles cost about $110 million; the 260 Tomahawk Cruise Missiles cost about $351 million and so on and so on. Many commentators have suggested that no one really knows or will ever really know the economic cost of the war.

Perhaps even more significantly, the cost to the American psyche and the unknown costs of continuing to ignore the serious domestic issues in this country are incapable of mathematical computation.

Some of these domestic issues are racially symbolized by the following facts:

There is a growing gap between the life expectancy for whites and Blacks; Black infants are twice as likely to die in their first year as whites; 45 percent of Black children live in poverty as compared to 15 percent of white children; a Black child's father is twice as likely to be unemployed as a white child's father; the proportion of Blacks in poverty is three times that of whites; median income for Blacks is 57.1 percent of whites; Black children are 15 times more likely to contract AIDS; Black males are 6 percent of the adult population but constitute 41 percent of those under sentence of death.

It was very disturbing to witness the patriotic fervor symbolized by the yellow ribbons, support-our-troops stickers and bring-our-boys-home-safely rhetoric. For many African Americans, it was difficult to express our disapproval and dissatisfaction with the war effort. How complicated the issue was to address in rational conversation with others who did not share our revulsion! The administration's management of the war, the media, and its public-relations campaign concerning the war was superb. Clearly those of us opposed to the war effort were outflanked and relegated to very defensive positions. Perhaps we thought it was Vietnam all over again, but as I said earlier, things change even though they remain the same.

Ironically, the deadline for the Iraqi troop withdrawal was Martin Luther King's Birthday. It occurred to me that when King was assassinated, I was in Vietnam. I can't recall the specifics of how I heard about it, but I remember how I felt and I recall the anger, isolation, sense of betrayal, and bitterness felt by many of my comrades at that time. Certainly the African-American experience in Vietnam and our neglect of domestic problems contribute to difference in attitudes about the war. Prior to the invasion, only 27 percent of African Americans supported the Gulf effort compared to 66 percent of whites. Even after the invasion, African-American support was only 48 percent as compared to roughly 80 percent support among whites.

Clearly the war was a growth industry for the United States, particularly for our military/industrial complex. Unfortunately, one domestic industry that seems to be growing as fast as our war machine is punishment. Today, prison construction is one of the fastest-growing components of local government, and on the federal level it may be the fastest-growing expenditure except for our war efforts. The total cost of incarcerating the more than one million Americans in prisons and jails today is $16 billion a year. A recent study indicated that Illinois needs to build 13 new prisons to accommodate its growth in sanctions and incarceration. As I recall, Illinois led the nation last year in its per-capita increase in prison population. A few months ago, I heard this state's former governor announce that one of his greatest accomplishments was building more prisons in his tenure as governor than all prior governors in the history of the state. It is said that prison construction in the United States rivals the construction of new homes. The U.S. incarcerated population has doubled in ten years, from 500,000 in 1980 to more than 1 million in 1990. The ratio of guards to prison inmates is one to three, while in most urban areas, there is one teacher for every 30 students in our public schools.

Our military and crime control policies have had a particularly harsh impact on the African-American community. Although African Americans are about 11 percent of civilians over the age of 16, they are 30 percent of the military; more than 20 percent of those on active duty today are African American and about 25 percent of those in the Gulf were African Americans. This disproportionate respresentation is greater in the criminal-justice system. Today, African-American males are incarcerated at eight times the rate of white males. A report by the Sentencing Project, Inc. revealed that Black males in America are incarcerated at a rate four times that of Black males in South Africa. Today, as I speak, there are more

African-American men incarcerated in jails and prisons in this country than in colleges and professional schools. So it seems that the only equal-opportunity employers in the United States for African-American men are the military or jails and prisons.

What conclusions can be drawn from all of this? I think there is a direct relationship between the percentage of African-Americans in jails and prisons and in the military. On some levels, African-American men are expendable. Our society is willing to spend whatever it takes, a fortune, to destroy Iraq, but is miserly in devoting resources to rebuild our inner cities. Is there a direct relationship between the misery and deprivation and killing visited upon the people of Iraq and upon African-Americans right here at home? Is there a relationship between the rise in so-called hate crimes and racial violence and our lack of concern for human rights around the world? Why is there no strategic plan to deal with the issues of poverty and racism? What is the relationship between police violence and the violence in Baghdad? What is the relationship between our government's willingness to devote billions to bail out the savings-and-loan industry while ignoring the calls by the Urban League and others for an Urban Marshall Plan to seriously deal with the crisis in this country?

It is somewhat ironic that in the wake of the Rodney King case, we hear pleas for more money for police training while the continuing pleas for job training, education, and prenatal care and drug treatment are discounted. Although it may be apparent that in the short run the United States has once again secured a military victory, in the long run the United States is the big loser. We have destroyed much of Iraq, but we have also ensured that our country will continue to endure poverty, hopelessness, and crime for many years to come because of our misallocation of resources. If these problems are not addressed one day, the war will come home, again, to roost in the streets of our cities.

As Bernadine Dohrn said in a recent speech,

We now can be certain that when the United States determines to do something, no cost, no resources and no mercy will be spared in pursuit of that goal. Halfway around the world, our young people are transported, weapons are amassed, one thousand nuclear warheads are deployed, an enormous support-and-supply system is implemented, military prowess is asserted. From our distance in the sky, no one appears to kill anyone; all that happens is satisfying blips on a computer screen. But the children of Baghdad are suffering the consequences; we can only imagine their fear today at the sound of an airplane overhead. We are told that more Iraqi children may die of starvation and disease after the ceasefire than during the bombing. Violent deaths, quietly executed. This inequitable distribution of national resources to the military is a major underlying cause of the conditions and "silent violence" in which so many of our children live.

What can we do to reverse this trend? I don't have all the answers, obviously, but I do believe that we have to deal with it on an individual as well as on an organizational level. A story sticks in my mind for some reason, a story I read a while ago. It was based on a Jewish legend or myth. The story of the *lamedvovniks:* the 36 righteous people who were sent by God to live and work among us. They were poor, unnoticed, not glorious, and according to myth, unaware of their own perfection. When a righteous person was discovered, according to legend, he or she would deny his or her identity, disappear, and reappear in another place. I do not pretend to be a religious scholar but I do believe that each of us has the responsibility to be "righteous": to speak out for those who are voiceless, to act for those who are restrained or confined. Recognition is unimportant.

Finally, more specifically in the area of criminal justice, a number of policy recommendations have been formulated by a variety of sources. For example, from the Sentencing Project in Washington, D.C.: establish a national commission to examine the high rate of incarceration of Americans, and African-American males in particular; fund pilot programs of the Justice Department to reduce the high rate of incarceration of African-American males; redirect the "war on drugs" to define drug abuse as a public-health problem and not a criminal-justice problem; redirect the focus of law enforcement to address community needs and to prevent crime; reduce the recidivism rate of prisoners by providing effective services; encourage our "leaders" to engage in a national and international dialogue on issues of crime and punishment.

Of course I could go on. There is no shortage of creative ideas; the problem is lack of commitment. As Dr. Martin Luther King noted, there will be difficult days ahead but we can be an inspiration to each other. The struggle continues and we must continue to struggle.

References

Barnaby Dinges, "Black Youths Are the City's Top Murder Risk," *Chicago Reporter,* February 1990.

"Constitutional Rights seen imperiled by War on Drugs," *News and Comments, BNA Criminal Practice Manual,* Volume 5, Number 18, September 4, 1991, p. 411.

"Homicide Rate up for Young Blacks," *New York Times,* December 7, 1990, p. A26.

Gerald David Jaynes and Robin M. Williams, Jr., eds., *A Common Destiny: Blacks and American Society,* Washington, D.C.: National Academy Press, 1989.

Marc Mauer, *Americans Behind Bars: A Comparison of International Rates of Incarceration,* The Sentencing Project, Inc., Washington, D.C., January, 1991.

Marc Mauer, *Young Black Men and the Criminal Justice System,* The Sentencing Project, Inc., February, 1990.

National Urban League, New York, *The State of Black America, 1988-1991.*

Charles Ogletree, "Does Race Matter in Criminal Prosecutions?" *The Champion* 15:6, July 1991.

John Powell and Eileen Hershenow, "Hostage to the Drug War: The National Purse, the Constitution, and the Black Community," *The University of California at Davis Law Review* 24:557, 1991.

Randolph N. Stone, "Crisis in the Criminal Justice System," *Harvard Blackletter Journal,* Spring 1991.

Randolph N. Stone, "The War on Drugs: The Wrong Enemy and the Wrong Battlefield," statement and testimony to Select Committe on Narcotics and Congressional Black Caucus, September 15, 1989.

CHAPTER 11

MINORITIES
IN THE MILITARY

Rachel L. Jones

Ain't life grand: in 1991 a Black man was running the United States military.

Racism in the United States is at its peak in recent history, replete with increasing self-segregation, racial isolation, and rampant resentment over meager minority gains during the last 25 years. Amidst that roiling stew, General Colin L. Powell's ascendancy is a mixed blessing at best. Fifty years ago in the military, you couldn't find a Black face outside of the mess hall, if you believed the John Wayne World War II propaganda being churned out non-stop. Hell, Black men didn't have courage, and Latinos couldn't shoot down five fighter planes and then land a burning jet on a tiny patch of airstrip. And, frankly, all Indians were good for was seeing in the dark and climbing steep hills. Leave the fightin' to the stalwart white guys, superior in all things heroic.

Poor Duke. He probably did a couple of backflips in his grave when Powell emerged as the chairman of the Joint Chiefs of Staff during America's latest hour of crisis.

Some older Black Americans view Powell's role as commander of the U.S. Armed Forces with the same pride afforded to a first-generation college graduate. He represents the first wave of Black soldiers who got a "fair shake," they argue—who entered the military as green and raw as any buck recruit, stayed the course, and rose straight to the top. It's living proof, they insist, that in the military, all you need is some discipline and longevity to succeed—regardless of your skin color.

Parts of this essay originally appeared in a January 1991 article by Rachel L. Jones in the *Chicago Reporter,* 332 South Michigan Avenue, Chicago, IL 60604.

It's estimated that the U.S. military is anywhere from 30 to 35 percent minority—mostly Black Americans. News of that percentage, coming hard on the heels of Operation Desert Storm, stirred some interesting debate about minorities and their relationship to the military, seriously criticizing this newfound compatibility. Powell was put on the defensive about the issue several months before Operation Desert Storm began, and his response was somewhat less than satisfying. In a *Washington Post* interview, Powell responded to questions about disproportionate numbers as follows: "What you keep wanting me to say is that this is disproportionate or wrong. I don't think it's disproportionate or wrong. I think it's a choice the American people made when they said have a volunteer army and allow those who want to serve to serve."

In sheer numbers, it may appear that Blacks don't have so much to complain about. For example, according to the Department of Defense (DOD), of the nearly 60,000 soldiers who died in the Vietnam War from 1961 to 1973, 12 percent were Black, which about mirrored their representation in the U.S. population at the time. Of 540,000 soldiers deployed for Desert Storm, 24.5 percent were Black, 5 percent Latino, 0.6 percent Native American, 2.1 percent Asian, and 1.7 percent "other." By March, the death toll from both Desert Shield and Desert Storm was 291; 74 percent were white, 18 percent were Black, 6 percent Latino, and the rest Asian and Native American and other.[1]

Observers are still debating those numbers, claiming that Blacks made up as many as 40 percent of Gulf forces, and that including other ethnic groups, the troops were more than 50-percent minority. But even if DOD numbers are accurate, percentages for Blacks are indeed higher than their representation in the U.S. population as a whole, which 1990 census figures put at 12 percent.[2]

And there's another sobering precedent for invoking the disproportionate-numbers issue. Some argue that in 1965 and 1966, when Blacks served in large numbers on the front lines in Vietnam, they made up more than 20 percent of the deaths. It took a manipulation of the numbers by government officials and a "spreading out" of Blacks among the ranks to bring the Black death rate down to an acceptable level.[3]

Statistics like that skew the minority-representation debate, knocking the wind from claims that people who join the army—regardless of race—know what they're getting into and shouldn't complain. Powell's answer would be more than adequate in a world where all things were equal and joining the army was just one of a myriad of options open to an 18-year-old minority youth today.

His response is fueled by the same sort of "even-playing-field" philosophy that's sprung full-grown from the head of racist backlash to affirmative action, along with fear of the dreaded "Quota Beast" that terrorizes our fair land. In Powell's perfect world, you either go to college, get a job, or join the army. But what about the 18-year-old minority youth, poised and ready to embark on the journey to adulthood and seeking some signposts to make sense of his or her future?

(This discussion of minorities in the military must be prefaced with this thought: Issues of discrimination and overrepresentation affect all minority groups dramatically. In fact, this essay will show that ultimately, Native Americans are the most overrepresented group in the military, given their small numbers in the general population versus their numbers in military ranks. But for the purposes of this essay, the emphasis will be on Blacks in the military, as there is an abundance of material on their military history.)

A city like Chicago offers an interesting microcosm in studying the issue of a disproportionately minority military. A January 1991 investigative study of Defense Department records by *The Chicago Reporter,* a monthly newsletter focusing on issues of race and poverty, revealed that in 1990, 80 percent of all recruits from the city of Chicago in all four branches of the military were minority—African American, Latino, Asian American, Native American, and other. The percentage was the same in 1989. Overall, from the entire Chicago metropolitan area, 50 percent of all recruits were minority.

What do those raw numbers mean? What sorts of statements can one make, just on the surface? In Chicago, do minority youths find the military more appealing than whites? Even in light of the inherent risks, do minority youths crave the discipline and camaraderie of the military at higher rates? Rather than go to college or take a job in his or her uncle's business, would a minority youth prefer to sign enlistment papers?

It's ludicrous to even hint at any of those notions. In stark terms, those numbers mean that for minority youths in this capitalist society, the military offers the best set of options available for employment, advancement, or a steady paycheck. Literally. Granted, one risks painting with too broad a stroke in concluding that *all* minorities view the military as their best option upon completing high school. There are in fact many possible avenues to explore in arriving at a conclusion.

Molefi Kete Asante, chair of the African-American Studies Department at Temple University in Philadelphia, explains Black participation in the military in three ways. "Blacks have gone into the military largely as a response to the economic situation of American society, and you'd be hard pressed to argue with that on any level," Asante says. Secondly, "The American military has been for African Americans a way of escape, probably since the time of the Spanish American War. It's been an avenue where people can get out of their current environments, however bleak. In a sense, it's the search for adventure," Asante added. Finally, there's the issue everyone is talking about—exploitation. "Whites, particularly middle-class whites and upwardly mobile whites, have seen African Americans and other minority populations as sort of cannon fodder, individuals whose lives are expendable," Asante says. "The war in the Gulf was when all of these motives and interests came together for the African-American community."

He forgot to mention one other reason: For many minority youths, there's nothing to lose by joining the military and literally putting their lives on the line in the process. Just take a look at the playgrounds, the corners, the major intersections of many Black American neighborhoods and view the Black manhood shriveling on the vine. Black men are imperiled, or imperiling themselves, at alarming rates. They face poverty and violence at alarming rates. They face racism and rejection at alarming rates. They face the question, why *not* join the Army?

Other minorities face the same stumbling blocks in education and employment, and some of the statistics are appalling. In Los Angeles, for example, during the 1989-90 school year, 18,521 students dropped out of grades 10-12, according to school district records. Of that number, 10,976 were Latino—59 percent.[4] It's a sign that Latino youth have reached a "crisis point" in their expectations of what society offers them, said Carlos Melendrez, a California consultant who joined forces with the Latino Issues Forum to open up debate on military participation during the war.

"We're extremely angry that the only institution in America that has any kind of progressive program, where there's any inkling of being an equal and having a fair shot at success, is the military," Melendrez said. The Gulf War signalled a shift in the overarching patriotism that has surrounded Latino participation in American wars. Latinos have joined the military and served in its ranks at a higher proportional rate than some other minority groups because they "wanted to display their patriotism. A lot of older Latinos we talked to felt that we should go out and participate regardless. Many new immigrants in particular felt they had to prove themselves to the dominant culture, prove they were willing to help protect all the things that their beneficent new homeland was offering them," Melendrez said.

In general, after Vietnam there was a significant shift in attitude about military service within the Latino community. As Melendrez saw it, during the 60s, Latino activists had aligned themselves with white liberals to oppose the draft and other social injustices, and found eager support. But in the interim years, with the draft eliminated and upper-class white youths largely out of harm's way, when the Latino community pressed for economic support and political empowerment, those same allies fell mute. When recent protests about Latino participation in the military ripped through communities in Los Angeles and San Francisco, Melendrez said, it was hard to find an interested ear.

"Basically, it's because we have no power in the board rooms, we have few voices in decision-making positions," said Melendrez. "[The government has] found a way to staff a military in such a manner where the least amount of the general public will be upset about sending people to war, and the way to do that is to staff it with minorities who have been cut out of other sectors," he added.

But in many ways, this issue transcends race. More than the color black for oil, brown for skin, or red for blood, the color of this issue is green—economics. Those who have shall debate, march, and picket. Those who have not shall fight, bleed, and die. Nothing more clearly delineated that fact than all the bickering and bluster arising from Congress, the gung-ho posturing and patriotic flag-waving that characterized the discourse in preparation for the Gulf War. While those country-loving, affluent white males raved about the war, they were unencumbered by worries about losing any of their offspring; only two of the 535 members of Congress had children fighting in the Persian Gulf.[5] "If you look at low-income whites in the military, you're going to find that they enlist in the army at very high rates as well," says Edward Lazear, a senior fellow at Stanford University's Hoover Institute. "Clearly, the issue then becomes opportunity, and the word poor has no color."

But race can't be given short shrift. Edwin Dorn of the Brookings Institution in Washington, DC, says, "Class and race are very different things conceptually, but it's very difficult to disaggregate their effects, when you're talking about this issue." He poses a compelling question: "Is a minority recruit confronting a lousy opportunity structure because he's poor, or because he's Black or Hispanic? Well, in large measure, he's poor because he's Black or Hispanic. Because you can't do anything about either of those things, you do what you have to do. You're more likely to sign on the dotted line."

For Barbara Carter, a Chicago mother whose daughter Mia served in a medical unit in the Gulf, the spate of protest from college students at campuses like Northwestern and Loyola Universities was infuriating. "Tomorrow, they're going to get out of their lily-white beds and go to their classes," Carter said just before the war began, "and my daughter will be out there dodging bullets."

Indeed, the pacifists who took the podium at Loyola University last December to announce the formation of Chicago Campuses United Against The War, jockeyed for position as the cameras rolled, each proclaiming their outrage and disgust about the blood being spilled for greedy corporations. By February, the demonstrations and "peace-ins" had ceased, causing a great deal of speculation about the demonstrators' commitment to the issue.

Meanwhile, Carter's daughter Mia left classes at a technical school and a part-time job at a local hospital to serve in Desert Storm, leaving Chicago in December of 1990. Though her grades weren't great and at 24, she couldn't pinpoint when she'd actually land a degree, Mia was continuing her schooling because of the monthly stipend she received from the Army Reserves. While she had re-enlisted twice, Mia was almost in shock when she learned she'd be going to the Gulf. "Why should I go to class?" she told her mother one morning before leaving. "You don't have to learn how to get your head blown off." The chances of that happening were high; Mia was one of the nearly 40 percent of women in the Army who are African American.[6]

It's obvious, then, that a major reason for a higher percentage of minorities in the military is the lack of options elsewhere. Said Dorn, "It's a commentary on the opportunity structures that exist in this society. In fact, the high representation of Blacks in the military is the best evidence that you could have that there is something wrong with the civilian opportunity structure."

A look at *Fortune Magazine's* top 500 U.S. Industrial Corporations for 1990 highlights his thoughts; not one is owned or operated by minorities. It also gives reasons for some of the vocal opposition to the war in the petroleum-rich Gulf; 10 of the top 15 companies listed, from General and Ford Motors to Boeing to Occidental Petroleum, depend directly on oil for their very existence. Yet another statistic clearly outlines the ominous lack of Black participation in this society overall, particularly in areas of power and decision-making: Of 30.6 million managerial and professional workers nationwide, only 6.2 percent are Black.[7] In Chicago, for example, only 13 of 625 top executives at the largest companies are Black.[8]

"We don't talk about white racism anymore," Asante explains, "but all the structural issues that sociologists have talked about are fundamentally predicated and based upon white racist supremacist notions. They're the people who set up the system. Such a system does not favor African Americans, and in fact punishes African Americans."

The military has become, then, "the major dumping ground for the surplus African American labor that's not being accommodated in other sectors of our society," Asante said. "It's not that this labor can't be used, but there's a lack of willingness by the people who run companies to usher these people into the higher levels in the private sector, largely because of the continuing presence of white racism."

In short, this overwhelming factor tends to create a "poverty draft," said Jamillah Muhammad, director of the Youth and Militarism Program of Chicago's Clergy and Laity Concerned. The program was formed in the mid-60s by Dr. Martin Luther King and others, at the height of King's objection to the Vietnam War. The group has a special focus on counseling youths, particularly those at largely minority high schools, about the consequences of military service. "Our kids are not only academically unprepared for college, they're financially unprepared. The military capitalizes on that," Muhammad explains, pointing to a $2.1 billion military recruiting budget as proof. "These kids sign up for service like it was going out of style, but once they're in, they find it's a much different experience."

Recruiting lures are especially attractive to minority inner-city youths. "Do you know what that would sound like to a kid who hasn't had much of anything his whole life?" Muhammad says. "They make it sound like the Promised Land. How is a kid supposed to resist that?"

She further likens the recruitment process to the street culture that many inner-city youths are all too familiar with. "They used to send out older veterans or gray haired officers to schools," Muhammad says. "Recruiters today aren't much older than the kids in school." For example, at Chicago's Roberto Clemente High School in December of 1990, where the student body is 80 percent Hispanic and Black, Muhammad counted five young black male recruiters from the Army alone. "You show up in a uniform, and you are somebody. That's the way the gangs recruit kids. They have their colors and their jackets, and they are a part of something, yet they rarely give the kids the full story." Still, even in light of the Persian Gulf crisis, Muhammad reports that youths "flocked to the recruiters. There were so many, I couldn't guess a number for you."

Lou Geraldi, an assistant principal at Clemente, estimated that less than 5 percent of students at Clemente go on to some kind of advanced schooling. Compare that to the 94 percent of students who go on to college at New Trier East High School in Winnetka, Illinois, an affluent suburb north of Chicago. Career counselor Nina Winter said only four or five students there pursue an interest in the military each year. "It's just not a part of what they're planning to do with their future," she said.

Lest this debate seems too mired in the plight of the Black soldier, a fascinating report by Tom Holm on American Indians and the military shows that, in terms of sheer numbers versus population representation, Indians are the most overrepresented minority group in the military. According to Veteran's Administration and census figures, there are nearly 160,000 living veterans who are American Indians. This means that fully

10 percent of all living Indians are military veterans. That's three times the rate of other groups, compared to their population numbers.[9] This has occurred since 1917, when American Indians served in the military far beyond their numbers in the U.S. population. For example in World War I, 10,000 Indians served; during WWII, 25,000 Indians served. By the Vietnam war, 42,000 Indian soldiers were stationed in Southeast Asia.[10]

Even with this record of honorable service, often undertaken because of a sense of "duty" felt towards a country that had grossly exploited and slaughtered their ancestors, Indians were once again debased and subjected to negative stereotypes held by whites. For example,

Almost immediately after America's entrance into the Second World War, the media began to exploit imagery built around the scout syndrome for propaganda purposes. Stanley Vestal, an ethnologist of high repute, wrote that the Indian "was a realistic soldier" who "never gave a quarter or expected anything." Even Harold Ickes, the Secretary of the Interior, stated in an article in a national magazine that Indians were "uniquely valuable" to the war effort because they had: "endurance, rhythm, a feeling for timing, coordination, sense perception, an uncanny ability to get over any sort of terrain at night, and better than all else, an enthusiasm for fighting. He takes a rough job and makes a game of it. Rigors of combat hold no terrors for him; severe discipline and hard duties do not deter him.[11]

That caricature of Indian soldiers as stoic scouts has dogged them through all successive U.S. wars. For example, Jack Miles, Indian veteran of the Korean War, said, "In Korea, my platoon commander always sent me out on our patrols. He called me 'Chief' like every other Indian, and probably thought that I could see and hear better than the white guys. Maybe he thought I could track down the enemy. I don't know for sure, but I guess he figured that Indians were warriors and hunters by nature."[12]

Fast forward to Desert Storm, where many young men and women are signing up in search of adventure, egged on by the blurbs in glossy magazines or between their favorite soap operas. As Muhammad explained earlier, once minority youths enlist in the military, many find a very different experience from the one portrayed on glossy videotapes and slick pamphlets.

For Army mechanic Lance Waters, serving in Kuwait proved a continuous test of his will and his nerve. In an article by Salim Muwakkil in *In These Times,* Waters related the racial tension, religious intolerance and even fear of violence that dogged Black soldiers in Desert Storm. A practicing Muslim, Waters said he was ridiculed for his religious beliefs and his outspoken racial views. "The atmosphere out there is one of sheer savagery," Waters said. "Everywhere you look, you see signs like 'Kill 'em all and let God sort 'em out' and 'We came thousands of miles to smoke a camel jockey' and those kinds of things. Most of the white troops call Iraqis and even the Arabs who are our allies 'sand niggers,' and they don't bother to hold their tongues in the presence of Black soldiers."

Waters said that Black troops comprised more than 40 percent of his unit—the 101st Airborne Division—but that virtually none of the leadership was Black. In his own company, 70 of 135 men were Black. "They openly called us niggers, and they disrespected my religion every chance they got," Waters said. "The people in charge tolerated the racism and the ignorant hillbilly shit that was going on in the ranks, and they accused us of undermining the morale if we complained. Their usual response was, 'Fuck you if you can't take a joke.' His story has been replayed throughout history, as the Black soldier learns, belatedly, that the only place there's true camaraderie in the military is in the foxhole, where the bullets whizzing past a white youth's head can make him want to kiss the "nigger" who just saved his rear.

But what about the future of the Black soldier, once he or she has fought for the country and paid his or her dues? Tom Wynn, director of the Milwaukee-based National Association for Black Veterans, says that when he travels the country talking about disproportionate numbers, he takes a different approach. "I'm dealing with it from a humanistic, moralistic, racial, equitable point of view," Wynn explained. "I'm dealing with what happens after the Colin Powells of the world get through with [minority recruits]." His organization has compiled this overview of some of the "rewards" of military service for America's 6.3 million Black veterans:

- For every one white unemployed military veteran, there are three minority veterans without a job.

- Veterans comprise about 35 percent of the prison population nationally. More than 50 percent of that population are Black veterans.

- Homeless veterans comprise nearly one-third of the total homeless population in some large cities, Wynn asserts. Nearly 50 percent of those homeless veterans are Black.

- During Vietnam, 507,000 soldiers received other than honorable discharges, issued administratively and without a military hearing, which was usually interpreted to mean that the soldier's performance was flawed in some way. Three hundred thousand of those soldiers were Black—nearly one out of every three Black soldiers who fought in the war.[13]

Dr. Earnest Webb, a psychologist at the Veteran's Resource Center in Chicago, says the minority vet has a compounded burden because of military service. "A lot of Blacks had experienced some trauma before they went to war, in terms of racism here in the U.S., then they experienced the trauma there, and then had to come back and deal with the trauma of being Black and a Vietnam veteran." While still in the military, Webb said, "There's no mentor system in the army, in terms of [Blacks] being brought up the ladder and taught proper procedures. They don't know what they're going to do or what they want to do."

Or as Jamillah Muhammad puts it, "They go into the army thinking they're going to work with computers and all they might do is wind up unloading them off a truck." She later added, "Basically, we send kids to the military, and they come out qualified to be janitors with a gun."

The psychic trauma of battle, coupled with a sense of frustration and hopelessness back home is stress on top of stress, Webb says. "I don't think there's a minority veteran who comes in here who doesn't talk about it. You think you've served your country, yet it doesn't seem like you've gotten any further than when you left."

Still, there are those Blacks who staunchly support the military, and find debate over disproportionate minority numbers almost offensive. Chicagoan Ted Saunders, a former Green Beret who did three tours of duty in Vietnam, thinks a discussion of minority casualties is actually the flip side of other criticism, wherein some of the same people who were complaining about Blacks being left out of the military before Desert Storm later cried about too many being in. "What we were afraid of, because qualifications were so high, was that minorities would be left out of the Army," Saunders said. Because many inner-city Black youths lack access to quality education, critics feared it might be difficult for them to pass the tougher military tests instituted since the early 70s. "I have no doubt in my mind that this was one of the schemes that was in place before Colin Powell came in," Saunders said.

An amateur expert on Blacks in the military, Saunders uses a lot of ammunition in making his point about the need for pride in Black America's military history. Indeed, the average Black child learns sometime during Black History Month that Crispus Attucks, an escaped slave, was the first to die when the Revolutionary War began on March 4, 1770. Saunders thinks Attucks's memory, and the memories of all Black soldiers in America's history, are tarnished when Black participation is criticized.

But Saunders' nationalistic pride is countered by a surprisingly large body of research done over the years on Blacks in the U.S. military. Most of that research—both military in-house studies and those by critical observers—conclude that equity and fair treatment for the Black soldier has been virtually nonexistent since day one.

One study notes that "Concepts such as democracy and community responsibility played nominal roles in determining the daily lives of Blacks in the military," and that in early wars, Blacks who served were largely still enslaved or freed solely for the purpose of filling gaps when white enlistment was down.[14] The same study notes that more than 5,000 Blacks served in the Colonial Army, though General George Washington had worked hard to exclude them. He changed his mind, however, when the need for men to fill manual-labor positions grew. Nearly 200,000 Blacks served as volunteers in the Civil War, and President Abraham Lincoln and others concluded that without their help, the Union would have lost the war. It was estimated that some 38,000 Black soldiers died—35 percent more than other troops.[15] Blacks displayed great bravery in ensuing conflicts, as exemplified by the all-Black Tenth Cavalry during the Spanish American War and the Black mess-hall mate Dorie Miller, who shot down six Japanese fighters during the invasion at Pearl Harbor. Still, Hope notes that Blacks returning to this country after wartime were often subjected to harsh treatment and outright racial violence from embittered whites deriding their wartime heroism.

The government responded with Executive Order No. 9981 in 1948, designed as a policy of equality for the military; on paper, anyway, the military was officially desegregated. Also, the elimination of a recruiting quota that controlled the numbers of Blacks resulted in a 28-percent increase in the number of Black enlistees within months in the early 50s. But by the end of the Korean War, Blacks accounted for more than 40 percent of the new reduction in Army personnel.[16]

Vietnam further underscored the inequities for Blacks in the military. In 1965, 27 percent of Black inductees were assigned to the infantry, compared to 18 percent of whites.[17] Dr. Webb, drafted in 1967 and wounded during the infamous Tet Offensive in 1968, says, "All the guys up on the hill with me were Black. I can't speak for anybody else, but that's what I saw."

One thing is certain: The advent of the volunteer army in 1973 drastically changed the composition of the armed forces. Whereas in principle, anyway, a draft cut across all economic boundaries for its ranks, the All Volunteer Force (AVF) changed the profile of the average soldier. The numbers of soldiers from more affluent or well-educated backgrounds dropped starkly, replaced by recruits from lower socio-economic and educational ranks.

In the late 60s, when large numbers of college-educated white males opted out of military service through deferments, or left the country to avoid the draft, the military lowered its required entrance-exam scores, which allowed more minorities and poor whites to enter. These recruits, who often had either little education or lower-quality schooling, comprise more than 90 percent of the men who received "other than honorable" discharges during the Vietnam war years, essentially casting yet another shadow over their already highly criticized participation in an "unjust war."[18]

In total, only 10 million of the potential pool of 18 million draft-aged men during the Vietnam years ever served in Vietnam.[19] Wynn and other veteran's groups say that these eight million others were largely middle- to upper-class, college educated males.

Dorn of the Brookings Institution says the volunteer army differs from the draft military in four important ways. It has: 1) a much higher percentage of Blacks; 2) a much higher percentage of women; 3) a much lower percentage of college graduates in the enlisted ranks; and 4) a much higher percentage of high-school graduates.

The military's tougher entrance requirements, such as background checks, drug testing, and the rigorous mental tests, weed out lots of applicants, many of whom might have been accepted 20 years ago, Dorn said. But in general, the AVF had swift results for Black enlistment. Their ranks had dropped dramatically from 1971 to 1972, from 41,326 to 26,599. But the following year, when the AVF began, that number rose by about 12,000, a near 20-year high.

Educationally, by 1988, more than three-fourths of enlisted recruits had high-school diplomas or GEDs. Among officer ranks, only 14,535 of the total 302,989 had less than a baccalaureate degree. But whereas the military is about one-third minorities, there are only 11 percent minorities in the officer ranks.[20] Dorn says it's directly related to the higher educational standards, and again, because Blacks and other minorities often don't have equal access to better or higher education, they are left out of officer ranks.

This relatively new focus on an educated military presents an ironic problem for Black America. It's not the kid who dropped out of school and is flirting with prison who gets into the military. In the Black community, it's often the above-average youth who is attracted to the military, and who because of financial reasons finds him or herself unable to go to the school of his or her dreams. In fact, those same students may even find that a state university is beyond their means, and the only avenue that will guarantee a college education is the military.

"You have to look at the kinds of Blacks and other minorities who are going into the military in order to assess whether or not they're going in because they're poor or poorly educated and have no choice," Dorn says. "Though often that's the case, many times they're bright young people who found themselves in financial constraints, or found their other choices unchallenging." In essence, the military is skimming off the "cream of the crop" of young Black males and females, whereas large percentages of their white counterparts, equal to them in every way except finances, may opt for other choices. For example, one 1982 study found that 42 percent of Black youths who met the military's requirements were enlisting, while only 14 percent of white youths were joining up.[21]

But there's a flip side to that: "Even when our kids test into the army, the largest percentage of them score as being eligible for combat training, not for being eligible for training as a technician or technologist," Wynn says. Though it's hard to find information about the variety of roles for Black soldiers in Desert Storm, or how many were on the front lines, it's probably safe to conclude that Colin Powell and Schwarzkopf's second-in-command Calvin Waller were probably the only persons of color present during war confabulations.

Some critics argue that not only is Powell's presence at the helm misleading, it's dangerous to assume that he will help smooth the way for Blacks coming up behind him. "Colin Powell is a product of the American white power structure, and it's predictable that he would not see himself necessarily as out front on issues that are significant for African Americans," Asante says. "Normally, when people become immersed in that system, they get to a position where they no longer see themselves from an ethnic or racial or cultural background. It's a mistake."

Indeed, the general has now been relegated to the status of "reluctant warrior," as *Newsweek* magazine called him several months after the war had ended. He's been characterized as unwilling to start the war, as someone who disagreed with Bush and wanted to continue with sanctions, and ultimately was a figurehead. How ironic that his more humanistic approach to the possibility of extinguishing thousands of lives is now being denigrated. It took a Black man to have the courage to say no to the killing machine, but Powell has risked his hero status in the eyes of the hawks in the war room.

But Powell aside, *have* minority soldiers been blatantly "used"?

History offers some insight into that question in an action taken by President Lyndon B. Johnson in the late 60s. Called "Project 100,000," its goal was to recruit 100,000 minority youths into the military, as the fighting escalated and numbers of troops began to dwindle. The program actually corralled more than 300,000 recruits who otherwise would not have passed Army tests. It was undertaken in light of sentiment that military training and discipline would help minority youths "overcome their disadvantages as they compete in the civilian sector."

But one 1990 analysis of Project 100,000 comparing participants in Project 100,000 with their civilian peers found that "In terms of employment status, educational achievement and income, those who never served appeared better off than those who had been in the military."[22] Project 100,000 veterans were found more likely to be unemployed, to have an average level of education significantly lower than non-veterans, and to make less money than non-veterans, the report says.

But how much were Project 100,000 participants, or in fact any of the minority men or women who've served in America's military, actually victims? Victims of economic conscription, victims of manipulative whites who've used them to further their own ends, or simply victims of a society that doesn't value or respect them on these shores, but is glad to have them shed blood on foreign soil? One can't be too hasty in deriving an answer to that question. One avenue that is underexplored for Black Americans, some think, is a widespread malnourished consciousness that leaves them blind to the machinations of a political and economic system only too eager to exploit them.

"What you must understand is that there is within our population a considerable amount of what I call naivete in regards to the political structure of the society itself," Asante states. "It is not so farfetched, as some of the white conservatives and others have said, that many of these African Americans who are fighting feel like they are indeed fighting for the same fundamental reasons as whites."

This "misorientation," as Asante calls it, creates a generation of Blacks who indeed view it as their duty to fight for a Commander in Chief who vetoed the Civil Rights Bill of 1990, which might have made their lives somewhat easier once they got back to the United States. In fact, "How many of those young Black males going to the Gulf, really understood what the Civil Rights Bill was about? That's what I mean about a lack of consciousness. If people are not aware of their situations and what's going on, then they will be used against themselves."

Asante explains that deadly void even further. "Most Blacks who are in the Army have basically a high-school education. And if they come through the educational system as African Americans, they have very little awareness of their own historical experiences in this country, and do not understand their relationship to either the nation or the military or the world. That is why it is so easy, particularly with the younger recruits, to convince them of any particular objective."

He adds a sobering footnote. "It's my opinion that if African American soldiers were asked for some reason to go and march on the Blacks in South Africa in order to support the white regime, that many of them would do so because of the notion of duty and that they are doing something for their country, without understanding the larger implications."

Perhaps. But perhaps not. In Chicago, a groundswell of activity occurred within the Black activist community as Operation Desert Storm progressed. But as one leader pointed out, there was no forum for those activists to be heard. In America, 1991, the last thing most whites want to hear is more "bellyaching" from minorities about fairness. Television cameras weren't seeking out the groups of Black mothers who took to the streets in protest. They weren't going to the Black churches and filming the candlelight vigils. And, sadly, for many people, if it doesn't make the television news, it's not worth considering.

Melendrez of California offers another interesting interpretation of the perception of inactivity. Recent polls have shown that most whites think minorities are less patriotic than they are, less willing to fight for their country. "As long as minorities are perceived as less patriotic, and whites feel they won't pull their load in the 'dirty work,' it's very hard to come out vocally in opposition. There's enough to deal with racism, poverty, health, and other issues to have your basic beliefs in the "ideals" of America challenged."

So what's the solution to Ethnic USA's dilemma, caught in the supposed "equal opportunity haven" of the military but still not able to pierce the armor surrounding other sectors of our society?

"Until we become unwilling to participate in battles to protect white hegemony around the world, we will always seek the military as the best way out," said Haki Madhubuti, founder of Chicago's Third World Press and most recently author of the renowned book *Black Men—Obsolete, Single, Dangerous?* He agrees with Asante's opinion that consciousness must be raised, but he was heartened by what he called a drumbeat of resistance that came from deep within the ranks.

"I don't believe that we're totally blind, and there were many young brothers who didn't think about the implications of what they were doing until they got over there," Madhubuti said. "Once they did get over there, though, their views changed. I think that if it keeps happening, those same people will gather the knowledge and courage to say no."

Whatever conclusion is drawn about minority representation in the military, the debate has at least forced Black Americans to reassess their contributions to patriotism and their service to a country that not only grudgingly made amends for past injustices, but has recently started the ominous process of reneging on earlier promises.

Or, summing it up more eloquently, "This issue does not exist in a vacuum," according to Michael Brown, national director of CENTERJE (Combined Efforts Nationally To Evoke Racial Justice and Equality), based in Chicago. "You cannot look at disproportionate numbers of African-American males on the front lines or in the Army as a whole, while on the other hand, their number in the officer ranks is disproportionately smaller, and not call that issue on the table," Brown said. "You cannot look at our history of inequities as an unconstitutionalized people and not talk about our reasons for not wanting to die on the front lines."

In fact, the signal must be sent that there is a national commitment that cuts across all racial and economic lines. Since the draft has been eliminated, it's fallen on the backs of minorities and the poor to "prove" their commitment to this country, to risk it all to protect our interests. "It's a wonderful situation for the liberals who've opposed the draft, because they're off the hot seat," Melendrez says. But we're shouldering their burden. The Gulf War was a perfect example of the people in power saying, "Let's get the disenfranchised of society, put them in the military, plan for an early, massive attack before you risk a rebellion at home, while the people back there sit dumb and happy in front of their televisions." It's dangerous to everyone involved, but particularly for people of color.

For minorities in general, the aftermath of the war is a time to ponder the true meaning of the word "power" within U.S. society. It can mean one of two things—first, the ability to stifle and crush your competition or enemy whether on the playing field, in the boardroom, or on the battleground, or it can mean having enough money or influence to remove yourself from the realm of concerns facing those less fortunate than you. Often, those concerns can be as simple as having enough to eat and finding shelter, or choosing between a minimum-wage job or a welfare check, or between state school or the Army. Minorities, who are hampered from the outset because of institutionalized racism, may always find themselves in the position of viewing the "three hots and a cot," the promise of an education, and the steady paycheck offered by Mother Military as the best deal of all, given the alternatives.

Notes

1. Department of Defense Statistics, from the DOD Office of Public Affairs, January 1991.
2. U.S. Census Bureau, 1990 census data.
3. Jack D. Foner, *Blacks in the Military in American History, A New Perspective*, New York, Praeger Publishers, 1974.
4. Los Angeles Public Schools, Office of Dropout Prevention, July 1991.
5. *Roll Call Newspaper*, Washington, DC, September 13, 1990.
6. Department of Defense, Office of Public Affairs, August 1991.
7. U.S. Bureau of Labor Statistics study, issued February 1991.

8. *Chicago Sun-Times* survey, August 1990.
9. Tom Holm, "American Indians and the Military, State Use of Ethnicity and the Process of Nativization," *State of Native America,* M. Annette Jaimes, ed., Boston: South End Press, 1992.
10. Ibid.
11. Ibid.
12. Ibid.
13. The National Council of Churches, the Incarcerated Veteran's Assistance Organization, the Senate Committee on Veteran's Affairs, and the Homeless Veteran's Reintegration Project.
14. Richard O. Hope, "Blacks in The Military, Trends in Participation," *Race: Twentieth Century Dilemmas—Twenty-First Century Prognoses,* Winston A. Van Horne and Thomas V. Tonnesen, eds., University of Wisconsin System Institute on Race and Ethnicity, 1989.
15. Foner, op. cit.
16. Ibid.
17. Ibid.
18. National Association For Black Veterans, Milwaukee, Wisconsin.
19. Ibid.
20. Department of Defense, Office of Public Affairs, January 1991.
21. Martin Binkin, *Blacks and The Military,* The Brookings Institution, Washington, DC, 1982.
22. "Effects of Military Experience on Post-Service Lives of Low-Aptitude Recruits," Janice Laurence, Peter F. Ramsberger and Monica A. Gribben, 1990 study.

CHAPTER 12

THE GULF CRISIS AND ANTI-ARAB RACISM IN AMERICA

Nabeel Abraham

The Gulf war triggered an outburst of flag-waving, blind patriotism, and jingoism not seen in this country since the Second World War. Some of the hyper-patriotism was directed at the media; Senator Alan Simpson's denunciation of Cable News Network reporter Peter Arnett as a "collaborator" and an enemy "sympathizer" was the most extreme. The brunt of the patriotic backlash, however, was directed at anti-war protesters. At Seton Hall, Marco Lokar, an Italian basketball player who declined to join his teammates in sporting the stars and stripes on his shorts, was booed and hissed off the court, and eventually off the continent. Actress Margo Kidder was similarly harassed after she spoke out against the war *and* demonstrated concern for Iraqi casualties. She encountered a torrent of opprobrium and abuse from loyal Americans who felt she had violated the sanctity of her on-screen role as Superman's girlfriend. Vanessa Redgrave experienced similar incidents, as did many others across the country who dared to question the White House's Gulf policies. Isolation and rejection was the order of the day once the country was at war. The spirit of the moment was aptly captured by George Mitchell, the Senate majority leader, who scolded dissenters, saying, "We have had our debate, now is the time to get behind our President," a 1990s twist to Senator Arthur Vandenberg's post-World War II quip that "politics stops at the water's edge."

The patriotic backlash was not limited to dissenters and anti-war protesters. It also touched the country's 2.5 million Arab Americans, as well as thousands of non-Arab Muslims and other Middle Easterners living in the United States. But, unlike the dissenters, Arab Americans and other Middle Easterners were not necessarily singled out because of their publicly professed opposition to U.S. intervention in the Gulf. Most, in fact, remained silent, intimidated by the zealotry swelling around them and by the knowledge that anti-Arab, anti-Muslim, anti-Middle Eastern racism lay just beneath the surface of U.S. society. Memories of previous outbursts of anti-Arab racism were still fresh in their minds.

Gulf Backlash: Anti-Arab Racism

Harassment, threats, vandalism, and violence against Arab Americans and others who could conceivably be mistaken for Iraqis characterized the Gulf crisis from the beginning. According to the Washington-based American-Arab Anti-Discrimination Committee (ADC), such hate crimes reached an "all time high" during the crisis, intensifying after the commencement of the air campaign on January 17. Before the crisis erupted in early August, ADC had logged five anti-Arab hate crimes during 1990. From the beginning of the crisis to February 2, 1991, the organization recorded some 86 incidents. Many others went unreported.[1]

The majority of crimes (48 out of 86 cases, or 56 percent) were directed at Arab-American organizations, political activists, and others who publicly dissented from official U.S. policy.[2] Several examples illustrate the nature of these incidents. On August 8, the day after Bush announced the dispatch of U.S. forces to the Persian Gulf, the ADC Los Angeles office received a highly offensive and threatening message. In Albuquerque, New Mexico, two Arab Americans were inundated by nearly 100 menacing phone calls after a local newspaper ran an interview with them. In Dearborn, Michigan, a caller threatened to kill the publisher of an Arab community newspaper "if any Americans in Kuwait are hurt."[3] Following the outbreak of war in mid-January, Arab and Muslim community institutions in Texas, Oklahoma, Michigan, and California were vandalized, bombed, or harassed in some way.

Being highly visible, such targets were inviting, and thus the incidents surrounding them were not wholly unexpected.

Less prominent targets were also attacked. Arab-owned businesses in Michigan, Florida, Ohio, Texas, and California were vandalized, several damaged by arson, though local police were reluctant to link some of the arson cases to ethnic hostility. Jingoism seems to have been behind much of the vandalism against Arab-owned businesses. In the inner cities, the attacks may have resulted from a combination of jingoistic hysteria and simmering resentment towards "foreign-owned businesses" in the African-American community. In reaction to the hostility, many Arab-owned businesses in the Detroit area, for example, prominently displayed American flags in their store windows, like talismans to ward off evil.

The most telling incidents were those directed at ordinary persons who had the misfortune of being in the wrong place at the wrong time, and who fit the American stereotype of "Arab." Such incidents reveal the depth of anti-Arab racism and bigotry in the United States. ADC logged 36 incidents (42 percent) against ordinary Arab Americans and others who were mistaken for Arabs for the period between August 8, 1990 and February 2, 1991. Several people were physically assaulted simply because they appeared to be Arabs. In Gaithersburg, Maryland, a road crew attacked an Iranian family, leaving the father partially paralyzed. Nine days later (August 24) in New York City, a gang approached a rider in the subway demanding to know if he was an Arab. The rider was beaten before he managed to flee to safety. In Toledo, Ohio, a Palestinian student was menacingly approached by a group of six men wanting to know if he was an Arab (September 14). He managed to talk his way out of trouble. Even Kuwaitis residing in the United States were not spared anti-Arab hostility. Two Kuwaitis were accosted at a shopping mall in Portland, Oregon. The attackers apparently were angered to find Kuwaitis enjoying some Christmas shopping while American troops were suffering the privations of the Saudi desert. Another Kuwaiti was beaten while delivering pizza in San Francisco, although it is not clear whether the attack was due to ethnic or other reasons. Perhaps the most perverse case of mistaken identity occurred in early January in Baltimore, when several drunkards verbally abused a Polynesian Jew, calling him "filthy Arab" and "Arab pig."

Anti-Arab assaults increased with the commencement of Operation Desert Storm on January 17. During the war, many Arab Americans feared for their safety. This was especially true among Arab immigrants, who were terrified by the jingoism swirling around them. In Dearborn, Michigan, for example, some immigrants reportedly refused to leave their homes during the first week of the war. Perhaps with good reason. Lebanese and Palestinian immigrant women, who often wear traditional Arab dress (head scarves and embroidered dresses), encountered hostility in the form of cold stares and verbal abuse when they ventured outside. In Bergen, New Jersey, a woman wearing a traditional headscarf was accosted by several women in a department store. In Fremont, California, a Sikh wearing a traditional headdress was angrily told by a customer in a store to "Go back home, you damned Iraqi."

Avoiding Middle Eastern dress did not always suffice to ward off trouble, however. One need only fit the American stereotype of an "Arab" and be overheard speaking some Arabic to trigger hostility, as a Lebanese student of mine discovered when he and a friend, also Lebanese, stopped for gas in a white, middle-class neighborhood on Detroit's east side. As they chatted in Arabic while pumping gas, they were approached by four youths demanding to know if they were Iraqis. The friend responded inappropriately, an altercation ensued, and my student received a gash across his forehead that required eight stitches to close.

Even at home, Arabs were not always safe from the swelling tide of jingoism washing over the country. Non-Arabs, probably driven by a combination of personal enmity, xenophobia, and hyper-patriotism, harassed their Middle Eastern neighbors across the United States. In the same Maryland town where the road crew attacked the family of Iranians, neighbors pestered a Palestinian family with threatening telephone calls. Eventually, the family's house was egged and the tires on their car were slashed. In two decades of living in the United States, the family had never experienced anything like it.

Anti-Arab racism took many guises and surfaced in the most unlikely places. As Operation Desert Storm swung into action, the basketball team at Fordson High School in Dearborn, Michigan, was told that the Wolverine A Conference, to which Fordson belongs, was considering a proposal to terminate competition in all sports for the rest of the school year. Ostensibly, concern for the safety of students was the reason for the proposal. The basketball players, however, knew the real reason: Fordson athletic teams are predominantly Arab; 11 of the 13 players on the basketball team are Arab-Americans. "People don't like me because I'm Arabic," said Haisam Abadi, a junior point guard. "It's like that wherever I go, even on the basketball court. In our last game (against Wyandotte Roosevelt) someone said: 'Go back to Saudi Arabia. You're not wanted here.' Every game something like that is said." An alarmed parent at a rival high school told the Fordson coach she would not attend a game in Dearborn because she heard "they blew up Telegraph" (a major metropolitan artery running through part of Dearborn). Another parent complained to the same coach that one of the Fordson wrestlers had "Hussein" etched across the back of his warm-up jacket. "She didn't think it was appropriate," the coach said, even though that was the boy's name.[4] In Gaithersburg, Maryland, a dark-skinned North African bearing the common Hussein surname was ridiculed at a social-services office. The social workers advised him to change his name if he hoped to find a job.[5]

Any attempt to gauge anti-Arab sentiment during the crisis must take into account the hype trickling down from the White House and other powerful institutions (Congress, the news media, political commentators, academia). Bush's characterization of Saddam Hussein as "the new Hitler of the Middle East" served to inflame passions among a politically unsophisticated populace, as did reports of alleged horrors perpetrated by the Iraqi army in Kuwait. The most notorious was the removal of babies' incubators from Kuwait's hospitals, a fabricated story that circulated widely.[6] Latent fears about a recurrence of the oil shortages and attendant price rises were also stirred by the Bush administration, which concocted reports of an imminent Iraqi takeover of the Saudi oil fields.[7] Such scare tactics fed on deep-seated anti-Arab, anti-Muslim sentiments extant in U.S. culture.

Although the anti-Arab tenor of the Bush administration's mobilization campaign was relatively restrained by the standards of the Reagan administration (see below), the anti-Arab message got through just the same.[8] Radio talk shows and other venues of popular culture (bumper stickers, t-shirts, pins, posters) percolated with anti-Arab sentiment.[9] Stand-up comedians parlayed blatantly crude anti-Arab jokes into wider audiences and greater profit, as did the enterprising merchants who peddled anti-Arab wares to a hyped-up public. A popular item was a poster depicting a bedouin on a camel in the cross-hairs of a rifle atop the slogan "I'd Fly 10,000 Miles to Smoke a Camel." Equally distressing to Arab Americans was the use of musical lyrics to convey anti-Arab messages. Lyrics that had been altered at the time of the 1980 Iranian hostage crisis ("I'm Going to Atomic the Islamic" and "Bomb Iran," the latter a takeoff on the Beach Boys' classic "Barbara Ann"), were retro-fitted to the new enemy. "Many of these songs go beyond being cute or patriotic," observed Lewis Carlson, professor of popular culture at Western Michigan University. "When Hank Williams Jr. sings 'Don't Give Us A Reason,' he's saying 'Don't give us a reason to wipe you off the map'." Carlson is probably correct in adding that such lyrics reflected the inner wishes of many Americans at the time.[10]

So far as can be determined, Pan Am was the only major corporation that engaged in crude anti-Arab discrimination, barring all Iraqis, even legal resident aliens of the United States, from all its international and domestic flights when the war broke out. Other airlines appear to have been more discreet. A United Airlines spokeswoman disclosed that "Iraqi nationality was 'one of several' factors taken into consideration when accepting passengers, cargo, and mail."[11] Protests by Arab-American and civil-liberties groups forced Pan Am to modify its "no Iraqis allowed" policy to allow resident aliens to board its planes, but the airline continued to bar other Iraqi nationals, even those with valid U.S. entry visas.[12]

Many companies in the Detroit area tightened security at their offices and plants during the Gulf buildup, reportedly at the direction of federal authorities who warned of potential "terrorist threats" emanating from Detroit's large Arab-American community.[13] In October, Northwest Airlines, which operates a large facility at Detroit Metropolitan Airport, was accused of subjecting two Yemeni women and other Árab travelers to excessive security measures, including body searches. The company's attitude was typical. According to a company spokesman, a passenger's ethnic background "could have an influence" on the decision of security guards to conduct searches. The previous June, Northwest hired an Israeli company, International Consultants on Targeted Security (incidentally, the same outfit used by Pan Am), to oversee its security operations.[14] The fact that the Arab-American community nationally has no history of terrorist involvement, and instead has been the *victim* of Jewish extremist terrorism and redneck violence, never seems to carry much weight with law-enforcement agencies. For them, as for most Americans, "Arab" is synonymous with "terrorist," irrespective of the facts.[15]

The fallout from the Gulf crisis was clearly a manifestation of the anti-Arab, anti-Muslim, anti-Middle Eastern racism endemic to U.S. culture. Unlike other forms of racism, anti-Arab prejudice is often tolerated by mainstream society.[16] This fact has been recognized by a number of commentators. After surveying the attitudes of 600 Americans in a telephone poll in the fall of 1980, researcher Shelly Slade concluded, "The Arabs remain one of the few ethnic groups who can still be slandered with impunity in America."[17] Similarly, recalling her attitude toward Arabs as a reporter for *The Chicago Daily News* in 1969, nationally syndicated columnist Georgie Ann Geyer writes:

> The Arab world was set up, largely subconsciously, to be sure, in the minds of the American people and even of the American press as a kind of "outcast" world. The unspoken expectation of editors, friends and even of oneself was that the Arabs were a decadent and backward people, left behind by history and even slightly abhorrent in their ancient and odd habits of past times.[18]

Some important work has been already done in the area of anti-Middle Eastern bias and stereotypes in the news media, literature, and Hollywood, and there is little need to rehearse it here.[19] Stereotypes, however, constitute only one aspect of the more fundamental problem of anti-Arab racism as evinced by the surge of anti-Arab incidents during the Gulf crisis. Curiously, anti-Arab incidents never reached the doomsday levels predicted by some during the Gulf crisis, which arguably was the most intense and sustained armed conflict involving the United States and an Arab country.[20] To be sure, the increase in the absolute number of anti-Arab hate crimes was dramatic, but the overwhelming majority of incidents (77 percent) was limited to threats and other types of harassment (verbal abuse, fake bomb threats). Based on previous experiences (see below), one might have expected greater and more serious repercussions from the Gulf War (e.g., bombings of mosques and Arab community organizations, community media outlets, ethnic businesses, coffee houses). With several notable exceptions, this did not happen.

One way of assessing this episode of anti-Arab racism is to compare it to others of similar nature and magnitude. The most relevant candidate would be the period encompassing the 1985 TWA and Achille Lauro hijackings, and Ronald Reagan's attacks on Libya the following year.

Anti-Arab Racism in the Eighties

For the better part of the 1980s, Arab Americans lived in an increasing state of fear as the Reagan administration waged its war on international terrorism, a euphemism for "Arab or Middle Eastern terrorism." The apprehension reached its zenith in 1985-86.[21] The hijacking of TWA Flight 847 to Beirut by Lebanese Shiite gunmen triggered an outpouring of anti-Arab anger in the United States. The June 14 hijacking began with the beating death of a young American aboard the plane, and ended 17 days later with the release of the remaining U.S. hostages. The incident received extensive coverage in the news media, much of it unabashedly sensationalist and hysterical.[22] The media hype may have contributed to the outbreak of violent attacks against Arab Americans and Middle Easterners that coincided with the hijacking, making 1985 a milestone in the history of violence against Arabs and other Middle Easterners.[23] Between June 16 and 22 Islamic centers in San Francisco, Denver, Dearborn, and Quincy (Massachusetts) were vandalized or received telephone threats. Arab-American organizations in New York and Detroit were also threatened. On June 22 the Dar es Salaam Mosque in Houston was fire bombed, resulting in $50,000 worth of damage.[24] A week later, on June 30, a woman known to be dating a Palestinian was raped in Tucson by two men who lightly carved a Star of David on her chest. On August 16 a bomb placed outside the door of the Boston office of the American-Arab Anti-Discrimination Committee (ADC) detonated, severely injuring the two policemen called to remove it.[25]

In autumn 1985 another Middle Eastern hijacking occurred, and again violence against Arab Americans and other Middle Easterners ensued. But this time the outcome was far more tragic. On the morning of Friday, October 11, a bomb went off at the Los Angeles office of the ADC, killing the organization's 41-year-old regional director, Alex Odeh.[26] The day before, Odeh had appeared on a local television news program, where he opined that the Palestine Liberation Organization (PLO) and its leader Yasser Arafat were not behind the hijacking of the Achille Lauro cruise liner in the Mediterranean. The murder of one of the ship's passengers, Leon Klinghoffer, had been confirmed on Wednesday, October 9. Odeh's statements condemning the hijacking and terrorism in general were edited out, possibly contributing to his murder, though it is difficult to be certain about this.[27] The FBI considered Odeh's murder to be the top terrorist act of 1985 in the United States. The agency strongly hinted that the Jewish Defense League (JDL), or a similar Jewish extremist group, was behind the bombing.[28]

In the 18 months following the Odeh murder, hostile attacks against Arab Americans and Arab organizations tended to follow a fairly predictable pattern. Less than two months after the Odeh killing, the Washington headquarters of the ADC were severely damaged by a mysterious fire that gutted major parts of the building.[29] The still-unsolved fire occurred on Friday evening, November 30, five days after Egyptian army commandos stormed a hijacked Egyptian airliner on the Mediterranean island of Malta. The rescue operation resulted in 59 dead from among the mostly Egyptian passengers and crew.[30]

In the early weeks of January 1986 the Reagan administration openly raised the possibility of a retaliatory strike against Libya following terrorist attacks at the Rome and Vienna airports on December 27 in which 12 persons died and 114 were wounded.[31] On January 7, Reagan publicly declared that there was "irrefutable" evidence linking Qaddafi to the airport attacks.[32] The tension of the period is reflected in the following headlines: "Libya Jets Buzz U.S. Plane on Patrol in Mediterranean," (New York Times, January 15); "Shultz Supports Armed Reprisals," (New York Times, January 16); "U.S. Navy Starting Maneuvers Off Libya" (New York Times, January 24).

On the night of January 17, 1986, Moustafa Dabbas, the 51-year-old publisher and editor of Arrayb (The Aim), Philadelphia's only Arabic/English newspaper, was beaten and mugged by several men. Dabbas says one of the men first inquired as to whether he was the editor of Arrayb. When he replied that he was, "the men beat him unconscious, leaving him with a fractured skull, a gash under one eye, and bleeding from the ears."[33] According to another report, Dabbas "was nearly beaten to death

ANTI-ARAB RACISM   263

and spent several days in intensive care with a blood clot on the brain, a fractured skull, 17 stitches and other complications."[34]

Dabbas, an immigrant from Syria, had experienced harassment before, but nothing like the assault against his person.[35] Ten days earlier in Washington, DC (January 7, 1986) "two ADC staff members were forced off the road on the way home from work by a car which sped away afterwards." In Milwaukee two days later, a Palestinian grocer was shot in the head by gunmen who took no money.[36]

By late January concern was still running high among Arab Americans.[37] In Flint, Michigan, three Arab Americans, two men and a woman, were arrested in a Hyatt Regency hotel on January 21 after an employee reported to local police that the three were part of a "Qaddafi hit team." "The three, all of whom are U.S. citizens, said the police abused them verbally and refused to explain the charges." The men told the Washington-based ADC that they were beaten by jail guards; one man reportedly suffered a fractured foot which allegedly went unattended until the next morning.[38] Mosques in southern California were also vandalized in late January. In Milwaukee, a Libyan student was allegedly harassed by the FBI and INS because of his nationality. Threats and abusive telephone calls were received by Arab-American community activists across the country.[39]

On February 19, several Arab-American leaders, joined by Alex Odeh's widow and brother, appeared before the U.S. Commission on Civil Rights, where they demanded an investigation into pernicious media stereotypes, as well as harassment, discrimination, and violence against Arab Americans. The Arab Americans faulted the news and entertainment media, Jewish groups, politicians, and government agencies. ADC Chairman James Abourezk, a former senator from South Dakota, accused President Reagan of exacerbating the problem, adding, the president has "'created a cowboy anti-Arab atmosphere' with his statements on terrorism."[40]

In March and April U.S.-Arab tensions reached an all time high. On March 25 and 26, the U.S. Navy attacked four Libyan ships in the Gulf of Sidra, destroying two of them; survivors were left to die. U.S. planes also conducted raids against the Libyan mainland, flying approximately eight miles into Libyan air space. The attacks left more than 50 Libyans dead, while the Americans suffered no casualties. The attack failed to provoke a Libyan counterattack or ignite terrorism against U.S. civilians, its apparent goal. "The Gulf of Sidra operation ... was plainly timed to stir up jingoist hysteria just prior to the crucial Senate vote on contra aid, coinciding with a fabricated Nicaraguan 'invasion' of Honduras," Noam Chomsky observes.[41]

In early April, bombs placed by unidentified terrorists aboard a TWA flight enroute from Rome to Athens (April 2), and in a West Berlin nightclub (April 5), left one American dead in each incident out of a total of five dead and scores wounded. The nightclub was frequented mostly by Black GIs and Third World immigrants, making it an unlikely target for a Libyan attack. Calling Libya's Col. Qaddafi the "mad dog of the Middle East," President Reagan vowed in a nationally televised address to retaliate if evidence revealed Libya was behind the bombings.[42] A week later (April 15) U.S. fighter planes bombed Libya in retaliation for Qaddafi's alleged complicity in the bombing of a West Berlin disco.

The April 14 attack was the first bombing in history staged for prime time television. As the subsequently published record shows, the bombing raids were carefully timed so that they would begin precisely at 7 PM Eastern Standard Time as they did (New York Times, April 18, 1986); that is, precisely at the moment when all three national television channels broadcast their major news programs, which were of course preempted as agitated anchormen switched to Tripoli for direct eyewitness reports of the exciting events.[43]

Given the climate of jingoism prevailing in March and April 1986 and the previous pattern of anti-Arab violence in the country, it was highly likely that violence would result again.[44] Indeed, that is what happened. On the night of the U.S. raid, the Washington headquarters of ADC received threatening calls with references to Libyans. In Dearborn, Michigan, several persons were arrested vandalizing Arab-American businesses, homes, and the local community center. Bomb threats were received by the Detroit ADC office, the Arab community center (ACCESS), and the local Arab-American newspaper, a routine occurrence during heightened Middle East tensions.[45] Two days before the U.S. bombing, five Arab students from the University of Syracuse (New York) "were beaten by a gang of Americans" in a bar; one student almost lost an eye in this outburst of anti-Arab hostility. Similar attacks were reported in Detroit and New Haven, Connecticut.[46]

Several weeks later on June 17 a mysterious fire damaged the offices of the United Palestine Appeal (UPA), the second Arab-American organization in Washington, DC to be struck in six months. The blaze caused over $60,000 in damage. The police determined arson was the cause, but added there was "no evidence the blaze was set by terrorists."[47] A former building custodian was later charged in the case, but his actual motives have never been established. UPA Director Bishara Bahbah told the Washington Post, "We can't help but think [the fire] might be motivated by the fact that we're Palestinians, but we do not know."[48]

The mounting violence and harassment of the previous twelve months, beginning with the June 1985 TWA hijacking, prompted Congressmen John Conyers (D-Michigan), Chairman of the House Subcommittee on Criminal Justice, to hold hearings on anti-Arab violence, the first ever.

The hearings were held on July 16, 1986. The Subcommittee on Criminal Justice heard testimony from over a dozen witnesses, including the widow of Alex Odeh. Norma Odeh seemed to encapsulate the frustrations of Arab Americans when she told the subcommittee: "While our government apprehends terrorists half way across the world, it seems helpless in the face of domestic terrorism directed against Arab Americans."[49]

Bush's War vs. Reagan's: Anti-Arab Racism in Perspective

The similarities between Bush's war and Reagan's are striking. The two events illustrate the continuity of U.S. policy toward the region as well as the extent of anti-Arab racism here at home. In the main, the Gulf War was a continuation of Reagan's aggressive stance towards Libya and others in the region (Lebanon, the Palestinians, Iran, Syria). Reagan's policy, in turn, was rooted in a long-standing U.S. imperative dating back to the Second World War, namely, control over the vast energy resources of the region.

With the tacit assistance of the major media, Bush and Reagan cynically demonized their Arab opponents. Bush's characterization of Saddam Hussein as the "New Hitler of the Middle East" echoed Reagan's earlier denunciation of Muammar Qaddafi as the "Mad Dog of the Middle East." The supposed threats posed by Libya and Iraq were exaggerations often based on outright falsehoods. Ronald Reagan alleged Qaddafi had sent a "hit team" to assassinate him and other prominent Americans. The FBI later sheepishly admitted that it had traced the notorious team to a propaganda mill located in the basement of the White House. Likewise, George Bush fabricated a string of Iraqi "threats" to justify the largest U.S. military buildup since Vietnam. Americans were told that Iraq was poised to invade Saudi Arabia following its occupation of Kuwait, raising the specter of Iraqi control over the Saudi oil fields and gasoline shortages here at home.[50] Satellite photos purchased from a commercial source revealed no such buildup. The Bush administration subsequently claimed that Iraq was on the verge of developing nuclear weapons, even though reliable information at the time indicated that Iraq was a decade away from producing even a crude World War II-type bomb.[51] The fact that the United States could have flattened Iraq using a tiny fraction of its enormous nuclear arsenal never seemed to enter into the administration's rhetoric or that of respectable opinion. The implicit assumption throughout was patently racist: Arabs (and other Third World peoples) are incapable of responsibly controlling such sophisticated weaponry and technologies, just as they are unable to exercise sufficient "self-restraint" in other areas of life.

The propaganda worked. A majority of Americans was stampeded into supporting the war of aggression. The prospect of fighting a war with the New Hitler of the Middle East sent Americans into a panic. Army surplus stores sold out their supplies of gas masks, and enterprising marketeers took to peddling masks through the *New York Times*. Americans not only refused to fly to European destinations during the normally busy Christmas holiday, they even canceled domestic trips within the continental United States—further testimony that the public had lost its grip on reality. The domestic airline industry was hurting so badly during the war that Barbara Bush took to traveling on a commercial airliner in order to reassure a wary public. Administration hype over potential Arab terrorism in the United States was so effective that "as the United Nations deadline for Iraq's withdrawal from Kuwait neared," the *New York Times* reported, "fear outpaced reality." "Some New Yorkers filled their bathtubs with water and stocked up on powdered milk."[52] Rumors had spread earlier that the city's water system had been poisoned by Arab terrorists.

In contrast to most Americans, Arab Americans were better prepared politically to see through the official propaganda and deceit. As Arab Americans were quick to point out, if Bush were truly standing up for principle in Kuwait he would have opposed aggression and occupation elsewhere: To wit, Israel's 24-year occupation of Arab lands, and its repeated aggression against neighboring Arab countries like Lebanon. As for the Reagan administration, its professed concern with deterring international terrorism hardly squared with the fact that it was at the very same time busy orchestrating a major terrorist war against Nicaragua, going so far as to prosecute the war secretly after Congress cut off funding.

As their alienation deepened, Arab Americans ironically found themselves under suspicion and attack from a populace agitated by the jingoistic rhetoric emanating from the White House and the corporate media. That was only part of their dilemma, however. In keeping with a practice dating back at least to the Nixon administration ("Operation Boulder"), the Bush and Reagan governments placed Arab Americans under the surveillance of federal agencies like the FBI and the INS, and introduced draconian "anti-terrorism" legislation in Congress (see below). These measures were doubtlessly designed to lend credibility to Washington's rhetoric regarding the "threat" from the Middle East. But they also further stigmatized Arab Americans and other Middle Easterners in the eyes of the public.

The depth of ignorance about, and racism towards, Arabs and the Middle East was so widespread that successive U.S. administrations could easily manipulate public opinion into supporting the detention and incarceration of large numbers of Iraqis (immigrants as well as U.S. citizens), Arab Americans, Iranians, and, in all likelihood, anti-war activists. I can still vividly recall standing before an all-white, middle-class church congregation in Dearborn, Michigan, on the eve of the Gulf War and witnessing the disbelief and suspicion in the faces of some church-goers when I denounced government surveillance of Arab Americans. Their attitude, openly expressed to me, was that if Arab Americans had done nothing wrong they should have nothing to fear. There was no acknowledgment that surveillance of an entire community merely on the basis of its ethnic heritage violated a basic principle of civil liberties, no recognition that the government was on the verge of repeating the mistakes of the past (i.e., the detention of Japanese Americans), and no sensitivity to the fears Arab Americans might be experiencing. If the authorities felt there was a threat, then their concerns must have merit.

Though no terrorist actions occurred in the United States during the entire duration of the Gulf crisis, no mainstream commentators took the trouble to wonder whether the White House had not merely conjured up the "threat" as a clever device to mobilize the country behind its aggression against Iraq. Doubtlessly, a few able commentators probably considered the task "unwinnable," akin to questioning the efficacy of amulets designed to ward off the evil eye. If no harm comes to you, it is because the charms "worked." If, on the other hand, misfortune occurs, it is because the precautionary measures were overpowered by malevolent forces.

Fallout from the Gulf War

Overall, Ronald Reagan's war against Libya and "Arab terrorism" uncapped a more lethal anti-Arab backlash than did George Bush's far more devastating war on Iraq. During the period March 1985 to June 1986, the zenith of Reagan's attacks, Arab Americans and Muslims suffered:

three deaths; 10 instances of serious bodily assault and seven other injuries; four bombings (one against a mosque and another against an Orthodox church); four cases of arson; 15 acts of vandalism (six committed against Muslim leaders and places of worship); 20 threats (five directed at Muslim leaders and places of worship); five complaints of harassment (two against law-enforcement authorities); and at least one break-in.[53] This period represented a peak of anti-Arab hate crime.[54]

In contrast, the wave of anti-Arab racism triggered by Bush's war, though deplorable, was relatively non-lethal. There were only five reported firebombings and cases of arson against Arab-owned businesses, and one pipebombing of a residential property during the seven-month long Gulf crisis/war.[55] No Arab or Islamic community organizations were bombed during that period, though many received threats and an incendiary device that apparently failed to explode was discovered at the American Muslim Council in San Diego. In comparison, on March 29, 1990, the Islamic Center of New England was the target of arson that resulted in one-half million dollars in damages. The incident occurred some four months *before* the Iraqi invasion, at a time when there was no Middle East crisis involving the United States. Although there were many reports of assaults against Arab Americans during the Gulf crisis, few resulted in serious injuries and no one was killed. Five incidents can be traced to the assassination of Rabbi Meir Kahane, the founder and spiritual leader of the Jewish Defense League. His murder in New York in November triggered a spate of death threats and harassment against prominent Arab Americans and others, including a drive-by-shooting in which no one was hurt. In all likelihood, these incidents had little to do with the Gulf crisis, being attributable instead to extremist Jewish hatred of Arabs.

Bush's Pious Words and Odious Deeds

It was probably fortuitous that the fallout from Bush's war was less lethal from the standpoint of Arab Americans than was Reagan's mini-war against Libya and "international terrorism." Nevertheless, it should be noted that Bush did something Ronald Reagan never did: He deplored hate violence against Arab Americans. Two months into the Gulf crisis Bush invited 200 Arab Americans to the White House for a briefing on U.S. objectives in the Gulf. He used the occasion to condemn "hate-mongers here at home," adding "death threats, physical attacks, vandalism, religious violence and discrimination against Arab Americans must end." "We [are] not going to stand for them," he intoned.[56]

Bush's pious-sounding statements should be weighed against his actual deeds. His destruction of Iraq, along with the resulting 200,000 deaths (based on a Greenpeace study) of soldiers and civilians, as well as his insistence on maintaining a stranglehold on Iraq's economy long after the cessation of hostilities and the attainment of his stated goal speak volumes about the president's concern for the value of Arab life. On the domestic front, after his meeting with Arab Americans, George Bush said or did little to allay their fears during the crisis and ensuing war. To the contrary, he made matters worse when in early January 1991, on the eve of the U.S.-led attack against Iraq, he ordered Arab Americans placed under surveillance. The Federal Bureau of Investigation immediately began "interviewing" community activists under the guise of inquiring about their "welfare." Its real mission was to investigate possible terrorist activities in the Arab community. In similar fashion, the Justice Department began photographing and fingerprinting persons entering the country carrying Iraqi or Kuwaiti passports. News of the government measures surfaced about a week before the start of the U.S.-led attack, and was no doubt timed to heighten American apprehension of "the Hitler of the Middle East."[57]

In this regard as in so many others, Bush's actions were in effect a continuation of previous White House policies, especially Reagan's. Under the Reagan presidency, the existence of a secret government plan to round up and detain up to 10,000 Arabs and Iranians was leaked to the press in 1987. The plan has never been revoked by either the Reagan or Bush administrations. The fact that the Bush administration did not try to implement it or some similar plan may have been due in part to the strength of the anti-war movement (a point to which we return). Fresh from his triumph in the Gulf, Bush sent a "crime bill" to Congress that loosely defines a "terrorist" as anyone who has raised money or recruited members for any organization that has engaged in violence. The bill effectively sets up a secret tribunal to hear the government's arguments that a "terrorist" suspect should be deported from the country and denies the defendant the right to question the government's evidence, which can include material gathered through illegal wiretapping. Moreover, if no country will accept the deported alien, he or she can be incarcerated indefinitely, even though not convicted of a crime.

Anti-Arab Racism in the Service of White House Policy

Both Bush and Reagan exploited latent U.S. racism towards Arabs and the Muslim world as a way of mobilizing public support for the projection of U.S. power overseas while promoting their domestic political agenda (expanding the national security state, increasing defense spending and attendant subsidies to the high-technology sector of the economy, savagely slashing social expenditures). As we have seen, the White House's anti-Arab machinations had negative consequences for Arab Americans and others domestically, not to mention tens of thousands more in the Middle East itself.

Whereas Reagan was able to mobilize popular sentiment merely by pandering to anti-Arab racism, Bush faced a more complicated task. Although Iraq was not the Germany of the 1930s that Bush made it out to be, it was not by the same token the underpopulated and underdeveloped Libya that Reagan had inflated to a world-class threat. The long buildup in the Gulf, coupled with the enormous scale of the enterprise, meant that Bush had to come up with justifications and arguments that went beyond Reagan's crude anti-Arab racism. The long debate over sanctions that seriously divided the elite, and by extension the media and the public, entailed greater refinements in Bush's brief for war; hence the string of fabrications and exaggerations about Iraq's "imminent" invasion of Saudi Arabia, its alleged development of nuclear weapons, its "deployment" of chemical and biological weapons, its "rape" of Kuwait, its regional ambitions, etc. The stakes were so high and the specter of major American casualties so large that crude anti-Arab racism was insufficient to convince Americans of the need to go to war.

In essence, however, Bush's brief ultimately rested on racist notions: Why should Iraq's invasion of Kuwait be opposed, but not its invasion of Iran? Why did Washington move heaven and earth to reverse Iraq's invasion but remain largely silent, even complicitous with regard to invasions by Israel, Turkey, Indonesia, South Africa, and Morocco? Why are Washington's invasions of Grenada, Panama, and South Vietnam not even called "invasions" in official newspeak, let alone the subject of criticism? How is it that the United States can drive 17 million Iraqis to near famine, inflicting epidemics and untold misery on an entire nation, all for the sanctimonious goal of stopping Iraq's crude uranium-enrichment program, but barely utter a word of criticism about Israel's sophisticated nuclear-weapons arsenal, or South Africa's program?

As usual, the major media loyally played along as they did during the Reagan years. The press conveyed the administration's propaganda line, amplifying it in the process. But toeing the line meant there was little real news to report to a news-hungry public. During the inordinately lengthy buildup in the desert, the media played up even minor incidents of anti-Arab hostility here at home. Some editorialists, cartoonists, and commentators were quick to deplore anti-Arab bigotry, while thinking nothing of supporting a near total naval blockade against a major Arab country, and, after the outbreak of war, one of the most devastating aerial bombardments in history.[58]

This contradiction was especially pronounced in places like Detroit, where the presence of a large and highly visible Arab-American community provoked intense local and national news media interest. For example, in the early days of the crisis the Detroit media seized upon a minor incident involving a Jordanian college student who had been harassed by two men waiting in the check-out lane of a Dearborn, Michigan, hardware store. One man told his companion, "We ought to nuke 'em," provoking an angry response from the Arab student who was within earshot. The latter retorted, "You can start with me, if you are big enough." The incident, trivial by any measure, was picked up by a reporter for one of the major Detroit dailies. In typical herd fashion, his story inspired several other reports in the local television media. In contrast, the grisly killing of 200,000 Arabs, Asians, and others by the U.S.-led forces provoked mild interest, if any, in these same media. The major media also criticized the government for unleashing the FBI on the Arab-American community, although they made it clear that they were not opposed to appropriate security measures to "prevent terrorism."

The domestic fallout from the Gulf War undoubtedly could have been much worse than it actually was. The fact that it was not is, I think, testimony to the size and strength of the anti-war movement across the country. The movement was able to take advantage of the long military buildup to educate segments of the population and, after the outbreak of the war, organize protests against it, albeit with uneven success. In addition, many years of work by Arab-American organizations helped make anti-Arab slurs and bigotry less acceptable in the public mind.

Sensitivity to anti-Arab stereotyping and racism has gradually spread throughout the liberal segments of society over the past decade (church groups, mostly Protestant denominations, some liberal Jewish organizations, human-rights, civil-liberties, and peace organizations). The news media, particularly the print media in cities with active Arab-American organizations, and belatedly some local television stations, have displayed greater awareness of anti-Arab bigotry. In a major departure from its previous track record of airing made-for-television movies with a decidedly anti-Arab bent, NBC aired an episode of "Shannon's Deal" several months after the Gulf War that portrayed Arab Americans sympathetically as victims of war-related bigotry. A sign of the times?

It is difficult to be sanguine when it comes to the major ideological institutions of American society. Hollywood, for example, remains reluctant to drop demeaning Middle Eastern stereotypes from its repertoire; apparently they are still a box office draw. The corporate media remain institutionally tied to the centers of power. Racism during the Gulf War was operative on many levels, not the least of which was the demonization of Hussein and the attendant notion that Arab life is dispensable. While anti-Arab violence was muted on the domestic front, it was multiplied 1000 times in the Saudi desert. The White House no doubt can be counted on to play the anti-Arab racism card again in future wars in the Middle East. Progress in countering racism must be measured not just by our success at home but by how effective we are in undermining its use in foreign policy.

Notes

1. American-Arab Anti-Discrimination Committee (ADC), *1990 ADC Annual Report on Political and Hate Violence,* Washington, DC, February 1991, and "Hate Crimes Chronology, Update," February 6, 1991. Unless noted otherwise, the data and incidents cited hereafter pertaining to the Gulf crisis are derived from these reports. C.f. "Incidents of Intelligence Gathering and Harassment Related to the Persian Gulf Crisis," *Movement Support Network* (New York: Center for Constitutional Rights, April 1, 1991).
2. This and subsequent extrapolations are based on the author's analysis of the incidents listed in the ADC logs. After breaking down the incidents into different categories, and discarding several incidents having inadequate or dubious descriptions, the total number of Gulf-related incidents was determined to be 86.
3. For other examples occurring in August 1990, see Fox Butterfield, "Arab-Americans Report Increase in Death Threats and Harassment," *New York Times,* August 29, 1990, p. A10.
4. Mick McCabe, "Fordson Confronts Prejudice," *Detroit Free Press,* January 18, 1991, p. 1E. Ultimately the Conference voted down the proposal to terminate the playing season, no doubt due to the adverse publicity the original proposal received ("Sports Suspension Rejected by Fordson's League," *Dearborn Press and Guide,* January 20, 1991, p. 1).
5. Jennie Anderson, "Blame the Arabs," *The Progressive,* February 1991.
6. On doubts about the story's authenticity, see Alexander Cockburn's "Beat the Devil" column in *The Nation,* February 2, 1991, and the magazine's Letters-to-the-Editor section, April 8.

7. On these and related matters see Knut Royce, "White House Distorted Iraqi Potential: Sources," New York *Newsday,* reprinted in *Ann Arbor News,* January 21, 1991. On the fabrication of the Iraqi threat to Saudi Arabia, see also the revealing story by Jean Heller, "Public Doesn't Get Picture with Gulf Satellite Photos," which appeared in the *St. Petersburg Times,* January 6, 1991 (reprinted in *In These Times,* February 27- March 19, 1991, p. 7).

8. Steven A. Holmes, "Arab-Americans Fault Bush Tone For Animosity Since Crisis in Gulf," *New York Times,* August 30, 1990, p. A11.

9. A Boston talk-show host made a national reputation for himself by calling on the Pentagon to go all the way. "War is not a tea party, and if it means a higher number of Iraqi casualties to take fewer American casualties and shorten the war, that's all to the good. Ultimately, even if civilian centers come under attack, it would probably shorten the war." (Cited in Martin Walker, "Patriotism in the Roar," *Manchester Guardian Weekly,* April 7, 1991, p. 23.)

10. Lisa Perlman, Associated Press, *Dearborn Press and Guide,* November 29, 1990, p. 4A.

11. Robert Reinhold, "Pan Am Is Barring Iraqis From Flights," *New York Times,* January 26, 1991, p. 9.

12. *New York Times,* February 7, 1991, p. A7.

13. Gerald Volgenau, "U.S. Security Systems Upgraded Quietly," *Detroit Free Press,* January 10, 1991, p. 13A.

14. Jeffrey S. Ghannam, "Northwest Gets Harassment Complaints," *Detroit Free Press,* October 29, 1990, p. 1B.

15. During the height of the Reagan administration's "war on international terrorism" in the mid-1980s (see below), a source close to a Detroit-area police force admitted to me that area police departments had developed contingency plans for a "Shiite uprising" in Dearborn. Coordination and leadership for the plans came from federal authorities.

16. Typical was the comment of a Wayne County Circuit Judge in Detroit who presided over an assault-and-battery case involving two Lebanese parties. According to the official transcript, Judge Harry Dingeman commented:
    "The case does involve parties of Arabic descent, and it would seem that two cultures are somewhat involved. These people ... [who are] apparently still pursuing their native cultures, appear to be of a mind that they can settle their own differences without the intervention of anyone else ... On the other hand, they are now living in a culture where law and order prevails..." (Cited in, "Judge Accused of Ethnic Slurs," *Detroit Free Press,* September 23, 1990, p. 1C.)
    In a different case involving a major insurance company and a Detroit-area Lebanese woman, the attorney representing the company made two references to her "Arabic" ethnicity. In a legal brief submitted before Wayne County Circuit Court (July 30, 1990), he observed:
    "She is an Arabic-speaking woman who lives alone with five children. Her husband has lived out of state for the last couple of years "looking for a job" ... This woman expects to recover money as an Arabic Defendant in front of a Wayne County jury under these circumstances. Sure."

17. Shelly Slade, "The Image of the Arab in America: Analysis of a Poll on American Attitudes," *Middle East Journal,* Spring 1981, p. 143. The survey revealed, *inter alia,*
    "A large percentage of the respondents [felt] that the Arabs can be described as 'barbaric, cruel,' (44 percent), 'treacherous, cunning' (49 percent), 'mistreat women' (51 percent) and 'warlike, bloodthirsty' (50 percent). Furthermore, when asked how many Arabs are described by a long list of traits, a large percentage view[ed] 'most' or 'all' Arabs as 'anti-Christian' (40 percent), 'anti-

Semitic' (40 percent) and 'Want to Destroy Israel and Drive the Israelis into the Sea' (44 percent)." (p. 147) (Cf. Michael W. Suleiman, *The Arabs in the Mind of America*, Brattleboro, Vermont: Amana Books, 1988.)

18. Foreword to Edmund Ghareeb, ed., *Split Vision*, Washington, D.C: American-Arab Affairs Council, 1983, p. vii. Two decades later, Flora Lewis could still write in her syndicated column:

"Many Mideasterners bemoan the fact their region seems to be losing significance now that they can't play Cold War tag. No doubt many more, muzzled by dictatorships, bemoan the fact their region hasn't joined the march to democracy. They suffer most from their own *sick* societies." [*New York Times*, April 28, 1990; emphasis added.]

19. On how the U.S. news media portray the Arabs, see Edward W. Said, *Covering Islam*, New York: Pantheon, 1981; Suleiman, *Arabs in the Mind of America*; Ghareeb, *Split Vision*. For a detailed examination of Hollywood's Arab stereotype, see Jack Shaheen *The TV Arab*, Bowling Green: Popular Press, 1984; Laurence Michalak, "Cruel and Unusual: Negative Images of Arabs in Popular American Culture," *ADC Issues*, American-Arab Anti-Discrimination Committee, Washington, DC, January 1984. On the Arab stereotype in popular literature, see Janice Terry, *Mistaken Identity*, Washington, DC: American-Arab Affairs Council, 1985, and Kathleen Christison, "The Arab in Recent Popular Fiction," *Middle East Journal*, Summer 1987. An illuminating study of the cultural antecedents of anti-Arab, anti-Muslim attitudes in western culture is found in Edward W. Said, *Orientalism*, New York: Pantheon, 1978.

20. See, for example, Stephen C. Fehr, "Backlash Feared in U.S. Against Arab Americans," *Washington Post*, August 9, 1990; Peter Applebome, "Arab-Americans Fear a Land War's Backlash," *New York Times*, February 20, 1991.

21. Material on this period is drawn from the author's "Anti-Arab Racism and Violence in America," in *Arab-Americans: An Evolving Identity*, Ernest McCarus, ed., Ann Arbor: University of Michigan Press, 1992.

22. An editorial in the *News Leader* (June 21, 1985, Richmond, Virginia), for example, suggested one Lebanese Shiite prisoner be executed every 15 minutes until the hostages were released. The *New York Post* (June 19), famous for its shrill tone, ran a front-page photo of a Dearborn man of Lebanese Shiite ancestry posing with the likeness of an AK-47 machine gun, wearing a camouflage vest, bandoleers and bullets under a banner headline, "'U.S.-Nation under Attack'/ Beirut U.S.A." The photo was obtained by an unscrupulous reporter who persuaded the Lebanese-American to pose for his camera. According to the accompanying article, the Dearborn man was said to have boasted that 5,000 armed Lebanese Shiites were poised to defend themselves in the Detroit suburb.

Even the normally staid *Wall Street Journal* (June 18) was not immune to the hysteria of the hour. In an editorial titled, "The Next Hijacking," the *Journal* unabashedly called for U.S. military retaliation, starting inexplicably with "strikes against Syrian military targets inside Lebanon."

23. According to the Los Angeles Human Relations Commission, 12 (16.9 percent) out of a total 71 religiously motivated incidents that took place in Los Angeles County in 1985 "were directed against Islamic mosques, centers or individuals of the Islamic faith." Commission officials noted this was the first time that any anti-Islamic incidents had been recorded in the six years records had been kept. According to the Commission's annual report the anti-Muslim incidents appear "to have been provoked by a number of events in the Middle East," specifically, the TWA plane and Achille Lauro hijackings, and the Rome and Vienna airport attacks (see below). "In each case, Americans were killed" (Bob Baker, "Anti-

Arab Violence Represents 17 percent of Racial, Religious Attacks in 1985," *Los Angeles Times,* March 1, 1986).

24. "The force of the blast moved the room's 15 x 30 foot wall nearly four inches from the foundation. The bomb went off less than one hour after the congregation of Dar es Salaam, which means the House of Peace, had left from the evening prayer... Three young men, one an Air Force veteran, were convicted in the bombing." (Written testimony of Sayed M. Gomah, President, Islamic Society of Greater Houston, before the Subcommittee on Criminal Justice, *Ethnically Motivated Violence Against Arab Americans,* Committee on the Judiciary, U.S. House of Representatives, 99th Congress, 2nd Session, July 16, 1986 (henceforth *Ethnically Motivated Violence)* pp. 200-201).

25. *Ethnically Motivated Violence,* pp. 57, 58, 64. See also "Men Carve Star Symbol on Woman During Rape Outside of Restaurant," *Arizona Daily Star* (Tucson), July 2, 1985, and Steve Lerner, "Terror Against Arabs in America," *The New Republic,* July 28, 1986.

26. Odeh was blown in half by the force of the booby-trap bomb wired to his office door. Cf. Dave Palermo and Gary Jarlson, "Bomb Kills Leader of Arab Group in Santa Ana Office," *Los Angeles Times,* October 12, 1985; David Reyes and Lanie Jones, "Odeh Becomes Victim of the Violence He Decried," *Los Angeles Times,* October 13, 1985; Mark I. Pinsky, "The 'Quiet' Death of Alex Odeh," *Present Tense,* Winter 1986; Robert I. Friedman, "Who Killed Alex Odeh?" *Village Voice,* November 24, 1987.

27. Especially distressing to Arab Americans was the lack of attention devoted to Alex Odeh's murder by the U.S. news media in comparison to that given to victims of Middle Eastern violence generally. In a memorial address for Alex Odeh on January 31, 1986, *Nation* columnist Alexander Cockburn compared the media's coverage of Alex Odeh's murder to coverage of Leon Klinghoffer's murder a few days earlier. "In the first three days after the killings, the *New York Times* devoted 1,043 column inches to the Klinghoffer killing and twelve and one half inches to the murder of Alex Odeh. Comparative figures for the *Washington Post* were 620 inches for Klinghoffer and 30 inches for Alex Odeh." (Cited in *ADC Times,* Washington, DC: American-Arab Anti-Discrimination Committee, February 1986, p. 15.)

Although most of the news reporting was straightforward, the *New York Post (October 12, 1985),* known for its sleazy sensationalism, ran the Odeh story under the headline, "Arafat Fan Killed, 7 Arabs Injured in Cal. Bomb Blast." The callously insensitive headline was set in boldface type. The *Post* shamelessly twisted Odeh's comments on the Achille Lauro hijacking, telling readers Odeh "had publicly praised Yasser Arafat's role in the seajacking," *without once* mentioning that Odeh was praising the PLO leader's mediation efforts, not his purported involvement in the actual hijacking. Odeh had in fact said, as some more responsible newspapers reported, " ... we commend Arafat for his positive role in *solving* this issue" (*Los Angeles Times,* October 13, 1985; emphasis added).

28. Judith Cummings, "F.B.I. Says Jewish Defense League May Have Planted Fatal Bombs," *New York Times,* November 9, 1985.

In Los Angeles, JDL head Irv Rubin told reporters shortly after the blast: "No Jew or American should shed one tear for the destruction of a PLO front in Santa Ana or anywhere else in the world. The person or persons responsible for the bombing deserves our praise for striking out against the murderers of Americans and of Jews," (cited in *New York Post,* October 12, 1985). Not one to mince words, Rubin told the *Washington Post* (October 13, 1985), "I have no tears for Mr. Odeh. He got exactly what he deserved."

29. "There's too much there for it to have been accidental but not enough to declare it arson, so we are classifying it at the present time as suspicious," was how Ray Alfred, a Washington, DC Fire Department battalion chief, assessed the fire. (Cited in Reginal Stuart, "Arab Office Fire Termed Suspicious," *New York Times,* December 1, 1985.)

30. Earlier that month, "Los Angeles police dismantled a bomb found on the steps of a school adjoining the Masjid al-Mumin Mosque in the city's downtown area..." (Pinsky, "The 'Quiet' Death of Alex Odeh.")

31. The attacks, which were completely incomprehensible to westerners, appeared to be the work of a renegade Palestinian faction led by Abu Nidal. Their purpose was to discredit the mainstream wing of the Palestine Liberation Organization (PLO), and block its attempts to gain admittance to the U.S.-sponsored Arab-Israeli peace process. (See my discussion of this incident, "The Real Target of the Airport Atrocities," *Middle East International,* January 24, 1986.)

32. In private, however, the President resisted calls for a direct military strike "pending a 'smoking gun'—some evidence linking Qaddafi to the airport bombings" (Seymour M. Hersh, "Target Qaddafi," *New York Times Magazine,* February 22, 1987, p. 71.) "The Italian and Austrian governments stated that the terrorists were trained in Syrian-controlled areas of Lebanon and had come via Damascus, a conclusion reiterated by Israeli Defense Minister Yitzhak Rabin." Officials of both governments reiterated the same position months later. In the words of the Austrian Minister of Interior, "there is not the slightest evidence to implicate Libya." (Noam Chomsky, *Pirates and Emperors: International Terrorism in the Real World,* New York: Claremont and Amana, 1986, pp. 135-136.)

33. Lerner, "Terror Against Arabs...," p. 21.

34. Bonnie Rimawi, "A Rash of Death Threats and Arson Followed Bombing of Tripoli," *The Guardian,* New York, July 9, 1986. Rimawi herself encountered repeated death threats, which forced her to resign from her job as ADC regional coordinator for New York City (see below).

35. Philadelphia police treated the incident as a robbery, "but Dabbas claims that nothing was stolen from him. 'I was attacked because I am the tongue of the Arab community here.'" In 1975, the year after he started his printing business, his printing machines were stolen and vandalized on two occasions, apparently by the local JDL, which boasted about the theft in the Philadelphia newspapers. (Lerner, "Terror Against Arabs...," p. 21.)

36. The Washington incident is found in Robert I. Friedman, "Nice Jewish Boys with Bombs," *Village Voice,* May 6, 1986; the Milwaukee incident in John Schidlovsky, "Arab-Americans Fear Growing Hostility," *Baltimore Sun,* August 10, 1986.

37. The prevailing hostility caught the eye of *Newsweek,* which observed that "the animosity grows with each new terrorist outrage overseas." ("Arab-Bashing in America," January 20, 1986.)

38. Tom Hundley, "State had Most Cases of Arab Harassment," *Detroit Free Press,* April 3, 1987. The news report is based on information gleaned from the 1986 annual log of anti-Arab harassment issued by ADC. Cf. Rimawi, "Rash of Death Threats and Arson ..."

39. "ADC Harassment and Violence Log," *Ethnically Motivated Violence,* pp. 64-66.

40. Mary Thornton, "Arab Americans Ask Rights Inquiry," *Washington Post,* February 12, 1986. See also, "Arab-Americans Call for Full Inquiry into Rights Violations," *ADC Insider's Report,* March 1986; and James Zogby, "Statement to the U.S. Commission on Civil Rights," *Issues 86,* Washington, DC: Arab American Institute, March 1986.

41. Chomsky, *Pirates and Emperors,* pp. 142-145. Seymour Hersh adds, "Qaddafi's failure to rise to the bait frustrated the N.S.C. [National Security Council] staff."

"The basic question for N.S.C. aides remained: how to convince the reluctant President that bombing was essential" ("Target Qaddafi," p. 74).

42. Reagan later claimed to have "direct," "precise," and "irrefutable" evidence linking Libya to the La Belle disco bombing. In fact, as Noam Chomsky found, there was never any proof of Libyan involvement:

In an interview on April 28 with a reporter for the U.S. Army journal *Stars and Stripes,* Manfred Ganschow, chief of the Berlin Staatschutz and head of the 100-man team investigating the disco bombing, stated that "I have no more evidence that Libya was connected to the bombing than I had when you first called me two days after the act. Which is none." (*Pirates and Emperors,* pp. 149-150).

43. Chomsky, *Pirates and Emperors,* p. 147.

44. Two days after the attack in the Gulf of Sidra, Joel Lisker, chief counsel of the Senate Judiciary Subcommittee on Security and Terrorism, raised the specter of Middle Eastern terrorists residing in the U.S., saying, "You have a cadre of individuals with Middle East connections, some of whom are American citizens, some of whom are 'green carders' [permanent residents], who have been trained in the Middle East since they've been here." Lisker's "warning" bears an eerie resemblance to government claims in the arrest of eight Palestinians and a Kenyan some nine months later on trumped-up charges of membership in a Palestinian "terrorist organization." Lisker also added that radical states like Libya, Syria, and Iran "could call upon any of their nationals in the United States 'presumably to act in solidarity... with Arab nationalism, or anti-U.S. sentiment, because of what is happening in the Gulf of Sidra.'" (Quoted in John McCaslin, "Terrorists Trained Abroad are Known to Live Here," *Washington Times,* March 27, 1986.) Ten days later on April 28, Attorney General Edwin Meese said he would study the issue.

45. During crises, threats are the norm. For example, during the Achille Lauro hijacking a caller telephoned the Houston Islamic Center threatening, "For every American killed, 10 of you... pigs will die." In early 1986, when promotions for the NBC movie special "Under Siege" were airing, another caller warned the Islamic Center to "go back to your home country or die" (*Ethnically Motivated Violence,* p. 202). The pattern was repeated elsewhere.

46. "ADC Harassment and Violence Log Sheet," *Ethnically Motivated Violence,* pp. 67-69. A closing note in the Detroit entry for this period states: "Many incidents occur that are not reported to ADC, but only to the police. Dearborn Police said on TV that there are more incidents than usual of anti-Arab attacks. Detroit FBI Director Walton asked the public not to direct hostility against Arabs in Detroit, since they had nothing to do with the current crisis" (p. 69). See also Colin Campbell, "Attacks on U.S. Arabs: The Middle Eastern Link," *New York Times,* July 20, 1986; Steve Hamm, "Anti-Khadafy Backlash Stings Foreigners Here," *New Haven Register,* May 11, 1986.

ADC found that "nearly 40 percent of all 1986 incidents of anti-Arab violence and harassment reported to the National Office were directly attributable to heightened tensions surrounding the U.S. bombing of Libya in April 1986. The incidents included acts of vandalism and threats of violence," *ADC Insider's Report,* Washington, DC, May 1987, p. 29.

47. "Arson Damages Palestinian Office in DC," *Washington Post,* June 18, 1986.

48. "Arson Damages Palestinian Office... ," *Washington Post.* Cf. *ADC Insider's Report,* July 1986, p. 32.

49. *Ethnically Motivated Violence,* pp. 106-107. The reference was to the U.S. Navy's interception on October 10 of an Egyptian plane carrying four Palestinians suspected of hijacking the Achille Lauro cruise liner. James Zogby, Director of

the Arab American Institute, struck a similar chord, saying "Every time a Palestinian greengrocer in Dearborn writes a check to the PLO, the FBI is swarming all over the place... Why haven't the FBI caught the Jewish terrorists?" (Cited in Friedman, "Nice Jewish Boys with Bombs.")

50. Meanwhile U.S. oil companies profited by exporting refined gasoline to Europe, Japan, and other overseas markets, earning $4 to $10 a barrel over the domestic market ("Gasoline Exports Rise Despite Concern Over Supplies, *Wall Street Journal*, September 17.)

51. See note 7.

52. James Barron, "U.S. Takes Steps to Curb Terrorism," *New York Times*, January 16, 1991, p. A9.

53. "ADC Harassment and Violence Log," *Ethnically Motivated Violence*, pp. 61-70. Again it is important to emphasize that these cases represent only those that came to the attention of ADC. That much of this violence did not figure in studies of racism and hate violence of the period is telling. A recent scholarly volume on violence in America briefly mentions the JDL, and only in the context of "American terrorism in foreign causes," not in the context of "rightwing extremism." Aside from an oblique, one-sentence reference to the murder of Alex Odeh, no mention of anti-Arab violence is made in this volume. Ted Robert Gurr, ed., *Violence in America*, Vol. II: *Protest, Rebellion, Reform* (Newbury Park, CA: Sage Publications, 1989), pp. 222-223.

54. By late 1985, violence against Arab-American targets had become so conspicuous that even the *New York Times* felt it necessary to comment that it had "taken too long for the rising violence against supporters of Arab causes in the United States to get the attention it deserves" (Editorial, December 15, 1985).

55. The businesses were located in Cincinnati, Detroit, Los Angeles, and Blissfield, Michigan. The pipebombing occurred at the home of an Indian family living in Lakeland, Florida. The family may have been thought to be Iraqi (*ADC Hate Crimes Chronology*).

56. *ADC Times Newsletter*, American-Arab Anti-Discrimination Committee, Washington, September-October 1990, p. 6. The *New York Times* referred to the meeting in passing, "U.S. Views Threat by Iraq As Strategy to Split Critics," September 25, 1990, p. A6.

57. "Scrutiny of Iraqis Stepped Up in U.S.," *New York Times*, January 8, 1991, p. 1; "FBI Questioning Worries Arab Americans," *Detroit Free Press*, January 9, 1991, p. 1; "FBI Has Secretly Investigated Local Arab-American Groups," *Detroit News*, January 10, 1991, p. 1. The Movement Support Network received reports of 40 Arab-American community leaders, activists, and others who were contacted by the FBI during the Gulf War. MSN also documented widespread government harassment of antiwar activists as well, *MSN NEWS*, Special Edition, 1991, Vol. 7, no. 1.

58. *The New York Times*, for example, deplored anti-Arab bigotry in a brief editorial relatively early in the crisis ("Arab-Americans and Ugly Americans," September 9, 1990). Coretta Scott King raised the issue in her nationally syndicated column ("Arab-American Bashing Can't Be Tolerated," *Detroit Free Press*, September 10, 1990). The major media were also quick to condemn government harassment of Arab Americans, particularly the FBI's plans to interview Arab-American community leaders and activists in an effort to gather intelligence about possible terrorism threats ("Singling Out Arab Americans," *Washington Post*, January 16, 1991; *Detroit Free Press*, "Crisis is No Excuse for Arab Harassment," January 10, 1991).

CHAPTER 13

MILITARY RESISTERS DURING OPERATION DESERT SHIELD/STORM

Tod Ensign

> Should military action be required, this will not be another Viet-
> nam... If one American soldier [goes] into battle, that soldier will
> have enough force behind him to win.
>
> President George Bush,
November 30, 1990 press conference.

True to his word, President Bush and his military commanders waged a war of unprecedented ferocity against Iraq. In just 42 days, the U.S.-led forces rained down more bombs and missiles on Iraq and Kuwait than they had used during the entire Vietnam War. Despite international laws and treaties which prohibit waging war without distinguishing between civilians and combatants, our warplanes demolished Iraq's electrical, communication, and sanitation systems. A UN team described "near apocalyptic" conditions that threatened to plunge the country into a pre-industrial stage of development.

There's no doubt that its quick and bloody victory over Iraq won the U.S. armed forces many new supporters. A poll conducted by *USA Today* just after the war ended found that 78 percent of those surveyed had a "great deal" of confidence in the U.S. military—the highest rating since polling on that question began in 1972.

America's journalists, for the most part, endorsed Bush's claim that this overwhelming blitz had exorcised the "Vietnam Syndrome" from U.S. political life, once and for all. For the past 20 years, it has been an article of faith among many military professionals that the Vietnam War was lost because timid civilian leaders had tied their hands, robbing them of victory. In his recently published memoirs presidential adviser Clark Clifford analyzed this belief. "The war was not lost at home," he wrote. "It was lost where it was fought, in the jungles of Southeast Asia and [by] our corrupt and incompetent allies."

Another pet theory of military careerists is that the massive anti-war movement that helped turn many GIs against the war was fueled by journalists who gave an anti-war slant to their Vietnam reporting. Despite several media studies that found that most wartime coverage was either pro-war or neutral, this myth persists.

It has often been said that America's generals spend much of their time fighting their last war—over and over again. This adage seems particularly true of the Vietnam conflict. The Pentagon has conducted innumerable studies and reports on every aspect of that war. Along with scrutinizing every battle and skirmish, the armed forces also have taken a very close look at the GI resistance movement and the larger anti-war movement that spawned it.

I believe that one goal of this analysis was to find ways to lessen the impact of future wars on the predominantly white, middle-income voter. Congress took a large step in this direction when it abolished conscription and instituted the "all- volunteer" force in 1973. Three reforms were implemented to help the armed forces maintain a two-million-member force without resorting to a draft.

- Pay and benefits were raised substantially so that the military could compete with civilian employers at least for semi-skilled workers.

- Ancient taboos against female soldiers were scrapped, and within a few years the percentage of women in uniform jumped from about 3 percent to 11 percent of the total force. (More than 32,000 female GIs served in the Persian Gulf.)

- The mission of the Reserves and National Guard was changed from that of a backup force to one with a primary combat mission. This change was to have great impact on many reservists during Operation Desert Storm, as we shall see.

Lessons from Vietnam

Once the decision was made to commit a substantial U.S. military force to Saudi Arabia, the Pentagon implemented a number of new policies that were intended, in my opinion, to stifle the growth of any significant resistance movement among GIs serving there. These new policies are as follows:

No troop rotation, leaves, or discharges

During Vietnam, many GIs deserted or made anti-war statements while on leaves and furloughs from the war zone. Others took strong anti-war positions as soon as they received their discharges. Fearing a repetition of this, the Pentagon simply stopped allowing anyone to leave the war zone or the military during the entire campaign.

Strict isolation of GIs in Saudi

In Vietnam, some GIs were influenced by the Vietnamese peace movement while others were in contact with Americans living in South Vietnam. Our Saudi hosts helped the military keep GIs almost totally isolated from Saudi society. In part, this was due to that society's repressive attitudes towards women, non-Muslims, and other "deviants." Since Saudi Arabia and the other Gulf states normally admit few, if any, visitors, foreign contacts were not a problem.

Refusal to acknowledge any resistance

During the entire seven months of Operation Desert Shield/Storm, inquiring reporters were told repeatedly that there was no perceptible anti-war opposition within the ranks. As one indicator, they were told that the application rate for discharge as conscientious objector (CO) did not increase after August 2, 1990. In recent years, CO applications by GIs have averaged between 800 and 1,000 per year. Two counselling groups, the War Resisters League and the National Interreligious Service Board for Conscientious Objectors (NISBCO) estimated respectively that 2,500 or 2,000 GIs attempted to file CO claims during the war period.

One scandal of Operation Desert Shield/Storm that has gone almost entirely unnoticed by the regular press is the military's refusal to approve almost any of the CO claims that were filed by GIs. An informal count by the War Resisters League in late July turned up less than a dozen successful applications. In the pre-war era, CO claimants enjoyed a success rate in the 50 to 60 percent range.

One means of harassing claimants was a change in army policy so that CO applicants were required to deploy to the Persian Gulf, even though processing of their applications was incomplete. This revised regulation was surreptitiously slipped onto the books by army headquarters in Washington in October 1990. Previously, an applicant would remain at a duty station until a final decision had been made on his or her CO claim.

A civilian lawyer, Robert Rivkin, has charged that the Marine Corps also manipulated its regulations to frustrate would-be COs. Not long after the Iraqi invasion of Kuwait, marine headquarters decreed that all CO claimants throughout the United States should be shipped to a special unit at Camp LeJeune, North Carolina.

The change implemented by the two service branches made it very difficult for claimants to present supportive witnesses at their CO hearings and to be represented by civilian lawyers of their choosing. In the case of those deployed to the Persian Gulf these rights were virtually annulled.

For years, military regulations have required that CO applicants be assigned to military duties that "minimally conflict" with their asserted beliefs. By shipping claimants to the war zone in the Gulf, the Pentagon basically scrapped this safeguard.

In October 1991, Congresspeople Ron Dellums and John Conyers formally requested that the GAO conduct an investigation into the Pentagon's handling of CO claims.

Strict rules against GIs talking freely to the media

As noted, career military officers have long distrusted journalists, at least in a wartime setting. From Day One of Operation Desert Shield, military censors clamped tight controls on reporters. Only those with "official" accreditation from the Pentagon were even allowed to travel to the region. Here, the military was assisted by the strict control our Gulf allies have traditionally exercised over foreign visitors. During the Vietnam War, by contrast, many independent journalists were able to enter South Vietnam or Cambodia without securing military approval.

Because reporters from liberal or progressive publications and broadcast outlets were denied press credentials, a number of them sued (unsuccessfully) in federal court in an effort to overturn these strict controls as violations of the First Amendment.

In the combat zone, GIs were allowed to talk with reporters only when a press officer was present to listen in. In one case, an Air Force enlisted man was threatened with punishment because he had the audacity to write letters home that were published in his hometown newspaper in Michigan. There were, no doubt, a number of prosecutions of GIs for breaching the military's wall of silence. As I was writing this, a Hispanic army sergeant called and reported that he was being court-martialed at Ft. Campbell, Kentucky for having written a girlfriend letters in which he described his unit's position as "60 miles from the Kuwaiti border." He claimed that he had learned this fact from watching CNN. After his correspondent vengefully turned over the letters to the military, a conviction brought his 14-year army career to an abrupt end.

During Vietnam, many anti-war and alternative newspapers circulated widely among combat troops, even on the front lines. One newspaper, the *Vietnam GI*, which was written by Vietnam vets, was particularly popular among the troops. While the command did what it could to suppress these publications, they were unable to isolate GIs from civilian influences.

In Saudi, on the other hand, the military's tight control was effective in isolating GIs from reporters and vice versa. This meant that acts of resistance such as combat refusals or other "disobedience" were hushed up so that they couldn't stimulate further resistance. Periodically, I heard rumors of racial confrontations and troop rebellions during Operation Desert Shield/Storm, but it was impossible to obtain further details. For its part, the media reported only the blandest accounts of GI "gripes" from the field.

While U.S. journalists have always been susceptible to a degree of censorship by the military command, Operation Desert Storm represented a new low in terms of media sycophancy and patriotic cheerleading. Even during the Korean war, when anti-communism was at its height, at least one Australian journalist, Wilfred Burchett, was allowed to file dispatches from the front lines that presented the Allied war effort—warts and all.

Conscientious Objection:
A Critical Look

Pacifism has been an important current within both the United States and European anti-war movements since World War I. For pacifists, the issue of employing violence in pursuit of political ends is elevated from a tactical question to a moral one.

In the aftermath of World War I, members of the newly-formed Communist parties in the West viewed armed struggle as a necessary component of the fight for basic social change. Pacifists argued that revolutionaries should eschew violence, relying instead on moral leadership and suasion in the ideological struggle with the capitalist class.

When the new Cold War order was formed at the end of World War II, the United States and its NATO allies (except Great Britain) instituted compulsory military service. For the United States, this was the first peacetime draft in its history. In response, U.S. pacifists formed the Central Committee for Conscientious Objectors (CCCO) to assist and support young men who sought deferment from military duty as COs.

During the early days of the Vietnam War, pacifist groups like the War Resisters League and CCCO played important roles in sparking what was to become a massive anti-war movement. Partly because the pacifists played a central role within the anti-Vietnam War movement, the actions of resisters who sought CO status prior to being drafted received prominent attention. By and large, these folks were white and well-educated.

When one considers the nature of the CO application process, either for a draftee appealing to a draft board or for an active-duty service member, it's not surprising that applicants tend to be middle-class whites. Not only does one have to be opposed to participation in war or violence in any form, but the lengthy application process requires one to be able to articulate his or her personal philosophy in response to a number of thorny essay questions.

Once the written answers have been submitted, the applicant must submit to intensive interviews by a psychologist and priest or chaplain. In the military, both of these professionals are active-duty officers. Both write reports on the applicant that are incorporated into the CO hearing, which is the next step.

In the military, an officer is detailed to conduct a hearing at which all the evidence is adduced and the applicant is again subjected to a barrage of questions about his or her moral, philosophical, or religious belief. Hearing officers have been known to grill applicants all day about their beliefs. Given that the process is highly technical and legalistic, those who can afford a civilian attorney to represent them have a real advantage.

Since conscription was ended in 1973, the U.S. military has been composed almost entirely of men and women from working-class backgrounds, with Blacks accounting for a quarter of all recruits. Not only are few of these young people familiar with pacifism, but I doubt that many would adopt it as personal philosophy, even if they did understand its tenets.

The legal standard which is required for one to qualify as a CO, i.e., opposition to participation in war in any form, also limits the number of eligible applicants. For instance, I counselled a number of Blacks who had become Muslims and were philosophically opposed to fighting other Islamic adherents. Under the law, their religious-based belief would not qualify them for recognition as COs. Also, many GIs would be philosophically opposed to fighting on behalf of racist or fascistic governments such as those in South Africa or El Salvador, but they would endorse military action against Nazi Germany.

Since many of those involved in military counselling today are pacifists, they often harbor unconscious attitudes toward those who have voluntarily (albeit for economic reasons) enlisted into the military. Their class and cultural differences from those they are counselling would also be a hindrance to understanding in some cases.

Another problem has to do with the training and experience of the majority of counsellors. Very few of them have been trained as attorneys or even as paralegals and few possess any direct experience with the military's criminal-justice system. Since the bulk of their training centered around the preparation of CO applications they understandably tended to steer their clients toward filing such claims. When the military simply rewrote its regulations so as to deny virtually all CO applications, these counsellors (and more importantly, their clients) were left high and dry.

Once the Pentagon began ordering tens of thousands of GIs and reservists to deploy to the Gulf, the volume of aid requests to counselling groups grew exponentially. This deluge placed an enormous additional burden on the existing counselling network. Because many of the callers had complicated claims and legal tangles related to their service, it was not humanly possible to provide many of them with competent (or even helpful) advice.

Despite all of these deficiencies and problems, the intense desire of thousands of GIs and reservists for information about alternatives to service in the Gulf was undeniable and impressive. During the Vietnam War, it was only after the war had raged with full U.S. participation for two years that GIs (as opposed to draftees) began seeking out counselling groups in any numbers. I attribute the change to a general skepticism about Bush's war aims in the Gulf and to a heightened concern among many GIs about foreign military interventions in general. Many members of the National Guard and Reserves who called for advice seemed genuinely surprised that they were being ordered onto active duty and sent to the war zone even ahead of many active-duty units. In many cases, their recruiters hadn't bothered to explain the new military strategy that targets reservists for deployment whenever offensive operations are planned. (About 20 percent of the 540,000 troops eventually sent to the Gulf were reservists.)

Resistance in the Ranks

Just days after the United States began sending military units to the Gulf, acts of resistance by GIs began to occur. Jeffrey Paterson, a 21-year-old marine stationed in Hawaii became the first public resister to announce that he would refuse deployment orders. His act of refusal attracted intense publicity in both the U.S. and international media. Members of the Maoist Revolutionary Communist Party (RCP) played an active role in defending Patterson and publicizing his case. While his exact relationship to the RCP is unclear, his decision to publicly wear the Bedouin headdress (*kaffiyeh*) often associated with the PLO probably undercut his appeal in some quarters. Paterson was finally court-martialed in December for refusing orders to board a Saudi-bound troop plane. However, the Marine Corps chose to abort the trial midstream and discharge him administratively, probably in the hope of dissolving the media interest in his case.

The first two army members to follow Paterson's lead were Matthew Brown and Patrick Colclough, who announced their decision to resist at the Vietnam Veterans Memorial Wall on September 18, 1990. Brown, 20, of Albany, California, and Colclough, 21, of Saugerties, New York, told a group of reporters that they considered the U.S. buildup in the Gulf to be a serious threat to world peace. Brown, a package handler at Federal Express in Oakland, had enlisted in the army three months earlier because he was promised medical training and a European assignment.

"When I joined in June, the Berlin Wall was coming down and *glasnost* was in the air," Brown told reporters. "Since then, President Bush has decided to send tens of thousands of Americans into the Gulf. I don't consider the emir of Kuwait nor cheap gasoline as valid reasons for thousands of young Americans to die." Brown later failed to report to training as ordered on October 4, 1990. Subsequently, he was separated from the army without court martial.

Patrick Colclough, enrolled in the army's Reserve Officers Training Corps (ROTC) at St. Lawrence University in upstate New York since 1987, told reporters that the Gulf buildup "crystallized my opposition" to current military policies. Because he stopped attending ROTC drills, Colclough faced activation as an enlisted person. Colclough told reporters that he would not obey such an order, even if it meant prosecution as a deserter. Legal and political support for the two men was organized by Citizen Soldier. Colclough later filed as a conscientious objector and his claim, handled by Boston attorney Louis Font, was one of the relatively few by a public resister to receive favorable action by the military.

After speaking with reporters in a field near the memorial, Brown and Colclough posed for photographers in front of the black wall listing the names of those killed or missing in Vietnam. "There are thousands of lives that could have gone on to be part of America," Brown mused. "There are so many names up there it sort of numbs you."

One of the first female GIs to take a public stand against deployment was army reservist Stephanie Atkinson, a 23-year-old from Murphysboro, Illinois. Atkinson was literally in the last weeks of her six-year reserve commitment when she was ordered to active duty.

"My conscience is my guide," she told me in a phone interview, "and it tells me not to take part in what President Bush is planning in the Gulf." Atkinson told me that if the United States hadn't decided to send troops that she might be a "clueless" punk rocker with spiked, purple hair. Like many others, she had originally joined the reserves in 1984 to earn the monthly training stipend.

Stephanie travelled to New York to consult with Citizen Soldier attorney Louis Font and to discuss her case in media interviews arranged by the non-profit group. On the "Sonya Freeman Show" on CNN, she handled herself like a seasoned professional, lucidly explaining to the skeptical host why she felt morally compelled to resist orders, even though it might result in a prison term.

On the morning of the first national anti-Persian Gulf War march in New York City on October 20, 1990, Stephanie joined nine other young resisters at a press conference organized by Citizen Soldier, War Resisters League, and the anti-war coalition that had organized the march. Initially, the march coordinators were opposed to the press event, probably fearing that it might detract from coverage of their demonstration. Eventually, they were persuaded that the two events would complement each other.

The press conference proved to be an emotional and inspiring event. One by one the 10 resisters, male, female, Black and white, walked to the dais covered with microphones and related the beliefs and feelings that had brought them to the decision to resist. Each possessed a kind of eloquence one associates with deeply-held principles.

Stephanie Atkinson probably spoke for all young resisters when she challenged a skeptical reporter's innuendo that the resisters were betraying a sacred oath. "What do you want," she asked with a sardonic smile, "that every 18-year-old who joins up stay at exactly that same level of political and moral understanding for the rest of his or her life?"

As thousands of GIs and reservists were inundating U.S. counselling groups with questions about their rights and duties, hundreds more were raising similar questions in West Germany. With over 200,000 troops stationed in that country, the requests for help and advice soon overwhelmed the scarce counselling resources. One Mennonite counsellor based in Kastellaun, Germany reported hearing from more than 400 GIs who wanted counselling in just that one area.

On another front, a lawsuit was filed by the Center for Constitutional Rights in New York City on behalf of an army reservist, Sergeant Michael Ange, who had been ordered to active duty. Ange sought an injunction against being deployed to the Persian Gulf, arguing that Bush's mobilization and activation orders violated domestic and international legal principles. The federal judge denied Ange's request. Later, after additional hearings, he dismissed the entire case, ruling that a federal court couldn't become involved in a "political issue" such as the legality of U.S. military operations in a foreign country.

The results from the November congressional elections had barely been tabulated when President Bush announced that General Norman Schwarzkopf and other strategists in the Southern Command would now begin planning for offensive, rather than merely defensive, military operations in the Persian Gulf. Of course, this meant that deployment orders would go out to tens of thousands of additional GIs. In turn, this brought forth a new spate of anxious phone calls and letters to the already-overburdened counselling network.

In late November, the first act of mass GI resistance to the war occurred when seven members of a marine reserve unit in the Bronx, New York, publicly refused to report. Sam Lwin, 21, a Burmese-American from Queens, New York, the informal leader of the group, had taken a public stand against the war a few weeks earlier. An ad-hoc group of students and faculty from New York's New School of Social Research calling itself the "Hands Off!" committee rallied in support of the Bronx reservists. Their regular leafletting and vigils outside the marine armory in the Bronx eventually induced seven reservists to join with Sam. They adopted as a slogan, "Don't let them turn the Fox Company into the Box Company."

Four of the seven held a public speakout in New York during which they explained their decisions to resist. "I felt like I should be proud to be a marine, but I wasn't," stated Colin Bootman, a 24-year-old Black New Yorker. A native of Trinidad who emigrated to New York as a child, Bootman explained that he'd enlisted in part to repay what he felt was a debt to America. Once in, however, his feelings changed. "Every drill session, I saw guys walking around with knives strapped to their hip and I'd think, 'Why don't I feel what they feel?'" Bootman also cited the U.S. invasion of Grenada as another reason for his decision not to deploy. "My aunt, a leader in the New Jewel Movement there, was assassinated as a result of the political turmoil. My family encouraged me to leave the marines because they saw no future in waging wars."

Another Black reservist, Keith Jones, a lance corporal like the others, said that when he joined the marines he was "close-minded" toward anti-war and other progressive organizations on his City College campus. His attitude changed, however, after he performed in two plays written by Vietnam veterans. "They say that at the stage I joined, I should have known what was happening," Jones wryly noted. "If I'd known then what I know now, I wouldn't enlist. This is insane."

For some reason, many members of the press and other commentators were perplexed that military reservists could serve with their units for months or even years without confronting the issue of killing other human beings. It seems obvious that if most reservists are serving primarily from economic motives, then orders to deploy to battle could easily stimulate profound moral questions that had heretofore lain dormant.

When members of the Fox Company Seven surrendered a few weeks later they were taken, like all other marine resisters, to Camp LeJeune, North Carolina and confined in a special barracks, which was promptly dubbed the "yellow building" by pro-war marines on the base.

From the start, the command kept up a steady campaign of harassment against the marine dissenters. Each was assigned to work details during the day, and then ordered to stand at least two fire-watches of two hours each during the night. This ensured that no one received a full night's sleep. In addition, each was regularly strip-searched, ostensibly to look for contraband or weapons. Guards routinely addressed the resisters as "cowards" and made them scream "I'm shit!" at the top of their lungs. At least two of the marines cracked under the pressure and had to be hospitalized for a brief period.

Throughout the war period, I was impressed with the political sophistication of most of the resisters. During the early years of the Vietnam War, the few GIs who dared to take public stands, such as the Fort Hood Three or Captain Howard Levy, MD, tended to be from politically active backgrounds. By contrast, Persian Gulf resisters generally made complicated connections between our military intervention and U.S. energy policy, Arab-Israeli politics, and the U.S. penchant for intervening in the Third World, in spite of their apolitical backgrounds.

The Camp LeJeune resisters are typical of Gulf War refusers in their diversity. Many are African American or Hispanic. One is a convert to Buddhism, while another now professes Islam. Several had been attending college with majors ranging from mathematics to pre-law to computer engineering. Others worked at various jobs such as elevator repair, carpentry, house painting, and greeting card design.

As this is written, all but three of the resisters at Camp LeJeune have been convicted by court martial and sentenced to "bad" discharges and prison terms ranging from one to 30 months. Nearly all were charged with two offenses: desertion and missing a movement. Many of the resisters chose to sign pre-trial agreements whereby the command agreed to limit punishment in exchange for a "guilty" plea. As noted earlier, the armed forces have virtually stopped approving applications for CO status. At Camp LeJeune, the command has uniformly denied every one of the 40 claims filed by resisters there.

It's important to note that the prosecution of resisters has been highly selective. Those who took a public stance against the war and then filed CO claims have been singled out for the harshest treatment. Hundreds of other reservists who simply failed to report when activated have been quietly discharged without court martial, provided that they didn't publicize their disobedience.

The Camp LeJeune resister who received the harshest sentence to date (30 months) had fled his native El Salvador in 1979 to escape the bloody repression of the U.S.-backed regime. Enrique Gonzalez, 24, of Yonkers, New York, had less than a month remaining on his six-year reserve hitch when he was summoned to active duty. He told reporters at Camp LeJeune: "My beliefs took a dramatic turn in 1989 when the United States invaded Panama and killed 3,000 people. Why, I asked, did we kill hundreds of people just to catch one corrupt person?"

Two marine resisters still facing trial, Eric Larsen and Tahan Jones, had their CO applications denied and now could be sentenced to five years if convicted of desertion.

As befits its status as governmental lap-dog, the national media virtually ceased to report on resistance in the ranks once President Bush flashed clear signals in early January that he planned to attack Iraq—no matter what. For instance, on January 9, Citizen Soldier held a press conference at the National Press Building in Washington, DC so that Captain Yolanda Huet-Vaughn could announce her refusal to serve. The event was well-attended by reporters from most major newspaper and television networks. Coincidentally, it ended just as Secretary of State Baker in Geneva was telling the press that talks with Saddam's foreign minister were a bust and strongly hinted that war was on the horizon.

From that moment, media interest in GIs who were resisting evaporated, not to return until "victory" was ours.

As U.S. warplanes were pulverizing Iraq, two large and spontaneous acts of mass resistance were taking place at army bases in Texas and Louisiana. Unfortunately, none of the national media felt that nearly 100 soldiers refusing to train for Gulf duty was worthy of their attention.

In one episode on February 7, 67 white members of the Louisiana National Guard left Fort Hood, Texas to protest inadequate training and inequitable leave policies. About 40 of them traveled home to Louisiana before the army succeeded in coaxing them back. This was done with promises of lenient punishment; nearly all the AWOL GIs were let off with a reduction in rank and loss of some pay. One Guard member reportedly is still missing.

The next day, about 60 members of a mostly Black battalion of the same National Guard brigade also held an angry meeting at Fort Hood, in which similar grievances were discussed. Three Guardsmen, Sergeant Robert Pete, Sergeant Dwayne Brown, and Sp/4 Derrick Guidry, all Black NCOs from Lake Charles, Louisiana, were charged with attempting to lead 100 fellow troopers in a work stoppage over training conditions and racism at the base.

This time, the military used the stick rather than the carrot. The alleged "ringleaders" were court-martialed for conspiracy to lead a strike and soliciting others to strike. Pete was hit with a six-year prison term while Brown received a year. Only one of the three, Derrick Guidry, was represented by a civilian attorney, and he was let off with only a "bad" discharge and no jail time.

The Military Strikes Back

As the Pentagon prepared for war in the early days of 1991, it adopted a more punitive stance towards those who resisted. In the last weeks of the old year, several well-publicized resisters like Jeffrey Paterson, Stephanie Atkinson, and Ronald Jean-Baptiste were given administrative "bad" discharges instead of being court-martialed.

In some instances, the military rode roughshod over individual rights by handcuffing anti-war GIs and dragging them aboard military planes bound for Saudi Arabia. At least five soldiers in Germany—Sergeant Derrick Jones, Sp/4 David Carson, and Privates Bryan Centa, Sean Hodder, and Robert Chandler—were treated this way even though each had filed a CO claim which was still unresolved.

Despite the gathering war clouds, some GIs continued to refuse deployment orders. An army reserve doctor from Kansas City became the highest-ranking resister. Captain Yolanda Huet-Vaughn left her newly-activated medical unit at Fort Riley, Kansas, and spent the month of January speaking to the media on the East Coast as well as at peace rallies like the large Washington anti-war march on January 26.

On February 2, she returned home and surrendered at a large protest/rally at a Black church in Kansas City, Missouri. The army sent her to Fort Leonard where she was charged with desertion with intent to avoid hazardous duty. Later she was also restricted to post, despite the fact that she had surrendered and was not a flight risk.

At a pre-trial hearing at Fort Leonard Wood, Missouri, in early May, Huet-Vaughn became the first resister to base her legal defense on international law. Her attorney, Louis Font of Boston, called several experts on international law and medical ethics to prove that she had legal authority to refuse duty given the war crimes that reasonably could be anticipated.

Former U.S. Attorney General Ramsey Clark, who conducted a fact-finding mission to Iraq in the midst of the Allied bombardment, testified and showed a video on the effects of systematic destruction of civilian targets, including hospitals, schools, and apartment buildings. The prosecutor objected that the cries of distraught Iraqi women in the video were "inflammatory." The hearing officer (the equivalent of a judge at a court martial) rejected his request that the sound be turned off. Asked who was responsible under international law for the carnage, Clark responded, "America's military and civilian leaders are guilty of war crimes under both Nuremberg and Geneva conventions."

Francis Boyle, a renowned international law expert, buttressed Clark's testimony. The University of Illinois professor outlined the international laws and treaties that are binding on the U.S. government and that the U.S. forces violated during Operation Desert Storm—including Hague and Geneva conventions. Boyle testified that to convict Huet-Vaughn of desertion, the army must prove that she absented herself "without authority." In his opinion, she had the necessary authority under international law. Boyle also endorsed defense requests (denied by the hearing officer) that high-level witnesses like General Norman Schwarzkopf and Colin Powell be called to determine if U.S. military planning before the attack on Iraq constituted "crimes against peace."

Huet-Vaughn risked prison as well as possible loss of her medical license because of her belief that she would have violated her physician's oath by serving in the Gulf. Dr. Victor Sidel, a New York physician and medical-ethics expert, testified that military doctors must follow a unique form of triage whereby slightly injured GIs are treated before more serious civilian casualties. This, he argued, would force Huet-Vaughn to violate her Hippocratic oath.

Sidel also discussed the military's controversial inoculation program in which thousands of Desert Storm GIs were injected with experimental botulism and anthrax vaccines, allegedly to protect them from Iraqi biological weapons. He noted that Huet-Vaughn could have been required to give these shots and that the Nuremberg Code (which punished Nazi doctors) forbids experimentation without the patients' informed consent. While the war was raging, the Public Citizens' Health Research Group unsuccessfully sued to stop the injections as medically unsound. Both Sidel and Boyle testified that no evidence has been offered that the Iraqis ever possessed biological weapons.

Since her public surrender on February 2, Huet-Vaughn had received the steady support of peace activists in the Kansas City area. Her supporters filled the courtroom for each hearing.

In August 1991, Captain Yolanda Huet-Vaughn was court-martialed for desertion with intent to avoid hazardous duty. During preliminary hearings, her lawyers had been able to present expert testimony on U.S. violations of international law as well as testimony on the ethical issues for physicians serving in the Persian Gulf. Huet-Vaughn's is the only case to date in which a resister has based his or her defense on a duty not to participate in military operations that could result in war crimes. But before the court martial began, the military judge made a number of very restrictive rulings that prevented the defense from offering any of this evidence on behalf of Huet-Vaughn. This meant that the jury heard only an open-and-shut case about Huet-Vaughn's refusing to deploy, with no discussion of her motivations or beliefs. They returned a verdict of guilty and imposed a sentence of 30 months and a dishonorable dismissal from the service.

While the harsh treatment of marine resisters at Camp LeJeune, North Carolina has attracted considerable attention, the other service branches have also been vengeful toward resisters.

- At Fort Riley, Kansas, the army reneged on a plea-bargain deal with Sergeant John Pruner that would have limited his punishment to six months in prison. Pruner was one of two soldiers who exposed the army's changed policy on COs in September. The policy made it more difficult for Saudi-bound GIs to win conscientious objector status. Pruner now faces a court martial, which can impose a six-year prison term.

- At least two GIs who refused deployment orders at Fort Bliss, Texas, have received six-year prison terms.

- An Air Force reservist in California was given a year in prison even though he had filed a legally valid CO claim.

- The Navy recently dropped charges against two Black sailors, both Muslims. The two sailors, 22-year-old Abdul Shaheed of St. George, South Carolina, and 21-year-old James Moss, of Columbus, Ohio, were accused of encouraging sailors aboard the U.S.S. Ranger to sabotage the carrier's aircraft-launch system and to kidnap the skipper in January. Subsequently the Naval command at Subic Bay, Philippines dropped all charges, but gave no reason for this action.

Another army doctor, Captain David Wiggins, had filed a CO application months before the Iraqi invasion of Kuwait. After his application was rejected, Wiggins complied with orders to deploy to Saudi Arabia. Once there, however, he refused to perform medical duties; instead he went on a hunger strike. Perhaps his commanders in the Gulf weren't sure what "signal" they should send, so they dismissed him from the military with "only" a $25,000 fine.

Lessons Learned

The U.S. military has a tradition of scrutinizing its campaigns and military operations with an eye towards summarizing the "lessons learned." The goal of this exercise is to pinpoint deficiencies and, hopefully, to take corrective action. Our movement in support of GI resisters should do no less. What follows is an attempt to draw some conclusions about our successes and failures in supporting resistance during the recently concluded war. With the president and the Pentagon enjoying the highest approval rates they've had in 20 years, it's reasonable to expect that the United States will engage in other military interventions in the years just ahead.

Based on my close contact with a large number of actual and "wannabe" resisters and with the groups that sought to assist them, I offer the following conclusions.

- A significant number of GIs and reservists were (and are) receptive to anti-militarist and anti-interventionist perspectives.

As an anti-Vietnam War activist, I can attest that anti-war attitudes spread much more slowly during that war than they did among troops slated to deploy with Operation Desert Shield/Storm. There are probably several reasons for this change. Among them, shrinking economic opportunity, a growing perception that the United States—awash with intractable social problems—is on the decline, and a more polyglot, pluralistic America in which the influence of white, middle-class values has diminished substantially.

Activists should always remember that a substantial percentage of people (probably a majority) join the military today primarily for economic reasons. Contrary to what some in the peace movement believe, only a small fraction of people in uniform (probably no more than one in 10) are infected with the "kill-all-the-gooks" Rambo virus. The vast majority have vague feelings of patriotism and a sense of duty, but they're willing to ask questions when they suspect they're being used for corrupt or reactionary national goals.

Since Schwarzkopf's elaborate battle plan necessitated marshalling 540,000 soldiers and sailors to the region, the mobilization of GIs and the activation of reservists was fast and furious. More than 200,000 "weekend warriors" from the National Guard and reserves were ordered onto active duty in roughly 100 days.

Although many military professionals harbored doubts about the combat capacity of these reserve units, they had no choice but to mobilize them. As I explained earlier, a greatly expanded role for the reserve force was part of the price that was paid for scrapping the draft. For instance, about 65 percent of the army's medical personnel today serve in the reserves, as do 70 percent of those who fly and service the Air Force's cargo flights.

Since many reservists have been recruited solely by appeals to their economic self-interest (tuition assistance, extra money, etc.) a goodly number of them were rudely surprised by orders sending them for active duty in a combat zone. Some reservists told me that they'd been told that only if they volunteered could they be placed on combat status. In retrospect, I think that our movement's outreach to potential resisters within the reserve ranks was mediocre at best. Of course, one reason many groups didn't conduct more outreach was because they were already swamped with requests for help.

- Counselling and legal resources to assist resisters were grossly inadequate in light of the need.

Since military counselling and advocacy work has never been popular with liberal foundations and wealthy donors, it's not surprising that the existing projects are relatively few in number and small in size. Second, it's not possible in a short period of time to do more than train counsellors in rudimentary advice-giving for what are often complicated personal issues. In the entire country, there are probably not more than 100 progressive and competent civilian lawyers who regularly do military-defense work. Once again, economics rears its ugly head; few GI-clients have the resources to pay much more than minimal fees. This makes military-defense work unattractive to young lawyers who might otherwise be interested.

In April, a GI counselling project in Germany issued an emergency call for volunteer lawyers to help defend almost 100 GIs who were facing court martials for their acts of resistance. Unless new resources can be mobilized to train and support counsellors, paralegals, and sympathetic attorneys, this situation will not improve. This means that the next military intervention will generate yet another cycle of frustration and missed opportunities for legal and political organizing.

• Existing counselling groups tend to emphasize case-work "solutions." Virtually no efforts were made to support GIs who made collective political demands.

As noted earlier, the Pentagon was able, by one device or another, to beat back most efforts by GIs to win designation as conscientious objectors. Because there was little, if any, political organizing around political demands, this left GI support work on the defensive.

During the Vietnam War, the GI coffeehouses, which sprang up around most military bases, played an important role in helping GIs frame issues and pose collective demands. Most of these projects regularly published newspapers that helped keep GIs informed and active.

As noted, two battalions of National Guard members from Louisiana protested racism and bad training conditions at Fort Hood, Texas during Operation Desert Storm, yet no anti-war group was even aware of their actions, much less able to do anything in support. There were probably other such acts of resistance, but our movement is not likely to have heard about them.

There was also a serious failure on the part of the two large anti-Persian Gulf War coalitions to do more than pay lip service to the cause of GI resistance. Once the shooting stopped, neither group did anything further in support of those who refused to go. Unless we can provide these brave young people with consistent political and legal support, how can we expect their younger brothers and sisters to listen to us when the next military intervention begins?

- The indifference of the counselling network to forms of resistance other than filing CO claims is reflective of its white, middle-class orientation.

During Vietnam, GIs developed highly diverse and creative ways of "gumming up the works" and frustrating their military commanders. Nearly half a million Vietnam era GIs "voted with their feet" by deserting their units.

As noted, almost a third of the army today is Black, with similar percentages in the reserves. Our network is going to have to do a much better job of involving people of color in this work if we hope to develop programs and demands that have a chance of reaching beyond the relatively small world of COs.

CHAPTER 14

REFLECTIONS FROM THE WAR ZONE

Robert Allen Warrior

Sam Donaldson crystallized the war for me on a "Prime Time Live" tour of Stormin' Norman Schwarzkopf's private quarters in the Gulf last February. As the camera panned the general's spartan room, I noticed two decorated eagle feathers, the kind Plains Indians wear as scalplocks, sitting on some high-tech security instrument.

As Sam jabbered about America's newest hero, I thought to myself, "They're doing it again." In World War II, American Indian nations made honorary chiefs of war heroes, including FDR, Winston Churchill, and Josef Stalin. Norm, apparently, had received the same honor. The camera zoomed in on the feathers and I hoped Donaldson would tell us which nation made Schwarzkopf a chief so I could give hell to people from that group.

"These objects," said Sam, "are American Indian feathers that General Schwarzkopf received when he was made an honorary chief of the OSAGE NATION." I screamed, fell to the floor, got up, and ran around my apartment looking for a wall to put my hand through. I wasn't so much surprised, angry, or embarrassed as I was frustrated that I would spend the next several months hearing about Chief Schwarzkopf from other Osages. This television scene was just one of many ironies visited upon me during the Gulf War.

War, to the great surprise of many people on the U.S. Left, is a problem to American Indian people not just because of the way it conveniently directs attention away from American Indian political issues that are nearly impossible to get anyone to care about even when the U.S.

A version of this essay appeared in *Christianity and Crisis,* March 4, 1991.

military isn't destroying entire regions of the world. As hard as it is to comprehend, people whose great-great grandfathers fought *against* the U.S. Army now fight alongside it and have been doing so in large numbers since World War I.

Oklahoma Indians, especially, are well-known in Indian country for flag-waving and VFW halls. The mother of all parades wended its way through Oklahoma in the summer of 1991 with powwows and special homecoming ceremonies for Natives returning from the Gulf. While these ceremonies often spring from a deep well of patriotism, they usually have most to do with honoring servicepeople, feting their safe return, and reintegrating them into the community.

Such festivities, of course, are not what people on the U.S. Left want to think about when they draw parallels between this war and the Indian wars of yesteryear and today. The timing of this war made such parallels, at least for me, difficult to miss. Not long before the war began, I was in South Dakota, covering the the Big Foot Memorial Ride that commemorated the 100th anniversary of the Wounded Knee Massacre. More than 200 horseback riders rode 150 miles through bitter cold and snow to ceremonially mourn the deaths that took place on December 29, 1890—I guess they would be called "collateral damage" these days—of more than 300 Minneconjou Lakotas.

On Christmas Day, the Pine Ridge Reservation's radio station, KILI, opened its phone lines for holiday greetings. Nearly every caller sent a greeting to some relative in Saudi Arabia. Many of the Big Foot Riders had brothers, sisters, husbands, and wives in the Gulf. As it turns out, at least 500 of 55,000 South Dakota Indians were in the Gulf. According to *Native Nations* magazine, at least 9,000 American Indians served the United States in the Gulf. These numbers may sound insignificant, but that rate is higher than the rate of African Americans and every other disproportionately represented group in the U.S. Armed Forces. If all people in the United States had been represented at the rate of American Indians, U.S. forces would have numbered approximately 1.2 million.

The same disproportionate figures held true in Vietnam. According to many of the vets I know from that war, American Indians often drew "point" duty during patrols. The reason given was always something about genetics—superior vision and hearing and all that. Of course, they knew that what was really going on was that their lives, as American Indians, were expendable.

Two Robert Warriors have risked their expendable lives in the U.S. military. My great-grandfather, the first Robert Warrior, was in the Army during a time when he could not even be a citizen of the United States. When he vowed to defend the Constitution, he had no rights under it. In

1919, the U.S. Congress made all American Indian soldiers citizens and in 1924 all American Indians became compulsory dual citizens of the United States and their Indian nations, whether they wanted to be or not.

My grandfather, the second Robert Warrior, entered the medical corps of the Ninth Army in 1942, saw action in North Africa, and was killed in Normandy on August 4, 1944. He was the second Osage of 27 who would die during World War II. My great-grandmother, Mamie Bolton, was one of several Osage women who started the Grayhorse War Mothers Dance in order to honor Osage veterans like my grandfather. Mamie never believed her son had really died in France, and she scanned papers and newsreels looking for his face until she followed him in death, heartbroken, three years later.

In the U.S. wars in which my grandfathers participated, American Indians became part of public consciousness through major media and Hollywood movies. A volunteer squadron of oil-rich Oklahoma Indians was well-known around the country as the "Millionaire Company." During the Gulf War, Natives appeared in the press twice, once when a general referred to the Kuwait-Iraq theater as "Indian country," a term used in Vietnam for the jungle. The other time was when the U.S. military would not allow Navajo families to send messages in Navajo to loved ones in the Gulf. Messages in Navajo are apparently a security threat.

During World War II, an all-Indian secret platoon of Marines trained in communications—the code talkers—were able to trade messages in Navajo without threat that the Axis powers would be able to understand a word. Many Indians thought that there would be an outpouring of good feeling toward the code talkers and other Native war heroes, and that this would create public sympathy for dealing justly with American Indians. Instead, those who returned alive were welcomed back with the termination policy that threatened to end the U.S. government's responsibility for Indian affairs. The great symbol of that period is Ira Hayes, the Pima who helped raise the flag on Iwo Jima.

During the war, he was a great hero. Upon his return, he and other Native veterans were all but forgotten by the society that had promised so much if they would be "good Indians." Hayes confirmed the other half of the old saying about "the only good Indian" ("...is a dead Indian") by drinking himself to death, drowning in two inches of drainage-ditch water after a night of hard drinking.

Those Indians serving in the Gulf now can expect the same kind of return. A major restructuring of the Bureau of Indian Affairs, rumored to be in the works for nearly a decade, looks to be another verse in the same old song of giving not enough resources to all the wrong people in all the wrong places. At best, Native nations will gain control over some existing

federal funding and that funding will remain in the hands of cooperation-
ist tribal governments. The fundamental issues of sovereignty and control
of natural and economic resources remain unaddressed.

The feds have done nothing to indicate that they intend to pursue
their new policy, "the new federalism," in good faith. Until the United
States does something to build trust and continuity in its Indian policy,
most Indian people will not be willing to put their hearts into the
experiment and perhaps less and less will continue to risk their lives in
the U.S. Armed Forces. Meanwhile, even progressives in the United States
remain all but completely ignorant of Native issues except for vague,
general notions of highly emotionalized situations such as the ongoing
Black Hills land claims, Big Mountain, and others. Progressive movements
or organizations that grew out of the anti-war effort will be unlikely homes
for most Native Americans. While most activists understand some of the
basics of the battles fought on foreign shores for control of resources, they
understand little about similar battles that have taken place here in their
own country.

One of the greatest ironies of having Osages fighting in the Gulf is
that this war for oil did not begin on January 15, 1991, August 2, 1990, or
any other date in this century. The United States began fighting its
petroleum wars in the 1890s in Oklahoma, and the Osage Nation was one
of its chief targets. In the three decades after 1871, when Osages purchased a reservation from land they had previously sold to the Cherokees
in Oklahoma, the U.S. government engaged in low-intensity warfare
designed to undermine every effort by Osages to organize our own
government and control our own resources.

The war intensified in 1896, when oil was discovered on the
reservation. Geologists, surveyors, speculators, and opportunists showed
up to exercise their God-given right to separate a nation from its only
wealth. Unlike other Oklahoma Indians, Osages maintained mineral
rights communally rather than individually and all within the nation
shared the wealth that came with oil leases. Like the sheikhs in the Gulf
States, this made Osages fabulously wealthy for several generations.

The wealth, now shared by so many descendants of those who split
it 2,229 ways in 1906 as to be negligible except for a few, was small
compensation for the paternalism and violence it engendered. Osage
County, in the 1920s, was much like Kuwait in the 1970s and 1980s (*sans*
beachfront). Europeans flocked to posh hotels in the county to observe
the then-wealthiest people in the world motoring around in luxury cars
while wearing traditional clothes.

Along with the tourists came speculators and swindlers from around
the world, killing Osages if necessary to separate the people from their

money. Osage gravestones in the county's cemeteries are marked with a disturbing number of young people's deaths between 1918 and 1930. The stones do not tell the story of how many of these deaths came from alcohol poisoning, murder, and medical malpractice. Of course, the greatest beneficiaries of all of this intrigue and money-making were Frank Phillips, E.W. Marland, and other white men who made lasting fortunes from Osage oil.

With the onset of the Great Depression, the money dwindled and did not return until the early 1970s. Since the OPEC petroleum embargo, Osages have been locked in a death dance with Middle Eastern countries who are now dependent on the United States's insatiable appetite for oil. Those groups, like Oklahoma Indians, were compelled to make fast adjustments to that appetite. At the turn of the century in the Middle East, oil companies, with full backing from the U.S. government, bulldozed villages, displaced the residents, and used coerced labor to build new drilling towns.

As these ironies in the Gulf developed while I was at the Wounded Knee Centennial and increased as I watched the subsequent attack after returning to New York, a quote from John Fire Lame Deer kept coming to mind: "I have seen pictures of Song My, My Lai, and I have seen pictures of Wounded Knee—the dead mothers with their babies. And I remember my grandfather, Good Fox, telling me about the dead mother with a baby nursing at her cold breast, drinking that cold milk. My Lai was hot and Wounded Knee was icy cold, and that's the only difference."

American Indian people are still picking up the pieces of Wounded Knee and the rest of the U.S. wars against us from the last century. So are the people of Central America and many other parts of the globe. When this war is over, the Middle East will be in the worst shape that it has been in for a century.

My great disappointment with those who protested the Gulf War was their lack of deep historical analysis of U.S. foreign policy generally and in the Middle East particularly. People in my age group, especially, seem to have protested on principle—war is bad—rather than with some specific alternative vision for peace and justice. Wounded Knees, My Lais, Panamas, and Iraqs are going to keep happening until people in the United States take the time and make the effort to do the hard work of understanding the full picture of how the United States imposes its will on the rest of the world.

As I watched the war through eyes that see Osage County, Wounded Knee, my grandfathers and great-grandmother, and cousins, and friends whose lives were and are at risk, I saw that the white man's burden is alive and well. On American Indian land, in the Middle East, and wherever else they might exist, the United States still considers oil and other resources to be its property—and those who try to stand in the way of this unfathomably evil idea had better watch out.

CHAPTER 15

WAR AS VIDEO GAME

Media, Activism, and the Gulf War

William Hoynes

In order to fully understand the meaning of the Bush administration's "New World Order" we need to see it as a sound-bite-sized slogan. In its search for a rationale for the Persian Gulf War, the Bush administration found a clever catch-phrase that was a hit with the national media. As such, the New World Order may have a range of meanings—depending on the particular context in which it is used. But, at bottom, it is about a world with only one superpower: the United States. As the notion of a New World Order has taken shape, the national media has played a fundamental role in spreading the word. In fact, during the Gulf War, media served as a veritable public-relations arm of the U.S. government. In retrospect, it is rather astonishing that the language of the New World Order so quickly became the frame through which the national media looked at the post-Cold War world—if only because the dispersal of the "peace dividend" seemed, only months earlier, to be so imminent.

In this essay I will examine the media coverage of the Gulf War, focusing on its importance for the Bush administration's ability to capture public support for the war. In particular, the mass media were seen as useful for the administration primarily as a tool for directing rhetoric—including rhetoric about the New World Order—at a domestic audience. That is to say, a great deal of the imagery and rhetoric emanating from the

White House—including support for the United Nations, the demonization of Saddam Hussein, and the vision of the New World Order—was
designed largely as a public-relations strategy to prevent the emergence,
at least in the short term, of a major political upheaval in the United States.

The political contest for the Bush administration was primarily a
domestic one, in which the administration sought popular support for this
particular war, as well as support for the more general strategy of military
intervention. At the same time, the war quickly pushed a variety of
domestic issues—in particular the growing recession and the savings-
and-loan scandal—off the front-pages, quickly refocusing attention on
the strength, confidence, and leadership of the president. In the wake of
the Gulf War, I also want to argue that it is increasingly important for
activists to see themselves not simply as peace-and-justice activists, but
also as "media activists."

Censorship

If the military learned one thing from the Vietnam War, it was to
control media images more tightly. While the Pentagon was able to rely,
particularly in the early years of the Vietnam War, on the editorial support
of the U.S. media, the military did not have control of the content—especially the visuals—of the war coverage. In the rehearsals for the Gulf War
that took place in Panama and Grenada we saw the military's media
strategy develop.

By August 1990, experience pointed to the formation of press pools
as the most effective strategy for handling the media. Alternative media
were excluded from these pools, and mainstream media—for fear of the
same fate—acquiesced to this arrangement with little opposition. Ultimately, the U.S. military became virtually the only source of information
from the Gulf region, supplied most of the visual material, and "cleared"
all reports from the Gulf. At the same time, military claims that such
censorship—although it was rarely labelled censorship—existed only to
protect the lives of U.S. and Allied soldiers seemed to resonate with the
public mood (or at least that mood registered by public-opinion polls),
with one poll indicating that 79 percent of respondents believed military
censorship was a "good idea."[1]

Whether or not the major media were pleased with the restrictions,
they did little to change them. When the Center for Constitutional Rights
filed a lawsuit on behalf of several independent publications and individual writers that challenged Pentagon censorship, major media did not join,

nor did they file friend-of-the-court briefs on behalf of the suit.[2] Moreover, most media outlets did not even report on the lawsuit in the many pages and hours of war coverage. Certainly, there were some exceptions: CNN's Peter Arnett in Baghdad and CBS's Bob Simon, who left the press pool and went out on his own, come to mind. But the networks and the major dailies did little to either change the Pentagon's policy of censorship or to provide the public with knowledge about the efforts of others to oppose it.

If military censorship were the entire story of U.S. media coverage of the war, the blame for the lack of information made available to the public would rest squarely on the shoulders of the government. However, the military censorship is only the beginning of how—and why—the U.S. press acted more as a public-relations arm for the U.S. military than as an independent media. Coverage leading up to the hostilities, and at home during the war, was so full of self-censorship that, in retrospect, it makes the official censorship almost seem peripheral.

Self-Censorship

While the networks and major dailies presented a steady stream of stories about the press restrictions, they rarely addressed the more important question of why the U.S. press was serving more as a transmission belt for official positions than as an independent investigator dedicated to providing citizens with a wide range of information. By restricting media criticism to discussion of the official censorship, the regular self-censorship never became an issue.

The most obvious way in which the major media restricted themselves was in the sources they chose to quote. The policy debate at home was, in particular, sharply limited by the choices made by the mainstream media. In the early months of the conflict—between August and December—the media were not as single-minded as they were during the war. Yet, the bounds of dissent only stretched as far as the debate inside the Beltway.[3] For example, there was almost no criticism of the Bush administration's decision to send troops to the Persian Gulf in August. Only when Democrats in Congress and a series of former generals began to question the effectiveness of war in the Gulf did the media begin to raise questions about the administration's policy. Still, the questions were largely circumscribed by the participants in the Washington policy debate, and revolved around the more effective strategy for destroying Saddam Hussein's Iraq. Often right-wing critics of the administration's policy were brought on the networks to question the wisdom of war, while the growing peace movement was almost entirely ignored.

One study found that spokespeople for the anti-war movement were completely absent from discussions during the first month of the crisis on ABC's "Nightline" and PBS's "MacNeil/Lehrer NewsHour," two of the most influential and in-depth television news programs.[4] The results indicated that not a single guest on "Nightline" argued against U.S. military intervention in the month of August, the crucial period in which one would expect an independent media to provide a wide-ranging policy debate. The study also found that nearly half of the guests (48 percent for "Nightline," 47 percent for "MacNeil/Lehrer") were current or former government officials, while only 3 percent of "Nightline's" guests and 4 percent of "MacNeil/Lehrer's" guests represented non-governmental citizen-action groups—of any political stripe.

This would be the case with mainstream reporting throughout the conflict, regardless of the restrictions imposed in the Gulf. Another study found, for example, that in the first two weeks of the war almost half (47 percent) of the sources quoted on-camera on the three network's evening news broadcasts represented U.S. or Allied governments, while only 1 percent represented the government of Iraq and less than 0.5 percent represented governments in the region that were officially neutral (Iran and Jordan). Furthermore, only 1.5 percent of the sources were anti-war protesters, and only one source (0.1 percent) was a representative of a national peace organization.[5] Other studies, including one of the Boston print media, found a similar pattern: a heavy reliance on U.S. and Allied officials, with little or no inclusion of opposition voices.[6]

Once the war began the networks brought on a host of analysts and experts, and each network had its share of former generals on hand to provide military analysis. The networks treated these ex-generals (including recently fired Air Force Chief Michael Dugan) as non-partisan experts, and viewers would have had little reason to believe otherwise. They analyzed the situation in a dispassionate manner, suggesting that questions about the war were primarily strategic—rather than political—problems.

The UN

The media also largely ignored the Bush administration's selective memory about the United Nations. As the administration focused on the UN Security Council as the proper instrument for approving war against

Iraq, the national media did little to inform the public about the Reagan and Bush administration's long-standing record of contempt for the UN. The *New York Times* noted in September[7] that the UN was "functioning as it was designed to...for virtually the first time in its history." But while the *Times* seemed pleased about this change, it did little to investigate either the history of the U.S. relationship with the UN or the means by which the Bush administration was buying its way to a Security Council resolution supporting war.[8]

With all of the fervor about the righteousness of the UN resolution, we rarely heard about the U.S. refusal to abide by the World Court's decision regarding reparations for Nicaragua. Nor did we hear about the UN resolutions condemning the 1982 Israeli occupation of Lebanon, or its current occupation of the West Bank and Gaza. Most striking, however, was the fact that the December 1989 U.S. invasion of Panama was almost never discussed.[9] The fact that the UN General Assembly condemned the invasion and that the United States vetoed two Security Council resolutions condemning the U.S. invasion did not enter the discussion about the UN in the Gulf. It was as if the UN only mattered when it supported U.S. interests. When it did not, the UN did not have to be ridiculed; it simply was ignored.

Once the war began, the United Nations vanished from the picture. While the war was ostensibly fought by the UN, viewers of American television certainly had no reason to believe that it was anything other than a U.S. war. The extensive use of American flags, the focus on American soldiers, and the fact that American politicians and generals were making the key decisions left no room for the United Nations. In fact, viewers would have been hard pressed to see any spokespeople from the UN after January 16, 1991. A study of Boston print media found that UN sources made up less than 1 percent of the sources of war coverage in the first month of the war, equal to the number of sports figures who were cited for their thoughts on the war.[10] It was as if the UN had done its job by providing the justification for the war, but was no longer needed once the fighting began.

Marginalizing Dissent

The anti-war movement in the United States organized and mobilized almost immediately after the sending of troops to the Persian Gulf in August. However, with rare exceptions, the major media largely ignored the existence of organized anti-war sentiment. Even when the debate appeared to be open to dissenting views—in November and December 1990—criticism of the administration's policy was almost exclusively articulated by members of Congress and former government officials. In the months leading up to January 1991 there was very little national coverage of anti-war organizing, despite the wide range of local and national anti-war actions. One study found that only 1 percent of Gulf coverage on the network evening news even mentioned opposition activity. And foreign-policy experts associated with the peace movement did not appear on any of the evening news broadcasts.[11]

Even when the movement became too large and noisy to ignore, the major media continued to marginalize dissent. While we saw and read slogans, chants, and heard occasional sound-bites from the crowd, there continued to be a virtual exclusion of spokespeople from anti-war organizations. Therefore, even when media covered anti-war events, they rarely provided readers and viewers with articulate arguments against the Bush administration's policy. Nor did the media explore in any depth the rationale for the anti-war position. Instead, anti-war activism was treated as a spectacle, with more interest in the look of the crowd than the substance of their criticism.

Most interesting, however, was the media treatment of the pro-war movement, which emerged in local communities in the early days of the war. While pro-war activities never rivaled anti-war activities in size, they generally received equal or more coverage. And the strategy of counter-demonstrating at anti-war activities paid big dividends for war supporters, who—despite their generally small numbers—became a central part of the drama: demonstrations by both sides about the war. This message obscured the fact that large anti-war demonstrations were occurring all over the country, and were part of a growing national anti-war movement.

The Language of War

The national media also picked up very quickly on the Bush administration's use of language. The labels attached to individuals and the words used to describe the combat played a subtle, but important, role in framing what the war was all about. That is why the Bush administration was so clear about its own use of language. What was astonishing was the degree to which the media adopted these terms and used them in their daily coverage. One of the most important terms which emerged during the Gulf crisis, and which continues to inform media discussions of U.S. foreign policy, was the New World Order. There was little investigation into the meaning of this term, or into the irony of initiating a "new" order with the old tactics of U.S. military intervention. Moreover, the war was regularly referred to as Operation Desert Storm by U.S. officials and media alike. Perhaps it made journalists feel more important to use the official military jargon, rather than their own words. Ultimately, the term was widely adopted in popular discourse—as entrepreneurs sold t-shirts and hats bearing the name "Operation Desert Storm." Furthermore, the "liberation" of Kuwait was not only accepted by the media as a legitimate goal, but was used extensively in reporting with only rare questions about what it means to liberate a country by returning it to dictatorial rule by a royal family.

Even more important, the media played the crucial role of demonizing Saddam Hussein for the American public. It should not have been surprising that by January 1991 public opinion polls indicated that many Americans saw Saddam as a monster who had to be eliminated at any cost. Within the extensive discussions of Hussein's responsibility for human-rights violations, there was rarely any discussion of why the U.S. administration had supported Iraq until August 1990. Nor was Hussein's brutality set in a context that suggested that the U.S. government had played an integral role in arming Iraq.

The media's demonization of Saddam Hussein exhibited a subtle, and sometimes not-so-subtle, brand of racism. Much like the anti-Iran sentiment in the early 1980s, harsh criticisms of Iraq were often little more than thinly veiled attacks on Arabs and Arab Americans. In one case, the *New York Times* printed an editorial cartoon which depicted a fly-infested Saddam as lower than a snake in a lineup showing the "Descent of Man." The portrayal of Saddam as sub-human fit well with the long history of Arab stereotypes in the U.S. media.[12]

The administration's rhetoric about the "evil" Saddam was reminiscent of recent negative campaign advertisements, in which hostility is directed at "the other." In this case, Saddam served as a kind of international version of Willie Horton for the Bush administration, and racist attitudes easily commingled with a fervent, patriotic support for the war.

Perhaps most disturbing, however, was the use by the media of antiseptic military terms to describe the fighting. Bombing raids became "sorties," civilian casualties became "collateral damage," and Iraq became "the enemy." Such language served the interests of the Bush administration so clearly that it must have been surprising even to the White House that these terms were repeated on the evening news without the batting of an eyelash. The combination of technical jargon to describe violent acts that kill, along with the high-tech Pentagon-provided pictures of the "smart" bombs, made the war seem more like a new video game than a bloody war. While the video-game metaphor has been used extensively, the importance of this should not be underestimated, and it is clear that the U.S. military placed great value on controlling the imagery for this very reason.

Once again, the primary target of this language and these images was the U.S. public, whom the government hoped to shield from the reality of the war. In fact, the government had a great deal of success in this endeavor. There were few enough U.S. casualties to prevent any generalized feeling of loss during the war (and no pictures of the returning coffins at Dover Air Base were permitted by the military). And there were almost no images of Iraqi casualties until after the war was over. In fact, an avid viewer of network television news could have watched daily coverage of the entire war without ever seeing a human casualty. In this regard, the media played an indispensable role in making the war a more distant—almost bloodless—experience for the U.S. public.

With the war taking on the look and feel of a video game, network television—no doubt driven by the ratings race—seemed intent on making the war coverage as similar to prime-time television as possible. Upbeat music, catchy slogans like "Showdown in the Gulf," and fast-paced images made the war coverage seem like a well directed Music Video. The point, here, however is that this top-rated video was produced and directed by the U.S. military, with only minor editing by the networks. And the familiar feel of the coverage made it easier to watch without disrupting one's daily life. It was little different from watching the newest action film or police drama. In fact, action films and prime-time television generally contain a great deal more violence than we ever witnessed in the coverage of the Gulf War. Perhaps most important, the media treated people as mere spectators to the war—glued to the drama unfolding on their television screens—rather than participants in any kind of national policy debate.

The Casualties of War

Once the war actually started, the networks provided us with an extremely limited view of the casualties of the war. While Baghdad was being bombarded and Iraqi troops were being "softened up," we rarely saw pictures of the damage. When we did see footage of casualties in Iraq, we were reminded that we were seeing Iraqi propaganda, as when NBC Correspondent Dennis Murphy concluded his January 27 report by noting that "until we get some western reporters and photographers in there to vouch for it, I think we'll have to call it propaganda."

When Peter Arnett of CNN stayed in Baghdad to report on the damage, he was widely denounced in the United States—particularly by U.S. Senator Alan Simpson—as a propaganda tool for Saddam Hussein. Such claims were never made about the reporters stationed at U.S. military bases in Saudi Arabia who were under constraints similar to those faced by Arnett in Baghdad. And CNN, anticipating such pressure, went out of its way to indicate that Arnett's reporting was subject to censorship by the Iraqi government.

When reporting did focus on the civilian casualties in Iraq—as it did with the February 13 bombing of the Baghdad bunker—Americans were reminded by the media that it was not our fault. Tom Brokaw of NBC made the point clearly when he noted, "We must point out again and again that it is Saddam Hussein who put these innocents in harm's way."

With little reporting of Iraqi casualties, the horrors of war focused primarily on the victims of Iraqi Scud missiles in Israel. While the Scud attacks were certainly newsworthy, the fact that the victims received so much more coverage than the victims of the U.S. air war tells us a great deal about U.S. media priorities. One study found that the two Boston dailies spent three times as many column inches on Israeli casualties as Iraqi casualties.[13] And the previously mentioned study of the sources on network evening news found that civilian sources in Israel were quoted almost four times as often as civilians in Iraq or refugees from Iraq and Kuwait.[14] It was clear who the American media saw as the victims worthy of our attention: Israelis. And it was equally clear that Iraqi victims of U.S. bombs were relegated to second-class status. A stark reminder of this point was Ted Koppel's January 21 comment that "aside from the Scud missile that landed in Tel Aviv earlier, it's been a quiet night in the Middle East." This comment came at at time when the United States was flying 2,000 bombing missions a day.

Public Opinion

Throughout the months leading up to January 15 the public seemed bitterly split on whether or not to go to war. Once the bombing began, however, polls indicated overwhelming support for the president. This may have been little different from other wars—American wars always seem to begin with a good deal of popular support. But the public's reaction to this war was far more complicated than simply changing sides to support the president and "our troops."

One reason why it is difficult to interpret public opinion is that the national media provided so little substantive debate about the war. This fits nicely with a U.S. political culture which increasingly seems to value slick images over informed debate. As such, it was not surprising that instead of providing far-reaching policy discussions the media quickly pronounced the return of patriotism in America.

The principal expression of this patriotism was the yellow ribbon—displayed widely on lapels, cars, and storefronts. While the media highlighted the abundance of yellow ribbons—and sometimes displayed yellow ribbons themselves, the meaning of the yellow ribbon was not as uniform as it was generally depicted. At its core, the yellow ribbon was an expression of concern for the safety of family and friends in the Gulf. But whether that implied fervent support for the president is not at all clear. It is not unlikely that, for many, the yellow ribbon was a sign of hope for an end to the war—regardless of the circumstances.

Public support for the war was also related to the fact that, as I have suggested throughout this essay, the national media did little to provide people with alternative interpretations of the crisis. Even people who may have been skeptical about the war had little reason to believe that their were any legitimate grounds on which to oppose the war. What better indication that a position has no legitimacy than its exclusion from national media discourse? And for those trying to find some alternative policy to war, both the content of the reporting and the "showdown" imagery suggested that, in fact, the storyline was unfolding in the only possible direction. The implicit message was that war was, indeed, the only option.

Perhaps most important for understanding public opinion and the war is the fact that, according to one study, the public knew very little about the situation in the Middle East.[15] For example, only 13 percent of those surveyed could correctly identify the U.S. position toward Iraq before its invasion of Kuwait. And only 31 percent knew that Israel was occupying lands in the Middle East. Furthermore, only 14 percent of respondents knew of the U.S. votes in the UN against a political settlement to the Palestinian/Israeli conflict. On the other hand, 80 percent of respondents knew the name of the missile that intercepts Scuds: the Patriot.

Most interesting, however, is how the knowledge of respondents correlates with their television viewing and their support for the war. The researchers found that little knowledge was correlated with lots of television viewing and high support for the war. Given what we have seen about national media coverage of the war, this might be what we should have expected. Those who watched more television news were likely to know less about the war and to support it more strongly than those who watched less television news. In fact, the study found that the only fact that avid television viewers were more likely to know was the name of the Patriot missile. Given that the missile was regularly championed in television reports, this finding is not surprising. It is however, as the researchers conclude, "a sad indictment of television's priorities."

The Lessons of Vietnam

If the Persian Gulf War marks the beginning of a New World Order—one in which the United States will be unchecked militarily—the role played by the media in preparing the American public for the "new" international role of the United States has been central. In particular, the national media has been the primary site where the administration waged the symbolic contest about the meaning of the war in Vietnam. With the Cold War "over," the primary remaining obstacle for U.S. foreign policy-makers was the reluctance of their constituents to support wars of intervention.

Analysts on both left and right have long indicated that American public opinion is a central battleground of American foreign policy. While the Central America movement in the 1980s was not able to stop the U.S.-sponsored contra war against Nicaragua, it made the direct use of U.S. forces politically problematic. The symbol of Vietnam was used effectively by activists—both in rallying public opinion and in pressuring sectors of the Democratic Party—to oppose U.S. intervention in Central America.

The symbolism of Vietnam was a powerful tool for opponents of U.S. policy in Central America. The notion of Nicaragua as "another Vietnam"—a quagmire for the American military—was the opposition argument most frequently picked up by the major media.[16] Even activists whose perspectives focused more on the right to self-determination for the people of Central America or on the need to provide solidarity to revolutionary Nicaragua often appealed to the American public's concern about "another Vietnam." But there were serious limitations to this framing of the issue—limitations that the Bush administration took advantage of during the Gulf War.

As much as anything, the New World Order is a code for the end of the "Vietnam syndrome." The very fact that the reluctance of people to support wars of intervention has been labelled a "syndrome" implied that it was something which was in need of a cure. The Persian Gulf War—at least as far as the national media were concerned—provided the antidote to the Vietnam syndrome. Peace-and-justice activists, however, are not blameless here either. The focus—especially during the Gulf War—by the peace movement on the high costs of the war in American lives provided the Bush administration with the opportunity to tackle the "Vietnam syndrome." For if the New World Order is about the ability of the U.S. military to use force unchecked, the key to gaining popular support is to prove that it can be done with relatively little human cost to the United States. If this could be accomplished, there was little reason to fear "another Vietnam," a seemingly endless quagmire.

The outcome of the war—six weeks of massive bombing, followed by a "100-hour" ground war, with less than 150 U.S. combat deaths—indicated that, indeed, the United States is capable of fighting wars of intervention without high costs in personnel. And the media's focus on the success of high-tech weapons, preparedness of U.S. troops, strategic planning by U.S. generals, and the political skill of the president all served to suggest in a not-so-subtle manner that there was no legitimate reason for Americans to be afflicted with this "Vietnam syndrome." In fact, national media so accepted the official interpretation of Vietnam that the notion of "fighting with one hand tied behind our back"—as George Bush described the Vietnam War—was largely accepted. In this version of history it was the American public—influenced by the "liberal" media—who constrained the U.S. military. It should be no wonder, then, that the national media went out of their way to make it clear that they "supported our troops" —in for example, editorials, gala television tributes to the troops, full-page yellow ribbons in newspapers, and in special "commemorative issues" of national newsweeklies.

The symbolic contest over Vietnam—its meaning and its lessons—was waged primarily in the mass media. What emerged from the Gulf War was a popular reinterpretation of the Vietnam experience, one which suggested that the United States has finally licked the wounds of Vietnam.

Explaining Media Coverage

There is no simple explanation for why the national media served the interests of the U.S. government so effectively during the Gulf War. Some will argue that it is the very function of the national media to serve as a propaganda arm for elites, and that the media did their job quite well. Others will suggest that the corporate media serves its own interests by promoting elite interests. Still others will argue that administration officials are so skilled at "news management" that the national media did not even know how well they were being manipulated. All of these interpretations may be largely correct. However, they beg the question of how working journalists who think of themselves as independent are so easily turned into U.S. public-relations specialists.

In fact, for peace-and-justice activists faced with a New World Order of U.S. military power, it is too easy to dismiss the media as stooges for the elite without trying to make sense of why alternatives are so frequently excluded. Understanding how and why the media serve elite interests—rather than simply denouncing the media—may provide clues for how to think about the media when the next war comes along.

First, as a general rule journalists are highly dependent on officials for information. Whether it be due to the rationalization of the news-gathering process—stationing reporters at sites of regular "news," like the White House, Pentagon, and State Department—or the fear of alienating one's sources, or the perceived need to make use of "legitimate," "credible" sources, the effect is still the same. The intention to produce "propaganda" and the actual production of "propaganda" do not necessarily have to coincide.

In any case, the overwhelming reliance on officials ultimately suggests that "news" is what officials say and do, and that "newsmakers" are people in powerful positions. These are, in fact, basic tenets of American journalism. The reliance on official sources of information—often to the exclusion of other sources—should be understood as the fundamental underpinning of "objective" reporting.

Second, news media, particularly television, are ahistorical. Coverage is driven by breaking events, not by long-term "issues." There is often little interest in the background leading up to events, or the historical context in which current events are unfolding. Key points of the argument opposing the Gulf War focused on the history of U.S. foreign policy and the history of the Gulf region. However, as events unfolded, the relevant history for the media seemed to begin in August 1990, when Iraq invaded Kuwait. It was not surprising, then, that journalists generally ignored the historically grounded arguments of opponents of the war.

Conversely, media rarely have much foresight. And when officials had no interest in encouraging such forward thinking, there was little likelihood that journalists would focus much attention on the long-term consequences of the war. Again, a major part of the peace movement's argument focused on the likely aftermath of a war, and the havoc that war would wreak on the entire Middle East. As such, it is difficult for opposition perspectives to enter media reports that have been framed so narrowly around the latest, breaking event.

Third, television is dependent on visuals. For network television, newsworthiness is fundamentally connected to the quality of the pictures that accompany the story. And the specific content of stories is necessarily connected to the content of the visuals. In the Gulf War—as in Grenada and Panama—the visuals were controlled, almost without exception, by the U.S. government. (Attacks on CNN were, in my estimation, largely motivated by the fact that CNN was the one source of visuals that was not controlled by the government. While reporting by CNN was not oppositional in nature, the relative independence of the pictures was seen as threatening by the publicity specialists at the Pentagon and White House.) If pictures tell the story, most of the work was already done before network correspondents even picked up a microphone. Furthermore, the peace movement had only a limited ability to create its own visuals—especially visuals that national news would pick up. As such, it was easy for the national media to largely ignore the peace movement. Even those visuals that the peace movement did create did little to illuminate why activists opposed the war. The pictures of angry demonstrators—often contrasted with patriotic war supporters—gave the public no insight into the reasons for opposing the war.

Fourth, journalists, perhaps like many Americans, want to be seen as patriotic. Especially when they perceive that their audience is exhibiting national pride, market-driven media will do the same. It is important to remember that the media in the United States are fundamentally *American* media. In times of national crisis, this makes the notion of an "independent" media more illusory than real. Even the most "liberal" portions of the U.S. media are likely to feel the pressure to, at least subtly, support the president—who the media generally depict as the symbol of the nation. For example, PBS postponed the broadcast of Bill Moyers' special on the Iran-Contra scandal, "High Crimes and Misdemeanors," in March, noting that "the program could be seen as overtly political by attempting to undermine the president's credibility."[17] And when journalists fear, whether consciously or not, the power of officials and their well-funded allies to label journalists "unpatriotic," it is even more likely that their identification with the "American" side will be less than subtle.

All of this suggests that the organization of the media, along with the socialization and attitudes of journalists, make for a national media who were unlikely to serve as anything less than cheerleaders for the war effort. This also suggests that room for intervention by peace-and-justice activists is severely limited. But given the importance of the national media as the fundamental arena in which national politics now takes place, it makes little sense for peace-and-justice activists to give up trying to influence it. However, such a recognition clearly poses several serious dilemmas for activists.

Dilemmas for Activists

While there is disagreement about the degree to which media affects what people think, critics have long recognized its "agenda-setting" function.[18] That is, by highlighting certain issues, while downplaying or ignoring others, the news media puts certain subjects and ideas on the public stage. In the case of the Gulf War, the avid news junkie who is trained in deciphering media messages may have been able to put together the clues which suggested that the war was not as simple as it appeared or that the New World Order had little to do with "democracy," "peace," or "countering aggression." But the constant replaying of certain themes—Saddam Hussein is evil, the United States is the guardian of democracy, the troops need the support of the American people, for example—made it difficult for the public to see alternative sides of the story. Instead, media attention focused largely on the families of the troops in the Gulf, the success of the weapons used in the Gulf, the atrocities committed by Iraqis occupying Kuwait, and the courage of the soldiers fighting the war. It is not surprising, then, that the public appeared to be concerned about similar issues.

If, indeed, the media can help to define what is important and what is not, it is also not surprising that officials have become more astute at using the media to set the agenda for the American public. It is not clear how peace-and-justice activists could have responded during the Gulf War in a way that would have decisively affected the political climate at home. But one could imagine that had the media examined the history of U.S. policy in the Gulf, U.S. hypocrisy in its relationship to the UN, or the various possibilities for a diplomatic solution to the conflict in the kind of depth with which media analyzed Saddam Hussein's or George Bush's character, the political debate in the United States may very well have been different. One major dilemma facing peace-and-justice activists, then, is how to engage in national political debates when the terms of the debate have been largely set by the White House.

Furthermore, even when alternative ideas do occasionally find their way into the national media, spokespeople often find themselves trying to express complex ideas in 15-second sound bites. When such ideas have been so marginalized by the media, their occasional inclusion may not resonate with a public that is entirely unfamiliar with these ideas. And since the position against the war was not only less familiar, but far more complex than a position to support the war, it is clear that national media cannot be the only place where activists attempt to articulate alternative perspectives. Still, introducing these relatively unfamiliar perspectives to a wider public remains important. Activists need to see the media as only one site amongst many for presenting interpretations which challenge dominant assumptions.

At the same time, the media's tendency to personalize events makes it difficult, for example, to get at the root causes of the Persian Gulf War. Instead, the media treated us to a kind of prize fight between George Bush and Saddam Hussein, chock full of sports metaphors and personal profiles. Again, this is the kind of terrain on which it is difficult for peace-and-justice activists to put forth alternative interpretations of events.

Lessons of the Gulf War

Given the high profile of the press during the Gulf War, it is not surprising that a great deal of peace activists' attention and anger was directed at the media. The reliance on ex-generals for commentary, the marveling at the high-tech weaponry, and the tendency to dismiss the peace movement—all spelled frustration for those opposed to the war. In their analysis of the war, peace activists have drawn a variety of conclusions about the role of media in social change organizing. However, several of their lessons are misguided.

First, many have argued that the U.S. people were somehow duped by the media into supporting the war. As evidence they point to the rapid shift in public opinion in the middle of January, apparently caused by the jingoism expressed in media coverage. Second, some have suggested that the national media, which is designed as a propaganda system for elites, is not malleable. It follows, therefore, that it does not make sense for activists to direct any energy at the national media. Instead, the alternative media needs to be supported as a challenge to the mainstream media.

There is no simple answer to the relationship between the media and public opinion. However, it is problematic for activists to lay blame for war support solely on the doorstep of the network news. The news media clearly played an important role in legitimizing the war policy and in limiting the range of acceptable positions on the war. Perhaps more important, when the war started the media played a major role in keeping the war distant from our lives: We did not see the "enemy" casualties, nor were there enough U.S. casualties to cause major dissent at home. But the reasons for such overwhelming support for the war are far more complex than a cheerleading media. And the notion that the public was simply duped by the media suggests that people are simply passive consumers of media imagery. For a movement that calls for a more participatory democracy, this line of reasoning is problematic.

More challenging is the argument that the Gulf War demonstrates the futility of focusing on mainstream media for social-change activists. The daily experiences of activists—who are regularly ignored by major media—lends credence to this interpretation. And it clearly is important to support and build the alternative media. Alternative media play an important role in social movement organizing—providing coverage of events that would otherwise go uncovered, room for the development of new perspectives and alternative analyses, along with space for debates about movement strategy. Without doubt, one of the lessons of the Gulf War is that activists need to work to strengthen alternative media institutions.

However, alternative publications have a limited reach, and have limited access to new readers. As part of a response to the New World Order, activists do need to build the circulation of the alternative press, and to promote these publications in new settings. New technologies are also making alternative television and radio easier and less costly to produce. Activists need to take advantage of the opportunity to produce alternative programming for the electronic media—on public-access stations and college radio stations, for example. A wide range of alternative publications, and the likes of Paper Tiger Television, the Gulf Crisis Television Project, and Pacifica Radio invested large amounts of resources into disseminating an alternative analysis of the war. But the sheer reach of the major media, especially network television, and its ability to set the terms of debates, makes it virtually impossible to fight political battles only through alternative media.

When the importance of building alternative media is tied to an argument for withdrawing from the mainstream media, it is a serious misreading of the lessons of the Gulf War. Even though movements are at a severe disadvantage, the media still must be seen as an important arena for political struggle. While the economic organization of the major media limits the change that is possible in the short term, it does not eliminate all together the possibility of media coverage that is more conducive to movement organizing. There are many arenas in which activists engage politically even though their analysis suggests the structural constraints that limit change. The media should be seen as one of these arenas, where limited, but still important, change is possible in the short term. The benefits of broadening the media to include a more wide-ranging debate are not inconsequential. And these benefits may be helpful in the future, when the democratization of institutions—in this case the corporate media—will be a central long-term project.

Clearly, activists are up against long odds—corporate-owned media that are becoming increasingly centralized. In the short run, activists can realistically hope to broaden the media and to gain increased access to national publications, television, and radio. As a start, activists need to begin to see media as a contestable terrain—one in which they will begin with relatively minor victories, but one around which a growing movement can continue to grow.

All of this must take place with an understanding that media discourse is severely limited by a variety of structural and ideological constraints. But the discourse is not fixed; and the range of possibilities varies depending on the specific historical context. One of the variables which can affect media discourse is the strength and organization of social movements. That is, opposition movements—while often marginalized by mainstream media—have the potential to significantly affect the content of stories that the public receives from the mass media each day.

Media Activism

Ultimately, one of the fundamental lessons of the Gulf War is that peace and justice activists need to become "media activists." Media activism is a relatively new concept that is still largely undefined. At its core, however, is a recognition that the media is not monolithic, that it is not impenetrable, and that it is an arena—like the electoral arena—in which activists need to organize. The Gulf War demonstrated starkly that late-twentieth-century wars are fought in the media as much as on the battlefield. The corollary to this is that U.S. politics are fought, in large part, in the media as well. While activists must be conscious of the constraints, the possibility of small, albeit important, changes should not be discounted.

The tactics of media activism vary widely, depending on the particular context of one's organizing. There are several ways in which peace-and-justice activists have begun to integrate media activism into their work.

Media criticism and media monitoring can play an important role for activists. Popular media criticism has traditionally been the domain of the Right in the United States. Thoughtful, well-documented media criticism—as in such publications as *Extra!, Lies of Our Times,* the *Nation,* and *Z Magazine* —can be a useful service to activists and non-activists alike. For activists it can help to clarify the problems with the mainstream media and provide helpful tools for direct organizing. When movement-oriented media criticism reaches a larger public, it can counter the myth that the media is "liberal."

Monitoring can also help provide activists with increased access to members of the mainstream media. For example, an anti-intervention group in Philadelphia prepared a detailed analysis of their local paper's coverage of Central America.[19] After presenting it to the paper's editors and disseminating it within the activist community, activists met with the editors. While the paper did not immediately change its coverage, activists put the paper "on notice" that it was being carefully observed. They concluded that the strategy was effective because it "shook up" the editors and gave the Philadelphia-area peace movement increased access to the *Philadelphia Inquirer.* A Central America group in Seattle used a similar strategy and found that the "action of the Media Project along with other citizen action groups in the area helped create greater public awareness and political representation on issues related to Central American policy."[20] Media monitoring can also provide the basis—and lay the framework for specific demands—for more action-oriented strategies directed at the media.

One strategy which has been used widely by media activists is organized media response. For both local and national media, activists have organized write-in and call-in campaigns in order to pressure the media to change. For example, in Boston, the volume of calls to one talk-radio station during the Gulf War persuaded the station to bring on Noam Chomsky. A few days later Chomsky appeared on the station's national-network "town meeting" on the Gulf. And phone and letter campaigns in several cities, including Los Angeles and Boston, saved the PBS program "South Africa Now" from cancellation in 1990. Even when there is no immediate result from this kind of organized response, activists should not despair. Such pressure is part of a long-term project, and it alerts the media to the fact that there is a movement capable of mobilizing an organized response. During the Gulf War, PBS's "Washington Week in Review" received so many letters complaining about its coverage that producers responded with a form letter.[21] The letter indicated that the most frequent complaints were "You are not getting the entire story; you are not getting all public views on the war (especially the anti-war view); the Pentagon is using the press as vehicles of U.S. military propaganda."

Other groups have tried legal challenges to the mainstream media. The Philadelphia Lesbian and Gay Task Force, after completing a study of "public-interest" coverage on Philadelphia television,[22] challenged the renewal of the licenses of several major television stations—arguing that women, lesbians and gays, and ethnic "minorities" were largely ignored by Philadelphia television stations. While the FCC took no action, enough publicity was generated to make the station owners uncomfortable. As a result, the issue of the responsiveness of television to the needs of the community was raised for a larger public, and the Task Force has gained increased access to a range of television and radio stations.

Public-access television also provides new opportunities for peace-and-justice activists. It gives them the opportunity to produce their own programming. In Boston, for example, a group of anti-war media activists produced an alternative talk show on the Gulf War with plans to air it on local cable stations.

There is also room, of course, for public mobilizations directed at the media. During the war, a group of 2,000 activists marched to the offices of the three networks and PBS in New York City. The demonstration demanded, among other things, more substantive coverage of the anti-war movement. The march helped to mobilize new activists. And several days later ABC News presented one of the few in-depth pieces on the peace movement.

In the wake of the Gulf War, activists in a variety of cities—including New York, Boston, Chicago, Los Angeles, San Francisco, Hartford, and Austin—have organized to continue to pressure the media. The specific tactics of media activism are likely to evolve in the coming years as some prove to be more effective than others. Where media activists have already succeeded is in exposing the inequities in media coverage. That is no small achievement.

Clearly the media is not the only terrain that is ripe for organizing, and activists should not focus on media work so single-mindedly that they neglect other important areas. In particular, the media may reach many more people than activists can in face-to-face discussion, but direct organizing is not something that can be sacrificed simply because we live in a high-tech, mass-mediated world.

It is central to remember that media organizing and other forms of political work are part of the same fight. At the same time, peace-and-justice organizations need to understand that their media work has to be part of their overall political work. What activists need to do is to think in terms of re-framing debates.[23] One place where this re-framing struggle needs to occur is in the media, though it is certainly not the only place. Activists will be most successful if they learn how the media works, and if they try a wide range of strategies for influencing the media. At the same time, organizing will be most successful if activists see that increased access to the mainstream media can help to promote alternative media, and that criticism of the mainstream media in the alternative media can help to build a movement of media activists. As such, media activism focused on pressuring the mainstream media and the building of alternative media need to be seen as complementary.

The Gulf War provided ample evidence that peace-and-justice activists need to think more strategically about the media. In particular, I am suggesting that activists need to see the media as an institution in which they can organize: building relationships with and feeding information to some journalists, pressuring—both privately and publicly—other journalists, and providing a wider public with an analysis of what is wrong with the media. Even if victories are small and temporary, peace-and-justice activists need to bring their organizing experience and strategic thinking—rather than simply public-relations skills—to their media activism.

Notes

1. Times Mirror Center for the People and the Press, Washington, DC. The poll was conducted between January 25 and 27, 1991.
2. See "Pressing Freedom," the *Nation*, May 6, 1991, p. 579; and "Spin Control Through Censorship: The Pentagon Manages the News," *Extra!*, May 1991, p. 14, for more on the Center for Constitutional Rights lawsuit.
3. See Hertsgaard, Mark. "Following Washington's Lead," *Deadline*, January/February, 1991, pp. 4-5.
4. "Nightline and MacNeil/Lehrer: Who Spoke on the Gulf?" *Extra!* 3:8 (November/December 1990).
5. "Gulf War sources survey—January 17-January 30, 1991," FAIR, February 22, 1991.
6. See "Scenes From a War: A Study of Boston Press Coverage," an unpublished report by Boston Media Action/Media Watch, March 20, 1991.
7. *New York Times*, September 24, 1990.
8. See Chomsky, Noam, and Z Staff, "Z Pullout: The Gulf Crisis," *Z Magazine*, February 1991, for a more complete analysis of the role of the UN.
9. See Naureckas, Jim, "Media on the March: Journalism in the Gulf," *Extra!*, November/December 1990 for a more complete comparison.
10. "Scenes From a War: A Study of Boston Press Coverage," op. cit.
11. "Survey Shows Anti-War Movement Marginalized by Networks," FAIR press release, January 16, 1991.
12. For a discussion of stereotyping in news and entertainment television, see Shaheen, Jack, *The TV Arab*, Bowling Green, OH: Bowling Green State University Popular Press, 1984.
13. "Scenes From a War: A Study of Boston Press Coverage," op. cit.
14. "Gulf War sources survey," op. cit.
15. Lewis, Justin; Jhally, Sut; and Morgan, Michael; "The Gulf War: A Study of the Media, Public Opinion and Public Knowledge," University of Massachusetts

Center for the Study of Communication, 1991.

16. See Hoynes, William, "Political Symbolism and the Central America Movement," Boston College Working Papers in Social Economy and Social Justice, December, 1987.
17. "Cleared By Self-Censors?" *Extra!*, May 1991, p. 15.
18. See Iyengar, Shanto and Donald R. Kinder, *News That Matters: Television and American Opinion*, Chicago: University of Chicago Press, 1987.
19. "An Analysis of Central America coverage in the *Philadelphia Inquirer*, September 1989-February 1990," Philadelphia Pledge of Resistance Media Committee, July 1990.
20. Bennett, W. Lance, *News: The Politics of Illusion*, second edition, New York: Longman, 1988.
21. Quoted in *Extra!*, 4:3, May 1991.
22. "Whose Public Interest: A Study of Attention to Women, Minorities, and AIDS in Issue-Responsive Commercial Television Programs, 1986-88," Philadelphia Lesbian and Gay Task Force, 1989.
23. For a discussion of re-framing, see Ryan, Charlotte, *Prime Time Activism*, Boston: South End Press, 1991.

FIGHT THE POWER

CHAPTER 16

WHERE DO WE GO FROM HERE?

Rebecca Gordon

It was around the second week in January when most of my friends realized that the war was really going to happen. Until then, many people I know believed that one of the men sitting at that poker table would fold his hand before the other called his bluff.

The week President Bush ordered the bombing to begin, we stood around in dazed clumps at demonstrations, eyeing the other dazed clumps, shouting to each other over the chants, all of us trying to figure out why it was going to happen, who could possibly benefit from it, and what it would mean for the future. One thing we were sure of: This war would change the rest of our lives. Ten years, fifteen years from now, we would refer to various events as occurring before The War or after The War. We meant, I think, that whatever the outcome for the people in whose countries it was being waged, this massive U.S. military mobilization would change our own country in ways we could not yet define. I think we were right.

This essay is an attempt to put into print my own small contribution to a process I think is happening all over the country right now. People are trying to figure out what to do next. None of us has the Answer, or even many answers yet. But every one of us has the right to apply her or his perfectly good brains to the problem. Now is no time to let the experts—even the experts of the Left—do our thinking for us.

Even if we had not just failed to prevent the United States from committing a massacre in the Middle East, this would have been a time

Reprinted with permission from the *Guardian Newsweekly*, 24 West 25th Street, New York, New York (212) 691-0404. Yearly subscriptions: $33.50.

for mulling things over, for thinking about the events of the last two years. A lot has changed, and no one has put it all together yet. We've watched the collapse of communism in Eastern Europe. We've seen the Nicaraguan revolution give way before the economic and military power of the United States—with tremendous implications for similar struggles in El Salvador and the rest of Central America.

All the political activists I know—feminists, solidarity workers, lesbian and gay activists, union organizers—are struggling with the practical question of where to direct their energy. But they're also struggling with something bigger—a new way of understanding history and their place in it. Is it all over for dialectical materialism? Probably not, nor even for my own favorite organizing principle for understanding the world, radical feminism, but if I were a paradigmatic worldview, I'd be feeling a bit nervous right now.

Thinking about where we go from here raises a couple of prior questions. Like, Who's "we"? and, Where are we now?

For me, that "we" must be a big group. It's bigger than just the men of the working class, traditional marxism's historical agent. And it's wider and less comfortable than the white middle-class peace movement. "We" includes poor people, permanently unemployed people, communities of people of color, many women, most queers, sex workers—all of us who can't afford to give in to despair. "We" is all of us who desperately need to build a just society, for our own physical, emotional, and spiritual survival.

And where are we now? We live in a country in serious, perhaps permanent, economic decline, teetering on the brink of genuine fascism. I mean fascism in the historical sense of the word, i.e., a popular movement supporting an authoritarian system of government based on an ideology of nationalism and a pseudo-science of gender and race.

The nightmares created by the eight most irresponsible years of government in my lifetime—the Reagan presidency—are just now coming into focus. We've seen the collapse of one of the country's biggest financial institutions, its savings-and-loans system, shortly to be followed by the banking system and insurance companies. We've watched the creation of sub-class of newly and perhaps permanently homeless people. Every state faces crises in health care and education, and the devastation of poor communities by AIDS and crack cocaine.

It's ironic—though not coincidental—that jingoistic nationalism once again has overtaken the country at this particular moment in history. Ironic, because I think we're also living through an unprecedented period of transition, as power passes worldwide from the hands of national elites to multinational corporations. (This process has been going on at least since the end of World War II, but recent developments in computers and electronic communication have tremendously accelerated the internationalization of money and its owners. Between New York, San Francisco, London, and Tokyo, the casinos stay open 24 hours a day now.)

As many observers have pointed out, in the "new world order," the military apparatus of the United States may function less as the world's policeman than as the world's paid enforcer. International capital can now hire the U.S. armed forces to make the world safe for its own interests. Far from reaping a peace dividend, we will probably see our economy even further deformed, as military power replaces automobiles and food as our major export on the world market. Such an economy based in military power can't help but have its reflection in a national ideology of militarism.

Now What?

So where do we go from here? These are hard, dry times. We can't force-ripen history. When the next movement of major historical importance comes along—and my guess is that in this country it will once again come out of the African-American communities—we'll recognize it. Here are a few things we can do in the meantime, so we'll be ready when it happens:

- Get organized! Break down capitalism's equation of lonely individualism with freedom. We don't often have the opportunity to experience the power of unified action, but there's nothing more electrifying and satisfying—or likely to keep you around for the long haul—when it happens. Being part of an organized group—a union, a neighborhood association, a parent organization—makes it possible to mount a powerful response in an emergency, whether it's a war in the Persian Gulf or school closures in your neighborhood.

  By the way, getting organized shouldn't mean attending endless meetings in order to be harangued by boring white men with their own agendas. When it works well, getting organized means agreeing to break the work up into smaller pieces so that it can all get done.

- Stay visible! Bumper sticker your car, bike, or wheelchair. Put that sign in your window. Stick that pin on your shirt front. Talk to the people you work with. Being visible helps political allies recognize each other, and it provides an extra dose of courage to those of us who feel we're drowning in a sea of flags and yellow ribbons. When a coherent movement emerges, among other things, we may want our own flag. Efforts by groups like Fairness and Accuracy in Reporting to get more women, leftists, or people of color on "Nightline" are great, but we're not going to take over the mass media any time soon. So in the meantime, we have to find other ways to be seen and heard, through leaflets, newsletters, house meetings, and public events.

Support your local alternative media, whether it's community radio, public-access television, or community publications. Here in northern California, we rely on listener-sponsored KPFA radio for news, analysis, and community access to the airwaves. KPFA's parent organization, the Pacifica Foundation, produces an excellent daily news program. You may be able to convince your local National Public Radio affiliate to carry it.

• Get real. Make real reality at least as interesting as that new electronic fad, "virtual reality"! It's hard to compete with Nintendo or MTV, but political action should offer people pleasure, empowerment, and an opportunity to exercise their creativity. Very few of us get to participate in the creation of our culture these days. Mostly culture is something you rent at the video store, and that's a crime. Given half a chance, people will astonish each with their capacities to imagine and create. When more than a 100,000 people came out in San Francisco to march against the Gulf War, almost a third of us were carrying some kind of homemade sign. Huge amounts of thought and effort went into those expressions of wit, grief, and outrage. (A personal favorite: "Bush, you schtupped us! Kuwaitus interruptus!")

We have to make political work fascinating, by calling on people to stretch and amaze themselves by what they can do, rather than what they can absorb. Otherwise, even if they're starving, people will quite reasonably wander away to something more pleasant and interesting, like watching reruns of "Cheers." Little things like incorporating music and theater in your political actions make a big difference. These are even more powerful when there's room for the "audience" to participate.

The Names Project's AIDS Quilt has put thousands of people's artistic impulses to powerful political use. Here in San Francisco, Hotel and Restaurant Workers Union Local 2 regularly resists the temptation to hold one more boring moving picket. Instead they do things like arranging a living 6:00-AM wake-up call for a union-busting hotel's guests— complete with music and noisemakers! Check out Queer Nation's lesbian and gay kiss-ins in shopping malls for an example of zaps with humor and tenderness.

- Reduce frustration. We get enough of it in the rest of our lives. Let people know how and when an action—whether a demonstration or an ongoing campaign—will begin and end. Give your actions clear, identifiable objectives (e.g., to deliver a 10,000-signature petition to a reluctant mayor by rolling it down the steps of City Hall). If we know what the goal is, we'll know when we achieve it, and we'll be able to do something else important—celebrate our victories.

- "And also teach them to read." People in this county learn too much of what they "know" through passive absorption of television. If there's one lesson to be learned from Nicaragua's revolution, it's that this country needs a literacy campaign, in the literal sense of teaching adults to read. The furor stirred by Jonathan Kozol's *Illiterate America* (published by Doubleday in 1985) seems to have died down in the intervening six years. But as much as a third of the country remains functionally illiterate today, excluded by illiteracy not only from decent employment, but from real participation in any political process. Even the majority of those who do make it through public schools emerge having learned two basic lessons—they are stupid, and the world is far too complicated for people like them to understand.

  By literacy, I mean both the actual ability to decode print, and the ability to decode one's own life. As literacy campaigns in the Third World have shown, teaching people to read can be a powerfully subversive activity. People come to realize that they have perfectly good brains and the right to use them to analyze their own situations. I can't think of a more revolutionary activity today than organizing campaigns to teach people to read and encourage them to think for themselves.

- Look out for each other. If the pessimists among us are right, and we're entering a period of increased repression, if not outright fascism, we need to be ready to protect each other. Our adversaries are not invincible, but they're not stupid either. They'll try to pick off people first who aren't respectable to the mainstream and may not have a lot of support—young people, people with green hair, people who call themselves queer, people with AIDS, members of small political sects. They'll focus on people with fewer resources, especially people of color. And they'll pick off people some of us may passionately dislike, precisely because they are the most vulnerable. We must defend every one. First, because it's the right thing to do, and second, because only by defending everyone, do we defend ourselves.

- Don't be afraid to tackle "divisive" issues. They won't go away just because we agree not to discuss them. A papered-over rift is not unity. Perfect agreement is not required, but a movement that's held together through a tacit consent not to talk about something—sexism, racism, homophobia, nationalism—will come apart at the seams when the issue in question inevitably surfaces. It took a war in the Persian Gulf to force the Left to think and talk about Israel, Palestine, and the Arab world.

- Sharpen our focus on what's happening in the United States, while we simultaneously deepen our international connections. Many—though by no means all—of us on the Left have spent the last 10 years working in solidarity with revolutionary struggles in other countries. We weren't wrong to do so, but international solidarity also has its pitfalls. We can't afford to to emigrate in our hearts to some revolution in another place, while giving up on the people of our own country. As the U.S. victory in Nicaragua demonstrated, only real change in the United States will keep our government off the backs of small revolutionary nations in this hemisphere. Besides, we need revolutionary change in this country for our own survival as well.

So it's time to pay some attention to what's going on here, while maintaining our internationalism. Some Ford workers in Minnesota are currently doing just that, by initiating a series of meetings with their counterparts in Mexican Ford factories to strategize about the impending "free"-trade agreement between the Mexican and U.S. governments. These Minnesota workers recognize that in an era of international capitalism staving off cutbacks and plant closures requires both political action at home and forming international alliances. As long as labor is cheap and non-union in other parts of the world, U.S. workers will suffer, too. These folks know that in the age of international capitalism, international solidarity is more than altruism, it's our lifeline.

These are just a few ideas of my own. What I really need now—what we all need—is to hear other people's ideas. I want to know what the people in my office think, what the woman who bags my groceries thinks, what the homeless man who sells me my monthly copy of the *Street Sheet* thinks. I especailly want to know what people 20 years younger are thinking. After all, they'll be living with the aftermath of this ill-begun decade longer than I will.

Wherever we go from here, we'll inevitably be going there together. The more of us who have a say in where that is, the more likely that when and if we get there, it will look something like home.

CHAPTER 17

AFRICAN AMERICANS AND FOREIGN POLICY

Salim Muwakkil

During the confusion churned up in this country's War of Independence, thousands of enslaved Africans escaped bondage and joined the British army. This action made good sense: the British "enemy" offered freedom to any male slave willing to bear arms, while the rebellious colonies that the slaves called home denied them basic human rights. Until a personnel shortage forced a policy change, Blacks were forbidden the right to serve in the Continental army. When that racial barrier fell, at least 5,000 Black men—including leaders like Prince Hall, Lemuel Haynes, and Peter Salem—signed up to fight the British. The paradox facing those Black soldiers was obvious: they were fighting for a system that allowed, indeed encouraged, their own enslavement. But the egalitarian rhetoric of that rebellious era persuaded many Blacks that participation in the battle against British colonialism could be a path to freedom. Black activists and intellectuals began utilizing the ideology of the American Revolution—the deism of the European Enlightenment, the Natural Rights doctrines of inalienable human rights, the pietistic religions of the white church—to fuel their anti-slavery arguments.

The ambiguous pattern set during the war that birthed this country still shapes the foreign policy attitudes of many African Americans. Unlike most other peoples in America's ethnic patchwork, the space separating "African" from "American" signifies dueling, as well as dual, identities. European Americans could avoid confronting the hypocrisy of a slaveholding nation founded upon the ideals of freedom and liberty, but Blacks

335

lacked that luxury; this country always has been more menacing than promising for people of African ancestry. For African slaves and their descendants, U.S. independence meant chattel slavery and racism. Black Americans are culturally disposed, therefore, to view the freedom-and-liberty pieties of the American myth with more skepticism than are white Americans. This is especially true when U.S. leaders evoke those pieties to marshal support for various military adventures. African Americans know better than anyone that U.S. victories over foreign evils have done little to lessen the evil of racism at home.

What's more, this country's foreign policy history is tainted by its racist effect. From the near-annihilation of Native American Indians to the ruthless acquisition of Cuba, Puerto Rico, the "Danish West Indies," Hawaii, the Philippines, the island of Dominica, and the Panama Canal Zone, the pattern of American imperialism clearly is one that subordinates darker people and exploits their resources. There should be little mystery about why African Americans are, at the very least, ambivalent about the use of military power in the service of this country's imperial ambitions.

Yet, many white Americans have interpreted Blacks' ambivalence as a lack of patriotism. From the period of the Revolutionary War, when many colonial leaders argued—correctly—that escaped slaves were betraying "their" country by fighting for their own freedom, Black participation in America's military adventures has been problematic. The problem was highlighted during last year's turkey shoot in the Persian Gulf. Mainstream (read: right-wing) pundits were troubled by poll findings that Blacks were considerably less enthusiastic about Operation Desert Storm than were whites. In the month following the high-tech overkill that blasted Iraq back into the preindustrial age, triumphalist editorials in publications across the country were generously peppered with putdowns of "too liberal" Black leadership.

Despite their well-founded suspicion of U.S. foreign policy aims, Black leaders generally have supported most of this country's major military adventures. During the Civil War, most recognized Black leadership—including Harriet Tubman, Frederick Douglass, Henry Highland Garnet, Martin Delany, and William Wells Brown—supported Union forces and the white Republicans who commanded them. Since most Blacks had always considered themselves at war with the Confederacy, this was a logical tactic. In fighting for the Union, African Americans were literally fighting for their own freedom. The war emboldened and enfranchised Blacks, but it also provoked an intense white backlash; the Ku Klux Klan and other white supremacist groups promoting anti-Black violence were born during this period. This pattern is repeated throughout U.S. history.

Black soldiers were among the first to serve in Cuba in 1898 during the Spanish-American War because someone in the War Department thought they were immune from tropical diseases. While soldiers from the all-Black Ninth and Tenth Cavalry accompanied Theodore Roosevelt's Rough Riders on their charge up Cuba's San Juan Hill, thousands of southern Blacks were being lynched on the home front.

When the United States entered World War I, some radical Black leaders like A. Philip Randolph and Chandler Owens spoke out against the idea that the victimized U.S. Black population should fight in a war for the victimizers. But most Black people supported W.E.B. Du Bois' 1918 argument that Black participation in an Allied victory would help expand democratic rights, lessen social injustices, and stop racial lynchings. Du Bois was a leading Black intellectual who at the time was editor of *Crisis*, the influential house organ of the National Association for the Advancement of Colored People (NAACP).

Forces put in motion by World War I are still operating in contemporary discourse on race relations and the problems of this country's predominantly Black inner cities. The concentration of African Americans into resource-poor urban centers is a reality easily traced to events surrounding World War I.

Southern Blacks, encouraged by manufacturers, the Black media, and a boll weevil plague, rushed northward to fill the labor shortage the war created. Not only were white soldiers leaving the factories, but the war also curtailed European immigration. During this period, the southern states were also experiencing a Ku Klux Klan revival and a concomitant increase in lynchings. Pulled by the promise of racial tolerance and industrial employment, and pushed by a recession and the growing danger of racist violence, an estimated one-half million African Americans left the South between 1916 and 1919 to start life anew in the cities of the industrial North. Nearly 1 million more followed in the 1920s.

When they arrived in the urban North, few African Americans found the industrial paradise they were led to expect. Instead, they ran headlong into violent white resistance. The NAACP charged that a "lynching orgy" had occurred in many regions of the country during 1918. After the war, racial tensions increased. The raised expectations of African Americans collided with the hostility and fear of those enamored of the racist status quo.

As if to discredit even the suspicion that the war had altered that status quo, Black soldiers were often specifically targeted for violence. In several southern states, white mobs disarmed, arrested, and confined Black members of the armed forces. The summer of 1919 has since been characterized as the "Red Summer" because of the racial violence that erupted then. Race-based riots had occurred before in the U.S., but never had this country witnessed racial violence that spread from one city to another. In the span of two weeks, racial outbreaks occurred in Omaha, Washington, Knoxville, and Chicago.

African Americans, especially war veterans, responded to this violence with an increasing militancy. Then, into this emotional setting came Marcus Garvey, a Jamaican-born pan-Africanist whose preachings struck a chord that still resonates strongly in the Black community. Within a period of about five years, Garvey's Black nationalist group, the Universal Negro Improvement Association (UNIA), became the largest Black organization in U.S. history, a title it still holds.

The war and its aftermath provoked movement on many levels in the Black community. Inspired by Garvey's Black nationalism, many Black activists and intellectuals increased their efforts to develop independent and analytical critiques of U.S. foreign policy. Hubert Harrison and John Bruce advocated internationalizing the Black struggle, and Du Bois went to Paris to help organize the second Pan-African Congress. Groups like Cyril Briggs' African Blood Brotherhood made explicit connections between anti-colonial struggles in Africa and the battles of African Americans. The Harlem Renaissance symbolized Black America's growing cultural confidence, and celebrations of the "Jazz Age" represented mainstream America's grudging acknowledgment of Black America's cultural wealth.

The period between the wars witnessed a further sophistication in Blacks' foreign policy analysis. Black leaders watched the depression-fueled growth of fascist governments in Germany and Italy with concern. Italy's 1936 invasion of Ethiopia triggered large protests in Harlem and Chicago. Increasing numbers of Black intellectuals were attracted by marxist ideology, and the Communist Party reaped bushels of positive p.r. in the Black community through its active—and perhaps principled— participation in several well-publicized causes, such as the defense of the "Scottsboro Boys" (six Black youths who were accused of raping two white women) and the organization of the Alabama Sharecroppers Union. Marxism provided perhaps the most comprehensive and cohesive theoretical framework from which to critique U.S. foreign policy, and it was easily adaptable to the situation of African Americans. Although marxism's widespread appeal soon waned, socialist ideals remain important in the philosophy of many contemporary Black organizations.

During this same period in Detroit, a small group of Blacks calling themselves the Nation of Islam (NOI), led by a Georgia migrant named Elijah Muhammad, began attracting converts. Utilizing a Garvey-like message of racial redemption and ancestral glories in the motherland,

Muhammad's group took hold. The NOI's foreign policy views were simple racial reductionism: white people were biologically disposed to take violent control over the non-white world and NOI members were forbidden to fight in "white men's wars." When Muhammad was jailed in 1942 for refusing to serve in the armed forces, he was accused of harboring Japanese sympathies. Muhammad's outright opposition to U.S. foreign policy was unusual. For, although Black Americans were reluctant to beat the war drums, they were even more reluctant to criticize openly this country's foreign-policy decisions. The public onus of blackness was bad enough; why add the label of "unpatriotic"?

In the days leading up to World War II, some Blacks did express admiration and a sense of dark-skinned solidarity with the Japanese. Those sympathies changed following Pearl Harbor and the consequent U.S. entrance into the war. While Blacks exhibited their traditional ambivalence about U.S. military adventures, the fascist enemy was a starker evil. But even in the midst of the war against fascism, anti-Black violence in this country continued apace.

A military draft had been instituted even before the formal U.S. entrance into the war that brought together thousands of Black and white conscripts; there were scores of incidents on military installations that pitted Black and white servicemen against each other. Most of these episodes involved brutal treatment of Black GIs and their attempts to counter that treatment. The question of racial violence in the armed forces was of deep concern to Black leadership, and it illuminated the irony of Blacks fighting for a country that yet regarded them as unworthy of true citizenship. In civilian society the event that caused the most concern was the bloody racial clash that broke out in Detroit in 1943, claiming 34 lives and wounding hundreds. Similar, though smaller, clashes erupted in Harlem, NY; Mobile, Alabama; Newark, NJ; and other places on Blacks' migratory route. The changes brought about by the war had again stoked simmering racial antagonisms within the country. Racial violence mocked the notion of national unity against fascism. Still, most African Americans acknowledged the legitimacy of the war effort, even as they pushed for their own rights. Black newspapers initiated a campaign designed to use the war's anti-fascist momentum to influence domestic racial policies; it was called the "Double V Program." The two "V"s symbolized a victory over racism at home and a victory over fascism abroad.

African Americans came out of World War II with an incipient civil rights movement and a growing sense of enfranchisement. This was another period when Black leadership emphasized the international implications of this country's racial struggle. Spanning the ideological spectrum, both the moderate NAACP and A. Philip Randolph's more radical National Negro Congress (NNC) presented separate documents to the United Nations calling for an international investigation of U.S. treatment of its Black citizens. As far as Black leadership was concerned, the Allies' victory over fascism completely discredited the racist ideas at fascism's core.

A new sense of empowerment began inspiring African American communities across the country. Although radicals like New York City's Reverend Adam Clayton Powell referred to the war as "Civil War II," an intramural European power struggle with little direct relevance to Black people, most mainstream groups seldom questioned the rationale for military confrontations. Instead they began pushing for implementing the complete integration of the armed forces, an action that had been ordered by President Harry Truman in 1948. Many Black soldiers fought and died alongside whites during the Korean conflict. In 1954 the *Brown v. Board of Education* ruling in the Supreme Court ended this country's legal apartheid. For a time it seemed as if America's promise was finally overshadowing its menace.

The Cold War years saw successive anti-colonial wars of national liberation in many Third World countries. It became clear that the United States' allegiances were with the former colonizers. Although the few radical groups that survived the war and McCarthyism questioned this country's policies, African Americans mostly toed the anti-communist line. The evolving civil rights movement altered this pattern in a significant way; by pushing for greater access to education, the movement opened doors for thousands of Blacks to enter college. It brought to prominence a young clergyman, the Reverend Martin Luther King, Jr., who helped to "legitimize" Black opposition to U.S. foreign policy.

The baby-boom generation was the immediate benefactor of civil rights struggles to increase educational access. The Black baby boomers who flooded the colleges from the mid-1960s to the early 70s were exposed to the views of the radical Black theorists in vogue during this period and developed political perspectives based on a vague but widely embraced Pan-Africanism that found solidarity with other Third World peoples. During the Vietnam era, this tendency was perhaps best exemplified by Muhammad Ali, who refused induction into the Army in 1966, saying, "no Viet Cong ever called me a nigger." Ali, a member of the NOI and a protege of Malcolm X, was stripped of his heavyweight boxing title and excoriated in the press, but his stance was supported by growing numbers of African Americans.

A year later, the Reverend Dr. King condemned U.S. involvement in Vietnam in a historic speech delivered at New York's Riverside Church. Although King's anti-war views were lauded by a growing number of

Americans opposed to the Vietnam conflict, many of his colleagues in the civil rights establishment were quite critical of his position. The slow decline of overt racism had widened the foreign policy disagreements between mainstream Black leadership and more radical political activists. Mainstream leaders focused their concerns on the treatment of Blacks both within the military and in society at large, while radical activists emphasized the political implications of U.S. policy decisions.

But after the United States invaded Grenada and Panama, bombed Libya, Lebanon, and Iraq—all nations of color—a widening range of African-American leadership began raising questions about the racial component of U.S. foreign policy. Even a superficial analysis of U.S. history reveals a clear pattern: The United States consistently aligns itself with the forces of reaction and white supremacy. This policy bias faces growing criticism from an African-American community that is more educated and politically sophisticated than ever before.

The dimensions of this changing situation was made manifest in the behavior of the Reverend Jesse Jackson in the early days of the Gulf conflict, before Desert Shield became Desert Storm. Ever eyeing mainstream respectability, Jackson initially offered tepid opposition to President George Bush's line-in-the-sand challenge to Iraqi leader Saddam Hussein. But after finding himself to the right of the National Baptist Convention—the largest African-American denomination—and the Southern Christian Leadership Conference—the group he left in 1970 to start Operation PUSH—Jackson readjusted his position. He later led the opposition to Bush's Gulf policy and even traveled to Iraq on a uniquely "Jacksonesque" mission as a diplomat/journalist. It could easily be argued that the two-time presidential candidate has been outpaced by a movement he nurtured. For it was Jackson's astute foreign policy critiques that helped shape the sensibilities of many present day critics. The 50-year-old president of the moribund National Rainbow Coalition was one of the loudest public voices opposing U.S. aggression in Grenada, Lebanon, Libya, and especially Panama. In fact, Jackson virtually personifies the transitional period between the time when King's anti-war sentiments received bad reviews in the Black community and the current period, when such views are much more widely held.

Indeed, in the early days of the 90s there seems to be growing foreign policy consensus among African Americans. Groups like the National African-American Network Against U.S. Intervention in the Gulf had unprecedented success in attracting the interest of a wide segment of the Black community. Secular activists eagerly joined with leaders in the clergy-dominated civil rights fraternity and a variety of Black Islamic groups to oppose the Persian Gulf conflict. King had a hard sell in 1967 with his anti-war views, but in 1991 virtually every Black Christian denomination lined up against the assault on Iraq. This sacred-secular convergence represents a rare opportunity to forge closer cooperation between forces often at odds and, with Black Americans reeling from a relentless series of socioeconomic shocks, the time is ripe for some concerted rescue efforts.

What's more, after their disproportionate service in Vietnam and Iraq, African Americans have earned their military stripes and need no longer fear the charge that they—as an entire race—lack patriotism, although that charge surely will fly again. The appointment of General Colin Powell, a Black man, as Chairman of the Joints Chiefs of Staff indicates this country's willingness to trust African Americans in military uniforms. Black leaders can now offer critical comments about U.S. policy without automatically being tagged with sweepingly disreputable labels.

But African Americans' success within the military has placed them in another dilemma. The proposed downsizing and restructuring of the military, made possible by the end of the Cold War, will have a dispro-portionate effect on Black citizens. According to a report by the Joint Center for Political and Economic Studies (JCPES)—a think tank that focuses on African-American issues—the Department of Defense projects a 25 percent reduction in active-duty military forces by 1995-96. And since African Americans comprise 20 percent of the military and are likely to remain at that level, approximately 100,000 fewer Blacks are expected to be on active duty in five years. That number could be even higher, since the army—which has the largest percentage of African Americans—is scheduled for the largest cut.

Those most affected, the JCPES report noted, will be young people coming out of high school. For the past several years, the services have lured Black high school graduates who score well on standard military aptitude tests and who are unburdened by arrest records or a drug habit. Although these young people are very employable they traditionally face higher unemployment rates than any other age group. Additionally, they will be entering a job market that, if current trends persist, will be inhospitable at best. Their options will be further limited by the shrinking military. So while Black leaders increasingly raise their voices in opposi-tion to U.S. militarism, they also are looking over their shoulders at an expanding group of young people seeking nonexistent employment opportunities. With murder and crime rates already mushrooming in most of the United States' resource-poor cities, the prospect that additional thousands may soon join the unemployment roles is not a pleasant one to ponder. Because of the peculiarities of their history, African Americans are obliged to consider a bewildering array of complexities before making choices other Americans find simple and straightforward.

Still, African Americans bring a unique perspective to the foreign policy debate and increasingly they are willing to add to it. The Congressional Black Caucus (CBC), for example, has increased its attempt to gain a greater voice in the conduct of international affairs. In fact, CBC member Representative Ronald Dellums (D-California), one of Congress's most eloquent advocates of military sanity, is chair of the House Armed Services Subcommittee on Military Installations and Facilities. For the most part, Dellums has managed to balance his congressional responsibilities with his often strident criticisms of U.S. policy. For many years Dellums was consigned to the left flank of Black public opinion and marginalized, but his views resonate more strongly in the African-American community these days and his political status has increased accordingly.

Among the most compelling reasons to intensify education and organizing efforts during this rare period of African-American consensus is to offset the growing appeal of racial demagogues. Just as more Blacks are questioning the racist biases of U.S. foreign policy, a growing number are affirming the racist reductionism of people like Louis Farrakhan and others who provide "divine" panacea or fanciful conspiracy theories. According to these groups, U.S. imperial ambitions are invariably encoded by nature, or commanded by Satan. And while such beliefs may stimulate a desire for further study, or help—to quote the quotable Jackson—"keep hope alive," they tend to discourage political engagement while fueling the fires of tribalism.

The intellectual precincts of Black academia are charged with discussion surrounding notions of multiculturalism and Afrocentricity, and their international implications. The vigorous debate has spilled over into the non-academic world. Hosts of Black talk radio shows across the country told *In These Times* newspaper that their audiences show much more concern with issues of foreign policy than in the recent past. Rap artists and other popular Black entertainers are addressing issues never before considered appropriate for the dancefloor. Public Enemy, a popular rap group, attributes U.S. foreign policy decisions to an emotion they identified on the title of their last album: the "Fear of a Black Planet." In a partial return to their role as rallying-points of Black resistance, African-American churches around the country increasingly are providing forums from which to discuss foreign policy issues as well as other vital concerns. Those interested in wounding the beast of U.S. imperialism could do no better work than to reveal its racist pattern to a newly receptive African-American public. In the history of African Americans' complex relationship to U.S. foreign policy, there may never be a better time.

CHAPTER 18

COMMUNITIES OF COLOR FIGHT FOR JUSTICE AND PEACE

Sandy Carter interviews Roots Against War

As I prepare this piece on the evening of February 28, all Bay Area newspapers are ablaze with bold headlines proclaiming Kuwait's liberation and Iraq's defeat. The CBS "Evening News" is pumping up the victory parties and Dan Rather is giving thanks to the Allied troops and their commanders. For families who have sons or daughters in the Gulf, it is certainly a time for celebration. But most of the people I encounter are neither boisterous nor ecstatic. Instead they seem to be breathing a sigh of relief and experiencing a quiet kind of national pride, a feeling that we did something good and something that had to be done. No one seems to be thinking very much about the thousands upon thousands of dead, maimed, and wounded Iraqis or the long-term repercussions in the Middle East of this "U.S. victory." No, although the mood is reserved, today is a day for basking in the glory of U.S. power and the myth of U.S. righteousness.

In this atmosphere it is heartening to recall that over the last four months an enormous amount of anti-war activism has been awakened across the country. Although no one would know it from the news coverage of the nation's mainstream media, this movement has been large and has involved a broad spectrum of the public. Compared to the early

Reprinted with permission from the April 1991 issue of *Z Magazine*. The Afterword was added in September 1991.

anti-Vietnam War movement, the anti-Gulf War movement has been more diverse along lines of race, class, age, and gender.

The January 19 and January 26 demonstrations in San Francisco brought out 100,000 and 200,000 people, respectively, and in both instances the demonstrators included high-school and college students, Vietnam vets, union members, families of soldiers, longtime peace activists, socialists, anarchists, liberals, women, gay and lesbian activists, people of color, public officials, clergy, and ex-military men. And all around the Bay Area spontaneous marches and actions against the war that began during the period of the Allied troop buildup have continued right up through the cease-fire and will likely continue through the coming weeks. Though the war was not stopped and the yellow ribbon/American flag fever is epidemic, a sizable expression of dissent remains visible and active.

One of the most encouraging aspects of the emergence of the new anti-war movement is the activism of young people. During the Reagan-Bush years both the mainstream press and people in the Left have had quite a lot to say about the apolitical, conservative nature of youth. The growing activism on college campuses has generally been discounted, and certainly the rising politicization and militancy of young people of color has been all but ignored. That is why I chose to interview a Bay Area anti-war group called Roots Against War.

The organization came into existence last December, ignited by an opposition to the impending war in the Gulf and particularly vocal about the war's impact on communities of color. Roots Against War (RAW) describes itself as an alliance of people of color including people of Asian, African, Native American, Arab, and Latino origins. About two-thirds of the group are women and most of the 35 to 40 members are in their mid-20s, although some members are as young as 17 and as old as 55.

Thus far the organization is largely based in San Francisco and Berkeley, where many of RAW's members were previously politically active on the campuses of San Francisco State University and the University of California at Berkeley. But RAW clearly cannot be described as a student organization. RAW's political commitments flow from a dedication to grassroots organizing among low-income, working-class communities of color. The RAW vision therefore stretches beyond anti-war mobilization toward long-term, fundamental social and economic issues facing their communities: jobs, housing, drugs, education, health care, and crime. Those domestic concerns are also tied to an analysis of international struggles, which means RAW's local activism is informed by a global definition of community. Though RAW is a very new and relatively small organization, its influence is being felt far beyond the numbers of its active membership. Through its street corner educationals, demonstrations, and rallies, RAW is helping communities of color on both sides of the Bay articulate their political voice on their own terms and in their own language.

The following interview was conducted in mid-February at a RAW member's apartment in the Fillmore district of San Francisco. Rahdi Taylor is a 22-year-old African-American woman from Los Angeles who became politically active while a student at UC Berkeley. Kareima McKnight, a 23-year-old African-American woman, grew up in Los Angeles strongly influenced by a mother who was active in the civil-rights movement. She also attended UC Berkeley, where she organized on issues of abortion rights, apartheid, and racism. Hatem Bazian, a 26-year-old Palestinian man, born in the West Bank, moved to Jordan at the age of five and came to the United States in 1983. Besides his activism in the Middle East, he has been involved in campus politics at Diablo Valley Community College and San Francisco State around apartheid, racism, and issues related to Palestinians and the Middle East. Naheed Islam, a 26-year-old woman from Bangladesh, came to the United States at age 18 to attend school at Ohio Wesleyan. She enrolled in graduate school at UC Berkeley in 1986, where she has been active organizing around racism, women's issues, and U.S. foreign policy.

Much of what RAW has to say reflects old, ongoing problems and divisions within the Left. They are sharply critical of what they term "white-dominated movements." In fact, the formation of RAW was given impetus by the unwillingness of predominantly white groups to come to terms with issues of race and their own racism. So they are finding their own way forward, driven by a politics that is passionate, idealistic, and defined by their own experience.

SANDY CARTER: Let's begin by talking about how and why Roots Against War was started.

RAHDI TAYLOR: RAW was started in December of last year. A bunch of us were at a forum where Tahan Jones, an African-American conscientious objector against the war, was speaking. At the end of the speech Abdi Jibril stood up and said, "I've been in a lot of functions and organizations against the war and most of them are not reflecting issues pertinent to me as a person of color. If there are other people here who feel the same way, maybe we could join up at the end of this meeting and see if we can do something." And so eight people came together and talked and agreed on a few things. Specifically, we felt that the organizations and meetings we had been a part of didn't offer any sort of analysis or action relevant in terms of race and class. Everything took off from there.

NAHEED ISLAM: Another thing that was in the minds of some of us who had been involved in campus politics on universities was some feeling that the elitism and framework of campus organizations separated us from our communities, elevated us above our communities. We felt that what we needed to do was go back to our communities and organize. We wanted to join in something that we thought was a larger struggle.

KAREIMA McKNIGHT: On campus we were organizing around issues of diversity, white supremacists, community struggles, and we had started to organize against the Gulf War early on because we could see that as people of color we were going to be disproportionately affected by the war, in terms of who would be doing the fighting and dying on both sides.

But through our involvement in various actions and protests we were finding that the white reaction to our participation was that we were alienating people by bringing up issues of justice and moving beyond issues of peace and war. We wanted to take the anti-war movement toward a movement that would continue after the war. We were asking what kind of society are we going to bring our soldiers home to after the war and we were making reference to the long history of the United States waging war on people of color. Many white activists felt that we threatened the broad or "mainstream" appeal of the anti-war movement by raising these issues.

SC: What kind of organizations were these?

KM: Mostly campus coalitions such as Direct Action Against Racism. And it was our experience that within these coalitions, white people, advertently or inadvertently, dominated the organizations. So we decided that we needed an organization that was for us. Someplace where we could do the educating, learning, and community work that we felt was needed.

SC: Obviously, RAW has a radical critique of the social inequality that is so deeply embedded in U.S. society. How do you describe your political perspective and social vision?

HB: We tend to be internationalist in our perspective. I don't think that you can look only at what's going on in the United States, because what's going on here is directly linked to international struggles. For us, issues of class, sex, and race in the United States can never be separated from their international implications. But as far as our organizing goes, we organize locally. We try to raise the consciousness of people who come in contact with us on a daily basis. And I would say that as far as reaching out to our people, our job is very easy. You don't have to convince them that they are oppressed. They already see the system as oppressive. The bigger problem is confronting people's hopelessness because the system is so large and powerful. So we have to demonstrate the ability and strength of the individual versus the system.

NI: I think your question implies whether we advocate any particular "isms." We are looking for an alternative framework, but we don't see any of the "isms" that are around right now as providing any chance of equality and justice. We are definitely critical of capitalist society and feel that it has to be dismantled. Imperialism is inherently violent; it creates and recreates genocide.

HB: The capitalist system makes money off the masses. You cannot have everybody rich. Issues of class and various forms of oppression are the result of money and resources being centered in a few hands and the rest of the population is there as labor.

KM: I think another important aspect of our principles is that we feel that liberation from capitalism and imperialism will not occur unless women and people of color are at the forefront of the struggle. We've seen what happens when groups or movements wait to address our issues while pressing on with some more important struggle or "the revolution." Only by people of color and women uniting together, finding our strength, and leading in liberation struggles can we begin to define alternative institutions that truly benefit us.

SC: Can you describe some of the work that RAW is doing?

RT: In the beginning, our outreach to our communities was in the form of tabling on street corners. That was kind of like a street office with a table of literature geared specifically to the people we were talking to: Latinos, high school students, or African Americans. We would be discussing issues such as the war, conscientious-objector status, racism, U.S. foreign policy, and so on. In the case of CO information, many organizations might have the information available, but it was not being put out in our communities and made accessible, say, to people who speak Spanish. Nowadays we continue tabling and we do teach-ins for community groups, in public transit stations, high schools, and on the streets.

NI: We also have a project going where we are trying to make videos using alternative news sources. Bearing in mind that the eight largest investors in network news are oil companies, it is not surprising that mainstream news blocks out a lot of information.

RT: Also the day of the war deadline, some of our work came together in a large march called the Night of Resistance. About 15,000 people took part and we had a number of speakers that we felt spoke to and for our communities—June Jordan, Angela Davis, James Garrett, representatives from the American Indian Treaty Council and the American Indian Movement, Zulu Spear, Abdul Malik, and other people representing the diversity of our people. The march went through the Mission and Fillmore districts in San Francisco and focused on an agenda relevant to people of color.

SC: What kind of response are you getting from your teach-ins at high schools?

KM: We get a really good response. A lot of what we do consists of just standing out in front of high schools and passing out literature that makes links between their experiences as teenagers. The schools we go to are predominantly Latino, Asian, and African-American, so we're drawing connections between local, national, and international issues that are related to these young people.

As for the Persian Gulf War, since a lot of kids are facing the "option" of employment in the military, or possibly down the road the draft, obviously that's a primary focus. And to get the message across we use a lot of popular music and rap lyrics. When we're invited inside a high school to make a presentation, we'll use videos, music, and answer questions. And you'd be surprised at how receptive people are. At first they kind of spew out things they've heard without really giving it too much thought. But when you discuss things with them and they start thinking about these issues, they come around and we see eye-to-eye. People can see the war is not about liberating Kuwait when you talk about what kind of government Kuwait has. They see it's not about protecting the world from Saddam when you talk about previous U.S. support for Saddam and various other imperialist and terrorist activities the Bush administration has been involved in. After considering some of these realities a lot of kids will just say straight-up, "Fuck this war, I ain't going." That's good to hear. But then you have to say, Hey, you need to consider your options. You need some information, because you can't go to Canada and you can't go to Mexico.

SC: What kind of response do you get from white students?

NI: The white students are not people we are targeting. They have other sources from which they get their information. But if they pass by we do give them our flyer.

RT: The schools are definitely segregated and we're going to the ones in our communities, places that have less access to information.

SC: What about the reaction in ROTC classes?

RT: Well, we haven't got any violently negative response. Usually classes will swing one way or another, but again, generally, the response has been positive.

SC: You spoke earlier of other anti-war groups lacking a class and race analysis of the Gulf War relevant to people of color. How does RAW see issues of race and class related to the war?

NI: We see race and class issues as two different but interrelated segments. One is internal or within the United States and the other is on the international level. Internally the war is certainly racist in the way it impacts on our communities. For instance, 60 percent of the front-line troops in the Persian Gulf are people of color and virtually all of the troops come from low-income backgrounds. And simultaneously with the fighting of the Gulf War, it is the poor and communities of color that are feeling the most severe effects from budget cutbacks, welfare and social programs being eliminated, tuition hikes, unemployment, the housing shortage, and so on.

Externally, when we look at the regimes the United States is supporting, it is clear that the United States is supporting monarchies and very stratified social systems, which to begin with are lands that were divided up to suit the economic interests of the West. These factors make it evident that U.S. policies are inherently racist.

HB: In regard to the Middle East, the United States and other Western powers are trying to maintain borders that they established, and they act as if they are the only ones who have a right to question or determine these boundaries. The United States, of course, would have people believe that its actions are supported by the United Nations. But this world body did not vote to destroy Iraq. Only 13 to 15 countries on the Security Council voted for the UN resolution and those voting for the resolution had their votes bought with loans, aid, and other economic factors.

NI: I'm from Bangladesh and the government was sort of "convinced" into sending 5,000 troops to Saudi Arabia, even though Bangladesh has been up in flames with protests against U.S. policy. So they send these troops without the people's consent. This is just one more example of how people of color are used as fodder in this war.

HB: I would like to add that, as for U.S. support for UN resolutions, let us not forget that 63 UN resolutions addressing the Palestinian question have been vetoed by the United States.

RT: And again, if we look historically at the wars and interventions of the United States, we are faced with this country's long legacy of murdering, thieving, and raping people of color.

HB: You could trace the roots of these atrocities all the way back to the rise of so-called western civilization. Simply put, the West and whites have considered this vast world theirs to cultivate, while the majority of the population that lives in this world are considered savages or barbarians, be they Arabs, Native Americans, Africans, Asians, or any number of other peoples.

NI: This is where the voice of RAW comes from, an intense anger at hundreds of years of oppression. And I think people both inside the United States and in Third World countries are sending a message that we are not going to take it anymore. I don't think policymakers in the United States are aware of the tremendous accumulated anger that people have all over the world.

KM: With people of color looking at our history, looking at the millions that died in the slave trade, all the lynchings, the millions killed in Vietnam, in Korea, the bombs on Hiroshima and Nagasaki... The reality is the United States feels it is OK to slaughter us all around the world, as well as here. The policies and institutions of this country have been designed to keep us on the bottom. And today we are becoming a surplus population. There are no jobs for us in industry anymore. Increasingly, we are a population with little left to lose. Yet as we see people all around the world resisting imperial dominance and recall the struggles from our history in this country—the Panthers, AIM, the Chicano movement, the civil rights movement, all the people who have fought before us—we are beginning to see people of color as one large community of struggle and one day there will be a high price to pay.

SC: Today there are about 30,000 women, a very high percentage of them of color, serving in the armed forces in the Gulf. How do you speak to their situation and sexism as it relates to the war?

KM: Well, just as you find a disproportionate population of men of color in the military, you also find a lot of women of color in the military. You have something like 50 percent of the women in the fighting force in the

Gulf are Black. You have to ask yourself why do so many women of color find it necessary to seek a career in the military? Is it because they have so few options in civilian society? Is it because they make half of what men make?

In essence the military functions as a poverty draft and a sexist draft, forcing women to die in order to support themselves and get an education. You have a lot of women saying the same things the men are saying: "I joined up so that I could get the education benefits of the GI bill, I wanted to make something out of my life." The military offered a job, a skill, a chance to be somebody instead of wasting away. Now a lot of women who took that option are being forced to make some hard decisions and many are becoming resisters.

NI: Here again we see issues of class, sex, and race linked together.

RT: And I think it is important to emphasize once again that none of these issues can wait until after the war ends. No, it's all happening simultaneously and it's all part of the same struggle.

HB: Which means that in terms of our own work we think it is important that women play a leadership role and define their own issues and that as men we must learn about and deal with our own sexism.

SC: Given RAW's diversity and commitment to deal with all these issues simultaneously, how do you go about addressing the conflicts and tensions that come up between different communities or genders?

KM: For a new group and a young group like us, many of these questions are just coming up. We're learning to deal with them as we go, but we're not going to run past them in order to deal with some "bigger issue." We can't pretend there's no racism going on between different racial or ethnic groups or there's no homophobia. That's bullshit. We're having these problems. We say, "Hey, I'm queer, I'm of color, are you going to deal with me? You better deal with me." So it's a process. You don't just take people out of a sick society and stick 'em in this group or any group and say you're well.

NI: Our openness to criticism means that we run the risk of falling apart, but this is absolutely necessary in order to deal with all the issues and their interconnections. So each meeting ends with a period of self-criticism.

RT: Another thing we're working on is establishing a women's caucus to frame issues of gender, homophobia, and sexism.

NI: I think it helps that we have such a diverse group of people. We have people from all different religious backgrounds, cultural backgrounds, racial backgrounds, people speaking different languages. That's what makes RAW unique. It makes for a very different kind of interaction. I think this diversity makes us feel empowered. After all, we are two-thirds of the world's people and artificial divisions have kept us apart, and we realize that we must be unified to get what we want. We are mighty in numbers, but we have been divided.

RT: Because of the mindset of people in the group, we are willing to learn from each other. I don't want to offend my sister. I don't want to be homophobic or sexist or racist. So when someone says I don't want to be referred to as a minority or as Black, we begin to talk about it. We are constantly learning about each other's culture and oppression.

SC: Historically the social movements of the Left have not been very comfortable environments for working-class people and people of color. Can you talk in a little more detail about your experiences in the current anti-war movement?

NI: Well, the general problem is that our issues are not on their agenda. We are used as token speakers, token representatives, and we will not accept that or be a part of that. This, of course, has been the history of white-dominated movements and that is why we started RAW…to establish our own agenda. Until white movements begin to question themselves about why people of color don't turn up in their organizations, then this is where we'll be.

I mean people of color shouldn't have to be in that room to educate white people again and again about what's going on. If they're activists, they should take it upon themselves to bring these issues into their groups and be willing to take some risks.

HB: I think a lot of people in today's anti-war movement have a nostalgia about the 1960s. For a lot of the younger people, all they know about that period comes from a few movies, television, and *Time.* Which means they see the 1960s in mostly white terms. And as for many of the older activists from that period, they seem to want to assert themselves and run things and say this is how it is, leaving us out of the picture. In the end, we get used only to fulfill a kind of affirmative-action standard.

So within these groups we face many problems. To mention a few, there are issues around the definition of racism, around dealing with the Palestinian situation, around whether the system should be changed or merely reformed and on and on. Our point of view on nearly all things is different. We have not been a part of the American Dream. The American flag does not represent freedom and justice to us. I cannot support the troops who are killing my brothers and sisters in Iraq, even if they are not completely aware of their actions or they didn't make the policy that put them there.

NI: The mainstream movement talks about patriotism, but how on earth do you talk about patriotism to Native Americans whose lands have been stolen and are still being stolen, to Black and Latino people living in barrios and ghettos?

KM: And there is also the problem of the paradigm of non-violent struggle. I think whites are much more apt to accept this paradigm because they have not generally experienced the violence of the system and because of their position in society they have more faith in the government and the legal system. And in many ways it does work for them. But this is not our experience and therefore we will struggle by any means necessary.

Maybe we are fighting for something they are trying to protect. Whatever, when you plan a march that doesn't take our experience into consideration, in so many words, you're saying "Fuck off." But we will express ourselves the way our history has taught us to express ourselves.

SC: You mentioned the problem of defining racism. Since the popular notion of racism is focused on understanding it merely as a set of beliefs or prejudices, I think it would be useful to hear RAW's definition of racism.

HB: Racism is a form of oppression that stems from people in the highest positions of power. It is a systematic form of oppression, meaning it is expressed through all aspects of society—the political process, the economy, the military, the culture, the dominant ideologies, etc.

NI: And it is at the very basis, the very foundation of western society.

KM: Personally, I have some problems with the term racism. Because many people understand it as something that applies to people of all races, I think it's confusing. I'm more comfortable with the phrase white supremacy, which is more specific and clearly suggests relations of power, not just isolated attitudes.

SC: Given these relations of power, as well as those of class and sex, you've stated several times RAW will continue its work after the Gulf War ends. What are some of the issues you will be organizing around?

HB: There are so many. I think we would like to be engaged in creating some alternatives to the educational system. And certainly economic issues like unemployment and homelessness are important. Childcare is extremely important, developing media alternatives, dealing with drug issues. And all issues of occupation and self-determination will be ongoing.

NI: Confronting sexism and homophobia must have a high priority. I think much of the Left still neglects and excuses these issues.

KM: Basically we are in it for the long haul. This means we must deepen our community roots, become involved in projects that serve our communities, and through these projects become known in our communities as people who are out there on the streets.

SC: Any final words for readers?

HB: I would simply add that in terms of the longer struggle, historically we are at a crossroads. When George Bush went into the Middle East with his vision of a New World Order he felt confident that the Soviet Union would not question his moves and therefore the United States has more room to maneuver. In that regard he is only partially right. The questioning of U.S. policy will not come from the Soviet Union. It will come from people of color, in the Middle East, and all around the globe where masses of people are saying, "No, we will not take this anymore."

EVERYONE: Amandla.

Afterword

CYNTHIA PETERS: In the eight or nine months since the Gulf War, what has been the focus of your political work?

HB: We have focused on many things: working with COs from communities of color and those facing court martials because they refused to participate in the Gulf War mobilization. Tahan Jones is one of the people we are trying to support. We're organizing rallies, demonstrations, and letter-writing campaigns to congresspeople asking them to drop all charges and grant amnesty.

We are also working with a large coalition of community groups participating in the pro-choice organizing that has gone on since the gag rule was introduced. Mostly, our work consists of tabling with information, petitionining, and running workshops to educate people about the issue. This fall we plan a big rally against the gag rule, the nomination of

Clarence Thomas, and against the increasing conservativism of the Supreme Court and the Bush administration.

We are working with Native American groups in preparation for the 500th anniversary of Columbus's landing. Replica ships are coming to the San Francisco Bay to celebrate the quincentennial. There will be a big protest, emphasizing 500 years of genocide of the Native American people. We are one of the few racially diverse organizations in this area that includes Native Americans so we are one of the few organized groups that is working closely with the Native American community on this project.

We are continuing our food program, where we provide food for the homeless in the neighborhoods. We raise money from businesses and people in the community, and do fundraisers to pay for the program.

Lastly, we have a study group on political issues so that we can educate ourselves as well as bring others into the education process. We've looked at many issues, including history, ideological frameworks, conflict resolution, media, and cultural differences.

CP: How big is your group?

HB: There are 60 people on our list. About 15 do the day-to-day organizing.

CP: What do you find are the biggest obstacles to your work.

HB: During the war everyone was interested and ready to work and organize. Since the war is officially over, a new feeling of apathy has set in. Feelings of laziness, giving up, and losing hope have taken over. That is our major obstacle: finding people that still have the drive to organize.

CP: How have you tried to deal with this obstacle?

HB: We have tried to bring people back on a social level. We have pot-luck events where we talk about issues other than politics. We hold sessions where people talk about their feelings, feelings about why they have lost so much hope after the war. People feel a great deal of loss about what happened during the war. It's worked some, but not much.

CP: How is RAW different from other organizations that grew out of the Gulf War?

HB: RAW focuses on the people of our community. Other organizations continue to focus only on a foreign-policy level, without making the links between what's happening abroad and what's happening domestically.

CP: Tell me something about the lessons you learned from your work.

HB: One important thing is that we've had to learn how to work around, work with, as well as confront the different ideological groupings that exist on the Left. Sometimes there is an element of disruption, sometimes our process is delayed while we try to work around our differences. It's been difficult, but in the long run we have been able to develop a process for negotiating people's different frameworks. We are able to juggle all the different ideologies in our group without having to come up with one overriding "ism."

Working in a multicultural setting has benefits but also has setbacks when differences emerge, taking away energy, causing divisions and arguments. We have argued over everything from small things like selecting the speakers so that there was a good race/gender balance to negotiating whether people of one community can speak to the needs and issues of another group. We have had to learn to work around these debates (at the same time that we have grown from them). We have learned to focus on similarities as opposed to differences.

Another key lesson is that if you *do the work* and *spend the time,* you are able to reach the people you need to reach. True, the media has a lot of influence but people are ultimately skeptical. If we can reach them and give them the needed support, they will come out and be our allies.

I would say that we also learned something about burn-out. We spread ourselves so thin during the war. We were just running around 18 to 19 hours a day, and that took its toll. We have to be better about allocating time equally to all the various things we do, including rest. A lot of people thought they were going to be able to change the world in two months. In fact, the only thing they could change was their health.

CHAPTER 19

ON GAINING "MORAL HIGH GROUND"

An Ode to George Bush and the "New World Order"

Ward Churchill

Since the onset of the Gulf War, we in the United States have been subjected to a relentless chorus of babble from George Bush and his colleagues concerning a supposed "moral imperative" for the United States to militarily enforce "international law, custom, and convention" because of "a dozen United Nations Security Council resolutions condemning Iraq's invasion, occupation, and annexation of Kuwait." Iraqi President Saddam (usually pronounced "Sodom" by U.S. officials) Hussein's "naked aggression cannot stand," Bush has solemnly and repeatedly intoned to wild applause. Kuwait's "territory must be liberated"; its "legitimate government must be reinstated"; its vast oil resources must be "returned to the rightful owners." Meanwhile, those Iraqi officials responsible for "the rape of Kuwait" should be tried for war crimes and/or crimes against humanity, says Bush, en route to gaining what he has taken to calling "the moral high ground." The net result of "the precedent we

This essay is the development of an excerpt from an introduction given to Angela Y. Davis at the University of Colorado in April 1991. An earlier version was published in *New Studies on the Left*, Volume XIV, No. 2, Summer 1991.

are now setting," according to the president, will be the ushering in of a "New World Order" predicated in "the rule of law" and, consequently, peace and civility among nations.[1]

Let's forget for a moment that it's George Herbert Walker Bush talking. Forget that Kuwait was never a nation in its own right, that it was historically part of Iraq, an area stripped away and established as an administrative entity by British colonialists, an expedient to landlocking and thus controlling the much larger Iraqi territory and population to the north. Forget that the "legitimate government" under discussion is the harshly anti-democratic regime of an emir propped up for more than 50 years by external neocolonial forces rather than the internal consent of the governed. Forget also that the actual "owners" of the oil fields in question have been always been a gaggle of transnational oil corporations rather than any Kuwaitis, even the emir. Forget all of this long enough to realize that intermingled with Bush's barrage of blatant untruths and self-serving rhetoric is the substance of some genuinely worthy ideas.[2]

Rather than pitching the baby out with the bath water simply because a figure as slimy as the president of the United States has articulated such principles, we might instead seize upon them, insisting that the U.S. government actually conform its behavior to the lofty posture described by its chief executive. To an extent which is startling, George Bush has unintentionally defined the contours of what should be the agenda for American progressivism. In a way, all that remains for us to do is demand consistency in the application of George's postulates. Well, that and to develop the muscle necessary to see to it that the government follows through. Even that, however, should be no overwhelming problem, given the sort of public sentiment George has whipped up while proving he's no wimp.

Unquestionably, we have a right to demand that all the millions of flag-waving patriots who've recently turned out at George's request to "support our troops" in their quest for victory over evil in the Great Gulf Crusade join us in holding the United States strictly accountable to its newly proclaimed "standards of human decency." After all, as any ROTC cadet or Daughter of the American Revolution will tell you, "That's what America stands for." For once, we are in a position to insist that everyone, left and right, rich and poor, young and old, male and female, white and "minority," straight and gay in the United States band together for a common glorious purpose. In such unity, we will find strength and righteousness. Together, we can help George and the boys put their performance where their mouths have been. You bet. Anyway, let's get on with it, proceeding to examine what will have to be done to mesh reality with recent official verbiage (set off herein by quotes).

International Law, Custom, and Convention

The president has said unequivocally that international laws "must be enforced. And they will be enforced. Period." This is certainly commendable, and something we should all be prepared to insist upon vociferously. Now that Iraq has been compelled to comply with "all relevant UN resolutions" by being battered into near-oblivion through an unprecedented application of high-tech "defensive weaponry," we progressives should demand that everyone who supported the Gulf War join us in calling for redeployment of the "force levels" evident in "Operation Desert Storm" to ensure that certain other, much longer standing, UN resolutions are honored. Let's start, say, with Israel's illegal occupation of Palestinian territories. This Israeli conduct has been, after all, the focus of more than a few UN condemnations over the years, as has Israel's occupation of the southern portion of Lebanon.[3] For that matter, there has long been a UN resolution equating zionism with racism, thereby rendering the ideology of the Israeli state illegal under the United Nations Convention on Elimination of All Forms of Racial Discrimination.[4]

For consistency's sake there must be a U.S. ultimatum, comparable to that delivered to Iraq, ordering the Israelis to leave the occupied territories immediately. In the alternative, it must be made plain, Tel Aviv will be flattened by massive air strikes, while every military installation in the country will be "surgically eliminated." In the event that Israel does begin an instantaneous withdrawal from Palestine and Lebanon, we should urge George to be somewhat more "magnanimous" in other respects. The people of Israel could, for instance, be given as long as six months to overthrow Yitzhak Shamir and his colleagues, dissolve the totality of their state bureaucracy, and reconstitute their polity on the basis of a non-zionist model. In the event they fail to accomplish this latter UN requirement, a U.S. suspension of aid and orchestration of comprehensive international sanctions should probably be sufficient to bring them around in a couple of weeks.

Then there is the matter of South Africa.[5] Its apartheid socio-political organization has been condemned by a series of UN resolutions beginning as far back as the early 60s. So have its large and persistent military invasions of neighboring Namibia (one is a bit unclear as to whether these aggressions have been of the "naked" or "fully clad" variety, but this is no time to be picky).[6] While it is true that previous U.S. administrations have sought to bring this "outlaw state" into line by "quiet diplomacy" (and the infusion of both military technology and tremendous quantities of economic support), there is still time for George Bush to "move things in the right direction."[7] "Diplomacy having failed," it's high time we played our "military card" to "set things right." U.S. martial prowess, when committed to such "appropriate objectives," obviously works much more quickly and leaves fewer loose ends dangling.

The Pretoria government could be given six weeks to dismantle its military and police apparatus, and a total of six months within which to conduct general elections under UN supervision. Should "responsible South African officials" refuse, the United States could stipulate that a major amphibious assault will occur at Capetown within "an unspecified but short interval," coupled to an airmobile invasion of the interior (spearheaded by "the redoubtable 82nd Airborne Division," and supported by "massive armored thrusts" from the coast). Given the relative size of the South African and Israeli military machines—as compared to "the world's fourth largest army,"[8] available to Iraq, but completely destroyed by the United States in just over 60 days—it is reasonable that we call upon President Bush to order Secretary of War (let's go back to calling this position by its right name) "Dick" Cheney to order middle America's favorite house negro, Colin Powell, to plan and initiate operations against both countries simultaneously. Once we "have a schedule," we can "stick with our scenario," "fight on our terms," and clean up these offenders against international order lickity-split.

Of course, there are a few other UN resolutions out there which might be a tad more difficult to handle. An example is the one that condemned U.S. mining of Nicaraguan harbors back in the mid-80s. Others condemned the U.S. invasion, occupation, and installation of a puppet government in Grenada a bit earlier.[9] More recently, a resolution condemned the U.S. invasion and subordination of Panama.[10] Then there are quite a number of such items accruing from U.S. activities in Southeast Asia during the 1960s and 70s.[11] These matters will undoubtedly prove most embarrassing to the multitudes who lately turned out wearing yellow ribbons in the belief that Saddam Hussein invented international aggression and was therefore subject to the first UN resolutions on record.

Short of calling in air strikes on Washington, DC, it is difficult to see how the Bush administration and "American public" might visit the same sort of consequences upon the United States they so gleefully laid upon Iraq for an ugly but somewhat lesser aggregate of offenses. Perhaps the public's sense of propriety—America having become obsessively concerned with international legality these days—could be satisfied that justice was being done if George were to deliver up some sizable assortment of perpetrators of the above-mentioned U.S. "excesses" to stand trial before an appropriate international body on charges of Crimes

Against the Peace, Crimes Against Humanity, and War Crimes.[12] After all, the president has suggested that just such a body be convened in the wake of the Gulf War. We progressives might well take the lead in advising that it see more extensive use than Bush originally had in mind.

An International Tribunal

The president has said that "Saddam Hussein and others" should be hauled in front of an "international tribunal" to stand trial for the "atrocities committed on their orders during the Iraqi occupation of Kuwait."[13] Fine. Carry on. Saddam and his compatriots have comported themselves for some time—with ample U.S. backing, it must be added—in the manner of the most brutal sort of thugs. The world would experience no loss were they to take a collective trip to the gallows. The problem is, to paraphrase no less a U.S. patriot than Supreme Court Justice Robert Jackson (during similar proceedings against the Nazis at Nuremberg in 1947), such things have legal validity only when the prosecutors are held to the same standards of accountability as the defendants, the victors put to the same test as the vanquished.[14] Hence, it is necessary that a few other folks, from countries other than Iraq, take their rightful places alongside Saddam Hussein in the defendants' dock.

This leads us, unerringly, to the ranks of U.S. officialdom itself. No tribunal of the sort George Bush has proposed, concentrating on the sorts of matters he has raised for its consideration, could neglect to include individuals like Robert McNamara, architect of the U.S. "intervention" in Indochina. Or William Westmoreland, the U.S. general who conceived the "strategy of attrition" his troops ultimately directed in genocidal fashion against the Indochinese population.[15] Or Henry Kissinger, the diseased mind behind the "secret bombing" of neutral Cambodia during that war, a process which itself accounted for thousands of victims lumped in with the toll extracted by Khmer Rouge "autogenocide" thereafter. Or Richard M. Nixon, who ordered the bombing of civilian targets in North Vietnam in order to attain "peace with honor," and whose "madman theory of diplomacy" provided the conceptual umbrella under which Kissinger functioned.[16] How could the list of defendants facing the tribunal be complete without the presence of Ronald Wilson Reagan, the mighty "Conqueror of Grenada?"[17] Or George Shultz and Elliot Abrams, kingpins of the contra campaign against Nicaragua?[18]

For that matter, how could Bush's proposed tribunal be complete without George Bush himself numbering among the defendants, perhaps for his roles in supporting Roberto D'Aubuisson's death squads in El Salvador, or in the smuggling of drugs to the youth of his own country in order to finance the clandestine butchery of peasants and poets abroad?[19] One would hope—and people of conscience will demand—that justice might prevail with regard to his participation in giving arms and other murderous support to petty dictators the world over while "serving" as director of the CIA, vice president and now president.[20] It is hard to conceive a performance more befitting the charges of Crimes Against the Peace and Crimes Against Humanity. At least he might be judged for that implausibly denied slit trench filled with some 4,000 slaughtered civilians his "Operation Just Cause" soldiers left behind in Panama.[21] Surely, the president will wish to continue to "do what's right" in his own case as well as the cases of his mentors, underlings, and opponents. And surely it is incumbent upon all Americans, particularly those who wave their flags so proudly, to ensure that he does. Justice Jackson, after all, required no less.

Liberating Territory, Reinstating Legitimate Governments

Truth be known, George Bush's recent speechifying has raised a range of issues much more fundamental than any mentioned thus far. If the swarm of supporters lately rallying to George's posture of ensuring the sovereignty of small nations against the designs of larger and more powerful predator states are in any way sincere, there is no shortage of action items to fill their agenda right here in North America. They can begin by insisting upon the honoring of all 400 treaties, duly ratified by the Senate and still legally binding, between the United States and various American Indian nations presently encapsulated within the United States.[22] This will mean, of course, that Bush will have to order "the immediate withdrawal" of all U.S. forces presently occupying each of the Native American national territories so clearly defined in the treaty texts, altogether totaling about a third of the land area the U.S. now claims as comprising the "lower 48" states.[23]

The president will also have to renounce the long-standing federal doctrine of exercising "trust" prerogatives ("annexation," by any other term) over all Indian acreage within the United States,[24] and forego the government's planned unilateral dissolution of Native land titles in Alaska (a move intended to open North Shelf oil to increased exploitation by U.S.

energy corporations).[25] Accomplishing this will require repeal of numerous federal statutes, beginning with the "Seven Major Crimes Act" of 1885 (through which the United States unilaterally extended its jurisdiction over Indian Country),[26] the "General Allotment Act" of 1887 (through which the United States unilaterally altered indigenous land-tenure patterns and declared some two-thirds of the treaty-guaranteed Native land base to be "surplus"),[27] and the "Indian Citizenship Act" of 1924 (through which the United States unilaterally imposed its citizenship upon native peoples, whether they liked it or not).[28]

Once American Indian national territories have been thus liberated—in conformity with what may come to be known as the "Bush Doctrine" of international affairs—it will be necessary that he engineer a repeal of the "Indian Reorganization Act" of 1934 (through which the United States unilaterally imposed a form of governance acceptable to itself upon most Native peoples).[29] This will allow legitimate American Indian governments to at last be reinstated after more than a half-century's outright suppression at the hands of the United States. These newly reconstituted and revitalized Native governments, functioning with full sovereign control over all the territory to which they are legally entitled by international treaty agreements, will finally be able to utilize the resources lying within and upon their land for the benefit of their own people rather than for the benefit of the occupiers. As the president has put it, "No benefits from naked aggression. Period."

This "restoration of resources to the rightful owners" means that about two-thirds of the uranium deposits the United States now considers as part of its own "domestic reserves" will pass from U.S. control. Along with the uranium will go approximately 25 percent of the readily accessible low-sulfur coal, maybe 20 percent of the oil and natural gas, such bauxite as is to be found within present U.S. boundaries, all of the copper, most of the gold, a lot of the iron ore, the remaining stands of "virgin" timber, much prime grazing and farming acreage, the bulk of the water throughout the arid West, perhaps half the salmon and other available fish "harvests," hunting rights over vast areas, and a lot more.[30]

There is also a big question as to whether the United States shouldn't also pay substantial reparations for having unlawfully and immorally deprived Native people of all these assets for so long, a matter which has induced incredible human suffering. Although the resources endowing American Indian treaty territories have always been sufficient to make Native people by far the wealthiest sector of the North American population, they have instead existed for generations as the very poorest. According to the federal government's own statistics, Indians receive the lowest per-capita income of any group on the continent. Their unemployment rate is far and away the highest, year in, year out. Correspondingly, they suffer—by significant margins—the highest rates of malnutrition, infant mortality, death by exposure, tuberculosis, plague disease, and teen suicide. The average life expectancy of a reservation-based American Indian man is presently 44.6 years; a Native woman may expect to live less than three years longer.[31]

Meanwhile, to select but one example among thousands, the Homestake Mining Corporation alone has taken more than $14 billion in gold from only one mine in the Black Hills of South Dakota, squarely in the middle of the treaty territory of the Lakota Nation.[32] It takes no Einstein to discern the relationship between this sort of wealth flowing into the economy of the U.S. occupiers on the one hand, and the abject poverty of the Lakota people on the other. The same situation prevails throughout Indian Country. This sort of thing has been going on for a long time now, and it hardly seems wild-eyed to suggest that some very serious payback is long overdue. We can hardly expect, given George Bush's continuous assertions that this is the world's leading "nation of conscience" and the general adulation he has received because of such utterances, that he and his admiring public will do less than "meet their just debts" and "measure up to [their] moral obligations" in this regard.

Before moving on, it seems appropriate to observe that once the president and his supporters have retired the "Indian problem" in a manner consistent with the "utmost good faith" pledged by Congress in 1789,[33] they will wish to act with equal swiftness to resolve a couple of other issues involving the outright U.S. occupation of land belonging to others, the theft of their resources, and/or usurpation of their governments. Undoubtedly, proponents of Bushism will wish to see him "stand tall" and order an immediate withdrawal of U.S. troops from their permanent bases in Puerto Rico, while the people of that island are finally allowed to conduct whatever process they decide upon in order to determine what political-economic relationship (if any) they wish to maintain with Washington, DC.[34] The same principle will certainly apply to the "U.S." Virgin Islands, "American" Samoa, Guam, the Marshall Islands, and several other chunks of geography scattered around the globe.[35]

American super-patriots will no doubt also wish to see Bush and his buddies ensure that the descendants of former Mexican nationals holding land grants issued by the Crown of Spain and Republic of Mexico in what are now the states of Texas, New Mexico, Colorado, Arizona, and California finally have their property restored. After all, the federal government promised "faithfully" to "honor and respect" these individual and group deeds under a provision of the 1848 Treaty of Guadalupe Hidalgo, through which the United States expropriated the northern half of Mexico and all the resources therein.[36] Between the treaty rights of Indian nations to their own territorial integrity and the extent of the acreage involved in the land grants, at least four of the states affected will for all practical intents and purposes cease to exist.The "undeniable skills" of "Stormin' Norman" Schwarzkopf may well be needed if the provincial governments seated in Santa Fe, Denver, Phoenix, and Sacramento are to be convinced to "get with the program." But, of course, no price is too high to pay while ensuring that "the Laws of Nations and common decency are adhered to."

Advantages to Progressives

The advantages of all this to progressivism in the United States should be obvious. Progressives, having never been able to articulate a viable and coherent agenda of their own—preferring instead to perpetually "bear moral witness," combat cigarette smoke amidst the nation's smog belts, and bicker with eternal meaninglessness among themselves about all manner of esoteric and irrelevant topics—will be glad that a visionary leader like George Bush has come along to clarify our priorities and give shape to our programs. He has completely crushed the false importance assigned to all those cutesy little carts most progressives have invariably attempted to place before their horses. Consequently, he has been able to energize and organize "the masses" in ways and to a degree we never have, and probably never could. All we need now is to tap into the dynamic he has unleashed and help him succeed in ways he and most of those parroting his rhetoric have yet to imagine.

In pursuing George's call for occupied national territories to be liberated, legitimate governments restored, expropriated resources returned, and transgressors punished, we can begin to dissolve the American Empire from within. Reasserting the territoriality and sovereignty of Native North America is not only "the right course of action" in itself, it inherently destroys the capacity of the United States to be what it is. Put simply, without the resources accruing from its ongoing occupation and "internal colonization" of Indian Country,[37] the United States would lack the material capacity to engage in the sort of military aggressiveness—both overt and covert—with which it has marked the second half of the twentieth century, most recently in the Persian Gulf. This has always been the case, a fact which should long since have established a leading prioritization of and emphasis upon American Indian rights within the progressive American consciousness. Unfortunately, progressivism has always managed to miss points so basic, and so it has been left to the president to point out, albeit in the most circuitous possible fashion, that "the First American must be our First Priority." For this, we owe him an immeasurable debt of gratitude.

Being a first priority does not, it must be noted, mean being the only agenda item, or the last. Certain things would stem inevitably from the liberation of Native North America. Consider that if the U.S. capacity to project military force were substantially diminished through erosion of its resource base, so too would its ability to exert corporate neocolonial control over the entirety of the Third World deteriorate. Similarly, the United States would rapidly lose the means by which it maintains literal colonial sway over external territories like Puerto Rico. And internal decolonization hardly ends with Native America. As the U.S. imperial potential recedes abroad, so too does its power to grasp the reigns of control over African America, the internalized Latino population, recent Asian immigrants, even the Scotch-Irish colony of Appalachia.[38]

Nor is this the end of it. As the physical reality of the U.S. status quo unravels, so too does its capability to impose continuation of the hegemonic socio-psychological structuration marking its existence, even among the "mainstream" population. The institutions of racism, sexism, classism, agism, homophobia, violence, and alienation that have defined U.S. life are thereby opened at last to replacement by forms allowing for the actualization of "preferable alternatives." Now, how's *that* for a "New World Order?" How's *that* for "moral high ground?" The seeds of such things really are integral to the notions George Bush has been voicing, regardless of how much to the contrary he intended his remarks. All of it is possible, all of it follows, but it can only be approached on the basis of "first things first."

So, it's time we progressive types paid the president his due. It's time we got out there to show our support for the real meaning embedded in his message, whether or not he knew or meant what he said. It's time we endorsed the valid principles underlying his script and pushed them along to their logical conclusions even though George may never have conceived the "end-game moves." It's time we set out seriously to strangle this country full of conservative jackanapes with the rope of their own contradictions. It's time we at long last brought things home, dealing with root causes rather than an unending series of grotesque symptoms. Let's don't allow ourselves to become bogged down in some sort of "U.S. Out of the Middle East Campaign," just as we bogged ourselves down in "U.S. Out of Vietnam" a quarter-century ago, and "U.S. Out of Central America" during the 80s. The only meaningful thing we can pursue is getting the

U.S. out of *North America*. Better yet, we should push it off the planet. And the hour is growing late.

Notes

1. For analysis of Bush's rhetoric and the media's handling of it before and during the Gulf War, see Cheney, George, "'Talking War': Symbols, Strategies and Images," *New Studies on the Left*, Volume XIV, Number 3, Winter 1990-91. Also see Doyon, Denis F., "Creating an 'Iraq Syndrome,'" in Greg Bates, ed., *Mobilizing Democracy: Changing the U.S. Role in the Middle East*, Common Courage Press, Monroe, ME, 1991.
2. The lies are dissected to a considerable extent in *Z Magazine* and *Lies Of Our Times* during the entire pre-war/wartime period.
3. For background, see Chomsky, Noam, *The Fateful Triangle: Israel, the Palestinians, and the United States*, Boston: South End Press, 1983.
4. The text of the convention may be found in Brownlie, Ian, *Basic Documents on Human Rights*, London/New York: Oxford University Press, 1971.
5. For general context, see Bunting, Ray, *The Rise of the South African Reich*, London: Penguin Books, 1964.
6. See Ya-Otto, John, *Battle-Front Namibia*, Westport, CT: Lawrence Hill Publishers, 1981. Relatedly, see Martin, David, and Phyllis Johnson, *The Struggle for Zimbabwe: The Chimurenga War*, New York: Monthly Review Press, 1981.
7. For details of U.S. support of the South African nazification process, see Western Massachusetts Association of Concerned African Scholars, *U.S. Military Involvement in Southern Africa*, Boston: South End Press, 1978.
8. The idea that Iraq's was the world's "fourth largest army"—never really substantiated to any extent, and grossly inaccurate in a number of ways—was dutifully parroted at least five times per day by CNN "military analyst" Wolf Blitzer from August 1990 through March 1991.
9. See O'Shaugnessy, Hugh, *Grenada: Revolution, Invasion and Aftermath*, London: Zed Press, 1984.
10. This led to the famous Bush retort that the United States was actually "enforcing the law" via its invasion of Panama by seeking to "serve a warrant" on the "international drug peddler" Manuel Noriega. As of this writing, however, federal prosecutors profess to "lack hard evidence" with which to bring Noriega to trial in U.S. courts, and even the DEA admits that drug trafficking through Panama has increased substantially since the defendant's ouster.
11. See Baird, Jay W., ed., *From Nuremberg to My Lai*, Lexington/Toronto/London: DC Heath and Co., Publishers, 1972, and Falk, Richard A., ed., *The Vietnam War and International Law*, New Brunswick, NJ: Princeton University Press, 1969.
12. Technically, a tribunal would not be required insofar as any nation is entitled to bring its own international criminals to justice. The mechanism is generally described in Lillich, Richard B., *International Claims: Their Adjudication by National Commission*, Syracuse, NY: Syracuse University Press, 1962.
13. Bush is on firm legal ground in making the suggestion. For the mechanics of how such a tribunal should function, see Appleman, John Alan, *Military Tribunals and International Crimes*, Westport, CT: Greenwood Press, 1954.
14. On Justice Jackson, the "Nuremberg Principles," their application against the Germans in 1946-47, and the leading role the United States assumed in formu-

lating them, see Smith, Bradley F., *The Road to Nuremberg*, New York: Basic Books, 1981; and *Reaching Judgment at Nuremberg*, New York: Basic Books, 1977. As concerns application of these principles against the Japanese during the same period, see Brackman, Arnold C., *The Other Nuremberg: The Untold Story of the Tokyo War Crimes Trials*, New York: William Morrow Publishers, 1987.

15. U.S. policymakers and military leaders were actually tried and convicted *in absentia* by a highly reputable tribunal convened to investigate events in Indochina during the U.S. intervention there. The United States, of course, refused either to turn over its own international criminals for punishment or even to end the offending policies. See Duffett, John, ed., *Against the Crime of Silence: Proceedings of the International War Crimes Tribunal*, New York: Simon and Schuster Publishers, 1968.

16. A detailed account of the "Nixinger" crimes in Cambodia may be found in Shawcross, William, *Sideshow: Kissinger, Nixon and the Destruction of Cambodia*, New York: Simon and Schuster Publishers, 1979. For a broader assessment of U.S. conduct in Southeast Asia during the Nixon era and immediately thereafter, see Chomsky, Noam, and Edward S. Herman, *After the Cataclysm: Postwar Indochina and the Reconstruction of Imperial Ideology*, Boston: South End Press, 1979.

17. On the Grenada adventure, see Searle, Chris, *Grenada: The Struggle Against Destabilization*, London: Zed Press, 1983. Also see Gilmore, William C., *The Grenada Intervention: Analysis and Documentation*, London: Bertrand Russell Foundation, 1984.

18. For a detailed summary of contra atrocities to that point, see Brody, Reed, *Contra Terror in Nicaragua*, Boston: South End Press, 1985. Ample documentation of the Reagan administration's crucial role in making this possible may be found in Sklar, Holly, *Washington's War on Nicaragua*, Boston: South End Press, 1988.

19. See McClintock, Michael, *The American Connection: State Terror and Popular Resistance in El Salvador* (two volumes), London: Zed Press, 1985. More broadly, see Chomsky, Noam, *Turning the Tide: U.S. Intervention in Central America and the Struggle for Peace*, Boston: South End Press, 1985.

20. For a survey of the liaisons at issue, see Chomsky, Noam, and Edward S. Herman, *The Washington Connection and Third World Fascism*, Boston: South End Press, 1978. Also see Herman, Edward S., *The Real Terror Network*, Boston: South End Press, 1982.

21. Removal of a portion of these bodies, the existence of which had been steadfastly and officially denied by the Bush administration, from the slit trench into which they'd been dumped by U.S. troops, was shown on a "60 Minutes" news program in April 1990.

22. The texts of 371 ratified treaties between the United States and various American Indian nations—formal and binding international instruments—may be found in Kappler, Charles J., *Indian Treaties, 1778-1883*, New York: Interland Publishers, 1972. The Lakota scholar Vine Deloria, Jr., has uncovered another two dozen ratified treaties that do not appear in conventional sources, as well as another 400-odd unratified treaties which the United States has elected to consider binding for purposes of vesting land title in itself, etc. This is aside from about 1,000 "agreements" of various sorts, engineered by the United States with indigenous nations, which even federal courts have acknowledged hold the same legal force and status as treaties. Plainly, even under U.S. law, "Indian affairs" are not merely an "internal concern" of the United States.

23. The federal government presently recognizes the existence of 482 "Indian tribes," although only about half retain some residue of their original land base.

Altogether, these "reservations" add up to about 3 percent of the 48 coterminous states. Actually indigenous entitlement to territory is more than 10 times this amount. For a depiction of those portions of U.S. territory federal courts have admitted were never legally ceded by indigenous nations—and to which the United States therefore possesses no *bona fide* legal title—see the map appearing in Churchill, Ward, "The Earth is Our Mother: Struggles for American Indian Land and Liberation in the Contemporary United States," in M. Annette Jaimes, ed., *The State of Native America: Genocide, Colonization and Resistance,* Boston: South End Press, 1992.

24. On U.S. "trust" prerogatives taken vis-à-vis Native America, a counterpart of what the federal government asserts is its rightful "plenary (full) power" over Indian Country, see Deloria, Vine Jr., and Clifford M. Lytle, *American Indians, American Justice,* Austin: University of Texas Press, 1983.

25. About 44 million acres are at issue. See the Alaska Native Claims Settlement Act of 1971, Public Law 92-203; 85 Stat. 688, codified at 43 U.S.C. 1601 et seq.

26. Ch. 341, 24 Stat. 362, 385; now codified at 18 U.S.C. 1153.

27. Ch. 119, 24 Stat. 388; now codified at 25 U.S.C. 331 et seq.

28. Ch. 233, 43 Stat. 25.

29. Ch. 576, 48 Stat. 948; now codified at 25 U.S.C. 461-279.

30. A summary of primary economic factors concerning Native North America may be found in Ammot, Teresa L., and Julie A. Matthei, *Race, Gender and Work: A Multicultural Economic History of Women in the United States,* Boston: South End Press, 1991. On water and fishing rights, see the relevant essays in Jaimes, op. cit.

31. For official statistics on Native American health and related factors, see U.S. Department of Health and Human Services, *Chart Series Book,* Public Health Service, Washington, DC, 1988 (HE20.9409.988).

32. On profits extracted by the Homestake Mine, see Weyler, Rex, *Blood of the Land: The U.S. Government and Corporate War on the American Indian Movement,* Vintage Books, New York, 1984, pp. 262-3.

33. The language accrues from the Northwest Ordinance (1 Stat. 50), in which the United States formally renounced "rights of conquest" in North America.

34. See López, Alfredo, *Doña Licha's Island: Modern Colonialism in Puerto Rico,* Boston: South End Press, 1987.

35. On the construction of this modern U.S. empire, see Zinn, Howard, *Postwar America, 1945-1971,* Indianapolis: Bobbs-Merrill Publishers, 1973.

36. See Weinberg, Albert K., *Manifest Destiny: A Study of Nationalist Expansion in American History,* Baltimore: Johns Hopkins University Press, 1935.

37. The concept of internal colonization is of English origin, pertaining to the incorporation of the Scots, Welsh, and others into "Britain." See Hecter, Michael, *Internal Colonialism: The Celtic Fringe in British National Development, 1536-1966,* Berkeley: University of California Press, 1975. For application to Native America, see Churchill, Ward, "Indigenous Peoples of the U.S.: A Struggle Against Internal Colonialism," *Black Scholar,* Volume 16, Number 1, January-February 1985.

38. The Appalachian example is far too little studied. See Lewis, Helen, et al., eds., *Colonialism in Modern America: The Appalachian Case,* Boone, NC: Appalachian Consortium Press, 1978. Also see Cunningham, Rodger, *Apples on the Flood: The Southern Mountain Experience,* Knoxville: University of Tennessee Press, 1987.

CHAPTER 20

REFLECTIONS OF A NATIONAL ORGANIZER

Leslie Cagan

It all happened so quickly. At the beginning of August 1990 most people in the United States probably didn't even know that a country named Kuwait existed, let alone where it is. It only took a few months before hundreds of thousands of U.S. and coalition troops were sent to the Persian Gulf and the world was in the midst of the first major post-Cold War crisis—a crisis that would end in the mass destruction that defines modern warfare.

In order to understand the anti-war movement during the Gulf crisis and war, it is important to recognize the state of the movement before that moment. As the 1980s came to a close, the extraordinary events of those 10 years receded into the background as we witnessed rapid changes in Eastern Europe and the Soviet Union. (Of course, those changes have by now been overshadowed by the most recent dramatic shifts in the Soviet Union.) While complete nuclear disarmament is still a long way off, there were the first signs that serious reductions in nuclear weapons might begin. The end of the Cold War, symbolized by the tearing down of the Berlin Wall, was trumpeted as the beginning of a new era of global peace and cooperation.

Of course, the world was not at peace. Social tensions, civil strife, fighting, and war continued as daily realities in much of Central America, Southern Africa, the Middle East, and other places. As 1989 came to a close, the United States invaded Panama, killing thousands of civilians. The functions of government were taken over by U.S. operatives and the economic situation was made worse for most Panamanians. It was only a matter of weeks until, at the end of February 1990, the Sandinistas would lose the national elections in Nicaragua. For those who bothered to think about it, it was clear that the government of the United States had learned its own lessons over the years. It was able and willing to use all of the tools at its disposal to achieve its foreign-policy objectives—from midnight bombing raids on civilians, to surrogate armies such as the contras, to direct involvement in another nation's elections.

By the summer of 1990 the anti-war, anti-intervention, nuclear-disarmament, and peace forces in our country were confused and lacked direction. While many groups continued to organize around Central America, there was a growing realization that our efforts had not been able to stop the U.S. government from achieving its objectives in Nicaragua. Additionally, as a movement, we had been caught off guard about Panama and could do nothing to stop that military action. The nuclear-disarmament movement, long suffering from a lack of direction since the collapse of the freeze strategy, seemed nonexistent as the United States and the Soviet Union discussed arms-control treaties. People here and worldwide celebrated the release of Nelson Mandela, but the Southern Africa activists lost energy after his historic tour of this country, and organizers searched for ways to maintain the pressure for sanctions.

In addition to the shifting international realities, we had just lived through the first decade of Reaganonmics and all that meant here at home: a re-ordered tax structure designed to make the rich richer while social programs were cut at every level of government; mounting federal and state debts, as more and more of our cities faced budget shortfalls that immediately translated into cutting services; a crisis in the savings-and-loan industry that taxpayers will be paying off for years to come; a deepening health-care crisis with AIDS at epidemic proportions and millions of people lacking any health insurance or coverage; upwards of three million homeless people; an environmental nightmare; and a crumbling infrastructure.

Perhaps the largest problem for the peace and anti-intervention movement was its historic inability to unite with those forces struggling for changes within this country. While many progressive and left activists understood the connection between domestic and foreign policies, as a movement our work had more often than not been separated. During the 1980s there was political growth within the peace movement as organizers began to see how U.S. military intervention and the nuclear-arms race were two aspects of a coherent U.S. foreign policy. And slowly the peace movement was beginning to articulate the ties between this country's foreign policies and the suffering of people in our own country. The peace movement took up the call to cut military spending and use those funds for meeting human needs here at home.

But there was always a flaw in the way those connections were drawn. What was missing was an understanding that military spending produces tremendous profits for major corporations, and that the protection and expansion of private profit is the cornerstone upon which most of this government's policies (be they domestic or foreign) are built. In fact, there has never been any reason to believe that money cut from the military budget would naturally or automatically flow into programs to create jobs, or build new homes, or provide quality health care. In a January 28, 1989 column in the New York Times, Russell Baker observed, "A conservative theory of that time [the early 1980s] held that loading up the Pentagon...could hold down liberal domestic spending for years to come. Because commitment to a new weapon becomes more expensive with each passing year, went the theory, there would be less and less money in the future for liberals to squander on wild-eyed socialistic do-good programs."

The other dimension of the problem was the inability to bring diverse constituencies into joint efforts beyond short-lived coalitions. Even when organizers theoretically understood how issues are connected, it was a rare instance when an organization acted on this insight. More importantly, the predominantly white peace groups did not have a history of programmatically making these links. For example, how often did peace groups become actively involved in local struggles against police brutality?

In the middle of the summer of 1990 our movement, while still very active, was not strong. Events around the world and here at home were unfolding at great speed and we were not politically, organizationally, nor programmatically able to keep up with it all. Our movement—the progressive movement for peace and social justice—was disorganized, fragmented, working with few resources, and suffering from a lack of political cohesion and direction.

Add to this one more critically important weakness. If there was a blind spot in the work of the peace and anti-intervention movement it was the Middle East. Since the 1960s we have been able to build mass movements that addressed the role of the United States in Southeast Asia, Central America, Europe, and Southern Africa....but never the Middle East. More of our country's foreign aid has gone to the Middle East than any place else in the world. For years, analysts believed that the Middle East was the most likely flashpoint for nuclear war. There has been a decades-old occupation of Palestinian land. And there has been sporadic warfare for years. But even with all of that, our movement could not come to grips with the Middle East and so it was continually excluded from our agenda.

It was with all of this as background that we woke up on that morning in early August of 1990 to hear that Iraq had invaded Kuwait. Within a few days it was clear to the whole world that the first major post-Cold War crisis was unfolding, and that the Bush administration was determined to not only draw a line in the sand, but to also use this crisis as a way to assert its authority in a quickly-changing world.

What We Did Well

Despite the movement's weaknesses, it was exciting to see the speed with which people were able to articulate and mobilize anti-war sentiment throughout the nation. Local organizers did not wait for national organizations or a major national coalition to provide leadership. Within weeks, certainly by mid-September, not only had groups formed, but they were out on the streets in cities across the country. Some groups did tabling with information leaflets and petitions to their elected officials, while others organized protest demonstrations. Virtually every group taking up the Gulf crisis organized public forums, educational events, and teach-ins. Organizers found people starving for information and receptive to a perspective different from the one coming from the Kennebunkport vacation home of George Bush.

Some local groups were built as a direct response to the Gulf crisis, while others were long-standing peace-and-justice centers or organizations. One could not help but notice that the backbone for many of the newer groups came from Central America activists. In part this had to do with the fact that many Central America activists had learned a great deal about how this government conducts its foreign policy—they knew not to trust George "CIA" Bush. The fact that much of the Central America movement was in disarray and people were confused about where that work was going perhaps helped make it a little easier for people to shift gears.

Local activists and organizers provided the leadership for this movement. They knew that the educational work had to be done; they knew pressure had to be put on Congress; they knew that it was critical to support the people within the military who declared their refusal to cooperate with the drive toward war; and they knew that public protest was an essential element in building an opposition force. As is always true, major national organizations moved somewhat more slowly than local grassroots groups. But by the end of September virtually every national peace, disarmament, and anti-intervention organization understood that it too had to address this crisis.

In the next six months, so much happened so quickly that it is impossible to present a definitive and detailed history of the anti-war movement. At last count, the National Campaign for Peace in the Middle East (one of the major national coalitions to come together during the crisis and war) had more than 400 local groups on its contact list, and we knew that was not every group that existed. There were probably thousands of teach-ins, hundreds of marches and rallies, scores of visits to elected officials, and countless encounters with the mass media. Very quickly an active and visible national movement came together—a movement that did a great deal but in the end was unable to stop the U.S.-led drive toward war in the Persian Gulf. But more on this later.

What we did best was mobilizing our base. For many years, people have been hard at work on many foreign-policy and domestic issues. It was those people who responded most quickly and took action against Bush's handling of the crisis. A lot of excellent educational work was done, as well as outreach to people not yet involved, but there were limits to how far that work could go. Events unfolded at a rapid pace with some new element of the crisis emerging almost every day. Not being a strong, unified, coherent movement to begin with, we were at a disadvantage. At the same time that we did the work to oppose the Bush administration, we had to do the work to build ourselves. Our movement was not organizationally prepared to jump into a major battle against our government. Of course, our lack of attention to the Middle East in the past meant that a lot of internal education had to be done simultaneously. In essence, we were working on several fronts all at once: opposing the administration, building ourselves organizationally, and trying to catch up on educational work we should have been doing for years.

It was the work of the anti-war movement which opened up the space and gave people the support they needed to express their opposition to the war. In hundreds of protests around the country, thousands upon thousands of people voiced their opposition to the government's handling of the crisis. In terms of numbers, the high point came on January 26th when at least 250,000 people marched in Washington, DC. There was a major demonstration in San Francisco that same day, and the weekend before 75,000 marched in Washington as over 100,000 demonstrated in San Francisco. I remember watching Bush on TV in early March as he declared that the war was over and there was no anti-war movement. I don't recall ever having been so happy that we had organized a demonstration. On January 26 we had stood together and shown the world that there were people—many, many people—in this country who publicly disagreed with the president. That mobilization represented the amazing organizing efforts people had been engaged in since September in communities around the country. Hundreds of thousands of people don't march in the middle of January if there has not been a lot of effective work taking place locally.

From the first moment Bush announced that he was sending U.S. troops into the area, the anti-war movement knew it had to figure out how to relate to the men and women in the military. We understood that many of the people in the armed forces were there primarily out of economic necessity, victims of the poverty draft. We knew this was not a case of people signing up to go to war. Indeed, many of those sent to Saudia Arabia were in the reserves. Engaging in combat was the furthest thing from their minds when they joined up.

Within a few weeks of the president's decision to send troops to the Gulf, the father of a young marine wrote an op-ed piece in the *New York Times*. Alex Molnar made his case clearly—if his son were to die in the Persian Gulf he would hold George Bush personally responsible. The response to his piece was quick and it came from around the country. Parents and relatives of people in the military knew they did not want their loved ones sent to fight and possibly die in a pointless and avoidable war. The Military Families Support Network was formed, and would grow to include thousands of people in chapters in over 30 states. At the same time, some active duty servicepeople as well as reservists publicly declared their refusal to participate in Operation Desert Shield and then Operation Desert Storm.

Long-term anti-war activists, including veterans of the Vietnam War, had never seen anything quite like this. It was clear that a new relationship between anti-war forces and people in the military was being built. This was a relationship that had to be handled carefully and with respect. The reality of who was in the military (and why) coupled with this new kind of anti-war voice from military personnel and their families led much of the movement to have as a core demand, "Support our troops—bring them home!" The anti-war movement wanted to be clear that reservists and enlistees were not our enemy.

What We Should Have Done Better

Once it was obvious that the United States was committed to an air war we should have realized that we were in a trap. Of course we didn't want our troops fighting and dying, but an air war meant there would be virtually no U.S. casualties. The problem was that we had not balanced our concern about U.S. casualties with the other reasons we opposed this war. We knew that in the mad rush to war, the U.S. government had not allowed room for a peaceful, negotiated resolution to the conflict. George Bush offered a string of rationalizations as he attempted to justify his commitment to war. Right up until the war began, most of the people of this country rejected them all, knowing that war only brings greater chaos and destruction.

We were opposed to this war and the use of military force to resolve the Gulf crisis even if none of our troops would die (which was practically the case!). We knew that innocent Iraqis would suffer and die, and we feared that most of the Middle East would end up directly involved in this war. Our movement knew that condemning the actions of Saddam Hussein and the Iraqi government did not mean that the Iraqi people deserved to be the targets of war. For the most part, so much emphasis was put on supporting our troops that our legitimate concern about the fate of the Iraqi people was lost. It was extremely difficult for us to shift gears once the air war was in full force. We had not laid the political groundwork that would have given people the tools needed to deal with the propaganda onslaught which came once the war started. Every yellow ribbon and American flag was flown in support of our troops. What made our support any different from the flag-wavers?

Our movement never found a way around this weakness. We, like everyone else, accepted the line from the Pentagon that this would be a bloody combat war. We assumed that it would take much longer than it did, and we believed that many more U.S. troops would be wounded and die. It was almost as if we didn't know what was in the U.S. arsenal and what it had deployed in the Persian Gulf. In fact, that information was fairly accessible. The problem was that we never made that an issue. We were focused on how many body bags were shipped to the Gulf and not on the number of bombs. We were politically unprepared to deal with the technology of this war, even though we had seen what the Pentagon had done in Panama and could remember the last phases of the war in Vietnam.

We should have learned one of the same lessons the Pentagon seemed to have learned from Vietnam. It is harder to maintain support for a ground war, but an air war can do as much (even more) damage and not lose support at home. And this seemed to be proven yet again in the Gulf War.

The shift in public opinion once the war began on January 16 was dramatic. Throughout the fall, most of the people of this country opposed or at least questioned the idea of going to war. The Bush administration had been unable to convincingly justify what might be thousands upon thousands of casualties. But as soon as the first bombs started dropping and our forces were actually in a war, the mood of this country shifted. We were bombarded with flags and yellow ribbons and statements by politicians and other prominent people lining up behind the president. With the beginning of the war, anti-war groups found a new level of resistance to their message. The mood of the country had changed.

The other technology we simply were no match for was television. Everything about the crisis and the war was filtered for the people of this country through the television screen. The great majority of people get their news from television, and during the crisis and war that was virtually all the news they got. We all know the story of the media and this war. What's important is that we begin to come to grips with the power of the mass media, and what it means that we have nothing that compares to its scale and scope.

The alternative media of this country, for the most part, did an incredible job of getting out another point of view. Innovative projects included the Gulf Crisis TV Project, which produced several dozen shows on all aspects of the war and the anti-war movement for cable television. Local organizers and cable producers made sure the shows were broadcast, and in so doing extended the reach of the anti-war movement. On January 12, the National Campaign for Peace in the Middle East produced a teach-in that was carried by more than 35 radio stations around the country. All of the movement publications had expanded coverage of the crisis and the war, and publications like Z Magazine, CrossRoads, and the Progressive used their resources to provide much-needed organizing materials.

But added all together, the alternative newspapers, radio stations, magazines, and now cable programming doesn't come close to reaching the numbers of people that the mainstream broadcast media reach. This is not to suggest that we should give up with attempts at alternative media. Just the opposite—that work needs to be strengthened. But our movement must also rethink its approaches to the mainstream mass media. They reach too many people for us to ignore them.

This war was clearly, amongst other things, a statement to the world—to economic rivals Japan and Western Europe, to the Soviet Union, to the developing nations of the Third World—that the United States is the one military superpower in this post-Cold War era. Not only does the United States have the most sophisticated and deadly weapons of mass destruction, but its leaders have the will to use them. The world had never seen a war like this one—massive concentrated bombardment designed to destroy a nation's infrastructure (roads, bridges, water purification plants, electricity plants, etc.) along with its military apparatus.

In preparation for war, the Bush administration played every card it had. It used everything, including economic coercion, to leverage support in the international community, more specifically at the United Nations. As a movement we have never been clear about our relationship to the United Nations, often dismissing it simply as an organ of the United States. In fact, the United Nations has been one of the few arenas in which the United States has been challenged. For many years, developing nations of the Third World used the UN as a vehicle for working together, often in opposition to the United States. Like many other institutions, the UN has its own complexities and possibilities for movement.

In this crisis most of the member nations of the UN did follow the lead of the United States, with the exception of Cuba and Yemen. It might have been worth our while to have mounted a serious campaign directed toward the nations on the UN Security Council. Although several small demonstrations were held at the UN, they had no real impact. We should have made sure that the UN heard directly from the people of this country and that we understood that the UN was charged with finding peaceful solutions to international conflicts, not giving the green light to a U.S.-led war.

Having won the support from the international community to go to war by January 15, the Bush administration only had to bring the Congress along. The fact that Congress discussed this issue for a total of three days should surely be recorded as one of the most disgraceful moments in that institution's history. For most of the crisis, Congress was not even in session. By late November and early December there was some discussion within the anti-war movement of mounting a campaign to pressure Congress to convene in special session to discuss the crisis. The goal of such an effort would be to have Congress play an active role in averting a war. But getting this off the ground was hampered in part by a concern that if we won and got Congress to convene, we could not be sure what action they might take! Throughout the crisis and war many people pressured their congressional delegations to take action or speak out against the president. But, as with so much of our work, the effort was never brought together as a national campaign. Could we all have done better had we been working as part of a more coordinated plan?

The anti-war movement started to connect domestic issues to the policies that led to the war. The consciousness about these connections was evidenced in the slogans, leaflets, posters, banners, chants, and speeches at rallies. Over and over again leaflets and speeches issued the call for money for health care, to fight AIDS, for housing and education, to clean up the environment. The anti-war movement called attention to the billions of dollars pouring into Operation Desert Shield and Operation Desert Storm. But, for the most part, the movement was not able to give programmatic expression to the connections we understood intellectually. Our movement would certainly have been stronger had we been able to make the concrete links in our work and not only in our speeches.

There were, of course, places where real breakthroughs happened, such as the organizing done in New Orleans and parts of the deep south by the Gulf Tenants Organizing Project. Building from their work as tenant organizers, they were able to make connections to the Gulf crisis in ways that resonated for people. For months they held demonstrations at local gas stations asking why our nation was spending billions of dollars planning for war over oil while people here lacked adequate housing, etc.

How We Hurt Ourselves

Regardless of what George Bush said, we know that we did have a movement, or at least the beginnings of a movement opposed to this war. Our greatest strength was our ability to activate and mobilize our base. In doing that, we helped an opposition movement find its voice. But our movement was not in a position to have stopped this war, and given the state of our movement when this crisis began, it would have been unrealistic and naive for us to believe that we could. There were forces in motion—in this country and internationally—that we could not begin to challenge. Stopping this war would have required the active participation of many more people, including some dissenting voices in Congress and some openings for our point of view in the mass media. Preventing or stopping this war would have required an expansion of our base that was beyond our capability.

For the most part, our inability to expand was directly linked to the state of our movement leading up to the crisis. But we can't lay everything on what happened earlier—there were also problems and difficulties within the work of this anti-war movement.

While there was a great deal of talk about the need to build a unified movement to oppose our government's handling of the crisis, there were several major political differences making anything more than tactical unity impossible—and sometimes even that tactical unity was elusive. For instance, overwhelmingly the movement in both its local and national expressions condemned the Iraqi invasion of Kuwait, while a minority felt that it was not our place to make such a condemnation. This was a very small part of the movement, but since condemning a military invasion is such a principled position for most anti-war organizers, the fact that some resisted it led to a lack of trust. In some ways the different positions over sanctions against Iraq were much more significant, in that those who opposed sanctions were almost as large a part of the movement as those who felt we should support sanctions (excluding medical and food sanctions) as an alternative to war. The point is that, while political differences existed, as a movement we lacked a vehicle to debate or discuss, let alone resolve, such differences.

Perhaps most importantly, our work suffered from the fact that historically the anti-war movement has not confronted and dealt with racism within its own ranks—let alone in the culture generally. For instance, while anti-war sentiment ran high amongst African Americans, many anti-war groups remained largely white. Our own awareness of the racism of this war and of the ways in which racism shapes this nation's foreign policies was not translated programmatically into our work. When anti-Arab racism escalated throughout the country, we were forced to confront the practical consequences of having neglected the Middle East for so long.

And the same can be said about sexism and homophobia. There was a new twist in this war as women took up combat positions for the first time and the issue of the participation of gay men and lesbians within the military came to public attention. Our movement did not address these complex issues. A movement which lacks a history of bringing diverse constituencies together into common work will of course find it hard to address issues that might seem divisive.

We need to be actively involved in the fight for women's equality and an end to lesbian/gay oppression. At the same time, as anti-war activists we should be clear that we do not believe advancement inside the military for women, gay men and lesbians, people of color, or working people is a primary objective. Far from it: the peace and justice movement needs to be consistent in our opposition to the U.S. military because of its role internationally as well as because of the ways it treats people inside its ranks. The fact that this anti-war movement was not able to address such concerns in a coherent way was only another reflection of its weaknesses and fragmentation.

Looking Ahead

The anti-war movement that developed throughout this country in response to the Gulf crisis did a lot of work that we can be proud of. There were problems, many problems, but given the limitations people were working with, a tremendous amount of positive organizing happened in every state of this country. The challenge we face now is to be honest about the weaknesses of that work and try to understand where they came from, including the baggage and problems we carried into the effort right from the beginning.

If there is going to be a peace-and-justice movement strong enough to actually make a dent in this government's policies, then we will have to come to grips with these realities and these difficult questions. We live in a different world than we have previously known. There is no counterbalance or block to the United States. Those in power are more than willing to ruthlessly use that power in all of its forms—militarily, economically, diplomatically, and through the media.

We live and work in a most difficult time, a moment in history that challenges us to rethink our strategies and bring new energy and creativity to our political work. For instance, we worked hard to bring people into the streets in mass mobilizations and demonstrations, and we needed to use those as a way to express the opposition that did exist. But have we not yet learned that marches and rallies alone can't do it? We need to put as much energy into building our organizations as we put into building demonstrations.

Dramatic changes in the world, the economic and social crisis within our own country, and the weakened state of the peace-and-justice movement could easily lead to confusion. The war against Iraq did not last long, but it marked a period of profound change in global relationships. For many in the anti-war movement the post-war period and the flood of parades and celebrations and television specials was particularly depressing. We saw the naked power of the United States, and we also realized the limitations of our own work. We saw the pain and suffering of the people of Iraq, and aside from some humanitarian aid efforts felt powerless to help. We see no real or lasting resolution of the conflicts in the Middle East as our own government, which justified its war by claiming to be against occupation, continues to support the Israeli occupation of the West Bank, Gaza, and the Golan Heights. And on top of all this we see and experience the crisis in health care, education, housing, etc., in our own country. We must rethink our work—it is time for some dramatic changes within our own movement.

We can no longer afford to have a peace movement on the one hand and a movement for social and economic justice on the other. This country needs a movement which brings people together based on an integrated political analysis and comprehensive strategy for change. We need a multiracial, multicultural movement strong enough to be a player in the political, economic, social, and cultural dynamics of this country. Making change is not a spectator sport where we sit on the sidelines and raise a banner of opposition from time to time. There is much to oppose and mobilizing people to express that opposition will always be a vital part of what we do. What are missing, and what are so desperately needed, are organizations capable of mounting serious challenges to power—in all its forms.

We are up against powerful and brutal forces—forces that will not give up their power and control easily or quickly. We must meet every crisis as it comes along, and we can be certain that there will be more, but we can never lose sight of what must be our long-term goals. Engaging millions of people in the process of change will require changes in our own movement that we have not even begun to imagine. Let us learn as much as we can from the Gulf crisis and use it to help build a mass movement for peace and justice as we look toward the future.

CHAPTER 21

LESSONS OF THE GULF WAR

Michael Albert

In January 1991, I wrote in *Z Magazine* that "George Bush, the White House, the Pentagon, the Congress, the Senate, the *New York Times,* the *Washington Post,* ABC, NBC, CBS, the mainstream national media, corporate capital, patriarchs, racists, and bigots together have unleashed a rain of destruction on the people of Iraq, and, before it's over, perhaps on people throughout the Mideast. Of course, they have showered economic hardship and therefore widespread death on the disadvantaged throughout the world all along. Peace and prosperity for the rich, war and deprivation for the poor. Business as usual. But now the scale of opposition is changing and that must further focus our attention and arouse our energies."

And I urged that "It does not deny your belief in human potential and your hope for humanity to admit the ugly truth. Bush, the White House, the Congress, the Senate, and the mass media do not care about the lives of U.S. troops [or anyone else] except insofar as loss of their lives might fuel resistance and thereby thwart war aims."

Masters of War

The book you have just read has made the same points. Our elite policymakers did not calculate for one microsecond the human travail that their policies would unleash on the people of Iraq or anywhere else, except insofar as that travail might provoke further resistance.

They did not respect national sovereignty or they would have opposed Iraq's war against Iran instead of supporting it, opposed Israel's violations of Lebanon's sovereignty instead of supporting them, opposed Turkey's violations of Cyprus instead of supporting them, opposed Indonesia's genocidal assaults on East Timor instead of providing aid to assist them. National self-determination obviously means nothing to those who invaded Grenada and Panama and mined Nicaragua's harbors in open defiance of international law.

The Bush administration, like its predecessors, did not care about democracy or removing a violent, oppressive dictator or it would not have supported Hussein before August 2, just as it would not have supported Pinochet, Somoza, Marcos, the Shah of Iran, and Noriega, and just as it would not now be supporting murderous dictators around the world or trying desperately to replace Violeta Chamorro with a contra thug more willing to reconstitute death squads to stamp out the legacy of Sandinismo. An aversion to justice is in fact the *best* credential for obtaining U.S. support. Murderers like Saddam Hussein fall out of favor with the United States *only* when they disobey "our" will.

Elite policymakers did not care about preventing the spread of weapons of mass destruction that they regularly produce and use, or they wouldn't produce them, wouldn't use them, and wouldn't obstruct all international efforts, including in the Middle East, to eliminate them. They cared only about implementing their vicious scenarios for enlarging their own power and wealth, and about that, there were no "buts" allowed.

The money that went to the Gulf War could have gone to ending hunger. Bush didn't care. Stephen Solarz didn't care. For that matter, not more than a handful of Senators and congresspeople cared. "Don't be silly," they would say if they had the courage to speak openly. "If we didn't use the wealth in war we certainly wouldn't use it to eliminate hunger. That would aid the poor. That would shorten the 'stick' we use to get the poor to do our bidding. It would reduce our relative advantage. It would be worse than war." These are the people we were and are dealing with. This is not rhetoric. It's not exaggeration. It sounds discordant because it is inconsistent with the megamillion messages we get to the contrary every day. Nonetheless, understand these truths and while each new affront to dignity and humanity will nauseate you, it will not sidetrack your activism.

The Institutional Causes Of War

In trying to situate the underlying causes of war and broaden the focus of our opposition, I also wrote in January that "Capitalism is theft.

It is brutality, corruption, lying, cheating, killing, all coupled to an almost infinite capacity for egoism. NBC worries about a terrorist attack somewhere in the United States, perhaps in some subway train or office building. Meanwhile the U.S. Air Force rains terror on a whole country."

Capitalism is private ownership of capital, hierarchical production, and free markets. It is hypocrisy. It yields not "surgical war" but "surgical morality" that applies whenever, wherever, and however the United States wants, which means never when moral accounting would interfere with the interests of U.S. elites.

Patriarchy is the institution of state- and religiously-ordained marriage coupled with sexist role definitions for male/female interactions in general, and particularly regarding procreation, sexuality, and child rearing. It is male domination. It represses human sentiment in order to preserve gender hierarchy. It is macho posturing built on sex discrimination, sexual harassment, woman-beating, and rape. It engenders a military mindset that celebrates destruction, enjoys obliterating defenseless opponents, and identifies courage with mindless obedience to anyone wearing more metal and ribbons on the chest.

Racism is a structure of diverse communities with unequal means to further their own cultural practices and beliefs. It includes denigrating attitudes toward one another, with some deemed superior and others inferior. It is mental and physical lynching with rules, words, money, culture, law, and clubs. And it is also elevation of self over others culminating in a nationalist crescendo that consigns people to a subhuman status to justify destroying them to save them.

The state is the armed might of a society hell-bent on domination. It is courts and police, missiles and troops. Bush is a surgeon who will calmly remove beating hearts and only limit carnage to diminish dissent. The state defends its own privilege and power while simultaneously propping up that of capital, patriarchy, and race as well.

The mass media is a product of capitalism, sexism, and racism, and subject to oversight by the state. The government put restraints on the media's access to the Gulf War battlefield, driving them away from the sights and sounds of war because in the throes of battle reporters may have let their hunger for Pulitzer Prizes interfere with their skill at obscuring the truth. But at home no such restraint is ever required. Media knows it was not their place to report on hundreds of thousands of anti-war demonstrators shutting down bridges, occupying post offices, stopping traffic, marching, teaching, and setting up peace-and-justice centers. Certainly NBC did not want to show a wide and welcoming movement that was serious and intent. But since they had to admit something was going on, their role was to pan in on a few vigils, some scenes of hippie protesters milling about, and a barrage of interviews with relatives of soldiers supporting the war juxtaposed with frequent shots of Young Americans for Freedom counterdemonstrating. This was the media's role: subservience to wealth and authority.

We must not let capitalism, patriarchy, racism, the state, and the mass media get us down. We must shut them down. We must replace them with better alternatives.

We Can Win

In 1964 and 1965, Boston anti-war rallies included only a few hundred people periodically listening to vague talks about the horrors of war. Most students at the Massachusetts Institute of Technology, my alma mater, ignored the events though a few eagerly threw rocks at assembled protesters.

By 1968 and 1969, Boston anti-war demonstrations included as many as 200,000 people listening to talks on the imperialist roots of war and the efficacy of resistance. Demonstrations often included civil disobedience. Most MIT students not only regularly participated but also elected a student-body president demanding no more war research, the payment of a $100,000 MIT indemnity to the Black Panther Party, no more grades or requirements, open admissions at MIT, and the redistribution of MIT's technical resources among local colleges.

In the four intervening years Boston had seen hundreds of teach-ins, dozens of major rallies, and many acts of civil disobedience, building occupations, and ROTC burnings. At campuses, cultural events, marches, classroom takeovers, sit-ins, building take-overs, and one-on-many and one-on-one late-night discussions transformed student life. Minds changed. Hopes rose. Anger surfaced. This trajectory of increasing resistance shows:

- Lesson one: Sustained organizing over an extended period can change people's consciousness, commitments, and values.

As the anti-war movement gathered momentum, a "Mayday" demonstration was called to convene in Washington, DC, where demonstrators would use mobile civil disobedience to shut down the government. Demonstration organizers like Rennie Davis and Tom Hayden toured the country rallying people to storm Washington to "Shut It Down" *now* and thereby end the war. This was "apocalyptic organizing": (1) Describe reality as careening toward catastrophe. (2) Urge that we have only one more chance before final disaster. (3) Urge that we can reverse the tide and win justice and victory *now* if everyone of good will drops everything and joins the action. (4) Commitments are given. Energy rises. Sparks fly. (5) Davis and Hayden leave for the next whistle stop, fists waving gloriously.

Other activists organized for Mayday with a different approach: (1) Explain that the war is fed by institutions that serve political and economic elites, nurtured by racism, sexism, and manipulative mainstream media, and orchestrated by leaders who will not give in easily. (2) Teach that our task at each demonstration is to strengthen our movement and attract new recruits. (3) Clarify that policy is *now* catastrophic and will *remain catastrophic* until we build much greater opposition. (4) Teach the methods of discussion and argument needed to spread the word and create local coalitions and organizations. (5) Preserve and combine the sparks to create more heat, channel the energy to avoid waste, nurture the commitment to get longevity.

Both approaches favored teach-ins, rallies, demonstrations, and civil disobedience. Apocalyptic organizing aroused demonstrators at raucous meetings, but when apocalyptically-organized demonstrators returned home from major anti-war events, they were unprepared to see the war continue without obvious change. Recriminations flew, frustration rose, and anger turned inward or toward cynicism. The result was well-meaning demonstrators who didn't know the detailed whys and wherefores of their actions. Finally, Davis left the movementt to support a two-bit "eastern" spiritual guru. Hayden left to enter a two-bit "western" secular party. Hundreds of thousands of apocalyptically-organized activists burned out.

In contrast long-term organizing gave people a reasoned perspective along with their passionate feelings. It provided the insight to look for signs of progress not in immediate Washington policy changes, but in the movement and the country. We looked at ourselves and not at their press conferences to see signs of progress. Were we getting better at organizing? At building institutions? At reaching out? At causing some decisionmakers to begin to take note? Demonstrators aroused by a long-term analysis better understood their actions and knew what indices of success to look for and what valuative norms to apply.

The argument that because the bombs are falling, we require an immediate massive outpouring aroused by apocalyptic rhetoric was *wrong*. First, change is nearly always longer-run than the next rally or demonstration. Second, elites can distinguish between (1) brief outbursts that can be weathered, and (2) resistance that will keep growing and will, if repressed, tend to grow still more. Only the latter worries them sufficiently to affect their policymaking. Thus follows:

- Lesson two: Apocalyptic organizing gets short-term results with limited staying power and impact. Long-view organizing gets a movement that can withstand the rigors it will face and sends a message able to reverse war policies and prepare for further future gains.

Nineteen-sixties organizers also favored two main focuses. Some, usually of the Davis/Hayden wing, said we always have to organize around the war alone. Sticking to this least-common-denominator politics and avoiding controversial stands on other issues will amass the greatest possible support. Others said we have to organize around the war, but also as much as we can around poverty, alienation, racism, sexism, and authoritarianism.

It was true that attention to violence against women, capitalist inequality, a local strike, or racism complicated matters. Some people who might have agreed with anti-war analysis might reject a stand on these issues. We needed ways new people could become involved even before feeling comfortable with wide-ranging analyses. Similarly, debates and disagreements about diverse issues would take time from outreach and had to be engaged in sensibly and not with an attitude that every issue had to be solved on every stage. But ignoring nonwar focuses had even more devastating costs.

Constituencies immediately concerned about domestic race, gender, or class issues didn't trust an anti-war movement that always slighted their concerns. Women who worked against the war reacted when male antiwar activists lacked concern for reproductive rights. Welfare rights workers who called out their constituents to demonstrate against the war reacted when the antiwar movement failed to fight for welfare rights. Finally, the single-issue approach also delivered a weakened message to elites. It said, "Yes, there is a growing anti-war movement, but its attention is narrowly on this war. If you can tough it out, this movement isn't going to challenge society's domestic class, race, political, and gender inequalities." A multi-issue approach risked alienating some people via controversial stands and debates. But done right it could reach more diverse constituencies and deliver a more threatening message. "If you don't end the war this movement is not only going to grow and become more militant and disruptive with regard to the war, it is going to develop similar strength and commitment with regard to racism, sexism, political participation, and capitalism." Therefore:

- Lesson three: Single-issue organizing appears less controversial and more popular but it carries the seeds of its own dissolution and sends a limited message to elites. Multi-issue organizing that preserves channels for participation and respect even for those who disagree is difficult to do well, but it is better insured against fragmentation, better oriented to maximum outreach, and sends a more powerful message to elites.

In my own 1960s organizing efforts I often addressed large groups for extended, highly emotional sessions. I would of course explain the criminality of the war for people who still believed the U.S. had a humane foreign policy. But especially on the campus, I invariably found that with sufficient facts I could correct this ignorance. Then, however, I encountered more tenacious obstacles to participation.

First, people who agreed that the war was immoral and only in the elites' interests, would often argue that nonetheless nothing could be done about it. Immorality was the way of the world. Hate, inequality, servility, and war are our nature. There was no point seeking a better world.

Second, even if our long discussions helped us overcome cynicism about ultimate human potentials, people would fall back on the notion that opposition could not succeed because the bad guys had the guns, money, and media. We couldn't beat them.

Third, if I could convince them that "the power of the people was greater than the Man's technology," the final impediment turned out to be distaste for left behavior and a fear of becoming our own worst enemy. People would say, "I know you are right that the war is wrong, but however good your ultimate aims may be, eventually you will just sell out your values and become as bad as those you now oppose." To address this I had to argue that movement organizations internally rejected the oppressive behavior that characterized the rest of society, sometimes a hard case. Thus, popular responses to organizing revealed that:

- Lesson four: Ignorance is only a part of the impediment to radicalism. Getting people to join radical opposition also requires overcoming cynicism about human nature and potential, fear of losing, and distaste for what activism seems to entail.

The United States did not drop nuclear bombs in Southeast Asia. We did not turn the whole region into a paved-over parking lot. Limits were placed on U.S. policy. Some aggressive acts were prevented and others reversed. Civil rights were won; women made major gains. Though the roots of inequities are structural, and permanent change requires transformed institutions, short-run victories do occur.

A look at the *Pentagon Papers*, newspapers, and the public record of Congress shows a remarkable fact. Whenever some politician changed from voting pro-war to voting anti-war, or whenever some corporate head went on record against the war, the explanation corresponded exactly to the variable deemed most important in official *Pentagon Papers* reports of policymaking as well.

There was never mention of the cost of losing American and Vietnamese lives, or of economic dislocation at home. When politicians and other elite figures switched from hawk to dove, and the *Pentagon Papers* listed factors considered in choosing among policies, what was mentioned was the cost of political resistance—our army is disintegrating, our streets are succumbing to militancy, the next generation is being lost to our corporations, the cost is too high; I am now for peace. With minor exceptions, no elite figure opposed the war because the United States was violating norms of morality. Nor did they change sides because the human carnage upset them. Nor was there any notion that the war was not "in U.S. (meaning elite) interests." The issue was rising social costs that threatened to undermine aims and relations that elites held even more important than winning the war. Their political power, their corporate economic control, racism, sexism, etc., were under increasing attack. That is:

- Lesson five: Moving people to raise the domestic social costs of war can constrain and reverse hated policy. The logic of raising the social cost for U.S. elites underpins the wisdom of lessons one through four and of all anti-war strategy.

So what does this imply? State and corporate elites are not stupid nor subject to moral persuasion. They promote heinous war policies not out of ignorance, but because the results serve state and corporate interests. To pressure them effectively, we have to avoid single-issue, apocalyptic organizing and opt for a multi-issue, long-run strategies We have to educate people about immediate facts and proximate causes, but also about the roots of injustice and the possibility of raising social costs to win immediate reforms and eventually restructure defining institutions.

Building An Anti-War Movement

So how might we build an anti-war movement that also builds left solidarity? Some ideas include:

(1) Every anti-war speaking engagement or teach-in panel or rally should include at least one speaker specially equipped to address the "totality of oppressions," and preferably numerous speakers adept at addressing war and peace and issues of domestic organizing. Moreover,

I am not talking only about someone whose primary agenda is anti-war work explaining how that work can benefit those primarily working on domestic class, gender, or race issues. I'm talking about the inclusion of feminists, labor organizers, and anti-racist organizers who talk about how *their* work is critically important in its own right and how assisting it will benefit the fight against war.

(2) The organization and culture of the anti-war movement has to be more empowering for diverse types of people. Women will not feel comfortable nor work well in a movement that is defined by the worst male habits of competitive and macho posturing amidst gender divisions of labor. We have to incorporate feminist principles in our anti-war movement. People of color will not feel comfortable nor work well in a movement defined by the most sterile cultural and behavioral characteristics of white culture. We have to incorporate diverse cultures into our anti-war movement. Workers will not feel comfortable or work well in a movement that is organized like General Motors and/or a lecture hall and characterized by the condescension familiar from their relations with managers, lawyers, doctors, etc. We must have working-class leadership and a way of organizing that incorporates working-class culture and priorities in our anti-war movement. Gays and lesbians will not feel comfortable in a movement that embodies sexual assumptions familiar from their daily encounters with homophobia. We must incorporate respect for sexual diversity in our anti-war movement.

A multi-constituency movement that inspires lasting commitment will have to be multicultural and disavow all the oppressive features common to gender, race, and class relations outside. This is difficult and we can't expect to attain perfection overnight. We shouldn't guilt-trip ourselves nor go to the extreme of making a movement that only the most culturally and socially "perfect" human being could feel comfortable in, but we must make steady and substantial progress at diversity to be credible.

(3) To promote the movement's growth and the strongest possible resistance and to give the movement a positive rather than always negative orientation, anti-war action should often target non-military sites and always make multi-issue demands. For example, they should be held:

- at the corporate headquarters of major war contractors, demanding an end to war and the reallocation of resources to production of food and shelter and infrastructure for better living conditions here and abroad;

- at Congress, demanding an end to war and the financing full-employment programs, massively progressive "soak-the-rich" tax reforms, two-term limits on elected officials, state-financed election funds, and binding public plebiscites on important policy matters;

- at drug hangouts or dilapidated drug treatment centers, demanding an end to war and creation of massive drug-rehabilitation and job-training programs;

- at army bases, demanding an end to war and conversion of the bases to industrial centers to build quality, low-income housing with the first units given to GIs from the base who decide to stay on as employees at the new construction firm;

- at television stations, demanding an end to war and initiation of massive funding for the arts and for independent radio and television under community control;

- at rape-crisis or day-care centers, demanding an end to war and massive funding for anti-rape, day-care, and affirmative-action programs for women;

- at run-down inner-city sites, demanding an end to war and funds for rebuilding infrastructure, enhancing housing, and providing jobs and job training;

- at inner-city schools, demanding an end to war and massive funding for education that will allow our youth to become more than mere mercenaries for a garrison state;

- at hospitals, demanding an end to war and conversion of resources to construction of new hospitals and local health centers and the imposition of universal free medical care.

(4) Local, regional, and national anti-war organizations should seek coalition support for anti-war actions from groups organized around gender, race, or class issues but should also give material and organizing assistance to groups, projects, and events organized around gender, race, and class issues whether they are explicitly requested to do so or not.

(5) To overcome cynicism, it is essential, of course, that anti-war activists explain as clearly as possible the magnitude and purpose of U.S. crimes and the real tenacity of society's oppressive institutions. But it is also essential that we not so inundate people with detailed descriptions of the venality of U.S. institutions that we corroborate rather than overcome cynicism.

People will ask, "What could you do that would be better?" and we have to go beyond repeatedly describing only how bad the system now is. "Bring the troops home"; "Bring the troops home and let the sanctions and international diplomacy do their work"; or even "Strengthen the UN, democratize it, and make everyone, including and especially us, subject to its will" are not enough. People are going to realize that if we are right that capitalism breeds imperialism breeds war, then unless we get rid of capitalism, war will recur. And, if war recurs, they will add, we have to be ready. And then they will bait us about how those nations who tried to institute alternatives to capitalism have recently rushed back to it. To reply effectively, we are going to need a compelling post-capitalist institutional vision encompassing economics, politics, gender, and race.

But even that isn't enough. To build a really large and lasting movement, we also need to describe activities that can promote lasting change, and show evidence that our movement can be humane enough, participatory enough, and sensitive enough to human desire to come through uncorrupted.

You may say revolution is not on the immediate agenda, so why develop these long-run revolutionary answers? You may say we aren't trying to get lifelong commitment, we are only trying to get people to fight against a war, so why worry about long-run aims and problems? But if so, you will miss the point.

People know that serious dissent can change their lives. They know that once they admit that U.S. crimes should be fought, they will either have to become radical, with possible loss of friends and job opportunities, or turn their backs on morality. People don't need long-run answers now because they think we may win tomorrow and will need to be ready; they need answers in order to believe that the struggle will be worthwhile in the long run and therefore worth joining now. People need to have a sense of self-worth to believe in what they are doing, especially if it entails sacrifices. Building a new sense of self only around hatred for war and its purveyors is not very sustaining. It even tends to create a bitter person who is unlikely to be an effective organizer. To become radical is to jettison one's old self-image and most of its assumptions. It is very hard to do this and maintain one's humanity without having a positive sense of where one is headed.

People who have been effective activists for decades believe in human potentials, believe in a better society, believe in the possibility of winning, and are sustained by these *positive* beliefs, not solely by hating a specific injustice. To get others involved just as deeply without helping them attain long-run confidence is ignoring our own politicization. To get people seriously involved in anti-war work means helping them to attain not just an understanding of today's crimes, but also of goals and strategies that can provide long-run confidence, so that they too can affirmatively answer even the immediate question, "Should I or shouldn't I demonstrate this weekend?"

The Gulf War Opposition

From August 2, 1990 to the end of the Gulf War in March 1991, people demonstrated against the war all across the country. Actions ranged from teach-ins to vigils, marches, civil disobedience, and blocking traffic, to taking over buildings and institutions. Participants came from every imaginable constituency. The goal of all this activity was to tell Bush and the powers that be that they were playing with fire.

The movement wanted to convey the idea that given the state of the economy, given the conditions of the cities, schools, and hospitals, the government was risking not only a massive anti-war opposition that would immediately prevent business as usual, but, even more important, the schooling of hundreds of thousands or millions of citizens in political action and political reasoning. The possibility that anti-war energy and commitment would soon extend beyond the Gulf crisis to address domestic social, political, and economic issues and institutions was what we saw as having the potential to rein in the masters of war.

While Bush and Co. would not hear movement analyses or moral pleas, they could potentially hear the threat of increasing and diversifying opposition. Though the opposition was not enough to prevent war from starting, we reasoned that if it grew it could nonetheless prevent the war's enlargement, prevent nuclear assault, end the war, curtail the further militarization of our society, and win conversion. We talked, organized, rallied, sat-in, occupied, and disrupted targets ranging from federal buildings and recruitment centers, to radio and television stations, ROTC offices, and research facilities. Regrettably, we never got around to focusing on dilapidated drug-rehabilitation centers, rape-crisis centers, soup kitchens, housing agencies, and the White House. We did not have the time or resources to follow all the "prescriptions" outlined above as well as we might. But our aim was to fight to shut down what should not be permitted and to fund what we needed. We thought we could do it with mass outpouring, a step at a time, starting with ending the war. And we were far better informed and had our eyes far more precisely on reality and on a sensible plan of action than the anti-Vietnam-War movement had at its outset, and even for years into its history.

Yet just a few weeks after the war's onset, the same anti-Gulf War activists who had spent months doing heroic and valuable work were depressed, and with ample reason. One-hundred-thousand or more Iraqis died in a "turkey shoot" inappropriately called a "war," a Nazi-like mass media campaign successfully manipulated public opinion, and Bush took a further step toward establishing a mercenary future for the United States.

As indicated in many articles in this book, U.S. elites went to war (1) to control Middle East oil as an international economic lever; (2) to ensure that Middle Eastern oil profits prop up our banks and now our construction industry ("we destroyed the country to rebuild it"); and (3) to establish that the United States is a gun for hire that will mercilessly repress any Third World country trying to establish the slightest control over its own destiny, regardless of whether it undertakes these actions from a right-wing or left-wing stance. Bush traveled far toward implementing this vision, and that is truly depressing.

But, more deeply, I think many activists are wondering, why am I doing what I do? Why am I radical, dissident, pacifist, feminist, antiracist, green, gay rights, anticapitalist? Why do I uncover every disgusting nook and cranny of oppression and brutality instead of doing what gives me the most pleasure? Is this sensible? Is it hopeful? Didn't some of the rampant depression that swept activist communities after the war stem from a fear that winning is impossible and we may be wasting our lives?

I don't think people who feel this way, whether over this war or another, will be dissuaded by calls urging that they "Don't mourn, organize." We did organize. And it galvanized tremendous opposition. *And it wasn't enough.* So what went wrong? In part, we made mistakes.

Support Our Troops?

At almost every rally and teach-in I attended the majority of speakers went to great pains to urge that we "support 'our' troops." To exaggerate only a little, I think that when this was elevated to a centerpiece of activism, it was borderline obscene and politically self-defeating.

In the first place, people who spend much of their time trying to demonstrate how they "support our troops" accept the terms of debate set by the administration and media. Any sane person supports our troops, Iraq's troops, and even the troops of a Hitler in the sense of wanting minimal deaths and killing. Beyond that, what one might sensibly ask is what attitude should one take toward the troops, though the far more important question is what attitude should one take to the war itself, and to the generals sitting in air-conditioned offices ordering people to kill and be killed.

What is the effect of endlessly talking about "supporting our troops," as if we were in a competition to see who cares most about their well-being?

The point to understand is that not to cheer the deaths of our fellow citizens and to work tirelessly to ensure that they don't have to die or kill is not the same as "supporting them." They are *our* troops insofar as they are our mothers and fathers, aunts and uncles, brothers and sisters, friends, and fellow citizens. When they go to war we want them back alive. But they are *Bush's* troops insofar as they are soldiers fighting an unjust war. We cannot support *that*.

We should not support GIs sitting in the sand of Saudi Arabia waiting to roll over Iraqi corpses. Yes, most of these ground troops were young folks looking for a better income or better education than they stood to gain by any other available route. Yes, most were caught up in a process whose scope and purpose they knew little if anything about. But while their ignorance and the dangers they faced should have made us feel sympathy and cause us to worry about their well-being, it should not have made us send messages of support. Of course we all wanted to help save the ground soldiers from having to kill or be killed. But we should have forthrightly *opposed* what the ground soldiers were doing.

For the pilots who rained bombs like deadly snowflakes on an essentially defenseless country, again we should have withheld support. Why did we give them the impression that if we were there on the tarmac when they arrived back from their bombing runs, we would have showered them with good wishes and praise? In fact, pilots are generally lifetime military personnel. Their business is death and destruction, and they study warmaking with a vengeance. They are highly educated and could easily learn the full meaning of what they are doing now and what their forebears have done in the past. Moreover, they do not have the largely valid excuse of operating under conditions of extreme danger in which they are constantly fired on, as ground soldiers often do. I do not cheer when their planes are shot down. But I want to remove their fingers from the deadly missile triggers.

To repeatedly claim that "we support the troops" not only distracted us from the real issues—policy and institutions—it also sent a message to soldiers fighting an unjust war that what they were doing was okay. They needn't worry that people at home were critical. They could go on about their business without thinking too hard about it. But soldiers in the Gulf should have been urged to think and to resist, go AWOL, refuse orders, become conscientious objectors, get out. An anti-war movement should make it hard for soldiers to follow warmakers' orders. Our attitude toward GIs should be that we want to save the lives of our fellow citizens while simultaneously preventing them from taking the lives of others. Our attitude toward war should be that it's a heinous crime. Our attitude toward the "masters of war" in the White House and Pentagon should be that they are war criminals.

If a tank commander rolling into some Third World capital refuses to fire on a building because he or she knows it houses civilians, we should support that act of "treason." If in the midst of fighting, dying, danger, and fear, a soldier fires on a building killing civilians, we should condemn that act of violence but understand the difficult conditions under which it came to pass. We shouldn't condemn every GI who ever kills an innocent person, or, for that matter, every GI who kills an enemy soldier in an unjust war that should never have begun. But even after they get home, I doubt that it does any good to tell GIs anything less than the whole, unvarnished truth about what we as a nation and they as individuals have done. As for the cold and informed decisions of the "masters of war," I believe the Nuremburg norms apply.

Finally, regarding these same issues, I am sick of hearing about how the Vietnam anti-war movement's attitude toward the troops was a mistake. At the outskirts of the movement there were certainly excesses. But the main, organized, Vietnam-era anti-war movement's activism, including the heroic and unstinting work of GI organizers, the courageous and committed sanctuary movements, and the endless demonstrations, rallies, civil disobedience, and disruptions, led to the near dissolution of Army command structures—not because we called GIs baby-killers (as the liberal media sometimes did, for example around the Calley case) nor because we spit at them (as crazed individuals sometimes did), but because we made GIs actually think about what they were doing. Moreover, GI rebellion was one of the primary factors in bringing the war to a close and implanting the "Vietnam syndrome." If criticizing the war *and* the process of carrying it out was painful for many, so be it.

Given the death and destruction suffered by Iraq, continually emphasizing that we "support our troops" is off the point and hypocritical. In fact, if our concern was *primarily* to support the troops, we would have to admit that Bush did a remarkably good job. Relatively few troops died. Most did not see the human travail they caused. But this is not a sign of success.

Moreover, as to the troops themselves, they will know we care about them even as we criticize their role and that Bush doesn't care about them even as he supports their role, if we fully address the real issues, including policy, motives, and alternatives, now and in the future. Caring about the troops means caring about unemployment, retraining, housing, education, health care, etc.

Strange Allies

Building movements is always difficult. For one thing, you have to get along with people you might otherwise avoid. But "getting together" can go too far. It is one thing to push for unity. It is another to unite with anyone, no matter how venal, so long as they agree to a key point or two.

James Webb of Reagan's war machine opposed the Gulf War. No one in the anti-war movement saw him as an ally. We all hoped his opposition, however hypocritical, would add to the pressures for peace and justice. But we did not welcome him to our anti-war organizations or respect his "politics."

But what about the Larouchites? Just exactly why did they turn up on speaker lists at so many events?

Everyone should have freedom of speech. But freedom of speech does not extend to freedom to become part of every project or movement that anyone anywhere initiates. There is nothing undemocratic about building an organization, project, or movement which excludes racists, sexists, classists, authoritarians, or anyone else. Whole societies can't and shouldn't exclude groups based on their views or lack thereof, but projects can and often must. Exclusion of any kind for a broad-ranging political project should certainly be a last resort. Most of the time it is unnecessary and unwise. But there are instances where views are so divergent and principles so contrary that it makes sense, and the Larouchites are a case in point.

A violation of freedom of speech and other freedoms would be to say that some particular people cannot participate in public events or build their own organizations. We should oppose that. We should not want the state to forbid Larouchites from holding their own rallies or attending the public rallies of any other group. But at the same time we shouldn't want to share a platform with them, nor to listen to them speak from a stage at an anti-war rally, march, or teach-in.

As a matter of ethics, allying ourselves with such groups is revolting. As a matter of organizing logic, it is horrendously self-defeating. What sensible person wanted to be part of a coalition that welcomed people who think that Queen Elizabeth runs the FBI, or whatever other inanity Larouchites were spouting? Defending Larouche's free speech doesn't require me to invite him into my living room *or* onto the stage of events I organize, and likewise for his followers. We shouldn't have done it.

Sects

And speaking of inanities, what do we do about marxist-leninist or other sects that have shown by their past practice an utter disdain for everyone around them? These sects are, remember, relatively small groups of adherents of one or another brand of marxism-leninism (or some other creed) who call themselves a revolutionary movement, party, pre-party, or whatever else, and who nearly always speak with one intonation and mindset. They have a "line" on nearly every subject imaginable and believe that the fate of humanity depends on their line becoming the uncontested belief of every citizen of the country. Moreover, to attain this end, sect members do anything they can get away with, usually to groups organized by folks who, not being full-time politicos, are not alert to sect behavior.

As a result, it is quite common, as at the national student meeting on January 27, 1991 in Washington, DC, to see large numbers of well-meaning people (in this case nearly a thousand students) stymied by a handful of sect members (in this case two groups of 10 to 15 each).

When they are a minority, sects vehemently urge vote after vote and harangue after harangue, regardless of the will of the body. Any resistance to their repeating the same points *ad infinitum* is labeled anti-communist, anti-working class, or even anti-democratic. Unless curtailed, this fosters audience attrition until only sect members and a few confused, exhausted, other souls remain. Then the sects ram through their line for an organization that no longer exists.

Sects also generally hold and endlessly proselytize for at least a few grotesquely inhumane or just insane views, thus disgusting nearly everyone they encounter. For example, they might support Saddam Hussein as a liberator of the Third World. Or they might propose that the Soviet Union has always been a workers' paradise and is failing due to the machinations of western capital. Or, they might be viciously homophobic. Sects come to other groups and projects not with an honest intention of working within the structure and principles established there, but with the preconceived plan of pushing their own oppressive view regardless of what anyone else thinks. Even when they have something insightful to say, sects almost invariably say it so destructively that the actual content of their message is lost.

At public rallies and meetings, where sects have every right to be, it ought to be possible to prevent those who disdain even the most limited notions of democracy and participation from disrupting. To do this requires patience and an ability to defuse and simultaneously clarify the situation even for those who have never seen this kind of behavior before.

Thus, movement people need to learn these skills. But there is no reason to include marxist-leninist (or any other) sects with a history of disruptive behavior in organizing groups, teach-in committees, well-defined organizations, or other non-public projects that uphold democratic principles and require a degree of mutual respect.

The Main Lesson: Episodic Organizing Is Dead

In any complex undertaking it is always possible things could have been done better. More of the opposition could have avoided accepting the turf defined by the administration and media—"Do we or don't we support the troops?"—and focused on the fact that U.S. Gulf policy was criminal and the war unjust. Instead of having two anti-war coalitions confusing people and dividing resources, we could have had one that was clear, principled, and eloquent. Sects could have been dealt with more effectively and less disruptively. Everyone could have worked just a little harder, demonstrations could have been a little better planned, speakers a little better prepared and more broadly focused, and leadership a little more willing to incorporate new ideas and energies.

But, the truth is, *given the starting point on August 2,* our anti-war effort was about as good as we could have hoped for. There was barely time to get started, much less become perfect. From Vietnam antiwar organizing we learned to try to avoid what I earlier called "apocalyptic organizing." The chief lesson of the Gulf War experience is that as a curb on warmaking, "episodic organizing" is dead.

Crises come and go. During crises, attention is aroused, energies grow, and activism naturally increases. By saying "episodic organizing is dead," I don't mean future crises won't spur increased activism. And I don't mean that the logic of raising the social cost of hated policies by education, demonstrations, and disobedience is mistaken. Nor do I mean that it's bad for people who were previously uninvolved to be roused for the first time to undertake critical initiatives during a crisis. But if there is not an *ongoing* infrastructure of grassroots and national movement institutions, the growth in energy that occurs with the onset of each new crisis will never be well-captured, long-retained, nor able to curb each new crisis it confronts. Therefore, building a lasting, systemically-focused movement must become priority number one for long-term activists.

The U.S. state and its agencies have learned the lessons of struggle taught by the 1960s and have modified their behaviors and that of the media, and of all classes with access to the media, accordingly. That transformation, coupled with the exit of the Soviets as a serious international force, has left a new organizing context. When war threatens, *if* anti-war movements organize from scratch, then by the time they attain an organizational capability to begin to wipe away media/government lies and confusions, the war is over. Media madness drowns out anti-war arguments until ticker-tape victory parades crowd anti-war demonstrations off the streets.

Suppose, instead, we had started on August 2 not from scratch but with well-established capabilities? Imagine, as one of many lost possibilities, that Jesse Jackson's Rainbow campaigns over the past decade had been primarily movement-building efforts with an electoral component as just one aspect. Imagine that, as many urged at the time, when Jackson and the Rainbow apparatus travelled all over the nation their chief priority was to help establish grassroots organizations, provide resources and skills, and build local structures that could later fight for local agendas.

Imagine also that after the elections, instead of gutting what could have been a community-based, institutionally-sound, multi-issue, multi-tactic Rainbow in favor of a narrowly defined, electoral machine, the Rainbow leadership had further democratized the Rainbow, developing new chapters, and steadily improving their means of national communication and education.

Suppose also that over the same years we had done more to develop alternative media. And suppose, too, that in the 1980s we had reached the obvious conclusion that we needed both the "autonomy" of movements and organizations clearly focused around particular oppressions— racism, battering, AIDS, housing, income distribution, foreign policy, schools, health care, conversion, etc.—and also an overarching alliance of all these in which a regular exchange of views, material aid, and energies was natural. And suppose we achieved a considerable degree of this "autonomy coupled with solidarity" through the Rainbow or some other union of all these movements.

Finally, suppose that after the Vietnam War (the contra war, Grenada, Panama, etc.), instead of moving on to other crises and leaving the field clear for mainstreamers to define the history and meaning of our past experience, we had done a better job of educating the public about exactly what had occurred and why, better preparing people to understand future events not as aberrations or errors, but as logical outgrowths of elite-serving national policy.

In this scenario, on August 2 there would have been thousands of local peace-and-justice groups, all with well-developed organizing skills, ties to their communities, and ties to one another. There would also have been a trusted representative organization to coordinate their crisis efforts, disseminate written resources for grassroots organizing, provide speakers for teach-ins, set dates for demonstrations, and even raise money to help sustain local work. And there would have been many more independent radio stations as well as far more visible radical print media able to provide mutual support, analysis, and aid.

Even if there weren't yet workplace, neighborhood, and union branches of this peace-and-justice movement, which would certainly be a necessary step on the way to lasting structural transformation, this level of activist infrastructure, political sophistication, and mutual support, would have been enough to force a negotiated rather than a military settlement of the crisis.

Moreover, since less than all this won't do, whether you see yourself as a revolutionary out to replace patriarchy with feminism, racism with intercommunalism, authoritarianism with democracy, and capitalism with participatory economics, or as a reformer intent on attaining justice within the system, you have a clear agenda. Yes, the revolutionary has to provide long-term vision while the reformer doesn't. But for short-term aims, both need to build a multi-focus, multi-constituency, grassroots-based, nationally-organized, institutionally strong opposition. Avoiding this to deal only with crises never made much sense. Avoiding it to focus entirely on single issues, no matter how important, never made much sense. Now, however difficult lasting, grassroots movement-building may be, to avoid it any longer makes no sense at all.

What's Next?

As I write this essay the country has been watching the Hill/Thomas hearings. Polls are showing majority popular support to put a reactionary, lying, opportunist, sexist on the Supreme Court. In Louisiana, David Duke, a Klan fascist, is in a runoff for governor. The public returning these sentiments has listened to my generation of leftists try to "raise their consciousness" for over a quarter century. We need to face facts.

Thirty years ago my generation of leftists began telling the truth about social problems, and people thought we were out of our minds. Most white students and community folks believed lawyers were honest; General Motors beneficent; workers well rewarded; the government just; women born to be housewives and mothers; and Blacks, Indians, Asians, and Latinos less than human. Moreover, they righteously rejected our "vile lies."

Thirty years ago we highlighted the causes of human suffering and people said we were crazy. The Vietnam War was to bring freedom to Asia, not wealth to ruling elites. The United States never, ever, killed innocent people. Campus teach-ins on the Vietnam War were raucous because students disagreed with what "Chomsky," "Dellinger," or "Zinn" said. But it became obvious to us that if we could convince people of what was going on and why, they would be transformed. So the Left offered more facts, images, and testimony and continually revealed the systemic causes of problems and began to convince people who then joined demonstrations and created more teach-ins, discussions, leaflets, and articles that convinced still more people. And the movement grew, and worked, but only for awhile.

Recruitment

Today, we still emphasize facts, images, and testimony about injustice, but our revelations have minimal impact. No one gets riled when we report corporate crimes and administrative horrors. At campus teach-ins most seem to calmly accept what "Chomsky," "Stockwell," or "Ehrenreich" says. Other than *apparatchiks* and cultural SWAT teams, no one calls us crazy. But when average folks accept our analysis, they do little about it.

So why did revelation recruit people to action then, while it doesn't now? Usually people say cynicism is the reason and leave it at that. But I think we need a deeper answer. Perhaps in the past 30 years the Left has done one job so well that now most people no longer believe that doctors, lawyers, capitalists, politicians, and even corporations and the government are dedicated to making life better. Perhaps people no longer find Left revelations so surprising. Perhaps leftists are more surprised when something venal is discovered than are ordinary people.

If this is true and people already know everything is rotten, repeatedly reporting injustices misses the point. If people think injustice, war, and degradation are just facts of life, naturally they resist radical recruitment regardless of facts about current oppressions. Believing things can't get better, people want to enjoy available pleasures and avoid dwelling on the unpleasant. Not wanting to feel guilty about this choice, they don't want to be constantly reminded of society's ills. To admit the systemic roots of injustice and to feel a desire to change them, and even to hear arguments on these matters, people first need to see how it is possible to beat Washington and Wall Street and that empowering and egalitarian institutions are possible—exactly what Left organizing largely leaves out.

Is there any evidence for my claims that people already know how bad things are? I am not saying everyone can give a major speech on the intricacies of capitalism, or enumerate the causes of violence against women, or explain racial income inequalities, or itemize all U.S.-sponsored Third World barbarism. I am only suggesting that everyone knows these type of things exist, but tries not to dwell on them since to do so while believing that fighting for change can't work and better institutions are impossible is painful and useless.

A popular Hollywood movie from 1990 titled *Air America* with major stars Mel Gibson and Robert Downey, Jr. portrayed the CIA using its private air force, Air America, to assist drug dealing out of Laos to raise money to finance the Indochina war. The Senate was portrayed as ineffectual, self-seeking yahoos, the president as supporting drug running to (a) American GIs in South Vietnam and (b) citizens in the streets of major U.S. cities like New York.

I suspect that nearly everybody who saw *Air America* found it entirely plausible. No one not in the employ of the *New York Times* or some Ivy League political-science department walked out outraged that U.S. largess should be so lied about. No public demonstrations called the film blasphemous. Instead, most viewers found the film's depiction of CIA drug running obvious. In the 1950s and mid- and late-1960s, this film would have created bedlam. Mel Gibson would have been as reviled as Jane Fonda was. *Air America* says the U.S. government pushes drugs and is arguably the main author of today's U.S. drug-addiction problem, and viewers take it for granted.

Or consider contemporary thriller novels, many of which appear on best-seller lists. These books nearly universally address international intrigue, including government, military, and corporate machinations. But with the exception of die-hards like Tom Clancy, today's best-selling thriller writers often imbue the CIA and U.S. political and corporate leaders with the most disgusting personalities and have them undertake the most vile behavior, all with obviously systemic causes. And though readers occasionally question this or that plot device, I bet they never question the negative portrayals of elites and elite institutions. These writers would have been labelled "reds" 25 years ago. Now their descriptions are commonsense backdrop.

Likewise, I don't hear a hue and cry over mystery novels, though in many instances they portray urban, class, gender, and racial issues in the United States as every bit as oppressive as anything the Left describes.

Or finally, consider the October 1990 issue of the very prestigious, MIT-associated *Technology Review,* a magazine primarily for engineers, scientists, and the science-watching public. Gar Alperovitz's cover story details the case he made a quarter-century ago, that the United States bombed Hiroshima and Nagasaki not to end the war with Japan, but to make a geopolitical point to the world. The war was ending anyway. We killed about a quarter-million people as an exclamation point, to indicate our strength, and, arguably, to research the bombs' effects. Thousands at least skimmed this article, but I predict that only a few academic hustlers and corporate cronies challenged its veracity, much less excoriated its "calumnies against our country." Yet 25 years ago all but a very few readers would have been horrified at the mainstream publication of such "lies." After all, this article claimed that the single most destructive military events ever undertaken were U.S.-sponsored for non-military, self-serving reasons.

Tell people that U.S. cows are fed grain instead of grass to make them more tender and therefore more profitable, and they will find it plausible. Explain that if the same grain were instead sent abroad, it would eliminate world hunger, and they believe it. It comes as no surprise that tens of millions of people die each year to enlarge corporate meat profits, though the specific fact will then be forgotten as quickly as possible. Instead of dwelling on this disgusting data, people will soon turn the conversation to the weather, or what's playing at the movies, or sports news. These things they don't have to feel responsible for.

So leftists not only need to continue revealing systemic oppression and explaining its causes, we also need to spend more time presenting alternative visions and describing possible short- and long-term strategies for attaining them so that people begin to class the horrors as things they "can do something about."

Retention

Once we get people to recognize the systemic roots of social problems and to want to organize and demonstrate for change, why do they drift back to passivity so quickly?

On this score, 1960s efforts weren't much more successful than those since. Again, we need to face facts. We are miserable at creating lasting commitment that preserves its activist edge. But if we can't do this, the thugs of the world will keep winning. Many factors influence people who become activist and drift away, but a few seem central.

• The Left Is No Fun.

I mean this seriously. Once people realize that change is not an overnight affair they inevitably come face to face with the prospect of having only Left friends and Left things to do for years on end. For most, this is not an appealing thought. It isn't that the Left doesn't know how to party. It is that by virtue of its beliefs the Left has a hard time getting pleasure out of most things society offers as entertainment. Movies are too violent. Sports are too commercial. Nice places to go are too full of yuppies. Everything is too classist, racist, and sexist. All this might be okay if the Left created alternative ways to have fun, celebrate, or just relax, but we don't. And because we are often on edge, critical, or being criticized, these absences take a great toll. Why trust that a permanently morose and maudlin Left will create a better future?

• The Left Infights.

Leftists rarely support one another. We compete for who is righter, who is better, which institution deserves more support. Ideas are personal property, almost like capital. You can tell who will be at a conference just by knowing the sponsors. Everyone finds fault with everyone else, with or without justification. We seek differences, not commonalities. And what solidarity there is, is often ridiculous. Consider this recent example. At *Z Magazine,* where I work, we not long ago received invitations to put paid ads in *In These Times'* fourteenth-anniversary issue and *Socialist Review's* twentieth. Each of the invitations indicated that coughing up some ad money was the supportive thing to do. Rubbish! For each periodical to put an ad in every other periodical's yearly anniversary issue saying how much it appreciates the other's work is supposed to be a big act of solidarity. But your supportive sentiments appear, please notice, in the periodical that you are complimenting, not in your own where they might actually do some good. It's like kids' birthday parties. The money merely goes round and round. As one obvious alternative, how about using one's *own* pages to boost other magazines? Most Left institutional relations are a little like high school. There are in- and out-groups and some occasional shuffling, and on the side everyone fundraises in private. Sensible people who don't have fanatical staying power generally decide the whole thing is pitiful and then leave.

• The Left Is Isolated.

The Left is supposed to talk about the most pressing needs and heartfelt aspirations of all of society's oppressed. But partly because the Left is depressed from rarely having fun, and partly because it's cynical from infighting, and partly because its culture is some kind of amalgam of politically-correct macho coupled with academic posturing, the Left is totally isolated from the rest of the United States. I mentioned earlier the Thomas confirmation hearings. At their close pollsters reported that over 50 percent of the public, even over 50 percent of women, and way over 50 percent of Blacks, believed Thomas, not Hill, and wanted Thomas confirmed. The fact is that leftists had no idea how to evaluate this. We did not know what people thought and felt. We did not know why. We could not predict reactions or even explain them after the fact. We were, and are, out of touch. It is hard to organize people you hate, and often the Left seems to hate everybody and everything. Or, at least it comes across that way.

- The Left Is Confused.

How about this for a series of Left admonitions: (1) Democrats are hypocrites and scum—Vote Democratic. (2) Mainstream media nearly always lie to serve vested interests—Curry favor with mainstream media to reach a wider audience. (3) Socialism is the way to go and the Soviet Union is socialist—The Soviet Union is a disgusting mess. (4) It is crucial to fight racism—Our organization has a lily-white culture and focus. (5) It is grotesque for one nation to oppress another and people's liberation struggles deserve militant support—Don't mention the Palestinians. (6) Hierarchical production relations deny worker's control—Maintain hierarchical work relations to keep your institution strong and respected. (7) Overthrowing capitalism is central to human progress—Don't mention class or capitalism publicly. (8) You can't motivate people without vision and win without strategy—We have no vision or strategy, and don't take time to read or debate. (9) Homophobia, racism, homelessness, poverty, imperialism, and sexism are all disgusting—Don't take a stand, much less invest resources, regarding more than one primary issue. (10) We need solidarity—Drop what you are doing and join our group. (11) Revolution is the only solution—Never say "revolution" in public.

To reduce and finally eliminate U.S. international terror we will have to demystify U.S. geopolitical, social, and economic motives and explain a viable alternative.

Strategically, we will have to recognize that Democrats no less than Republicans defend elite control and respond only to pressure, not argument. Thus, we will have to dissociate from Democrats and influence them not by kissing ass, but by raising the social costs of advocating oppressive policies. We will have to develop lasting, grassroots, organization.

Tactically, we will have to realize that media coverage will vary directly with either (a) the extent we sell out our principles, or (b) the extent we become strong enough so that we cannot be ignored. To not sell out our principles, we will have to never curtail our movement's political and organizational development on grounds of not alienating NBC, ABC, CBS, the *Washington Post,* or the *New York Times.*

When the movement gains headway, people will ask what we want. They will ask our alternatives for U.S. foreign policy, to U.S. government, economic, and social institutions. To recruit effectively, we'd better have answers ready.

Moreover, if we want to build a Left that lasts past one crisis, we will have to develop Left culture, Left ways of having fun, Left supportiveness, and Left solidarity. We will have to respect the whole array of concerns of constituencies we need to incorporate, not only in the targets we protest, but in our own organizations and behavior as well.

There are two reasons to be a radical, protester, green, pacifist, feminist, gay or lesbian rights advocate, antiracist, and/or anti-capitalist. (1) Because it is right. (2) Because it is right *and* can succeed. The first reason can sustain a relatively small movement undertaking endless episodic organizing that rarely if ever wins anything. The second can sustain a powerful movement that educates the public and organizes lasting institutions, thereby winning reform after reform on the road to a transformed society. To begin to make the second reason real and turn back the post-Gulf War tide of depression, those who have the energy and endurance to accept the challenge must build a new movement with roots, and practices worth supporting.

To do the whole anti-war, antipoverty, antisexist, antiracist thing still another time and get it wrong again because a few leaders want to retain ties to respectable Democrats, or bask in a media spotlight, or not make their own projects democratic, or not develop vision or strategy, or not deal with more than one issue, or not get down to the real tasks of long-term, grassroots organizing, would be a horrible shame. Our program is simple to understand, hard to undertake. We must learn from our past and get down to taking a real vision and strategy into the workplaces, dining halls, and living rooms of America. Anything less isn't worth the effort.

THE CONTRIBUTORS

Nabeel Abraham lectures and writes about the Middle East, Arab Americans, U.S. foreign policy, and the news media. He is co-editor (with Sameer Abraham) of two books, *The Arab World and Arab-Americans: Understanding a Neglected Minority* (1981) and *Arabs in the New World: Studies on Arab-American Communities* (1983).

Michael Albert is co-editor of *Z Magazine* and a founder of South End Press. He has written and edited numerous books, including, most recently, with Robin Hahnel, *Looking Forward: Participatory Economics for the Twenty-First Century.*

Leslie Cagan has worked as the coordinator of the National Campaign for Peace in the Middle East; campaign coordinator in David Dinkins' New York City mayoral campaign (1989); and organizer for several national demonstrations, including the 1982 disarmament rally in New York City, the lesbian/gay rights march on Washington, DC in 1987, and many other major actions. Her articles have appeared in *Z Magazine*, the *Guardian*, and other progressive journals, and she is a co-author of *Liberating Theory*. She is currently the coordinator of the Cuba Information Project.

Sandy Carter writes about music and politics in a monthly column for *Z Magazine*. During the last two decades, he has been active in organizing around workplace, community, and mental health issues. His writing has appeared in *The San Francisco Chronicle, The Guardian, State and Mind*, and other newspapers and journals.

Noam Chomsky, professor of Linguistics at the Massachusetts Institute of Technology, writes and speaks extensively on U.S. foreign policy. He is a columnist for *Z Magazine* and is the author of numerous books, including *Necessary Illusions, Deterring Democracy*, and *On Power and Ideology*.

Ward Churchill (Creek/Cherokee Métis) has served, since 1980, as codirector of the Colorado chapter of the American Indian Movement. He is associate professor of communications and coordinator of American Indian Studies at the University of Colorado/Boulder. A regular columnist for *Z Magazine*, Churchill is also editor of the journal *New Studies on the Left* and has published widely in a number of other periodicals. His books include *Marxism and Native Americans, Culture versus Economism, Agents of Repression, Critical Issues in Native North America, The COINTELPRO Papers*, and *Fantasies of the Master Race*.

Cynthia Enloe, professor of Government at Clark University, is the author of *Does Khaki Become You? The Militarization of Women's Lives* and *Bananas, Beaches and Bases: Making Feminist Sense of International Politics*. She lives in Massachusetts.

413

Tod Ensign, a lawyer, is director of Citizen Soldier, a non-profit GI rights advocacy project based in New York City. His latest book is *Military Life: The Insider's Guide*.

Abouali Farmanfarmaian is an Iranian freelance writer who lives and works in Canada. His main work is with Iranian refugees in Montreal.

Rebecca Gordon is a bookkeeper and editor of *Lesbian Contradiction: a Journal of Irreverent Feminism*. She lives in San Francisco.

Eric Hooglund is an editor of *Middle East Report*, and is the author of *Land and Revolution in Iran*, and *Crossing the Waters: The Arabic-Speaking Immigration to the United States before 1940*.

William Hoynes is a member of the Boston College Media Research and Action Project and a FAIR (Fairness and Accuracy in Reporting) Associate. He is completing a study of the politics of public television.

Rachel L. Jones is an investigative journalist at the *Chicago Reporter*. She is a recipient of the Robert R. McCormick Fellowship in Urban Journalism and has received reporting awards from Women in Communications and the National Hospice Organization. She is a member of the National Association of Black Journalists, whose 1991 Midwest regional conference she helped plan.

Michael T. Klare is an associate professor of Peace and World Security Studies at Hampshire College in Amherst, Massachusetts and the author of several books on U.S. military policy. He is the defense correspondent of *The Nation*.

Ann M. Lesch is the author of numerous articles on Middle East international issues. She is also co-author with Mark Tessler of *Israel, Egypt and the Palestinians*, and author of two earlier books on the Palestinians.

Arthur MacEwan teaches Economics at the University of Massachusetts/Boston. His most recent book is *Debt and Disorder: International Economic Instability and U.S. Imperial Decline*.

Cynthia Peters is a member of the South End Press collective.

Joni Seager is a Canadian feminist who teaches Geography at the University of Vermont and Women's Studies at MIT. She is very interested in bringing humanistic and feminist perspectives to bear on the environmental debate—"leaving environmental issues in the hands of the 'sci/tech' boys (and gals) is bound to get us all into deeper trouble." She is the author of, most recently, *The State of the Earth Atlas*, and a forthcoming book on feminism and the environment.

Holly Sklar is the author of *Washington's War on Nicaragua* and *Trilateralism: The Trilateral Commission and Elite Planning for World Management* and coauthor of *Poverty in the American Dream*. She is presently coauthoring two books: one on the National Endowment for Democracy, the other on community planning and development focusing on the revitalization of a Boston neighborhood.

Randolph N. Stone, formerly Public Defender of Cook County, Chicago, Illinois, is a clinical professor of Law at the University of Chicago Law School.

Joe Stork is the co-founder of the Middle East Research and Information Project (MERIP), and editor of *Middle East Report*.

Robert Allen Warrior (Osage) is a scholar and freelance journalist whose work has appeared in *The Village Voice, The Progressive, Lakota Times, Native Nations, News from Indian Country, Lies of Our Times, The Guardian*, and others. He is currently completing his doctoral dissertation on religion and politics in twentieth century Native America at Union Theological Seminary in New York City.

INDEX

About South End Press

South End Press is a nonprofit, collectively-run book publisher with over 150 titles in print. Since our founding in 1977, we have tried to meet the needs of readers who are exploring, or are already committed to, the politics of radical social change.

Our goal is to publish books that encourage critical thinking and constructive action on the key political, cultural, social, economic, and ecological issues shaping life in the United States and in the world. In this way, we hope to give expression to a wide diversity of democratic social movements and to provide an alternative to the products of corporate publishing.

Through the Institute for Social and Cultural Change, South End Press works with other political media projects—*Z Magazine;* Speak Out!, a speakers bureau; the Publishers Support Project, and the New Liberation News Service—to expand access to information and critical analysis. If you would like a free catalog of South End Press books or information about our membership program—which offers two free books and a 40% discount on all titles—please write to us at South End Press, 116 Saint Botolph Street, Boston, MA 02115.

Other titles of interest from South End Press:

Storm Signals
Structural Adjustment and Development Alternatives in the Caribbean
Kathy McAfee

The Sun Never Sets
Confronting the Network of Foreign U.S. Military Bases
edited by Joseph Gerson and Bruce Birchard

Prime Time Activism
Media Strategies for Organizing
Charlotte Ryan

Necessary Illusions
Thought Control in Democratic Societies
Noam Chomsky

State of Native America
Genocide, Colonization, and Resistance
edited by M. Annette Jaimes

DATE DUE

GAYLORD

PRINTED IN U.S.A.